ANCIENT
WISDOM

FOR THE
GOOD LIFE

ANCIENT
WISDOM

FOR THE
GOOD LIFE

RALPH K. HAWKINS

HENDRICKSON
PUBLISHERS

an imprint of Hendrickson Publishing Group

Ancient Wisdom for the Good Life

© 2023 Ralph K. Hawkins

Published by Hendrickson Publishers
an imprint of Hendrickson Publishing Group
Hendrickson Publishers, LLC
P. O. Box 3473
Peabody, Massachusetts 01961-3473

ISBN 978-1-61970-885-3

Library of Congress Control Number: 2023945508

Printed in the United States of America

First Printing — December 2023

Middle Eastern town cover illustration © iStock.com/vividvic. City landscape cover
illustration © iStock.com/venimo.

Cover design by Karol Bailey.

To the blessed memory of my grandparents, Chervis and Ora Isom, who sought to model wise living for their grandchildren. And to my own children, Hannah, Sarah, Mary, and Adam, to whom I would commend the words of the sages:

The beginning of wisdom is this: get wisdom,
and whatever else you get, get insight.

(Proverbs 4:7)

❧

CONTENTS

ILLUSTRATIONS

ACKNOWLEDGMENTS

I would like to thank the outstanding staff of the Blount Library over the past several years for their help with this project. As always, they went above and beyond the call of duty in helping me secure resources. I am also thankful to the congregations where I have presented sermons on portions of this book, including New Market United Methodist Church, Faith United Methodist Church, Calvary United Methodist Church, and Kerns Memorial United Methodist Church. My appreciation goes to the students in my Studies in the Psalms and Wisdom Literature class, who helped me think through many of the issues about which I have written in this book. I would like to thank William P. Brown, David Allen Calhoun, Daniel Fredericks, Richard S. Hess, Will Kynes, and Mark Sneed, all of whom discussed various aspects of this project with me. I appreciate their collegial support and acknowledge that any deficiencies in the work are my responsibility. As always, I am grateful to my wife, Cathy, and to our children, Hannah, Sarah, Mary, and Adam, for their love and support. Finally, I would like to thank Hendrickson Publishers for the opportunity to write this volume. I am grateful to Paul Hendrickson as well as Patricia Anders, my editor, for helping me see this project through to the finish line. When I contracted a severe case of COVID-19 early in 2021 that resulted in Long COVID conditions that persist even to this day, they granted me repeated extensions and even prayed for me. Although their patience with me may not have rivaled that of Job, I think it came close! I am so grateful to them for allowing me to complete this volume with Hendrickson, and my prayer is that it might be a blessing to many. *Soli Deo Gloria!*

RALPH K. HAWKINS
DANVILLE, VIRGINIA
FEAST DAY OF HILDEGARD OF BINGEN

ABBREVIATIONS

AB	Anchor Bible
ABD	*Anchor Bible Dictionary.* Edited by David Noel Freedman. 6 vols. New York: Doubleday, 1992
ABRL	Anchor Bible Reference Library
ANET	*Ancient Near Eastern Texts Relating to the Old Testament.* Edited by James B. Pritchard. 3rd ed. Princeton: Princeton University Press, 1969
AOT	*The Apocryphal Old Testament.* Edited by Hedley F. D. Sparks. Oxford: Clarendon, 1984
AOTC	Abingdon Old Testament Commentaries
ARA	*Annual Review of Anthropology*
AYB	Anchor Yale Bible
BASOR	*Bulletin of the American Schools of Oriental Research*
BBR	*Bulletin for Biblical Research*
BCOTWP	Baker Commentary on the Old Testament Wisdom and Psalms
BibSem	The Biblical Seminar
BJS	Brown Judaic Studies
BNTC	Black's New Testament Commentaries
BSac	*Bibliotheca Sacra*
BSS	Biblical Seminar Series
BZAW	Beihefte zur Zeitschrift für die alttestamentliche Wissenschaft
CANE	*Civilizations of the Ancient Near East.* Edited by Jack M. Sasson. 4 vols. New York, 1995. Repr. in 2 vols. Peabody, MA: Hendrickson, 2006
CBQ	*Catholic Biblical Quarterly*
CorBR	*Currents in Biblical Research*

CC	Continental Commentaries
EBC	Expositor's Bible Commentary
EncJud	*Encyclopedia Judaica*. Edited by Fred Skolnik and Michael Berenbaum. 2nd ed. 22 vols. Detroit: Macmillan Reference USA, 2007
ESW	Ecumenical Studies in Worship
GBSOT	Guides to Biblical Scholarship—Old Testament Series
HALOT	*The Hebrew and Aramaic Lexicon of the Old Testament*. Ludwig Koehler, Walter Baumgartner, and Johann J. Stamm. Translated and edited under the supervision of Mervyn E. J. Richardson. 4 vols. Leiden: Brill, 1994–1999
IEJ	*Israel Exploration Journal*
Int	*Interpretation*
IRT	Issues in Religion and Theology
JAAR	*Journal of the American Academy of Religion*
JATS	*Journal of the Adventist Theological Society*
JBL	*Journal of Biblical Literature*
JETS	*Journal of the Evangelical Theological Society*
JPSBC	The JPS Bible Commentary
JSOT	*Journal for the Study of the Old Testament*
KEL	Kregel Exegetical Library
LAI	Library of Ancient Israel
LCL	Loeb Classical Library
LGRB	Lives of Great Religious Books
LNTS	The Library of New Testament Studies
MBPS	Mellen Biblical Press Series
NAC	New American Commentary
NIB	*The New Interpreter's Bible*. Edited by Leander E. Keck. 12 vols. Nashville: Abingdon, 1994–2004
NICNT	New International Commentary on the New Testament
NICOT	New International Commentary on the Old Testament
NIDB	*New Interpreter's Dictionary of the Bible*. Edited by Katharine Doob Sakenfield. 5 vols. Nashville: Abingdon, 2006–2009

NIDOTTE	*New International Dictionary of Old Testament Theology and Exegesis.* Edited by Willem A. VanGemeren. 5 vols. Grand Rapids: Zondervan, 1997
NIGTC	New International Greek Testament Commentary
OTL	Old Testament Library
PHSC	Perspectives on Hebrew Scriptures and Its Contexts
REP	*Routledge Encyclopedia of Philosophy.* 4 vols. Ed. Edward Craig. London: Routledge, 1998
SBLAILit	Society of Biblical Literature—Ancient Israel and Its Literature
SBLDS	Society of Biblical Literature Dissertation Series
SBLMS	Society of Biblical Literature Monograph Series
SP	Sacra Pagina
StudBib	*Studia Biblica*
TBN	Themes in Biblical Narrative
TDOT	*Theological Dictionary of the Old Testament.* Edited by G. Johannes Botterweck and Helmer Ringgren. Translated by John T. Willis et al. 8 vols. Grand Rapids: Eerdmans, 1974–2006
TOTC	Tyndale Old Testament Commentaries
TynBul	*Tyndale Bulletin*
VT	*Vetus Testamentum*
WBC	Word Biblical Commentary
ZAW	*Zeitschrift für die alttestamentliche Wissenschaft*

INTRODUCTION

THE QUEST FOR THE "GOOD LIFE"

What do you think of when you hear the expression "the good life"? Here are some definitions from a few dictionaries:

> A life abounding in material comforts and luxuries. (Dictionary.com)

> If you say that someone is living the good life, you mean that they are living in comfort and luxury with few problems or worries. (Merriam-Webster.com)

Particularly regarding its usage in the United States, the "good life" primarily refers to:

> The kind of life that people with a lot of money are able to have. . . . [Someone who] grew up poor [but is] now . . . living the good life. (Merriam-Webster.com)

All of these definitions have two things in common. First, they define the "good life" in *comparison* to the lives of others. In this view, we experience the "good life" only when we attain a quality of life monetarily and materially superior to the lifestyles of others. Second, these definitions are all based on *external* qualities. In this view, we measure the "good life" by the clothes we wear, the car we drive, or where we live.

This is one of the great misconceptions of American society: that the attainment of the "good life" has to do with what we acquire on the outside. Our culture venerates those who are the fastest, the toughest, the most beautiful, who drive the fanciest cars, or who have the most impressive homes. Our culture has bought into the idea that it's what on the outside that matters, that this is what defines the "good life."

It should be obvious, however, that the accumulation of wealth and material possessions doesn't really equate to a good life. For example, the infamous Columbian drug lord Pablo Escobar (1949–1993) founded and led the Medellin Cartel. Through his monopolization of the cocaine trade into the United States in the 1980s and early 1990s, he became the wealthiest criminal in history, worth $30 billion at the time of his death. His luxury estate, Hacienda Nápoles, contained a colonial house, a sculpture park, and a zoo with animals from all over the world, including exotic birds, giraffes, elephants, and hippopotamuses. In the States, he had a 6,500-square-foot waterfront mansion in Miami Beach, Florida. He also owned an enormous Caribbean haven on Isla Grande, one of the twenty-seven islands that comprise the Islas del Rosario. In addition to these properties, he had race cars, boats, helicopters, and private jets. At the height of his power, he was smuggling 15 tons of cocaine per day—worth more than half a billion dollars—into the United States. Escobar and his Medellin Cartel were involved in the murder of numerous civilians, police officers, judges, and politicians. The battle for supremacy among the Columbian cartels made it the world's murder capital, with 25,100 violent deaths in 1991 and 27,100 in 1992. In 1991, Escobar surrendered to the Colombian government but escaped the following year. On December 2, 1993, at the end of a sixteen-month manhunt, he died after being shot through his ear, leg, and torso.[1] While Escobar may have acquired the outward trappings of success during his forty-four years, did he live the "good life"? After all, he had all the outward trappings of success. But if we're honest, we'd have to say no.

Throughout history, people have debated how to define the "good life." In the Classical period (from the eighth century BC to the sixth century AD), the good life was a common subject of discussion among Greek philosophers. In his *Apology*, Plato (428/7–348/7 BC) recounted that Socrates (c. 470–399 BC) taught that the unexamined life is not worth living. In his view, if we blithely go through the same old routine day after day—getting up, going to work, coming home, eating dinner in front of the television, and then going to bed—we are not living the good life. Instead, he says we should spend time examining what we value and why and then set about to master ourselves. For Socrates, mastering ourselves means reigning in our tendency to give in to our animal instincts, such as lust and pleasure; we should cultivate more noble behavior on the basis of reason, such as engaging in self–reflection, living justly, and serving society. If we can live a life that includes virtuous conduct, then we might just attain the good life.

Aristotle (384–322 BC), Plato's student, also wrote about the good life. In his best-known work, *Nichomachean Ethics*, he deliberated over what would amount to the highest good for a human being. He observed that most people think that their highest good can be attained by acquiring wealth, honor, or the satisfaction of their desires, and so these are what they pursue in life. Aristotle argued, however, that none of these lead to the good life. We can attain the good life only by contemplating and learning, which leads to the acquisition of intellectual and personal virtue. Intellectual and personal virtue, in turn, then produce the good life.

While Plato, Socrates, and Aristotle all taught that justice, moderation, and courage were keys to the good life, they also taught that contemplation, learning, and reason were necessary. But what was it that must be contemplated, learned, and reasoned out? Like all the Classical Greek philosophers, they believed that it is wisdom (*sophia*) that leads to the other virtues and produces the good life. Socrates recognized that there are particularized forms of wisdom, such as those related to particular crafts. Skilled artisans, for example, are wise in their craft, whatever it might be.[2] For Socrates, however, this particularized wisdom was not the kind of wisdom that produces the good life. As Nicholas Smith explains,

> Wisdom, for Socrates, invariably requires the possession of knowledge, and not just any knowledge, but that which provides the basis for infallibly good judgment in decisions pertinent to how one should live. Wisdom, then, is the possession of such knowledge plus the disposition and skill to use this knowledge in the right ways.[3]

Plato, especially in his later works, virtually ignored craft-related wisdom and eventually identified wisdom "only with the kind of knowledge that permits one to be infallible in judging the good."[4] In his *Republic*, he imagined an elite class of philosophical rulers with an extensive education in math and dialectic that prepared them to understand the Form of the Good. With their ability to determine which institutions and political decisions were most just, these philosopher-rulers would have the power to make infallible judgments on the state level. While Aristotle was critical of some of Plato's ideas and brought his own nuance to the discussion of wisdom, he accepted the Socratic and Platonic idea that wisdom could produce an infallible ability to judge the good and attain the good life.

The idea that someone has to develop an infallible wisdom seems to guarantee the failure of the ordinary person in ever attaining it. In fact, some of the Classical philosophers taught that even *trying* to attain the good was not for everyone. A person needed a certain level of moral virtue before even embarking on the task; and since this could be attained only through contemplation, this meant that only philosophers could attain it. Aristotle concluded that the ability to perform the good was "rare and laudable and noble."[5] In the end, it seems that the good life, as conceived by the Greek philosophers, is out of reach for the common person and attainable only by an elite class of philosophers.

The quest for the good life, though, is an old one and predates the Classical world by centuries. Pursued throughout the ancient Near East as early as the third millennium BC, each culture produced wisdom literature to aid those who sought the good life.[6] Located on the crossroads of the ancient Near East was the tiny country of Israel, which was about the size of the modern state of New Jersey. It was there, however, that God stimulated ancient Israel's sages to produce an inspired body of wisdom literature, though none of it actually uses the expression "the good life." "Good" and "life" are used throughout the wisdom literature of the Bible to talk about "a desirable state of happiness and prosperity," which is certainly commensurate with the good life.[7]

Throughout the wisdom literature of the Hebrew Bible or Old Testament, many of the promoted behaviors—such as marriage, work, prudence, and emotional self-control—are all associated with longer lifespans. This is reflected, for example, in a father's invitation for his children to accept wisdom:

> Hear, my child, and accept my words,
> that the years of your life may be many.
> I have taught you the way of wisdom;
> I have led you in the paths of uprightness.
> When you walk, your step will not be hampered;
> and if you run, you will not stumble.
> Keep hold of instruction; do not let go;
> guard her, for she is your life.
> Do not enter the path of the wicked,
> and do not walk in the way of evildoers.
> Avoid it; do not go on it;
> turn away from it and pass on.
> For they cannot sleep unless they have done wrong;
> they are robbed of sleep unless they have made someone stumble.
> For they eat the bread of wickedness
> and drink the wine of violence.
> But the path of the righteous is like the light of dawn,
> which shines brighter and brighter until full day.
> The way of the wicked is like deep darkness;
> they do not know what they stumble over.
> My child, be attentive to my words;
> incline your ear to my sayings.
> Do not let them escape from your sight;
> keep them within your heart.
> For they are life to those who find them,
> and healing to all their flesh.
> Keep your heart with all vigilance,
> for from it flow the springs of life.

Put away from you crooked speech,
    and put devious talk far from you.
Let your eyes look directly forward,
    and your gaze be straight before you.
Keep straight the path of your feet,
    and all your ways will be sure.
Do not swerve to the right or to the left;
    turn your foot away from evil. (Prov. 4:10–27)

This father believed that if his children embraced a lifestyle informed by wisdom, then they would live longer, fuller, healthier lives (v. 10). Those who reject the way of wisdom, on the other hand, are described as already living deep in the realm of the dead, even though they might not be aware of it (Prov. 9:17–18).

Along this line, various nicknames are used for wisdom that point to its life-giving qualities. It is referred to as a "path of life," "a fountain of life,"[8] and even as a "tree of life." The expression "tree of life" is used for wisdom or its effects four times in the book of Proverbs. In Proverbs 3, which explains that Wisdom (personified as female) and her instructions lead to refreshment, physical healing, and long life, Wisdom is described as "a tree of life to those who lay hold of her" (3:18). In Proverbs 11:30, the fruit of the righteous, who have lived life in accordance with wisdom, is described as "a tree of life." Proverbs 13:12 explains that the fulfillment of desires informed by wisdom is a "tree of life," and Proverbs 15:4 teaches that "a gentle tongue," which is a form of wise communication, is also a "tree of life."

These comparisons of Wisdom and her effects to a "tree of life" are especially important because they call to mind the tree of life in the Garden of Eden. In the garden, this tree seemed able to actually prevent death (Gen. 2:9). But then the fall disrupted the created order, and under sin, pain and futility seeped into every aspect of life. The sages seem to be saying, however, that whenever God's people live in accordance with God's wisdom and God's instructions, we may experience something of the good life once enjoyed in the garden, where there was harmony with God and among humankind.[9]

Another profound feature of biblical wisdom is that ancient Israel's sages claimed it is for everyone. In Proverbs 8, for example, wisdom is personified as Lady Wisdom, who stands at the crossroads and urges everyone to learn from her:

Does not wisdom call,
    and does not understanding raise her voice?
On the heights, beside the way,
    at the crossroads she takes her stand;
beside the gates in front of the town,

at the entrance of the portals she cries out:
"To you, O people, I call,
  and my cry is to all that live.
O simple ones, learn prudence;
  acquire intelligence, you who lack it.
Hear, for I will speak noble things,
  and from my lips will come what is right;
for my mouth will utter truth;
  wickedness is an abomination to my lips.
All the words of my mouth are righteous;
  there is nothing twisted or crooked in them.
They are all straight to one who understands
  and right to those who find knowledge.
Take my instruction instead of silver,
  and knowledge rather than choice gold;
for wisdom is better than jewels,
  and all that you may desire cannot compare with her.
"I, wisdom, live with prudence,
  and I attain knowledge and discretion.
The fear of the LORD is hatred of evil.
Pride and arrogance and the way of evil
  and perverted speech I hate.
I have good advice and sound wisdom;
  I have insight, I have strength.
By me kings reign,
  and rulers decree what is just;
by me rulers rule,
  and nobles, all who govern rightly.
I love those who love me,
  and those who seek me diligently find me.
Riches and honor are with me,
  enduring wealth and prosperity.
My fruit is better than gold, even fine gold,
  and my yield than choice silver.
I walk in the way of righteousness,
  along the paths of justice,
endowing with wealth those who love me,
  and filling their treasuries." (Prov. 8:1–21)

Lady Wisdom's invitation goes out to all with the promise that anyone can grasp God's wisdom, understand it, and receive its benefits. In the chapters that follow, we will introduce the wisdom literature of the Scriptures and explore what these books have to teach us about experiencing the good life today.

ANCIENT ISRAEL'S WISDOM LITERATURE

In the Old Testament, the books viewed as containing the most "wisdom" have traditionally been referred to as "wisdom literature." This includes the books of Job, Proverbs, Ecclesiastes, some of the psalms and, I would argue, the Song of Songs. There is a growing awareness, however, that genres are not pure forms with hard lines of separation and that texts can participate in multiple genres.[1] Along this line, recent research emphasizes that wisdom permeates all the different parts of the Old Testament.[2] While I agree that other texts throughout the Old Testament can certainly share these affinities, I also agree with Tremper Longman that Job, Proverbs, and Ecclesiastes "have a 'significant affinity' with each other that justifies the modern perception of them as participating in a genre that has been labelled 'wisdom.'"[3] In this chapter, we will introduce the concept of "wisdom," consider its relationship to wisdom in the ancient Near East, and reflect on the place of wisdom through the worldview of ancient Israel. We will introduce the books of Job, Proverbs, and Ecclesiastes, along with the so-called wisdom psalms and the Song of Songs and conclude with a discussion of how these different texts interlock to provide a comprehensive worldview.

The Nature of Hebrew Wisdom

In ancient Israel, "wisdom" (חָכְמָה) was not viewed primarily as abstract knowledge but as skill for living.[4] Biblical wisdom is about the "ways" of things—how they're meant to exist and work—and it deals with all kinds of activities, everything from sewing to farming, to building, to communicating, and so on. The purpose of biblical wisdom, however, is not just to provide insight into how to perform these activities most effectively, but also how to find their meaning in the whole of God's created order. It's about how to do these things in a way that's in harmony with God's order for the world. Each of these wisdom books addresses different aspects of God's world, so that the wisdom literature is comprehensive in its nature.

Raymond van Leeuwen offers four points to help us understand this "totalizing" nature of Hebrew wisdom.[5] First, wisdom begins with the "fear of the Lord" (יִרְאַת יְהוָה). The book of Proverbs begins with this statement (Prov. 1:7), but van Leeuwen points out that it is carefully embedded in the structure and theology of the wisdom books as a whole. It appears thirteen more times in Proverbs: at the beginning (1:7), in the middle (9:10), and at the end (31:30). It also appears in modified form in Job 28:28 and Ecclesiastes 12:13.

Walter Eichrodt (1890–1978) calls the "fear of the Lord" the "predominant trait in the personal relationship of Man with God in the Old Testament."[6] He says that it expresses "the sense of the gap between God and Man," an "oscillation between repulsion and attraction, between *mysterium tremendum* and *fasinans*."[7] Israel's reaction to the crossing of the Red Sea provides a classic example:

> And when the Israelites saw the great power of the Lord displayed against the Egyptians, the people *feared* the Lord *and put their trust in him* and in Moses his servant. (Exod. 14:31; my italics)

In this passage, the fear of and attraction to the Lord are clearly juxtaposed. Bruce Waltke calls these two reactions the "unified psychological poles" of relationship with the Lord.[8] He points to Deuteronomy 10:12 as a prime example of how these are supposed to be manifest in our relationship to God:

> "So now, O Israel, what does the Lord your God require of you? Only to fear the Lord your God, to walk in all his ways, to love him, to serve the Lord your God with all your heart and with all your soul."

He says that "the heart that both fears and loves God at one and the same time is not divided but unified in a single religious response to God."[9]

In Rudolf Otto's classic work *The Idea of the Holy: An Inquiry into the Non-Rational Factor in the Idea of the Divine and its Relation to the Rational* (1917), he uses a term that is probably best translated into English as "awe."[10] Eichrodt points out that the expression "fear of God" is used "with remarkable regularity from the earliest to the latest times."[11]

Gerhard von Rad (1901–1971) explains that the "fear of the Lord" shapes Israel's whole theory of knowledge (epistemology):

The thesis that all human knowledge comes back to the question about commitment to God is a statement of penetrating perspicacity. . . . It contains in a nutshell the whole Israelite theory of knowledge. . . . There lies behind the statement an awareness of the fact that the search for knowledge can go wrong . . . because of one single mistake at the beginning. To this extent, Israel attributes to the fear of God, to belief in God, a highly important function in respect of human knowledge. She was, in all seriousness, of the opinion that effective knowledge about God is the only thing that puts a man into a right relationship with the objects of his perception.[12]

Second, wisdom is concerned with the general order and patterns of living in God's creation. Wisdom literature is always talking about the "ways" of things. In Hebrew, the word for "way" (דֶּרֶךְ) literally refers to a "way" or a "path," and the authors of wisdom literature believed that the Lord built "ways" or "paths" into the world order. Accordingly, there are places for us to walk and ways for us to live.

Third, wisdom helps us discern the particular order of our lives. At times, our lives may seem random, but wisdom assures us that there is still an order that God created for any dilemma we face.

Fourth, wisdom is grounded in tradition. The word *tradition* has come to be scorned in recent times. In today's society, people tend to value what's new. In Hebrew society, though, they valued *tradition*, passing on traditional stories, customs, laws, and values from generation to generation. In the *Shema* (Deut. 6:4–9), for example, Moses describes the process of transmitting traditional knowledge. In examples from the New Testament, the apostle Paul talks about the importance of tradition with regard to liturgical practices at Holy Communion (1 Cor. 11:23–24) and passing on ethical precepts (1 Cor. 11:2–16; cf. also 2 Thess. 3:6). The teaching in wisdom literature is similar. In the book of Proverbs, for example, these sayings provide memorable ways for parents and teachers to pass on wisdom to children and students (e.g., Prov. 1:8–10; 2:1; 3:1). In this way, traditional wisdom is preserved in the community of God's people and handed down through traditions about God's precepts, ethics, and instructions.

Wisdom Literature in the Ancient Near East

In addition to the work produced by writers in ancient Israel, wisdom literature existed in cultures throughout the ancient Near East. For example, in particular, Egypt and Mesopotamia both produced significant collections, which we will briefly review.

EGYPTIAN WISDOM LITERATURE

Egypt has a rich and glorious past and had an expansive empire for much of its history with a stature that reached far beyond its pyramids and mummies. The writers of the Old Testament constantly testify to its influence on Israel: readers encounter Egyptians in the stories of Abraham and Joseph, and even during the time of Jeremiah. The Israelites were constantly under the influence of Egypt. In terms of wisdom literature, this influence is evident in the books of Job, Ecclesiastes, and especially Proverbs.

Egyptian wisdom has both similarities and dissimilarities with biblical wisdom. Like Israelite wisdom, Egyptian wisdom is grounded in creation, tied to its monarch, and handed down through family tradition (cf. Prov. 1:1–7; 3:19–30; Ps. 104:19). Another similarity can be found in the role of the Egyptian goddess Ma'at, who shares parallels with Wisdom (חָכְמָה) as we find her in the Bible. J. A. Wilson says that Ma'at was "the cosmic force of harmony, order, stability, and security . . . and the organizing quality of created phenomena."[13] In this way, Ma'at was similar to biblical Wisdom. Egyptian wisdom is dissimilar, however, in its "consubstantial" view of reality in which gods, humans, animals, water, and nature are all part of one spectrum of being or substance.

There are several groups of wisdom writings in Egypt. The first consists of hymns and prayers, similar to the book of Psalms. These consist of hymns to the gods, the pharaohs, the sun, and the Nile. A second group was comprised of instructional texts. The Egyptians probably produced more wisdom than any other ancient Near Eastern culture, and they developed schools (often attached to temples) whose main purpose was to produce "full-scale manuals of behavior" in collections known as "instruction" or "teaching."[14] This material provides a close parallel to Israelite wisdom literature. Books like the Instructor for Mirika-re (fifteenth century BC), the Instruction of Ani (ca. eleventh to the eighth centuries), and writings by Ptahhotep are especially significant. Such instructional materials are typically addressed to a "son," who is being given advice and encouragement to use wisdom to be successful in life and often in kingship.

When we study Egyptian wisdom literature, it's evident that these writings have more parallels with Proverbs than any other ancient source. There's one collection, in fact—that of Amenemope—that has especially close parallels in Proverbs 22:17–24:22. The table on the following page provides some examples.[15]

Finally, there are a number of ancient Egyptian wisdom writings that resemble the autobiographical form of instruction we find in Ecclesiastes. Examples include the Instruction of King Amenemhet, the Instruction of Prince Hor-Dedef, and the Instruction of Amenemope.

Amenemope	Proverbs
Do not carry off the landmark at the boundaries of the arable land, nor disturb the position of the measuring chord; be not greedy after a cubit of land, nor encroach upon the boundaries of a widow. (7:15)	Do not remove the ancient landmark that your ancestors set up. (22:28) Do not remove an ancient landmark or encroach on the fields of orphans. (25:10)
Do not eat bread before a noble, nor lay on thy mouth at first, if thou are satisfied with false chewings, they are a pastime for spittle. Look at the cup which is before thee, and let it serve thy needs. (23:15)	When you sit down to eat with an official, observe carefully what is before you, and put a knife to your throat if you have a big appetite. Do not desire an official's delicacies, for they are deceptive food. (23:1–3)

TABLE 1.1. A comparison of selected material from Amenemope and Proverbs

MESOPOTAMIAN WISDOM

Whereas Egypt had a consubstantial worldview (that is, all reality is in one harmonious spectrum), it was much more fragmented in Mesopotamia. Scholars have speculated that this worldview may have evolved out of an unpredictable climate. Since they considered the elements of nature as gods, and their weather was erratic, this meant that the gods were not in harmony and therefore their mythology is characterized by chaos. Their mythology—which includes stories such as Enuma Elish and the Gilgamesh Epic—are characterized by impulsive sexuality and violent battles. There is no Mesopotamian parallel to the Egyptian Ma'at.

Mesopotamian wisdom literature dates back as early as 2700 BC, with four main categories:

1. *Wisdom and Poetic Writings.* There are two famous collections in which a father gives advice to his son. These are Shurappak (versions date from 2500, 1800, and 1100 BC) to his son, Ziusudra, and Shube'awilum (second millennium BC) to his son. There's also a collection of counsels and sayings from Ahiqar (sixth century BC) that is similar to Proverbs.

2. *Theodicy.* These are texts that grapple with the question of how a good deity can allow evil and injustice. Mesopotamian theodicies resemble the book of Job. These include *The Worm and the Toothache* (ANET 100–101), *Man and His God* (ANET 589–91), and *The Babylonian Theodicy* (ANET 601–604). *The Man and His God* is a

Sumerian version of the book of Job, and *The Babylonian Theodicy* is a poem about a man and his friends that is similar to the dialogue between Job and his friends (Job 3–37).

3. *Poetry.* These are hymns and prayers, including praises of gods and creation lamentations, and psalms.

4. *Legal Writings.* These include law codes and treaties.

Wisdom and Worldview in Ancient Israel

The relationship between Israel's wisdom literature and its ancient Near Eastern neighbors is clear. When we do a comparative study, the similarities help us understand the context in which the Israelites composed their literature. It is often, however, the differences that help us understand their work the most. Although the Israelites used the forms that were common in the ancient world, they transformed them to express their distinctive theology, religion, worldview, politics, and ethics.

As already noted, the most important element of Israel's wisdom is that it begins with "the fear of the LORD" (Prov. 1:7; 9:10; cf. Job 28:28; Eccles. 12:13). Their wisdom has a single origin and a single religious path. This produced a unified system of thought that is a unique product of Israel's monotheism. Their religious view of wisdom thus critiqued the naturalism and pantheism of their neighbors by encouraging lives of faith and obedience that testified to the Lord as the one true God of all, and it affected every area of Israelite life. This can be illustrated as follows in Table 1.2 on the following page.

The foregoing chart illustrates how Old Testament wisdom sought to frame a worldview for Israel, one grounded in creation and in the Torah (that is, the law). God intended this wisdom literature to direct the Israelite people onto a "way" or "path" (דֶּרֶךְ) of life that would lead to successful living, thinking, relating, and working in this world.

The Book of Job

The issue of suffering is at the heart of the book of Job. Since everyone shares the experience of suffering, this book has a universal appeal. Its message is timeless. More specifically, the main character of the book suffers even though he is apparently not the cause of his suffering. When his physical

	ANE Wisdom	Israelite Wisdom
Divinity	Henotheism = many gods, often in conflict; pantheism = gods in nature, worshiped as such	Monotheism = only one God
Creation	Chaotic, violent, sexual, purposeless	Ordered and purposeful; humankind bears the *imago Dei* and has dominion
Nature	Consubstantialism = all is one	God is holy = literally, "separate"
King	Divine and the origin of law and wisdom	Rules on the Lord's behalf, under the God's law and wisdom, and is an example to the people
Wisdom	Cultural variety; strong humanistic overtones	Begins with the "fear of the Lord"; ethical and religious
Sexuality	Fertility cults; not monogamous	"Good"; monogamous; for the building of the promised nation

TABLE 1.2. A comparison of ancient Near Eastern and Israelite wisdom

suffering is compounded by his mental anguish, he asks, "Why me? What have I done to deserve this fate?" This book raises one of the most perplexing questions facing people everywhere: Are God's ways just? This is the question of theodicy. The book of Job is complex, and it is difficult both to translate and to interpret.

DATE, AUTHORSHIP, AND HISTORICAL PERIOD

The date and authorship of the book of Job are unknown. Technically, the author is anonymous. Although there are some indications about the setting of the book, there is really nothing definitive. The story seems to be set in the patriarchal period. Job is a patriarch like Abraham, whose great wealth is measured in terms of the number of his cattle and servants (1:3; 42:12). He was also the head of a large family for whom he served as priest, much like Abraham did for his family. He offered sacrifices (1:5), which would have been unthinkable after the formal priesthood was established at Mount Sinai. Also, his age exceeds the ages of the patriarchs. He lived 140 years after his restoration (42:16).

It seems clear that Job was a non-Israelite. Although it's not clear where "Uz" was located, it seems that a convincing argument can be made that it was not in Israel.[16] It appears that Job lived before the Abrahamic covenant, which limited the covenant community to a particular family.

This may situate the plot in the patriarchal period or even the pre-patriarchal period, but that doesn't necessarily mean that the book was *composed* during that time. Some argue on the basis of the book's language or its developed angelology that it was written later in the history of Israel, but the date of composition is simply unknown. Fortunately, there's nothing theological that hinges on knowing the author or the date of composition of the book.

CONTENT

A simple outline of the book of Job can be delineated as follows:

1. Narrative prologue (1:1–2:21)

2. Dialogues about Job's suffering (3:1–42:12)

   - Job's dialogues with his "friends" (3:1–42:12)
   - Elihu's monologue (32:1–37:53)
   - The Lord questions Job and his friends (38:1–42:12)

3. Narrative conclusion (42:13–30)

This book has a "sandwich" structure. That is, it begins with a narrative prologue (1:1–2:21), switches to a poetic dialogue, and then switches back to narrative for the conclusion. In this way, the beginning and end provide a narrative frame for the book. The prologue opens the narrative by introducing the main characters and the setting. It begins with God praising his servant Job to the "accuser," who then challenges God to allow him to put Job to the test. God grants the accuser's request, and Job immediately experiences terrible trials that include property loss, the deaths of his children, and attacks on his health. Since Job is unaware of the conversation between God and the accuser that took place in the divine council chamber, it seems to him that he suffers for no reason. Thus the prologue raises the problem that needs to be resolved: Job's suffering despite his apparent innocence.

The dialogue section (3:1–42:12) begins with a lament (ch. 3) where Job bemoans his fate, even wondering why he was born. His lament is similar to those found in some of the psalms. Chapters 4–27 contain three cycles of dialogues in which each of Job's three "friends"—Eliphaz, Bildad, and Zophar—address Job to which he then responds. These three each advocate a sort of mechanical view of "retribution theology": the idea that God blesses the righteous and curses the wicked. Job's friends therefore argue that if Job is suffering, then he must be a sinner in need of repentance (4:7–11; 11:13–20).

Job reacts strongly against this. Although he has been afflicted, he insists that it's not because he has sinned. He never claims that he's totally without sin, and he agrees with Bildad that no one can be righteous before God (9:2). But he does question whether he can get justice from God. In 9:21–24, he boldly repudiates the wisdom of his friends, and he brazenly asserts that God "destroys both the blameless and the wicked" (v. 22). In chapters 27–31, Job gives a speech in which he broods on how his life used to be when he enjoyed God's blessings (ch. 29), and he argues again of his blamelessness and insists that he doesn't deserve the suffering that's befallen him.

In the midst of this section, in chapter 28, is a poem on divine wisdom. In this poem, Job bows before God's superior wisdom but then complains again in the following chapters. This sudden change in temperament suggests that the poem may be out of place,[17] or that Job has a moment of insight before lapsing back into depression.

At this point (chs. 32–37), an unknown character named Elihu enters the dialogue. Up until this point, he hasn't appeared in the book, but he enters the story as a sort of brash young man who thinks he has all the answers. Really, though, he doesn't have anything new to say, and he basically repeats the same old theology of retribution: Job is suffering because he has sinned (34:11, 25–27, 37).

Throughout the dialogues, Job holds out hope for an interview with God (23:2–7), which takes place when God appears to him in the form of a storm (38:1–42:6). Usually when God appears in the form of a storm, it's a symbol of judgment (e.g., Pss. 18, 29; Nah. 1). Even though God finally grants Job the interview for which he has longed, God never directly answers Job's questions but only rebukes him for casting aspersions on his divine reputation. He asks Job,

> "Will you even put me in the wrong?
> Will you condemn me that you may be justified?" (40:8)

God doesn't really answer the question of justice but instead addresses the question of the real source of wisdom: that God alone is wise. The Lord speaks from the storm and asks Job a series of questions that sets the stage for the next few chapters—questions that only God could possibly answer:

> "Who is this that darkens counsel by words without knowledge?
> Gird up your loins like a man;
> I will question you, and you shall declare to me." (38:2–3)

The questions that follow demonstrate God's full knowledge and control of the natural order that he has created, which contrasts with Job's ignorance. The implication is that the same is true for the moral world: It too is beyond Job's comprehension. After this, the Lord asks Job a series of rhetorical questions about the source of wisdom:

> "Where were you when I laid the foundation of the earth?
>   Tell me, if you have understanding.
> Who determined its measurements—surely you know!
>   Or who stretched the line upon it?
> On what were its bases sunk,
>   or who laid its cornerstone
> when the morning stars sang together
>   and all the heavenly beings shouted for joy?
>
> "Or who shut in the sea with doors
>   when it burst out from the womb,
> when I made the clouds its garment
>   and thick darkness its swaddling band,
> and prescribed bounds for it,
>   and set bars and doors,
> and said, 'Thus far shall you come and no farther,
>   and here shall your proud waves be stopped'?
>
> "Have you commanded the morning since your days began
>   and caused the dawn to know its place,
> so that it might take hold of the skirts of the earth,
>   and the wicked be shaken out of it?
> It is changed like clay under the seal,
>   and it is dyed like a garment.
> Light is withheld from the wicked,
>   and their uplifted arm is broken.
>
> "Have you entered into the springs of the sea
>   or walked in the recesses of the deep?
> Have the gates of death been revealed to you,
>   or have you seen the gates of deep darkness?
> Have you comprehended the expanse of the earth?
>   Declare, if you know all this." (38:4–18)

This litany of rhetorical questions concludes when the Lord asks Job,

> "Who has put wisdom in the inward parts
>   or given understanding to the mind?" (38:36)

Forced to recognize God's power, Job responds humbly and penitently, and he submits himself to the Almighty God of the universe and his will.

The epilogue (42:7–17) brings the story to a happy conclusion when Job is reconciled with God and his fortune is restored to him. God blesses him and allows him to live a long life. Even though he grew frustrated, Job found favor in God's eyes because he didn't "curse God and die" as his wife advised him, nor did he give into the facile arguments of his friends who had advocated a mechanical version of "retribution theology." When Job was finally confronted by God, he responded appropriately with repentance and submission.

LITERARY BACKGROUND OF JOB

There are a number of books that bear strong similarities to Job, which shouldn't be surprising since the book deals with universal questions of suffering and especially how suffering relates to piety. This is a question people everywhere, in all religious systems, still ask today. In Francis I. Andersen's classic commentary on Job, he includes a discussion of similar books from Sumer, Egypt, Babylonia, Ugarit, and even India that span nearly a dozen pages.[18] The two most famous parallels are the "Babylonian Theodicy" and another piece titled "I Will Praise the Lord of Wisdom," both of which were mentioned above.[19]

Although Job is certainly not the first book written that deals with the question of why the righteous suffer, among other books of its genre, it is somewhat unique. If it is intended to be a theodicy, then it raises the question of theodicy without resolving Job's questions about why he suffers. God's only answer is that the ultimate explanation is beyond the comprehension of the human mind.

One scholar proposes that a better designation for the literary genre of Job is "wisdom debate."[20] He points out that the question of the source of wisdom is at the heart of the book, and that each of the parties involved claims it for themselves and disputes the wisdom of the others.

IS JOB A HISTORICAL BOOK?

The question of historicity complements the discussion of genre, since both could potentially include the question of whether or not Job is a historical or fictional book. Evangelicals tend to *assume* that the book is historical, based on the premise that all biblical material must be literally true in order to be valid. Scripture, however, contains parables, fables, and metaphors that are not "historical," but this doesn't make them any less "true." So, we should at least consider the possibility that Job could be a fable or a folktale.

The cycles of well-crafted dialogues in chapters 4 through 27 may be an indicator that we're not reading transcripts of conversations. First, these dialogues are written in verse as poetry and are highly artistic—people in antiquity didn't speak to one another in poetry any more than we do today.

Second, the dialogues are also highly structured. In each of the three cycles of dialogues, one of the friends addresses Job and then he responds to each one in turn. The order is always Eliphaz, Bildad, and then Zophar. The book is a sophisticated, artistic literary product, and its poetry elevates it to a position of timelessness.

Third, aside from its artistic structure, the circumstances of the story seem unrealistic or staged. The idea seems unrealistic that God would allow the adversary to wreak havoc in a man's life, who would then be satisfied by simply having all his family replaced with a new one along with his lost wealth. From this perspective, the story of Job seems like a parable created to explore theological ideas.

On the other hand, Job is mentioned three times outside of the book, two times along with two other historical figures from the Old Testament, Noah and Daniel (Ezek. 14:14, 20). He's also mentioned in James 5:11, although we might argue that this reference doesn't necessarily imply that Job was a historical figure. After all, we often refer to fictional characters to make a point. I have heard countless people quote Frodo or Gandalf, for example, because they relate so well to their experiences even though they are fictional. People in antiquity could also relate to fictional characters. And so, although we should not be dogmatic about it, we should probably leave open the possibility that the book of Job could be a fable or a folktale.

THE THEOLOGY OF JOB

The book of Job reflects on several key theological ideas, two of which are divine wisdom and human suffering. God alone is the source of wisdom, and the proper response to God is repentance and submission. Regarding human suffering, the book counters a wooden or mechanical view of retribution. Of course, the Bible teaches that both obedience and sin have appropriate consequences. Deuteronomy 28 says that those who follow the law will be blessed, while those who defy it will be cursed. The books of 1 and 2 Kings bear this out when the sins of the kings lead to the exile. And Proverbs says that those who follow the way of wisdom will "live in safety and be at ease, without fear of harm" (2:33). So there is some truth to the idea that sin leads to suffering. Job's friends, however, warp the idea of retribution theology to say that if you suffer, then you *must* have sinned. The difference in perspective is profound. Instead of saying that sin leads to suffering, they're saying that all suffering is explained by sin. The book of Job is a corrective against this type of faulty reasoning. Personal sin is not the only reason for suffering in the world.

APPROACHING THE NEW TESTAMENT

The story of the relationship between God and human suffering doesn't end with Job. The New Testament claims that God reveals his love for humankind by sending his Son Jesus, the Messiah, to die on the cross. Jesus is the true innocent sufferer. He voluntarily submits himself to suffer for the benefit of sinful humanity. Andersen says, "That the Lord himself has embraced and absorbed the undeserved consequences of evil is the final answer to Job and all the Jobs of humanity."[21] The early Christian community recognized the connection between Job and Jesus, and it was a common practice to read the book of Job during Holy Week.[22]

The Wisdom Psalms

The wisdom psalms appear in the book of Psalms, which is a collection of one hundred and fifty poems often referred to as ancient Israel's hymnbook. In order to study the wisdom psalms, we must first look at the book of Psalms as a whole, including its authorship, setting, and the types of psalms included in the collection. We will then examine the wisdom psalms and their distinctive features.

AUTHORSHIP, SETTING, AND CONTENTS OF THE PSALTER

There are two aspects to consider in terms of the authorship of Psalms, including: (1) the authorship of each individual psalm, and (2) the author or editor who compiled the Psalter as a whole. Of the 150 psalms, 115 of them are associated with a named person or group of persons in the title. Seventy-three are connected with David, Psalm 90 is associated with Moses, and some are identified with the "sons of Korah" and others with "Asaph."

In terms of the entire book, we might wonder if there is a rationale for the inclusion of each particular psalm recorded in the Psalter; it seems unlikely that every psalm ever recorded in ancient Israel found its way into the book. What was the rhyme or reason in the process of compiling the book? How were the psalms arranged? There have been many suggestions.

Since the Pentateuch was divided into 153 sections for reading in the synagogue, the question has been raised as to whether there may have been some correlation with the format of the Psalms. In modern Bibles, the book of Psalms is broken into five separate books, and this fivefold division is actually present in the oldest manuscripts of the Psalms as follows:

Book I: Chapters 1–41
Book II: Chapters 42–72
Book III: Chapters 73–89
Book IV: Chapters 90–106
Book V: Chapters 107–150

Based on evidence, there have been efforts to identify smaller groupings, as follows:

Pss. 3–41 are related to David
Pss. 42–49 are connected with the Sons of Korah
Pss. 51–56 are another Davidic grouping
Pss. 73–83 are associated with Asaph
Pss. 84–88 are another group connected with the sons of Korah
Pss. 95–100 are grouped as a congregational praise
Pss. 111–17 are grouped as a hallelujah
Pss. 120–34 are songs of ascent
Pss. 138–45 are another Davidic grouping
Pss. 146–150 are another congregational praise grouping

In the copies of the Psalms among the Dead Sea Scrolls, there is some variation in this order, which may indicate that the order of the Psalter was still in flux even as late as 200 BC.

The Psalter was not assembled arbitrarily, though, and there is some evidence of its arrangement. John Walton proposes that there are "seam psalms," which can be traced through the entire book, that share the theme of the vindication of God's people through the maintenance of the Davidic line.[23] This proposal suggests a clear purpose for the compilation of the Psalter. In this view, the book of Psalms in its entirety provides an inner reflection on the history of Israel. While this is somewhat speculative, its strength is that it proposes a purpose for the Psalter as a whole. While modern readers tend to focus on individual psalms, as if there were no connection between them, it makes sense that an editor would not compile a book with no overarching purpose.

TYPES OF PSALMS

Most or all of the psalms were probably meant to be sung or accompanied by music. Hermann Gunkel (1862–1932), who was a pioneer of "form criticism," identified five major literary categories among the psalms: (1) hymns, (2) community laments, (3) individual thanksgiving songs, (4) individual laments, and (5) poems of mixed types.[24] He thought that each of these genres originated in the context of Israel's worship.[25] Others, however, have argued against a cultic interpretation and claim that the psalms originated as individual expressions of Israelite piety.[26] Still others have cautioned against associating the psalms too closely with the temple or identifying them too strictly with fixed genres.[27] Recent studies are much more cautious about trying to identify a cultic origin, liturgical use, or the historical referentiality for each psalm.[28] Today, most scholars recognize six main types of psalms: (1) hymns of praise, (2) thanksgiving psalms, (3) individual laments, (4) community laments, (5) royal psalms honoring either the Lord as king or the earthly king as his representative, and (6) wisdom or didactic psalms.

In this volume, our interest is in the last category of the wisdom psalms. Ever since the time of Hermann Gunkel (1862–1932), there has been debate about whether the wisdom psalm is actually a distinctive form of psalm.[29] Most scholars recognize, however, that many psalms use the literary techniques of wisdom literature, such as proverbs, alphabetic acrostics,[30] comparisons, instruction, and admonition. Wisdom psalms typically seek to teach on a specific topic or address a particular problem, such as the prosperity of the wicked or the proper use of wealth.

There are a number of psalms that are widely accepted as wisdom psalms, including Psalms 1, 19, 36, 37, 49, 73, 78, 112, 119, 127, and 128. There are many other psalms that share wisdom features, either in whole or in part, and could be categorized as wisdom psalms.

THE THEOLOGY OF THE PSALMS

While our use of the psalms in this volume is limited to the wisdom psalms, they share the theological views reflected in the Psalter as a whole. Some of the main theological ideas in the Psalter are connected with ancient Israel's views of God and the world.

1. *View of God.* Many psalms express both the transcendence and immanence of God. On the one hand, God is high and exalted and far removed from humankind while, on the other hand, he is mindful of us and made us only a little lower than himself (e.g., Ps. 8).

2. *Relationship with God.* The psalms reflect both individual and corporate aspects of a relationship with God.

3. *Understanding of sin.* The sinfulness of humankind is blatant in the psalms (e.g., Ps. 51).

4. *View of nature and creation.* Throughout the Psalter, there is much emphasis on nature and creation. Part of the reason for this, of course, was that ancient Israel was an agricultural society. Many of the blessings and curses of Deuteronomy 28 focused on land and nature. However, the psalms always clearly distinguish God the Creator from his creation. Although God is never considered a part of creation or nature, nature is part of the creation over which he is in total control.[31]

TOWARD THE NEW TESTAMENT

The book of Psalms is quoted in the New Testament more often than any other book of the Old Testament. The New Testament authors often connected Jesus' ministry with various ideas from the psalms. For example, on one occasion, when Jesus was disgusted with the money changers in the temple and threw them all out, the disciples identified his actions with Psalm 69:9, "Zeal for your house consumes me."

The apostle Paul frequently quoted from the psalms, both in his speeches and in his letters. Understanding that the psalms had looked forward to the Messiah who would suffer and be glorified, Paul identified Jesus as that Messiah.[32] In Acts 13, for example, while Paul was preaching the gospel in a synagogue in Antioch, he explained to his audience that the messianic promises of the Old Testament had been fulfilled in Jesus. At the conclusion of his sermon, he cited four passages from the Old Testament to make his point, two of which are psalms he applied to Jesus.[33] He quoted these passages specifically to affirm Jesus' Sonship and resurrection.

There are plenty of other examples of New Testament authors who interpreted the psalms in light of Jesus' coming. Suffice it to say, the New Testament bears witness to the effect that the identification of Jesus as the Messiah has on reading the psalms.[34]

Since we are primarily interested in the wisdom psalms, we should consider what bearing the identification of Jesus as the Messiah might have on our understanding of them in particular. The wisdom psalms call us to be wise and righteous and to follow God's law (e.g., Ps. 19). The New Testament, however, makes it clear that we cannot be wise in ourselves and that we have to turn elsewhere for wisdom. According to Paul, we find this in Jesus Christ, "in whom are hidden all the treasures of wisdom and knowledge" (Col. 2:3). Identifying Jesus as the Messiah compels us to see him as the ultimate source of all wisdom and therefore as the lens through which we read the wisdom literature.

The Book of Proverbs

As we have already looked at the literary background of wisdom literature, we do not need to plow that ground again for the book of Proverbs. Instead, let's turn to the issues of authorship and date.

AUTHORSHIP, DATE, AND CONTENTS

The traditional view is that Solomon wrote the entire book of Proverbs, which seems to be supported by the titles in Proverbs 1:10, 10:1, and 25:1. We are told that Solomon was a wise man who wrote proverbs and collected sayings from other wise men (see 22:17–24:34). He is said to have "composed three thousand proverbs" and that "people came from all the nations to hear the wisdom of Solomon" (1 Kings 4:32, 34). There are a couple of sections of the book that are said to be written by Agur (30:1) and Lemuel (31:1), and those who hold to Solomonic authorship argue that these were pseudonyms for Solomon. Contemporary scholars recognize, however, that Agur and Lemuel were probably not pseudonyms for Solomon but are proper names. Also, 22:17–24:34, with its own title and purpose statement, closely mirrors the Instruction of Amenemope and is thought to be a separate collection that was added to Proverbs. Furthermore, the title of 1:1, which is usually thought to head up 1:1–9:18, may not actually refer to these chapters. It may simply be the heading of the whole book in its final form and may not necessarily indicate that the first nine chapters are from Solomon.

Many critical scholars suppose that few of the proverbs are actually by Solomon himself. Otto Eissfeldt, for example, says that only "one or another of the sayings" goes back to Solomon.[35] Ellen Davis suggests that some of the proverbs in chapters 10–29 may date to the period of the monarchy, but she presumes that much of the material in the book dates to later periods and suggests that it "assumed final form in the postexilic period, after the collapse of the nation-state before the Babylonian army (587 B.C.E.)."[36] She speculates that the rise of the kingship and its eventual collapse were two crisis points that caused people to pull together their traditional wisdom as a way to find some stability. It became a means of preserving their identity, traditional values, and culture. Her views represent common scholarly views about the compositional history of the book of Proverbs.

I suggest that the book of Proverbs cannot be dated to the postexilic period merely because it speaks to crises. While it does indeed address times of catastrophe, it's also true that its literary structure, themes, and overall structure can be clearly seen in parallels dating far earlier than the exilic period,[37] which we discussed above. A closer look at these titles may bring additional clarity to the issue:

- The heading in 10:1 clearly credits Solomon for at least some material that follows.

- In 10:1–22:16, some surmise there may be two collections (Prov. 10–15; 16:1–22:16) on the basis of the greater variety of parallelism in the second group.

- The heading in 25:1 also affirms that Solomon was the author or editor of a collection that the scribes of Hezekiah's court copied.

- There are some stylistic differences between chapters 25–27 and chapters 28–29, which include more illustrative parallelisms and grouping by topics in the first group and greater randomness in the second group.

- There are also titles in the book that are non-Solomonic, such as the collections of Agur (30:1) and Lemuel (31:1) mentioned above.

It is highly possible that Solomon may have been responsible for 10:1–22:16 and maybe all or part of chapters 25–29. There's no reason that wisdom sayings like these couldn't have been composed and collected during the Solomonic period. After all, the age of Solomon was a time of national consolidation, the organization and development of temple staff, and the collection of traditional literary works, including wisdom sayings. Most scholars see some dependence of 22:17–24:34 on the Instruction of Amenemope. While the nature of that dependence is not clear, it may be that Israel knew these sayings by the time of Solomon. The age of Solomon was a period of broad international exchange as he had many alliances and trade contacts, and he would have had scribes of foreign lands in his courts. It's therefore easy to see how similarities between Proverbs and other ancient Near Eastern literature could have developed. The prologue of 1:8–9:18 would have been added at the end to form an introduction. A simple outline of the book of Proverbs can be outlined as follows:

1. Speeches of Solomon: Introducing Wisdom (1–9)

2. Wise Sayings of Solomon: First Collection (10–22)

3. Sayings of the Wise (22–24)

4. Wise Sayings of Solomon: Second Collection (25–29)

5. Sayings of Agur: Advanced Wisdom (30)

6. The Teaching of King Lemuel's Mother (31)

AUDIENCE

Who was the intended audience for the book of Proverbs? This continues to be a subject of debate. The instruction in other ancient Near Eastern wisdom literature often comes from a royal father concerned with preparing his son to replace him. In such cases, the father is trying to teach his son self-control in terms of temperament, speech, and action so that he might be successful. Some biblical scholars argue that these provide analogies for the book of Proverbs, which must have also been written as a handbook for the elite classes.[38]

Ellen Davis points out, however, that "far from presenting a royal perspective, many of the proverbs uphold the values of peasant culture—that is, of the agrarian, kinship based, locally governed society that Israel was before the rise of the monarchy."[39] She notes that several of the proverbs deal with agriculture, such as taking care of the soil (24:30–34) and the problems the poor encounter in trying to hold onto their land (13:23; 30:14). Proverbs like these are considered "proverbial wisdom": they're what ordinary people know, and they represent grassroots knowledge, not elite knowledge.[40] As a whole, these proverbs tend to do the following:

- Focus on individuals rather than the nation.

- Apply to all people at any time who face similar issues (1:20; 8:1–5).

- Build on respect for authority, traditional values and teachings, and the wisdom of mature teachers (24:21).

- Provide immensely practical advice for developing personal qualities that are necessary for anyone to achieve success in this life and to avoid failure and shame.

Proverbs that deal with these kinds of ordinary, day-to-day issues probably represent the earliest stage of the proverbial material as traditional teaching.[41]

There are also many proverbs that indicate an urban background and may have originated among the elite classes or even been written by court sages. In the first nine chapters of Proverbs, for example, Wisdom is personified as a woman who stands at the city gates and calls out to young men in the streets to come in and learn from her. In other examples, there are proverbs that prescribe court etiquette (23:1–2; 25:6–7) or talk about the prestige of the king (16:10; 21:1).

Clearly, different sections of the book of Proverbs point to diverse contexts, with some reflecting a "family" or "tribal" stage and others an urban or even a "court" context. At some point, an educated, literate group must have been responsible for writing down and collating these proverbs. Katharine Dell suggests that this probably happened in the preexilic era, and she points to a number of factors that could lead to such a conclusion, such as: historical echoes of Kings Solomon and Hezekiah, literary evidence of earlier and later sources, social context, the theological outlook found in Proverbs, the links of its wider worldview with other parts of the Old Testament and the development of ideas, and its links with the ancient cultures of the Near East.[42]

THE THEOLOGY OF PROVERBS

There are more than 375 unrelated sayings in the book of Proverbs. These are not usually religious per se, nor do they deal with the problems of the religious community or with theological problems such as election, redemption, or covenant. Instead, they largely deal with human problems in general. On the other hand, Proverbs is not a secular book. Its teachings are grounded in the "fear of the LORD" (1:7), which connects all the proverbs with morality and spirituality.[43] Elsewhere in the book, it says that the "fear of the LORD" is manifested in a life of obedience, confessing, and forsaking sin (28:18) and doing what is right (21:3). These are said to be the believer's task before God (17:3). Proverbs also ties the way of wisdom to the Torah (28:4; 29:18). Rabbi Gunther Plaut says, "There are no 'secular' proverbs which can be contrasted with 'religious' ones; everything on earth serves the purposes of God and is potentially holy."[44]

TOWARD THE NEW TESTAMENT

In the New Testament, various authors draw on the book of Proverbs, which clearly means they appreciated its religious value. The following chart provides some examples of passages New Testament authors have either quoted or alluded:

Proverbs 25:6–7	Luke 14:7–11
Proverbs 3:11–12	Hebrews 12:5–6
Proverbs 3:34	James 4:6 1 Peter 5:5
Proverbs 11:31	1 Peter 4:18
Proverbs 25:21–22	Romans 12:20
Proverbs 26:11	2 Peter 2:22
Proverbs 3:11–12	Hebrews 12:5–6

TABLE 1.3. Select examples of proverbs used by New Testament authors

The Book of Ecclesiastes

Ecclesiastes is one of the most beguiling books of the Bible, and its apparent pessimism caused its inclusion in the canon of Scripture to be questioned. Ultimately, it was accepted because it was thought to be the work of Solomon.[45]

AUTHORSHIP AND DATE

The question of the authorship of Ecclesiastes is controversial. In verse 1, the author is identified first as *Qoheleth* (קֹהֶלֶת), which is typically rendered "Preacher" or "Teacher."[46] Qoheleth, however, doesn't mean "preacher" or "teacher" but is from the noun *qahal* (קהל), which means "assembly." A literal translation would be something like "Assembler" or "Gatherer." Throughout this discussion and the remainder of the book, we will leave the term untranslated and simply refer to the author of Ecclesiastes as Qoheleth.

Traditionally, Qoheleth is identified as Solomon. This may be implied in the opening verse, where Qoheleth is identified as the "son of David, king in Jerusalem." Again, at 1:12, the text says, "I, Qoheleth, was king over Israel in Jerusalem." Solomon *was* at the forefront of trade and culture. He did have important contacts with Egypt, including an Egyptian wife, and Egypt had a wealth of wisdom literature. This literature includes poems that grapple with the problems of life. For example, one of these is a dispute over suicide.[47] In Mesopotamia, examples include the Epic of Gilgamesh[48] and A Pessimistic

Dialogue between Master and Servant.[49] Surely, Solomon would have been familiar with these. He may have collected them and then added his own contribution to the corpus of Near Eastern wisdom literature. Unfortunately, Solomon didn't stay true to the wisdom tradition. He failed in his moral commitments as he grew older, both in the concessions he made to his wives (1 Kings 11:4–6) and in the way he treated his subjects (cf. 1 Kings 12:14).

Based on some vocabulary and grammar issues, most scholars today date Ecclesiastes to the end of the Persian period (528–323 BC), around the third century BC.[50] On the basis of a reevaluation of Qoheleth's Hebrew, Daniel Fredericks has argued that it is possible that the date could be somewhat earlier.[51] There is nothing in the text, however, that requires it be viewed as being written by Solomon since he is never actually named as the book's author. Any king of Judah could be identified as a "son of David," just as every man is a "son of Adam" and every woman a "daughter of Eve." Whoever Qoheleth was, he was a Solomon-like figure and a believing Israelite gifted with exceptional wisdom.

UNITY AND CONTENTS OF ECCLESIASTES

Scholars have often surmised that Ecclesiastes had more than one author. There are at least two reasons for this: (1) variations in literary forms, and (2) what some have viewed as a blend of unorthodox and unorthodox statements. Some have suggested that there are complaints about something being vanity, and that these are then followed by orthodox correctives, with a completely orthodox conclusion that brings the book to a conclusion. Among those who see the book as a unified whole, there are a number of approaches:

- It is the work of a single author augmented by editorial glosses along the way.

- The author presents the claims of conventional wisdom only to refute them from his wealth of experience.

- The author records his changing viewpoints over the years.

- It represents a dialogue between the author and a philosophical antagonist.

The book concludes with an epilogue (12:9–14) written in the third person, which has led many interpreters to conclude that it was written by a later editor who reacted to and maybe even corrected Qoheleth's troublesome teachings.[52] This view is clearly mistaken, however, as a careful reading demonstrates that the author of the epilogue clearly endorsed Qoheleth's teachings (vv. 9–11) and located him within the tradition of Israelite wisdom (vv. 11–12).[53] If the epilogue was written by an editor or compiler, then it was someone who essentially agreed with these teachings. Whoever the author or editor may have been, this person brings the book to a close with a brief postscript that clinches Qoheleth's reflections with an orthodox conclusion (vv. 13–14).

In the end, I am inclined to view the book of Ecclesiastes in its canonical form as a unity. A simple outline of Ecclesiastes may be presented as follows:

1. Superscription (1:1)

2. Introductory poem on the transience of life (1:2–11)

3. Qoheleth's failed quest for meaning (1:2–26)

4. A time for everything (3:1–22)

5. Work and the benefits of companionship (4:1–16)

6. Fear the Lord (5:1–9)

7. Wealth and satisfaction, the Lord's sovereignty, and the transience of life (5:10–6:12)

8. A collection of sayings (7:1–29)

9. Wisdom's elusiveness and some samples of traditional court wisdom (8:1–17)

10. Death, joy, and the superiority of wisdom (9:1–18)

11. Another collection of miscellaneous sayings (10:1–20)

12. The value of diligence (11:1–6)

13. Youth and old age (11:7–12:8)

14. Fear God and keep his commandments (12:28–36)

THE THEOLOGY OF ECCLESIASTES

After being introduced to Qoheleth as a "son of David, king in Jerusalem" (Eccles. 1:1), readers may expect to encounter the lofty thoughts of a royal philosopher who has affinity with the man (David) after God's own heart (1 Sam. 13:14). They may be shocked when they get to verse 2, which introduces a refrain that is repeated throughout the book: that everything is "vanity" (KJV). The Hebrew word is *hebel* (הֶבֶל) and its translation as "vanity," along with Qoheleth's fixation on death,[54] has suggested to many that the author is saying that world is completely and utterly without value. This has led many commentators to view Ecclesiastes as "pessimistic literature."[55]

It seems more likely, however, that Qoheleth was evaluating life in light of the fall and its results, and therefore he uses wisdom to study life and provide direction for surviving and succeeding in a fallen world.[56] This interpretation hinges on several factors, including a more positive translation of *hebel*, an understanding of the use of the phrase "under the sun," and recognizing the rhetorical argument associated with the structure of the book.

TRANSLATION OF *HEBEL*

Most commentators have consistently and overwhelmingly understood that the Hebrew word *hebel* has to do with valuelessness. It was Jerome's translation of *hebel* into Latin as *vanitas* that charted the path for it to be understood as "vanity"; this has remained the standard view up to the present time.[57] In addition to "vanity" (KJV), it has also been rendered as "meaningless" (NIV), "useless" (GNB), and "absurd" (Fox). All of these translations (and others like them) understand *hebel* as conveying valuelessness. This has led many Christian interpreters—from ancient to modern times—to conclude that Qoheleth was saying that the world was completely and totally without value.[58] While outside of Ecclesiastes, *hebel* sometimes does have to do with valuelessness,[59] its usage in Ecclesiastes does not focus on transience.[60] Qoheleth agrees with other Israelite and ancient Near Eastern sages who were concerned about the brevity of life.[61] *Hebel* literally means "vapor" or "breath" and in Ecclesiastes is used to convey the idea that everything in life is transient, like a breath.[62] Since the translation of Daniel Fredericks, which is included in his commentary on Ecclesiastes,[63] is the only one I am aware of that renders *hebel* this way, I will cite it often.

Commentators, both ancient and modern, have also noticed that there is a relationship between the books of Ecclesiastes and Genesis 4, which recounts the story of Cain and Abel.[64] In Hebrew, Abel's name is exactly the same as the Hebrew word *hebel* (Gen. 4:4). Although Abel was the righteous one in the story, his life was cut short when his brother murdered him. Abel's life was the epitome of transience. Qoheleth takes the idea of the transience of Abel's life and makes it the theme of his book, expanding it to everything in life. When he applies the word *hebel* to someone or something, he is saying it is "Abel-like" or has some aspect of "Abel-ness." As Russell Meeks explains, "Not only is Abel transient, but everyone and everything in life is subject to the reversal of fortunes that he experienced."[65]

This theme is introduced at the very beginning of the book in Ecclesiastes 1:2, which Daniel Fredericks translates as follows: " 'Breath of breaths,' said Qoheleth, 'Breath of breaths. Everything is temporary!' " This opening refrain is then followed by a poem about death and the fleeting nature of life (1:3–11), subjects discussed throughout the book. The writer brings the book to a conclusion by repeating the refrain: " 'Breath of breaths, everything is temporary!' says Qoheleth" (12:8). The repetition of this refrain at the beginning and end of the book provides bookends that summarize its thesis: Life is like a fleeting breath in a broken world without a reverential awe of God (12:13).[66]

THE PHRASE "UNDER THE SUN"

The expression "under the sun" is introduced at the beginning of Ecclesiastes (1:3). Michael Eaton observes that it reflects a "heaven-earth dichotomy" that is held in tension throughout the book and is essential to its interpretation.[67] He points to Qoheleth's observation that God dwells in heaven while humankind inhabits the earth (5:2). This is an underlying assumption throughout the entire book, where humankind lives out their lives "under the sun," "under heaven," or "on earth." This heaven-earth dichotomy features in other ancient works—such as in Babylonian, Phoenician, Sidonian, and Greek texts—and would have been "easily comprehensible in the ancient world."[68] Eaton explains,

> The Preacher's point is that what is to be seen with sheer pessimism "under the sun" may be seen differently in the light of faith in the generosity of God: mankind gains nothing "under the sun" (1:3); the "earth" which is dominated by futility "goes on forever" (1:4); no new thing can take place "under the sun" (1:9–11). As for the scope of the Preacher's research, he sought out what was done "under heaven" (1:13) and evaluated what resources could be found "under the sun" (1:14). His quest for pleasure likewise found no hope of gain "under the sun" (2:11); what is done "under the sun" was grievous to him (2:17f.).[69]

Qoheleth's account of life lived "under the sun" seems to describe life lived with a finite perspective that leaves God out of the account.

> Then dramatically the Preacher introduces God and all changes. The "under the sun" terminology falls into the background or lapses altogether (2:24–26; 11:1–12:14); instead he refers to the "hand of God" (2:24), the joy of man (2:25; 3:12; 5:18, 20; 9:7; 11:7–9), and the generosity of God (2:26; 3:13; 5:19).[70]

Eaton concludes that "Ecclesiastes is thus an exploration of the barrenness of life without a practical faith in God."[71]

THE RHETORICAL ARGUMENT

The structure of the book of Ecclesiastes, which is made up of the opening and closing refrains about the transience of life (1:2; 12:8) along with the poems about the brevity of life and the finality of death (1:3–11; 11:7–12:7), reveals a rhetorical argument. Life lived "under the sun" is brief and fleeting, and so Qoheleth makes the case for giving the Lord a central position in our lives. The message is not agnostic, skeptical, or pessimistic. It is a message "of hope and vivid instruction on how to make one's life count despite the brokenness of the world due to sin."[72]

TOWARD THE NEW TESTAMENT

Christians might ask how the stress on enjoying life tallies with the New Testament command to "not love the world" (1 John 2:15). The answer is that Qoheleth would agree with John's next statement that "everything in the world—the cravings of sinful man, the lust of his eyes and the boasting of what he has and does—comes not from the Father but from the world. The world and its desires pass away" (vv. 16–17). It would be hard to find a better statement of the whole theme of Ecclesiastes than this (e.g., Eccles. 2:1–11; 5:10). Life in the world has significance only when people remember their Creator (Eccles. 12:1).

> There always have been two kinds of teaching about the way to holiness. One is by withdrawal as far as possible from the natural in order to promote the spiritual. The other is to use and transform the natural into the expression of the spiritual. While each kind of teaching has its place, some people need one emphasis rather than the other. Ecclesiastes definitely teaches the second.[73]

The Song of Songs

This short book titled the Song of Solomon is also known as the Song of Songs (Song 1:1), which is a superlative meaning "the best of all songs." Despite the lofty claim of the Song's first line, there was great uncertainty among the rabbis about whether it really belonged in the Old Testament canon. A major part of their reasoning was that it wasn't clear to them whether the Song was sacred or secular. While it mentions the name Solomon and refers to known places in Israel, which establish its identity as Israelite literature, the usual marks of biblical literature are absent such as religious themes, institutions, and practices. There are no references to law, grace, sin, salvation, or prayer. In fact, there's not a single, indisputable reference to the Lord in the text. In the end, however, it was retained in the canon and even lauded by Rabbi Akiba as its "Holy of Holies."[74]

AUTHORSHIP AND DATE

Traditionally, the Song of Songs was attributed to King Solomon, for several reasons: (1) Song 1:1 refers to "the Song of Songs, which is Solomon's," which many readers understand as an attribution of authorship; (2) Solomon had a reputation as a song writer (cf. 1 Kings 4:32); (3) Solomon's name is mentioned six times in the book, and there are references to a king in several other passages;[75] and (4) Solomon's massive harem of "seven hundred princesses and three hundred concubines" (1 Kings 11:3) has led people to think of him as a romantic, to put it mildly.

Although Solomon is mentioned a few times in the book, it is unlikely that he was its original author. The reference to the Song of Songs, "which is Solomon's," is not necessarily a statement about authorship. The Hebrew phrase rendered as "which is Solomon's" could be just as easily translated as "which was to Solomon" or "which was for Solomon." The statement could be explained by any one of a number of scenarios. For example, he could have commissioned it, or it was written much later and dedicated to him. Solomon is never the speaker in the book; and in the passages that mention him, it is in the context of an explicit comparison (Song 1:5; 8:11–12). In the references to a king, the female speaker is probably making an implicit comparison between her beloved and Solomon. There is no clear evidence for when the book may have been written, although the use of the Persian word for "garden" in 4:13 has led some scholars to conclude that it should be dated to the postexilic period.

CONTENTS

The Song of Songs is made up of a number of songs, although exactly how many is unclear. In *Love Lyrics from the Bible*, Maria Falk identifies thirty-one poems in the book.[76] Tremper Longman recognizes twenty-three poems[77] while John Collins distinguishes only eleven. Because of its brevity, I'm including an adaptation of it here:[78]

1. The woman expresses her longing for the beloved and introduces herself to "the daughters of Jerusalem." She compares herself to a vineyard, which she "has not kept." (Song 1:2–6)

2. A conversation between man and woman, which begins with requests for a meeting and climaxes in mutual praise. (Song 1:-2:7)

3. A poem recounting an encounter with the beloved. (Song 2:8–17)

4. A description of the search for and discovery of the beloved. (Song 3:1–5)

5. A poem describing a wedding procession of King Solomon, which may be an implied analogy, comparing the grandeur of the beloved to the glory of Solomon. (Song 3:6–11)

6. A poem describing the physical beauty of the woman. This kind of poem is called a *wasf* and is typical of Near Eastern love poetry. (Song 4:1–5:1)

7. A dialogue between the woman and the daughters of Jerusalem, which includes a description of the man in the style of a *wasf*. (Song 5:2–6:4)

8. A *wasf* poem voiced by the man in praise of the woman. (Song 6:5–12)

9. Another *wasf* in adoration of the woman. (Song 7:1–9)

10. A poem by the woman expressing her desire. (Song 7:10–8:4)

11. A series of brief poems that serve as an epilogue or conclusion. In 8:12, the woman refers to "my vineyard, my very own," which echoes the opening verses. (Song 8:5–14)

Throughout the Song, the couple repeatedly separates and then reunites. Beyond that, the Song explores the intensity of desire in increasingly ways throughout its stanzas.

WISDOM LITERATURE

The Song of Songs has been identified with multiple genres, including wisdom literature, allegory, drama, and love poetry, and even pornography. There is a long tradition—in both Judaism and Christianity—of identifying the Song of Songs with wisdom literature. This goes back at least to the Septuagint, when the Song was grouped together with the other wisdom books.[79] Brevard Childs argues that the superscription (Song 1:1), which connects it with Solomon, indicates that it was intended to be read as wisdom literature.[80] Several commentators have observed that there are didactic refrains addressed to the "daughters of Jerusalem" that feature throughout the book. Rosalind Clarke suggests that these provide a framework for the entire Song, "in which the female character instructs these 'daughters of Jerusalem' about the dangers and joys of love."[81] There are also a number of proverbs, sayings, and riddles in the book.[82] Michael Sadgrove proposes that the riddle of the vineyards, which begins in Song 1:6 and concludes in 8:11–12, provides a frame for the whole book as a "wisdom puzzle."[83] Gerhard von Rad observed that the primary subject of the Song, love, is itself a frequent theme in the wisdom literature.[84] There are also numerous additional wisdom themes such as waiting, pursuit, the female initiation of sexual encounters, seduction, entrapment, riches and material wealth, nature, spices, the tree of life, peace, and death.[85] All of these suggest that the Song of Songs "could be a wisdom text, or, at the very least, a book with strong connections to the wisdom tradition."[86]

ALLEGORY

Throughout much of the history of biblical interpretation, this book has been understood as allegorical. Jews saw the Song of Songs as a depiction of the relationship of the Lord to his chosen people, Israel. Likewise, Christian interpreters understand it as a statement of the love of Christ and his church.

This approach has led to all kinds of unusual interpretations. For example, Jewish scholars identified the bride's breasts as Moses and Aaron, Moses and Phineas, or Joshua and Eleazar. Christian interpreters identified the bride's breasts as the church from which we feed, the two testaments, the twin teachings of the love of God and neighbor and the sacraments of blood and water. There are at least three major problems with interpreting the Song of Songs allegorically:

1. Nothing in the text suggests that the author intended to allegorize.

2. The people, places, and experiences seem to be real, not literary devices. In a work like *Pilgrim's Progress*, it's evident that it's intended to be an allegory.

3. It does not have the progressive storyline expected in an allegory.

DRAMA

Since Late Antiquity, many interpreters have understood the Song as a dramatic dialogue made up of speeches by multiple parties. Two versions of this interpretation have been proposed. In one, there are two primary characters: a Shulamite maiden and her shepherd love (Solomon), along with a chorus. In another, the shepherd and the king are two different characters. In either approach, the drama consists of several acts, each set in a different location and with various changes the refrains recited by the chorus.[87] There are no indications in the earliest texts, however, that the author intended the book to be understood as a drama. It is unclear how many characters feature in the text or which speeches would be assigned to whom. There is no clear structure for such a drama, and verses are often repeated without any clear pattern.[88]

LOVE POETRY

Since the earliest decipherments of Egyptian love poetry in the late nineteenth century, its parallels with the Song have dominated the discussion about genre. John White and Michael Fox published pioneering studies of the numerous parallels between the Song and the lyrical love poetry of Egypt.[89] There is a near consensus today that the Song is an example of love poetry, although scholars disagree about the unity of these poems. Some believe the book is an anthology of unrelated poems with no overall formal structure,[90] while other interpreters argue that it's a literary unity.[91] Hess contends that it is a single love poem.[92] Whether it is a collection of lyrical poetry or a single love poem, the Song of Songs praises the love that a man and a woman share for each other.

Rosalind Clarke, however, points out that the identification of the Song as a compendium of love poetry "is drawn primarily on the basis of the parallels with the other Ancient Near Eastern love poems" and that "caution needs to be exercised with respect to these parallels."[93] She provides five caveats we should keep in mind with regard to the identification of the Song as love poetry: (1) not all the parallels are as persuasive as they first appear, (2) there are no examples of ancient Near Eastern love poetry in the extended form we find in the Song of Songs, (3) none of the parallels contain abstract reflections on the nature of love similar to that in the Song, (4) none of the ancient Near Eastern parallels share the Song's Israelite setting, and (5) none of them have the same context within Jewish and Christian sacred literature.[94] The Song probably did not originate as a miscellaneous collection of love poems but as a single unified composition.[95]

PORNOGRAPHY

There is one additional label some interpreters today give to the Song of Songs: pornography. David Clines, for example, identifies the Song as soft-core pornography written for male entertainment.[96] In this view, its presence in the Old Testament is evidence of the influence of the male power elite who influenced the selection of books for inclusion in the Old Testament canon. For some of the same reasons considered above, Hess concludes that this is an example of how *not* to read the Song of Songs![97]

INTERPRETATION ISSUES

As we can see from the foregoing survey of approaches, the interpretation of the Song of Songs has been incredibly controversial.[98] Coogan and Chapman report that "the consensus of recent scholars . . . is that the book [was] originally secular," and they "marvel" at its presence in the Bible.[99] On the surface, it seems to be a collection of ancient Hebrew love poems celebrating the experiences of a lover and his beloved as they experience the beauty, power, agony, and joys of human sexual love. However, the repeated appearance of the word *bride* in the Song demonstrates that the relationship is one of marriage.[100] And yet, the question that has plagued the history of biblical interpretation—both in Judaism and Christianity—is whether its inclusion in the Jewish-Christian Scriptures is appropriate.[101] The fact, however, is that it is in the Bible and has had a significant impact on both Judaism and Christianity. In Judaism, it's read on the eighth day of Passover, and during the first fifteen centuries of the church, most major commentators wrote about it. It's had an abiding impact on both Judaism and Christianity.

In this section, I want to focus on the tradition of Christian interpretation of the Song of Songs, which has tended predominantly toward the allegorical approach. Why has Christianity been so insistent on interpreting the book allegorically? It has to do with the fact that early in the history of the church, a negative attitude arose toward marriage. In AD 325, there was a proposal made at the Council of Nicaea that all clergy cease living with their wives. The proposal didn't pass, but the negative view of marriage continued to grow. For example, the fourth- to fifth-century theologian Saint Augustine associated lust and depravity with sex and said that marriage was legalized depravity. This negative view of marriage culminated in Pope Siricius's command in AD 386 that all priests be celibate. For those who were already married when ordained, even they were required to take vows of continence. Eventually, it became standard to refuse to ordain anyone who was married to the priesthood.

Celibacy then became the symbol of supreme piety: Sexuality should be sublimated, and Christ should be our Bride. This view had a major impact on the interpretation of the Song, which came to be understood as a picture of the ecstasy of that better way.[102] The result of this was that the medieval church had a love affair with it and the eroticism prohibited at the human level was permitted at the divine level. And so, between the time of Augustine (354–430) and Luther (1483–1546), many allegorical commentaries were written on the Song.

For those Christians wondering whether this rejection of marriage and sexuality is biblical, we can be clear that the Bible absolutely does not share this negative perspective. In the Old Testament, human sexuality was of divine design (Gen. 1–2); God instituted marriage and pronounced it as good (Gen. 2). That assessment has never changed (Prov. 5:15–20; Eccles. 9:9; cf. Prov. 31), and connubial joy in marriage is encouraged. In the Old Testament, neither virginity nor celibacy were ever considered better but were instead seen as curses (Judg. 11:34–40). The Hebrew language doesn't even have a word for "bachelor" because, at least in the ancient Israelite mind, there weren't supposed to be any. Every patriarch was married; the priests were married, including the high priest who entered the Most Holy Place on the Day of Atonement; and every prophet, except for Jeremiah, was married. The sign of the covenant was circumcision (Gen. 17), which probably represented the idea that sexuality served the sanctified purpose of building the people of Israel.

Today, the prevailing view among biblical scholars seems to be that the Song of Songs is a compendium of love poetry. Katherine Dell observes that in discussions about the Song's genre, wisdom is seldom mentioned.[103] Many contemporary interpreters view it as a settled matter and categorically say that the Song of Songs "is not a wisdom book" but "a collection of love poems."[104] As we noted above, however, the superscription, the inclusion of proverbs, sayings and riddles, and the themes all suggest that the Song is a wisdom text. Hess points out that in Egyptian papyri, scribal and wisdom texts can be mixed in with love poetry.[105] The Song of Songs, therefore, is probably a wisdom book with a didactic framework that includes love poetry.[106]

RHETORIC

Karl Möller argues that the Song of Songs invites us to consider human sexuality from a perspective of "good news, with God's good creation, with original blessing rather than original sin."[107] He identifies three kinds of rhetoric that pervade the Song, including aesthetic appreciation, desire, and intoxicating pleasure.

First, the rhetoric of aesthetic appreciation is evidenced by four descriptive poems in which the lovers dwell at length on the beauty of each other's bodies. Three of them are from the perspective of the man: 4:1–7, in which he praises his beloved's body parts; 6:4–7, which is in many ways a repetition of chapter 4; and 7:1–7. In Song 5:10–16, the woman praises her husband's "radiant and ruddy" appearance (v. 10).

Each of the songs is organized as a list made up of zoological, topographical, and architectural comparisons, and each has a rhetorical function. The man's songs tend to be restricted to the visual, while the woman's songs move beyond the visual to also describe taste and smell. The function of all the songs is to express an unembarrassed delight in the body. This is in sharp contrast to traditional Christian views of the body.

The second kind of rhetoric is the rhetoric of desire, which suffuses the Song from beginning to end. For example, the woman yearns for her lover's kisses (1:2) and union with him (2:5), she pines for him at night (3:1–4), and she invites him to share a night of pleasure (2:17). She bids him to see whether the pomegranates are in bloom, which Möller interprets as an invitation to sex (7:11–8:2).[108] She wants to give him spiced wine to drink and the juice of her pomegranates (8:2), which Möller thinks is an allusion to "the sweet and powerful liquor of her kisses (and perhaps more than that) to drink."[109] Based on these and other examples from the Song, Möller argues that it's not mainly a hymn to the beauty of love but a longing for sexual union.

The third kind of rhetoric Möller identifies is the rhetoric of enjoyment and consummation. While many scholars argue that sexual love is never consummated in the Song, Möller concludes otherwise. He suggests, for example, that an intimate encounter is clearly described in 1:12–14, where the male lover is described as spending the night between his beloved's breasts.[110] In another particularly provocative example, he interprets the woman's description of her lover feeding among the lotuses in 2:16 as a clear allusion to consummation.

In the latter case, ancient Near Eastern parallels demonstrate that the lotus is a symbol of rejuvenation and has life-renewing powers. For example, in a painted ivory from the tomb of Tutankhamun, his Great Royal Wife Ankhesenamen holds a bouquet of lotus flowers and love apples under his nose (fig. 1.1). These seem to imply the rejuvenating powers of sex and were intended to arouse his love. Notice that Ankhesenamen's lower abdomen is bare, which suggests her readiness to receive her husband's love.

FIGURE 1.1. Ankhesenamen trying to arouse Tutankhamen's love. (Drawing by Sarah A. Hawkins.)

The most suggestive passages are found in 4:12–5:1, which are replete with sexual imagery. Verses 12–15 are especially controversial, and translations vary as to how they render them. The NRSVue reads thus:

> A garden locked is my sister, my bride,
>   a garden locked, a fountain sealed.
> Your channel is an orchard of pomegranates
>   with all choicest fruits, henna with nard,
> nard and saffron, calamus and cinnamon,
>   with all trees of frankincense,
> myrrh and aloes,
>   with all chief spices—
> a garden fountain, a well of living water,
>   and flowing streams from Lebanon.

The locked garden and the sealed fountain (v. 12) are clearly erotic images and may refer to female sexuality in general or the vagina in particular.[111] The mention of her "channel" (v. 13) seems to be an obvious metaphor for her pudenda.[112]

In 4:16 and 5:1, we find a repetition of the Hebrew word verb *bo'* (בּוֹא), which means "to come" or "to enter" and can be used as a euphemism for sexual intercourse.[113] In 4:16, the woman longs for the man to "come" to his garden and eat its delicious fruit; and in 5:1, he says he has "come" into the garden, gathered his myrrh and spices, eaten his honeycomb with his honey, and drank his wine with his milk (5:1).[114]

In the end, what we have in the Song of Songs is a powerful celebration of erotic desire. This is not insignificant and actually quite meaningful. For, as Möller observes, "desire is a vital aspect of our humanity, essential for our survival and well-being."[115]

THEOLOGICAL VALUE

Since the biblical canon does indeed include the Song of Songs, we must ask then what it is trying to teach us about sexual desire and abouts the nature of desire. In order to answer this question, it may be helpful to think about how desire is portrayed in the Old Testament more generally. In the wake of the fall (Gen. 3), the blessings that God originally bestowed on Adam and Eve unravel. The hardships the woman would now experience are of particular interest here. In Genesis 3:16, the Lord decrees, "Your desire shall be for your husband, and he shall rule over you." The Hebrew word translated here as "desire" is *teshuqah* (תְּשׁוּקָה), which expresses an "urge," "craving," or "impulse."[116] This is a negative desire. After Adam and Eve are exiled from the Garden of Eden, the effects of sin begin to radiate outward and animosity spreads among humankind. When God accepts Abel's sacrifice but rejects Cain's, "Cain was very angry, and his countenance fell" (Gen. 4:5). God warns him that "sin is lurking at the door; its desire is for you, but you must master it" (4:7). The sin that lurked at the door of Cain's heart had the same kind of "desire" (*teshuqah*) that Eve had for her husband—an urge, a craving, or an impulse to overtake him.

J. Cheryl Exum observes that throughout much of the Old Testament, desire is viewed as something negative and dangerous;[117] it is a harmful male attribute that needs to be repressed and controlled. This is evident in the laws about sexual relations, the advice of Proverbs to young men, and the "lessons" taught by the examples of heroes like Samson and David who were led astray by their libidos. Richard Hess suggests that the Song was written to turn this negative expression of desire into something positive.[118]

Several commentators have observed that the lovemaking that takes place in the garden in the Song[119] should remind us of the Garden of Eden.[120] In that garden, the eyes of Adam and Eve were opened, "and they realized they were naked; so they sewed fig leaves together and made coverings for themselves" (Gen. 3:7). Raymond Dillard and Tremper Longman point out that the Song presents us with a reversal of those conditions. "In the Song of Songs, we see the man and his wife in the garden naked and feeling anything but shame!"[121] Renita Weems points out that "as a result of what happened in Eden, there is a rupture in creation, disharmony between the first human couple, resulting in the subjugation of the woman and, by implication, the demise of mutual sexual fulfillment. In the garden of Song of Songs, by contrast, mutuality is reestablished and intimacy is renewed."[122] In sum, "The Song of Songs redeems a love story gone awry."[123] It "pictures the restoration of human love to its pre-Fall bliss."[124]

The final verses of the Song culminate in a confession of the power of love (8:6–7), which is stronger than any force in the universe. Several commentators have noted that the Song doesn't end with consummation but with a continued sense of separation and a longed-for reunion (8:13–14). Diane Bergant points out that this characterizes the nature of human love: "Human love knows no definitive consummation, no absolute fulfillment. Loving relationships are never complete; they are always ongoing, always reaching for more."[125] This sense of unfulfilled longing in even our most intimate relationships mirrors our longing for the divine.

TOWARD THE NEW TESTAMENT

The New Testament upholds this view. In Matthew 19:3–9, Jesus reaffirms the sanctity of marriage, and Hebrews 13:4 tells us that the marriage

bed is pure and marriage should be honored by all. Paul teaches that it's prefer-
able for elders and bishops to be married and that they be model family men
(1 Tim. 3:4; Titus 1:6–7).[126] And yet, even married sexual love cannot ever
provide complete fulfillment in this life; it points us toward something greater
and more complete. From a canonical perspective, this love points us toward
the consummation of all yearnings for a more complete love, a fulfillment
achieved in the marriage of the Messiah to his Bride, which will occur at the
culmination of history as described Revelation 19:6–9,

> Then I heard what sounded like a great multitude, like the roar of rushing waters
> and like loud peals of thunder, shouting:
>
> "Hallelujah!
> For our Lord God Almighty reigns.
> Let us rejoice and be glad
> and give him glory!
> For the wedding of the Lamb has come,
> and his bride has made herself ready.
> Fine linen, bright and clean,
> was given her to wear."
> (Fine linen stands for the righteous acts of God's holy people.)
>
> Then the angel said to me, "Write this: Blessed are those who are invited to the
> wedding supper of the Lamb!" And he added, "These are the true words of God."

Interlocking Wisdom

In the foregoing pages, we have surveyed the books of wisdom literature, but
it's important to note that they're not meant to function independently of one
another. When we consider the subject matter each of them covers and how
they complement one another, it becomes clear that all the pieces of wisdom
literature interlock to cover the entire field of wisdom (fig. 1.2).

In view of this, it becomes clear that the overall thrust of wisdom literature
as a whole is to help us develop a unified worldview with God at the center.
This brings us back to the claim that the fear of the Lord is the beginning of
wisdom. We bring order to the chaos of our lives and our world by having
such an integrated worldview.

FIGURE 1.2. The interlocking nature of wisdom literature.
(John H. Walton and Andrew E. Hill, Old Testament Today: A
Journey from Ancient Context to Contemporary Significance, 2nd
ed. [Grand Rapids: Zondervan, 2014], 334. Used by permission.)

THE BEGINNING OF WISDOM

In the sectarian tradition in which I grew up during the 1970s and '80s, fear was one of the predominant feelings that shaped the spiritual sensibilities of young and old alike. On the basis of a narrow approach to biblical interpretation, leaders in this tradition viewed the Bible as providing a pattern for correctly reconstructing the process of salvation, the order of worship, and the organization of the church. Limiting oneself to these patterns meant that there was no room for deviation. Conversions, worship, and church organization all had to be carried out exactly as the pattern prescribed. Ministers would often appeal to the fact that Nadab and Abihu were struck down because they offered "strange fire" to God when they burned incense that "he commanded them not" (Lev. 10:1–2 KJV), in order to show that God expects his people to unswervingly obey his patterns or risk eternal punishment themselves.[1]

One of the implications of this approach was that decisions were often made out of fear of divine reprisal. Baptism provides a good example, since the tradition held a unique position on it. Baptism must be by full immersion, for "the remission of sins" (Acts 2:38), and the candidate for baptism must fully understand its meaning and role in salvation in order for it to be effective. If any of these three criteria were not met, then the baptism was not considered effective. This meant there was some degree of fear connected with baptism. When I was seven years old, I "went forward," confessed my faith in Jesus Christ, and said I was ready to be baptized. The minister, however, was afraid I didn't know enough and that the baptism would therefore be ineffective, which would mean that I would remain lost. He insisted that the baptism be delayed for several years until I "knew enough" for it to work.

Several years later, when we were teenagers, my older brother became anxious that he hadn't known enough when he was baptized and that he may still be lost. The minister, along with some elders, interviewed him. After determining that he had indeed not fully understood what he was doing when he was baptized as a pre-teen, they agreed that the fear of remaining lost was real and allowed him to be rebaptized.

I recall that some years later, there was an elderly woman in the congregation who wanted to be baptized but was frightened by the prospect of being plunged under the water. The minister told her that the only way for her to be saved was to be fully immersed, but that if it would ease her fear, she could hold onto his shoulder with one hand when he submerged her. Later, some of the church members who had witnessed her baptism told her that since the hand with which she had clung to the minister's shoulder had not gone under the water, she had not really been baptized and was still lost. Terrified, she went to the minister and expressed her fear that she may still be in danger of going to hell.

Eventually, I became deeply disillusioned with this approach to Christian faith and left that tradition. A similar unease with the idea of the fear of God has led to its neglect in recent years by scholars and pastors alike. In this chapter, we will explore how the perception of the fear of God has changed over time, beginning in the ancient world and working our way up to the present. Then we will look at what ancient Israel's sages said about the "fear of the LORD" and conclude with a brief glimpse at how that idea features in the New Testament.

Changing Perceptions of the Fear of God

Throughout human history, fear of the gods has been a universal religious sensibility. In fact, many of the classical philosophers—including Democritus of Abdera (c. 400 BC), Epicurus (died 270 BC), and Lucretius (died 55 BC)—believed that it was fear that had originally given rise to religion.[2] The Greco-Roman poet Statius (AD 45–96) summarized this view in a now famous line from his epic Latin poem *Thebais*: "At the beginning of the world, fear created the gods."[3]

There's no question that the "fear of God" was a primary feature of ancient Near Eastern religion. In a classic article, Robert Pfeiffer proposed that "the fear of God" was "the earliest term for religion in biblical Hebrew, and indeed in Semitic languages in general."[4] In ancient Egyptian, Mesopotamian, and Ugarit texts, fear of the gods features as a prominent religious sensibility.[5] In each of them, the divine nature is beyond human understanding, hidden in impenetrable darkness, which evoked fear of the deity.

In the Classical (500–336 BC) and Hellenistic (323–146 BC) periods, fear of the divine was a prominent feature of religious practice. In his second-century travelog, for example, Pausanias describes a man who emerged from a consultation with the oracle of Tryphonius as paralyzed with fear.[6] It was also commonly believed that the gods were vindictive and vengeful, which naturally fueled human fear of them. This is a common subject throughout Greek mythology. In Homer's *The Odyssey*, Odysseus constantly has to cope with the capriciousness of the gods who unleash their anger on mortals, often including the innocent. This fear of the gods led people to be wary of offending them lest the gods seek revenge. This convoluted sense of fear was the status quo and part of Greek life.

There were several authors in antiquity who argued that religion should *not* be motivated by a fear of the gods.[7] Pieter De Villers cites Plato (427–347 BC) who argued that "traditional myths about punishment by the gods were fables and fairytales of which the main function could be to scare uninformed people into choosing a good life and not an evil life."[8] Epicurus (341–270 BC) believed religion was inextricably tied to fear, and therefore his whole project was devoted to rendering religion irrelevant.[9] Nevertheless, the fear of the gods persisted as a primary religious sensibility throughout antiquity.

In the medieval period, "the image of a wrathful God, a deity to be held in fearful awe, had occupied the shadow side of much Christian thought."[10] The experience of Martin Luther (1483–1546), before his discovery of grace and his launching of the German Reformation, illustrates this fear. Although Luther had planned to go into law, in July 1505, he had a brush with death that caused him to change course completely.[11] While he was traveling to see his family, he was caught in a thunderstorm, and a nearby lightning strike knocked him from his horse. Terrified that the next lightning strike would kill him and that he would be eternally condemned, he pledged that if God would spare him, he would become a monk.[12] Although he did quit law school and became a monk, his fear of eternal punishment continued at the monastery, where he practiced extreme mortification in an effort to conquer every human desire that might evoke God's wrath. He fasted to the point of collapse, prayed in an unheated cell, and kneeled at the altar until he passed out. None of these efforts, though, lessened his fear of God's judgment. But when he discovered justification by grace through faith, it launched the Reformation.[13]

Even after his discovery of grace, however, Luther still believed that the fear of God played a vital role in conversion. He held that "the terrified conscience was the means by which God revealed justice to the sinful believer."[14] Likewise, Luther's friend and fellow reformer Philip Melanchthon (1497–1560) understood that when people heard the demands and warnings of the law and realized they couldn't live up to them, they would became afraid, which would then lead them to the gospel of forgiveness.[15] For both Luther and Melanchthon, as well as for many other reformers, embracing the consolation of the gospel was the only way someone could be protected against being consumed by their fear of God.

In the eighteenth century, Enlightenment thinkers increasingly came to see the fear of God as in complete and in total opposition to the love of God. Friedrich Schleiermacher (1768–1834), sometimes referred to as the father of liberal theology, concluded that the fear of God was irreconcilable with the love of God. He gave primacy to 1 John 4:16, which says that "God is love," which he viewed as the primary attribute of the divine essence. He continued with 1 John 4:18: "There is no fear in love, but perfect love casts out fear; for fear has to do with punishment, and whoever fears has not reached perfection in love." He concluded that "love alone and no other attribute can be equated thus with God."[16] Throughout his work, Schleiermacher insisted again and again that fear does not belong to Christian faith.[17]

In this period, the fear of God continued to erode and there were those who argued that its loss had the damaging effect of watering down God's fundamental incomparability. One such defender of the fear of God was John Henry Newman (1801–1890), who was first an Anglican priest and later a Catholic priest and cardinal. Several of his sermons particularly address the fear of God. In "Reverence, A Belief in God's Presence," he protests the way that burgeoning liberal Christianity was discarding the fear of God.[18] He argued that this rejection was based in a refusal to acknowledge sin and one's own sinfulness. He believed that awe and fear of God were appropriate responses for a mature Christian toward a holy and transcendent God, and that healthy awe and fear would lead a believer to seek to abandon sin and pursue holiness. Newman's preaching and writing provide evidence that, in modernity, Christianity was in a crisis of which the deletion of the fear of God from social and religious thought was its major symptom.[19]

By the early twentieth century, William James observed that the fear of God played a vastly diminished role in contemporary religious life. In his classic work *Varieties of Religious Experience*, originally published in 1902, he described the "typical modern man."[20] He asserted that feelings of fear were incompatible with healthy religion, and he even attributed the idea of God itself to "ignorance, fear, and a general lack of knowledge of Nature."[21] James observed that a change had occurred in Christian sensibilities and that many Christians, including clergy, were no longer concerned with sin. Many "ignore, or even deny, eternal punishment, and insist on the dignity rather than on the depravity of man."[22] In 1927, self-proclaimed atheist Bertrand Russell famously asserted that "religion is based primarily on fear" and publicly defended his rejection of Christianity.[23]

The erosion of the fear of God was not something limited to the so-called mainline denominations, liberals, or even atheists, but it also occurred among conservative evangelicals. The conservative evangelical mystic A. W. Tozer (1897–1963), for example, complained that "in the majority of our meetings, there is scarcely a trace of reverent thought, . . . little sense of the divine Presence, no moment of stillness, no solemnity, no wonder, no holy fear. But always there is a dull or a breezy song leader full of awkward jokes."[24]

My own sense is that in the twenty-first century, the erosion of the fear of God has worsened. A number of factors have contributed to this, including a drop in religiosity, a weakening of belief in the inspiration and authority of Scripture, a decline of belief in hell, and a falling-off of the idea that God would ever judge anyone at all.[25] The erosion of the fear of God has also occurred in the church, both in mainline and evangelical denominations. In the broader world of evangelicalism, one of the most public expressions of the rejection of the fear of God is Rob Bell's book *Love Wins*, in which the author insists that the idea that God would ever judge anyone is just "toxic."[26] Bell argues that no one has any reason to fear God and that all people will ultimately be reconciled to God.[27] He goes on to say that God is love and that Jesus' kind of love "simply does away with fear."[28] In the end, "God's love is a party," where there's only laughter and fun, and no one will ever be afraid.[29]

Many conservative pastors branded Bell a heretic, and *Love Wins* ultimately led to Bell's leaving the congregation where he had served as pastor—and apparently, the church as a whole. But not before the book had sold half a million copies, which led to his being featured on the cover of *Time* magazine and befriended by stars such as Oprah Winfrey. Even today, more than a decade after the book's publication, I often see cars with bumper stickers proclaiming, "Love Wins!" Apparently, the message of *Love Wins* resonates with a culture that can no longer tolerate a God whose majesty and holiness might evoke fear.

Ancient Israel's Sages on the Fear of the Lord

In spite of the modern disparagement of the idea of the "fear" (יִרְאָה) of the Lord, ancient Israel's sages taught that it "is the beginning of knowledge" (Prov. 1:7). In fact, this idea is carefully embedded in the structure and theology of the wisdom literature as a whole.[30] These sages clearly viewed the fear of the

Lord as the vital foundation of wisdom. But what did this mean to the ancient Israelites? How did it affect the way they understood and related to God?

BACKGROUND OF THE IDEA OF THE FEAR OF THE LORD

In his classic work *The Idea of the Holy,* Lutheran theologian Rudolph Otto explores the universal importance of fear in all religions. He observes that it seems to have two aspects. First, it's a natural response to what he called the *mysterium tremendum,* or the tremendous mystery of the divine.[31] This mystery does not inspire an ordinary negative fear but instead "the hushed, trembling, and speechless humility of the creature in the presence of . . . that which is a *mystery* inexpressible and above all creatures."[32] He suggests that such an emotion might be conveyed by the German word *Scheu.*[33] *Scheu* can be translated as "fright," but it can also mean "shyness," "timidity," "reserve," or "awe."[34]

Its second aspect is fascination. Otto explains:

> These two qualities, the daunting and the fascinating, now combine in a strange harmony of contrasts. . . . The . . . divine object may appear to the mind an object of horror and dread, but at the same time it is no less something that allures with a potent cham, and the creature, who trembles before it, utterly cowed and cast down, has always at the same time the impulse to turn to it, nay even to make it somehow his own. The "mystery" is for him not merely something to be wondered at but something that entrances him; and beside that in it which bewilders and confounds, he feels a something that captivates and transports him with a strange ravishment, rising often enough to the pitch of dizzy intoxication.[35]

In *Theology of the Old Testament,* theologian Walter Eichrodt (1890–1978) accepts Otto's explanation of fear and uses it to elucidate the fear of the Lord in the Old Testament.[36] He identifies this as the "predominant trait in the personal relationship of Man with God in the Old Testament."[37] It appears "with remarkable regularity from the earliest to the latest times," and it always involves an "oscillation between repulsion and attraction, between *mysterium tremendum* and *fasinans.*"[38] A classic example of this dual response to the Lord can be found in the narrative account of Israel's crossing of the Red Sea: "When the Israelites saw the great power of the Lord displayed against the Egyptians, the people feared the Lord and put their trust in him and in Moses his servant" (Exod. 14:31). This example clearly demonstrates the response of simultaneous fear and attraction.

But is this dual response inherently contradictory? Not according to Bruce Waltke, who views these two reactions as the "unified psychological poles" of relationship with the Lord.[39] As an example of how these two responses are supposed to manifest in one's relationship with the Lord, Waltke points to Deuteronomy 10:12 in which Moses says:

> "And now, O Israel, what does the LORD your God ask of you? Only to fear the LORD your God, to walk in all his ways, to love him, to serve the LORD your God with all your heart and with all your soul."

Waltke explains that "the heart that both fears and loves God at one and the same time is not divided but unified in a single religious response to God."[40]

It may be that in order to express these different aspects of the fear of the Lord, we need a new vocabulary for the concept. As Nancy deClaissé-Walford observes, although "fear" is a good translation of the Hebrew word, "in today's culture, the idea of fear is usually connected with the basic human instincts to run, defend, or retaliate."[41] A few contemporary versions have provided alternate renderings like "respect" (NCV) and "reverence" (GNT), but few have deviated from the traditional translation of "fear." Daniel Fredericks translates the verb as "revere," John Goldingay as "awe,"[42] and Tremper Longman suggests:

> Perhaps the closest English word is "awe," but even that word does not quite get it. The "fear" of the "fear of the Lord" is the sense of standing before the God who created everything, including humans whose very continued existence depends on him. The emotion is appropriate for wisdom because it demonstrates acknowledgement that God is so much greater than we are. He takes our breath away and makes our knees knock together. Such fear breeds humility and signals a willingness to receive instruction from God.[43]

I would suggest that translating the Hebrew word for "fear" as "reverential awe" might express these various aspects of fear encompassed by it when it is used with reference to the Lord.[44] Throughout this chapter, however, I will generally use the traditional rendering "fear of the LORD," since this is what most readers find in their Bible translations.

THE BEGINNING OF WISDOM

So what did ancient Israel's sages mean when they said that the "fear of the LORD is the beginning of wisdom"? They understood it to be the beginning of wisdom in the sense of a "first principle."[45] As such, it shaped ancient Israel's whole theory of knowledge (epistemology). Gerhard von Rad (1901–1971) explains:

> The thesis that all human knowledge comes back to the question about commitment to God is a statement of penetrating perspicacity. . . . It contains in a nutshell

the whole Israelite theory of knowledge. . . . There lies behind the statement an awareness of the fact that the search for knowledge can go wrong . . . because of one single mistake at the beginning. To this extent, Israel attributes to the fear of God, to belief in God, a highly important function in respect of human knowledge. She was, in all seriousness, of the opinion that effective knowledge about God is the only thing that puts a man into a right relationship with the objects of his perception.[46]

Ancient Israel's sages believed that if God's people had a right understanding of the Lord, respect for the Lord, fear of the Lord, and an accurate understanding of the Lord's nature and character, then they would be able to make right decisions about everything else in life. God's true nature and character are reflected in the Torah, or law, which means that if we truly understand him, then we'll make all our decisions on the basis of that Torah.

JOB

In the Christian canon, the book of Job appears at the beginning of the wisdom literature. This position was clearly intentional. As we saw in chapter 1, one of the main theological themes in the book is countering a wooden or mechanical view of the principle of divine retribution. Lindsay Wilson insightfully argues that the book also counters a perfunctory view of the fear of the Lord.[47] In the prologue, the author establishes that Job was someone who "feared God" (1:1) and that God himself repeated this affirmation (1:8; 2:3). Furthermore, Job was someone who "turned away from evil" (1:1), which should be understood as a testimony to his fear of the Lord.[48] The author of the book wants to make it "very clear that the disasters that befall Job in chapters 1 and 2 occur in spite of the fact that Job has 'feared God.' "[49]

In the dialogue between Job and his "friends," they conclude that the tragedies he suffered must have befallen him because he no longer feared God. Repeatedly, they recommend the fear of God as a solution to his problems.[50] "This advice must be viewed ironically by the reader," Lindsay observes, "since the prologue has demonstrated that this is not the reason for Job's sufferings."[51] The analysis of Job's friends is mistaken, and God himself corrects their misguided reading of the situation later in the book (42:7–8).

After three rounds of dialogue in Job 3–27, the debate is interrupted in chapter 28 by a majestic poem about the quest for wisdom.[52] While it clearly provides "the peak of the 'fear of God' idea in the whole book," a lack of fear for God is not Job's problem nor is a return to it the solution.[53] After his friends urge him to turn away from evil and return to the fear of God, the poem seems to serve as Job's protest: He *already* fears God and *already* avoids evil, and yet his suffering continues.[54] Following this interlude, in chapters 29–31, Job resumes his protest and complaint.

The Elihu speeches (Job 32–37) mainly sum up the arguments of Job and his "friends" and render a verdict on Job. At the end of his last speech, Elihu states the idea of "fearing God" and concludes that the Lord regards only those who fear him (37:24). Like the earlier dialogues, Elihu's arguments don't provide any resolution for Job's problems; they simply repeat the assertion that Job needs to renew his fear of God in order to return to God's good graces.

The idea of fearing the Lord is not mentioned in God's response (38–41) or in the epilogue (42), which further indicates that the author of the book did not intend to say that fear of the Lord was the solution to Job's suffering. The narrator (1:1), God (1:8; 2:3), and even Satan (1:9) all agree that Job did indeed fear God.

In the end, this book seems to challenge a formulaic view of the fear of the Lord. In the same way that it qualifies the principle of divine retribution, it also demonstrates that while "the fear of the LORD is the beginning of knowledge" (Prov 1:7), it does not guarantee a life free from problems and crises.[55]

PSALMS

The expression "fear of the LORD" is found in Psalms 34 and 111, two "wisdom psalms," both of which are alphabetic acrostics. Acrostics probably serve multiple functions.[56] They certainly express literary creativity and artistic design as well as totality in that they cover their subject "from A to Z" according to the Hebrew lettering. The format of acrostics may have also facilitated memorization, which would have made them useful for instructing the community.

Psalm 34 is usually identified as an individual thanksgiving hymn, but about half of it (vv. 8–22) features wisdom elements, which suggests to some that it should be categorized as a wisdom psalm.[57] It can be divided into two halves, with verses 1–10 comprised of thanksgiving for God's goodness and justice, and verses 11–22 instructing God's people on how to attain wisdom. The author of Psalm 34 opens with personal praise in the form of a hymn (vv. 1–3) and then recounts how when he sought the Lord, the Lord answered him (vv. 4–5). He wasn't alone in his experience of the Lord's salvation, however, and he points to someone else in the community as an example of others who had experienced it (v. 6). He exclaims that "the angel of the LORD encamps around [all] those who fear him, and delivers them" (v. 7). The psalmist invites everyone to "taste and see that the LORD is good" (v. 8). To taste something means to try it and decide whether you like it. The psalmist is convinced that if people will try the ways of the Lord, they will "see"—meaning discover through experience—that he is good. The wise "taste" the Lord's goodness when they "take refuge" in him and submit to his way of life (vv. 8–9).[58] A second call is directed to his "holy ones"—those who are already devoted to God—to fear him (v. 9). In this case, this is not a call for an emotional response but to obedient devotion.

In verse 11, the psalm shifts to teaching readers how to attain wisdom, and the vocabulary and themes of wisdom literature pervade the second half. The psalmist summons his students and announces that he wants to teach them "the fear of the Lord," which is the foundation of the wisdom tradition. It is clear that for the author of Psalm 34, the "['fear of the Lord'] is a summary term for the proper attitude of one with whom God has established a right relationship."[59] This fear is expressed by embracing his ways, and the psalmist gives three examples, including honest speech (v. 13), turning away from evil and doing good (v. 14a), and seeking and pursuing peace (v. 14b). Doing this leads to "life" and "many days to enjoy good" (v. 12), which combine to refer to a long, full life characterized by the rich rewards of wisdom.

The psalmist, however, doesn't have a magical view of the fear of the Lord, and he recognizes that even the righteous have cause to cry out from time to time (v. 15). There is still evil in the world (v. 16), and the righteous still experience trouble and need to seek help (v. 17). There are still times when they are "brokenhearted" and "crushed in spirit" (v. 18). In fact, the righteous will experience "many" afflictions (v. 19). When they do face trials, though, the psalmist promises that God will watch over them (v. 15), hear their cry and rescue them from trouble (v. 17), save them (v. 18), rescue them (v. 19), keep their bones from being broken (v. 20), redeem them, and prevent them from being condemned (v. 22). The idea that fearing God is no guarantee that life will be free from the problems common to humanity is one of this psalm's most important perceptions.[60] While the fear of the Lord is the foundation of wisdom and should generally lead to a long and happy life, Peter Craigie explains:

> It is not a guarantee that life will be always easy, devoid of the difficulties that may seem to mar so much of human existence. The fear of the Lord establishes joy and fulfilment in all of life's experiences. It may mend the broken heart, but it does not prevent the heart from being broken; it may restore the spiritually crushed, but it does not crush the forces that may create oppression. The psalm, if fully grasped, dispels the naiveté of that faith which does not contain within it the strength to stand against the onslaught of evil.[61]

Like Psalm 34, Psalm 111 is typically classified as a hymn. It praises the Lord for his saving and revelatory work in ancient Israel's history, and its acrostic form indicates the content of that praise from A to Z. It's also clearly concerned with wisdom, which has led some interpreters to classify it as a wisdom psalm.[62] It begins with an individual worshiper giving thanks to the Lord in a context of public worship (v. 1). He proclaims the greatness of God's works and deeds (vv. 3–4), which testify to his gracious and merciful character (v. 4). These qualities are the first two of the divine attributes that God revealed to Moses at Mount Sinai (Exod. 34:6–7), although in reverse order.[63] In Jewish tradition, these divine characteristics are known as the "Thirteen Attributes" and in academic literature as the "Divine Attribute Formula," which presents an inventory of divine qualities that emphasizes God's love and mercy.[64] The qualities mentioned in the Divine Attribute Formula "are all clearly intended to create the cumulative impression that the Lord is a loving and gracious God."[65]

In the verses that follow, the psalmist outlines these works and deeds. In a clear allusion to the Lord's provision of food for his people after the exodus (Exod. 16), he proclaims that God "provides food for those who fear him" (v. 5a). He exclaims that God will remember his covenant forever (v. 5b) and that God began to fulfill his covenant promises when he demonstrated his "power" in the exodus and at the Red Sea and then gave his people the land of Canaan, which he had promised to their ancestors (v. 6).[66] In the same way that God's works are "faithful and just," his "precepts" are also "trustworthy" (v. 7). He "established" them when he provided "redemption" to his people through the founding of the covenant (vv. 8–9). God's mighty, redemptive work on behalf of Israel demonstrates that he is "holy and awesome" (v. 9), a laudatory expression with a meaning far beyond the formulation used to utter it. Allen Ross elaborates on the significance of the psalmist's adulation of God:

> There is no one like him—in power, in justice, or in faithfulness. No power in Egypt, physical or spiritual, could prevent or forestall the exodus; when he delivered his people from the bondage of the world, he destroyed all the gods of Egypt (Exod. 33:6). And no power on earth could prevent his giving the land of Canaan to them as their inheritance. There simply was no one like him, in heaven or on earth. Moreover, the many ways that God revealed his holiness were so amazing that they also showed him to be awesome (s.v., Ps. 2:11).[67]

It is only natural that after rehearsing God's wonderful works and holy character, the psalmist would conclude by affirming this foundational principle of the wisdom literature—that "the fear of the LORD is the beginning of wisdom" and that "all those who practice it have a good understanding" (v. 10). This response flows directly from the description of God as "holy and awesome" (v. 9). In this case, since the psalmist has reviewed the works that God has done on Israel's behalf, he probably doesn't mean that his readers should run away in terror, but that they should respond in grateful and awe-filled obedience.[68]

PROVERBS

The book of Proverbs begins by asserting that "the fear of the LORD is the beginning of knowledge" (Prov. 1:7) and then repeats it in the middle (9:10) and at the end (31:30) of the book. If we take the first occurrence of the expression in 1:7 as a thematic statement, and its last occurrence in 31:30 as the climax of the book's final poem (the "Ode to a Capable" wife in 31:10–31), then "the entire book is framed by the motif of fear of God."[69] The motif, which is sometimes stated with the variant wording "the beginning of wisdom," is also scattered throughout the book of Proverbs.[70] In contrast to the passages we considered in our discussions of Job and in certain wisdom psalms, the authors of many of the sayings collected in the book of Proverbs tend to understand this fear of God through the lens of retribution theology.[71] Virtue has its own rewards, and those who live virtuous lives will reap them.

There is a close relationship between this fear and wisdom itself. Proverbs 15:33 teaches that "the fear of the LORD is instruction in wisdom." Bruce Waltke understands this to mean that the instruction that gives wisdom is the fear of the Lord itself.[72] Since the "fear of the LORD" is mentioned here in parallel with "humility," it probably means that we should respect God as God. Together, fear of the Lord and humility cause a person to be open to instruction and discipline. In that sense, the fear of the Lord in and of itself is indeed wisdom.

Fear of God also keeps people from sinning. Proverbs 8:13 contains the words of wisdom personified as Lady Wisdom, who teaches that "the fear of the LORD is hatred of evil," and it is this disdain for evil that deters people from sin. She continues by giving some examples of the kinds of sin that this fear compels God's people to hate, including "pride and arrogance and the way of evil and perverted speech." These are fundamental vices that provide the springboard to many other kinds of sin. Pride and arrogance can lead people to disregard God's authority, pursue their own selfish interests, and engage in evil behaviors, until even their speech reflects an upside-down view of morals and ethics.[73]

One of the ways people might be lured into sin is through their envy of sinners, for which the fear of God can provide a powerful antidote. Proverbs 23:17 advises,

> Do not let your heart envy sinners, but always continue in
> the fear of the LORD.

The Hebrew text actually contains a play on the verb "envy" or "be jealous of" that is often missed in English versions. In his recent translation, John Goldingay captures the sense of the original: "Your mind must not be jealous of wrongdoers, but rather of [people who live in] awe for Yahweh all day."[74] The word that Goldingay translates as "awe" is literally "fear." So, while people should avoid being envious of sinners, they *should* be envious of those who fear the Lord. The first form of envy is negative and destructive, while the second is healthy and life giving. It leads the wise to avoid evil and turn away from it when they encounter it (16:6).

The rewards for "fear of the LORD" are many and include "riches and honor and life" (22:4). In Proverbs 22:4, "fear" is side-by-side with "humility," which suggests that in this context they share the same meaning. In other words, "those who fear [the Lord] and thus know their place in the cosmos are by definition humble. . . . They are not the center of the universe."[75] People who understand this are truly wise and thus more prepared to live in a way that leads to riches, honor, and life. In Proverbs, riches are often named as one of the rewards of wisdom.[76] "Honor" means having a good name. "Life" as a reward for "humility and fear of the LORD" imply the idea of the good life. In the end, fearing God leads to life (cf. Prov. 10:27; 14:27; 19:23; 22:4) and is in and of itself better than wealth (15:16).

ECCLESIASTES

The expression "fear God," or some variation of it, appears seven times in the book of Ecclesiastes. Many interpreters understand Qoheleth's view of the fear of God negatively. Michael Fox, for example, argues that Qoheleth's God is a God "who can be feared but not loved."[77] Similarly, Tremper Longman maintains that Qoheleth encourages his readers to be afraid of God and avoid drawing God's attention.[78] I disagree with these and similar interpretations. As we discussed in chapter 1, the structure of Ecclesiastes reveals a positive rhetorical argument. Life lived "under the sun" is brief and fleeting, and so Qoheleth makes the case for giving the Lord a central position in one's life. The message is not agnostic, skeptical, or pessimistic. It's a message "of hope and vivid instruction on how to make one's life count despite the brokenness of the world due to sin."[79] It reflects the Deuteronomic ideal that the fear of the Lord is the foundation of a life well lived.[80]

The first appearance of the theme occurs in Qoheleth's discussion of the rhythmic order of what happens in the world (3:1–22). He explains that God has established the workings of the universe and made people to live forever (3:14). For this reason, they should fear God. Longman understands this as a negative fear that comes from not being able to penetrate God's timing. He reasons that "Qoheleth believes that God acts the way that he does to frighten people into submission, not to arouse a sense of respectful awe of his power and might."[81] I argue, however, that this is a healthy fear. As Peterson explains, "Due to a person's lack of understanding of the future and eternity, the best thing that a person can do is to live a good/moral life while experiencing the rhythms of God's creation, even if it is broken due to the fall. After all, only God knows the beginning from the end (v. 15)."[82]

The theme features in a series of admonitions about the appropriate attitude that people should have before a holy God in a broken world (5:1–7). Whether we're approaching God in his sacred dwelling place (5:1) or speaking to him (5:2–6), we should do so with care. Qoheleth completes his instructions with a bit of an obscure saying: "With many dreams come vanities and a multitude of words" (5:7a). The nature of the "many dreams" Qoheleth refers to is unknown. His conclusion, however, is clear enough: We should approach God with "fear" (5:7b). God-fearing men and women will avoid thoughtless vows and vain dreams and instead live in humble reverence before God.

The idea appears again in a series of instructions for living a righteous and wise life (7:15–22). In this fallen world, life is unpredictable and death comes to everyone (7:15). In response to this unpredictability, Qoheleth advises:

> Do not be too righteous, and do not act too wise; why should you destroy yourself? Do not be too wicked, and do not be a fool; why should you die before your time? It is good that you should take hold of the one without letting go of the other, for the one who fears God shall succeed with both. (7:16–18)

It's not that Qoheleth is advising against righteous and moral behavior or approving of wicked behavior. Instead, his advice here should be understood as having to do with living a balanced life, one that avoids "both excessive righteousness and excessive wickedness."[83] The "excessive righteousness" that Qoheleth counsels readers to shun has been understood in various ways, including self-righteousness, hypocrisy, and righteousness that is flaunted.[84] Those who truly fear God, who have a view of God shaped by reverential awe, will embrace genuinely righteous and wise behavior.

One of the major themes in Ecclesiastes, which we discussed in chapter 1, is the brokenness of the world due to sin. Life "under the sun" is often characterized by experiences that run counter to God's good purposes. An example of this is that oftentimes wicked people whose hearts are full of evil don't receive a speedy judgment (8:11). Instead, they enjoy long life, go in and out of the temple as hypocrites, and then receive an honorable burial (8:10).

Some interpreters view this passage as an example of Qoheleth's pessimism.[85] On the contrary, it reveals his claim to certainty.[86] Qoheleth views this kind of injustice as "temporary" (8:10).[87] Even "though sinners do evil a hundred times and prolong their lives," in the end, "it will be well with those who fear God, because they stand in fear before him. "Yet because the wicked do not fear God, it will not go well with them, and their days will not lengthen like a shadow" (8:12–13). There will be an eventual retribution for the wicked, and an eventual reward for God-fearers.[88]

The final appearance of the "fear of the LORD" theme is in the book's epilogue (12:9–14), in which the author or editor affirms the teachings of Qoheleth and calls them "truth" (v. 10).[89] He concludes that the sayings of the wise "are like goads" (v. 11) used by herders to guide their animals, which emphasizes the disciplinary aspect of the wisdom tradition. Like ox goads, the sayings "sting and provoke" and "prod people to better behavior."[90] In a brief postscript, he states:

> The end of the matter; all has been heard. Fear God, and keep his commandments, for that is the whole duty of everyone. For God will bring every deed into judgment, including every secret thing, whether good or evil. (12:13–14)

Whatever doubts and concerns the author or editor may have expressed throughout the book, in the end, he affirms that "fearing God is the most important thing a person can do to live a wise life (cf. Deut. 6:2, 24; 10:12, 20; 14:23; 17:19; 31:12–13)."[91]

Toward the New Testament

Not limited to the Old Testament, the fear of the Lord continues throughout the New Testament. In her song of praise, Mary the mother of Jesus exclaims that God's "mercy is for those who fear him from generation to generation" (Luke 1:50). The wording here is drawn from Psalm 103, which is not an expression of servile fear but of thanksgiving for the Lord's goodness, which lasts forever. Psalm 103:17 proclaims that "the steadfast love of the LORD is from everlasting to everlasting on those who fear him, and his righteousness to children's children." Mary appropriates this phraseology to say that God's merciful bounty is shown "to those who recognize and reverence his sovereignty."[92]

Jesus himself recognized the fear of the Lord. When he sent out his disciples, he told them that they should expect some rejection and even persecution (Matt. 10:16–18). He encouraged them not to be afraid, however (vv. 26, 31), and explained that those who might persecute them did not have ultimate power over them. "Do not fear those who kill the body but cannot kill the soul; rather fear him who can destroy both soul and body in hell" (Matt. 10:28). Eugene Boring emphasizes that "these sayings are not concerned with the initial confession of faith in conversion"; they are "addressed to disciples who already profess Christian faith, but are fearful of bearing public witness to it in the church's mission."[93] Jesus was not threatening his disciples but reassuring them that their opponents could not do any permanent harm to them.

In the book of Acts, Luke describes the early Christian community as "living in the fear of the Lord and the comfort of the Holy Spirit" (Acts 9:31). By saying that they were "living" in the fear of the Lord, he's saying that this was "a way of living for these early Christians."[94] He introduces the idea in order "to enhance the wisdom that characterized early Palestinian Christians."[95]

The apostle Paul was heavily influenced by the Old Testament idea of the fear of God, and he often drew from it. In a discussion of the early Christian community as the temple of God (2 Cor. 6:14–7:1), for example, he called on the Christians at Corinth to "make holiness perfect in the fear of God" (2 Cor. 7:1 RSV). They were to maintain holiness by separating themselves from unbelievers, keep the temple free of idols, and cleanse themselves from any all defilement. The fear of God is "the sphere in which the perfecting of holiness takes place."[96] In another example from the "Household Codes,"[97] Paul instructed the Ephesians to "be subject to one another in the fear of Christ" (Eph. 5:21 NASB). In this case, the "fear of Christ" provides the reason for the congregation's mutual submission. Interestingly, this is the only occurrence of the expression "fear of Christ" in the entire New Testament, and it provides the foundation for Paul's entire discussion of the household codes in this epistle.[98] On another occasion, in a discussion about imitating Christ, Paul wrote to the Philippians, "Just as you have always obeyed me . . . work out your own salvation with fear and trembling" (Phil. 2:12). Morna Hooker emphasizes that "such fear and trembling are not caused by any uncertainty regarding their salvation, but are the appropriate attitude in the presence of God," which she suggests would be better described in English as "awe."[99] Clearly, Paul believed that this sense of awe should compel believers to obey the Lord, just as the sages explained in the wisdom literature.

The author of the Epistle to the Hebrews saw a contrast between the early Israelites' terrifying experience before God's presence at Mount Sinai and salvation through Christ. Regarding Mount Sinai, he writes:

> You have not come to something that can be touched, a blazing fire, and darkness, and gloom, and a tempest, and the sound of a trumpet, and a voice whose words

made the hearers beg that not another word be spoken to them. (For they could not endure the order that was given, "If even an animal touches the mountain, it shall be stoned to death." Indeed, so terrifying was the sight that Moses said, "I tremble with fear.") (12:18–21)

By contrast, he explains to those who believe in Christ,

But you have come to Mount Zion and to the city of the living God, the heavenly Jerusalem, and to innumerable angels in festal gathering, and to the assembly of the firstborn who are enrolled in heaven, and to God the judge of all, and to the spirits of the righteous made perfect, and to Jesus, the mediator of a new covenant, and to the sprinkled blood that speaks a better word than the blood of Abel. (12:22–24)

In approaching God through Christ, believers do not stand in a place of terrifying judgment but rather in a place of joyous fellowship with God.[100] Despite this contrast, however, the chapter ends with an appeal to worship God "with reverence and godly fear: for our God is a consuming fire" (vv. 28–29 KJV). Gareth Lee Cockerill concludes, "Recognition of such potential judgment only heightens the awareness that God is good in providing not only a way of escape, but a way that his own can enjoy eternal fellowship with him."[101]

Similarly, the apostle Peter based his call for holy living on a recognition that God is the one who will judge all people: "If you invoke as Father the one who judges impartially according to each person's work, live in fear during the time of your exile" (1 Pet. 1:17). Even though these early Christians called God Father, they would not be exempt from judgment. And yet the fact that the one who would judge was also the one they called Father meant that their fear could include a sense of "confident reverence."[102] At the conclusion of his discussion on how to live as servants of God, Peter urged his readers to "honor everyone. Love the family of believers. Fear God. Honor the emperor" (1 Pet. 2:17). In a pluralistic society, the emperor and all his subjects should be respected, but only God warrants reverence.[103]

First John contains the passage that led Enlightenment thinker Friedrich Schleiermacher to conclude that the fear of God is in opposition to the love of God. John writes, "So we have known and believe the love that God has for us" (1 John 4:16), and then, "There is no fear in love, but perfect love casts out fear; for fear has to do with punishment, and whoever fears has not reached perfection in love" (v. 18). Schleiermacher concluded that love was the primary attribute of the divine essence and that "no other attribute can be equated thus with God."[104] A closer reading of 1 John, however, makes it clear that this verse doesn't pit the fear of God as incompatible with love. Instead, it states that "those who have experienced the divine love have no fear for punishment on the day of judgment."[105]

In this chapter, we have seen that the fear of the Lord is viewed in wisdom literature as a positive sensibility rather than as a negative one. Resistance to the idea that God should be feared in any sense is a result of the influence of modernity. Some of the leading values of contemporary culture are: "Anything goes," "If it feels good, do it," or "How can it be wrong when it feels so right?" If we have those kinds of values, then we can't tolerate the idea of a God who inspires fear of any kind. Instead, it becomes necessary to jettison the idea of the fear of God in favor of a God who loves and accepts anything and everything. Accordingly, our culture has turned God into a doddering old grandfather who sits on his throne, nodding, and patting everyone on the back, regardless of how they behave in this world.

This was not how ancient Israel's sages viewed God. The idea of the fear of God is foundational for Deuteronomic theology, and it shaped the thinking of ancient Israel's sages. In wisdom literature, those sages teach that the fear of the Lord—a reverential awe of God—is the vital foundation of wisdom. It is deeply embedded in the structure and theology of the wisdom books as a whole. Ancient Israel's sages believed that God's majesty and power should evoke fear, and that such fear should lead people to put their trust in the Lord, to love him, and to follow his ways. This view is certainly not confined to wisdom literature or even the Old Testament; it features throughout the New Testament as well. Now, in the third millennium, "Christianity needs a new vocabulary of the fear of God, a renewed striving for that virtue, and a yearning openness to fear as God's saving gift of love."[106]

· 3 ·

———

INTEGRITY

It seems as if there's been a general erosion of integrity today. In *Empires of the Mind*, Dr. Denis Waitley explains how he would throw a wallet into the middle of his high school classroom and then tell his students that it contained a driver's license, credit cards, photos, and eight $100 bills. When he asked them what they would do if they discovered the wallet on a deserted street, he found the answers uncomfortably revealing. Typically, some say, "Wow, that would be awesome! I'd keep the money as my reward and mail back the wallet with the credit cards." Others suggest actions like not putting a return address on the envelope so the owner couldn't call and ask if there was money in the wallet when it was found.[1]

I remember reading a story in the paper a few years ago about some guys in New Jersey who found a bag of $150,000 in cash at an ATM that apparently had been left behind by ATM workers by mistake. Video camera footage showed a person getting out of a van and grabbing the bag. Not long afterward, one of the passengers purchased an SUV with $46,000 of the cash. The driver of the van was caught and held on $125,000 bail and charged with "theft of mislaid property."[2]

Although we could certainly find other examples from every arena of life, they all lead us back to the same question: Why is there such a lack of integrity and what can be done about it? In this chapter, we will explore the roots of integrity's decline and what the sages would advise about recovering integrity today.

Whatever Became of Sin?

In 1973, Dr. Karl Menninger, cofounder of the Menninger Clinic in Topeka, Kansas, wrote a book called *Whatever Became of Sin?*[3] In it, he traced the decline of integrity to the abandonment of the concept of "sin" in our culture. He says that this abandonment is due in part to the rise of scientific psychology, which replaced the word *sin* with nonmoral words such as *mistake, error,* or *weakness.* Indicative of this shift, crime came to be understood as the symptoms of one's circumstances or even as an illness. And how can you blame someone for their circumstances? Or for being ill?

This trend of explaining self-destructive behavior as a symptom of social circumstances, economic conditions, or oppressive systems has only increased since Dr. Menninger's time.[4] This has had a profound impact on our society, in that the idea of "sin" has been practically erased from our national consciousness. Everything is now understood as an illness or as genetics. Nobody's to blame for anything. A recent *Time* magazine article, "Infidelity: It May Be in Our Genes,"[5] proposes that adultery may be caused by genetics. In other words, it's a medical sickness and not something for which someone can be held responsible or need to repent of. Already in 1973, Menninger saw where these trends were headed, and he asked, "Is no one any longer guilty of anything?"[6]

More recently, David Brooks, a leading social commentator and columnist for the *New York Times* who often appears on PBS and CNN, wrote *The Road to Character.* In the book, he makes what many would consider a shocking statement: *Sin* is a word that is impossible to do without and that we need to reclaim in our culture "because it reminds us that life is a moral affair." He writes:

> No matter how hard we try to reduce everything to deterministic brain chemistry . . . no matter how hard we strive to replace sin with nonmoral words, like "mistake" or "error" or "weakness," the most essential parts of life are matters of individual responsibility and moral choice. . . . When modern culture tries to replace sin with ideas like error or insensitivity, or tries to banish words like "virtue," "character," and "vice" altogether, that doesn't make life any less moral; it just means we have obscured the inescapable moral core of life with shallow language. It just means we think about talk about these choices less clearly, and thus become increasingly blind to the moral stakes of everyday life.[7]

His argument is that sin should indeed be a vital part of our worldview, because if we don't know we have a disease, then we won't be all that interested in curing it.

The Ancient Problem of Human Corruption

Israel's sages certainly believed that sin was the real reason for the problems of humankind, and they also believed that sin was almost as old as humankind itself. The primeval history of Genesis 1–11 recounts when Adam and Eve disobeyed God's instructions in the Garden of Eden and were driven out of paradise and away from God's direct presence (Gen. 3:23–24), a consequence referred to in the Christian tradition as the "fall."[8] As their family grew outside the garden, it seems they passed on this proclivity toward sin to their children, for in the very next scene, their eldest son Cain murders his younger brother, Abel (Gen. 4:1–16). In the genealogies that follow, as the growth and spread of Adam and Eve's descendants are traced out, the constant refrain is "and then he died." The effect is an impression that, as humankind grew and spread, so did the realization of the effects of the fall: "You shall die" (Gen. 3:3). The effects of sin were so pervasive that eventually "the wickedness of humankind" became "great in the earth," so that "every inclination of the thoughts of their hearts was only evil continually" (Gen. 6:5).

The idea that humankind had somehow been tainted by the disobedience of the first human couple was deeply ingrained in the ancient Israelite consciousness. This belief is powerfully illustrated in the apocryphal book of 2 Esdras, which may have been written around AD 70, when the author(s) laments:

> Better never to have come into existence than to be born into a world of wickedness and suffering which we cannot explain! . . . We are all of us sinners through and through. Can it be that because of us, because of the sins of mankind, the harvest and the reward of the just are delayed? . . . O Adam, what have you done? Your sin was not your fall alone; it was ours also, the fall of all your descendants. What good is the promise of immortality to us, when we have committed mortal sins; or the hope of eternity, in the wretched and futile state to which we have come. . . . [W]e have made depravity our home.
>
> (2 Esdras 4:12, 38–39; 7:48–50, 54 NEB)

Ancient Israel's sages inherited this tradition, and it is reflected in their wisdom literature. For example, the author of Psalm 14, which is a poem of instruction clearly influenced by Israel's wisdom tradition,[9] echoes this idea that humans are innately corrupt:

> Fools say in their hearts, "There is no God."
>> They are corrupt, they do abominable deeds;
>> there is no one who does good.
>
> The LORD looks down from heaven on humankind
>> to see if there are any who are wise,
>> who seek after God.
>
> They have all gone astray; they are all like perverse;

> there is no one who does good,
>> no, not one. (Ps. 14:1–3)

Israel's proverbial wisdom likewise affirmed the belief that sin pervades the human heart and leads to death. One proverb expresses the idea that those who live in sin are spiritual corpses (Prov. 9:18).[10] Another reflects the idea that sin clouds the mind and prevents people from reasoning properly:

> There is a way that seems right to a person,
>> but its end is the way to death. (Prov. 14:12)[11]

Another asks,

> Who can say, "I have made my heart clean;
>> I am pure from my sin"? (Prov. 20:9)[12]

Israel's sages were under no illusion that men and women just make some "mistakes" from time to time, that their decision to have an affair was an "error in judgment," or that embezzling money from a business was the result of a momentary "weakness." They believed in sin and its terrible effects.

Recovering Integrity

"THE FEAR OF GOD IS THE BEGINNING OF WISDOM"

First, we must go back to the foundation discussed in chapter 2: that "the fear of God is the beginning of wisdom" (Prov. 1:7). There, we noted the close relationship between the fear of God and love and reverence for his Torah or law (תּוֹרָה).[13] In one of the wisdom psalms, the psalmist invites children to come to him so that he can teach them the fear of the Lord, and then he proceeds to teach them the importance of God's Torah (Ps. 34:11–22). In another example, the writer of Ecclesiastes sums up his quest for wisdom by concluding that the "whole duty of everyone" is to "fear God, and keep his commandments" (Eccles. 12:13). This reflects a main emphasis within the Torah itself. When Moses summed up its essence, he said,

> "So now, O Israel, what does the Lord your God require of you? Only to fear the Lord your God, to walk in all his ways, to love him, to serve the Lord your God with all your heart and with all your soul, and to keep the commandments of the Lord your God' and his decrees that I am commanding you today, for your own well-being." (Deut. 10:12–13)

The connection between the fear of the Lord and reverence for his Torah has important implications: It keeps people from sinning,[14] and when people who have a healthy fear of the Lord are caught in sin, this fear causes them to turn away from their sin.[15] If people don't have belief in God or reverential awe for him, then they won't believe in or care about his instruction.

EMBRACING GOD'S INSTRUCTIONS

If the first step in recovering integrity is recovering a fear of the Lord, then the second step is to accept and embrace God's instructions. Looking for connections between the Torah and wisdom has been somewhat controversial. Since at least the mid-twentieth century, some biblical scholars have argued that because of the sharp division between the genres of law and wisdom, there are virtually no traces of Mosaic legislation in wisdom literature.[16] More recent scholarship, however, argues that there is integration across the canon of Scripture, so that there is a "broad interconnectedness" of the whole Bible.[17] Along this line, intertextual studies reveal that Torah and wisdom are complementary.[18] William Brown, for example, conducted a thorough reexamination of the book of Proverbs and found that it portrays the law and wisdom as equivalent.[19]

The book of Proverbs provides the perfect entry into a consideration of wisdom and law because of its wealth of references to Mosaic legislation. According to the sages, a person with a "wise heart" accepts the commandments (מִצְוֹת). They also teach that "those who respect the commandment [מִצְוָה] will be rewarded" (Prov. 13:13), and that "the teaching of the wise [תּוֹרַת חָכָם] is a fountain of life" (13:14). A similar saying reads that "those who keep the commandment [מִצְוָה] will live," whereas "those who are heedless of their ways will die" (Prov. 19:16). These and other sayings refer to "a concept of wisdom that is determined by divine law . . . [a] nomistic, *torah*-oriented concept of wisdom."[20] Reflective of this orientation, Proverbs is full of both direct and indirect verbal links to the Ten Commandments. Among the most obvious are allusions to the command to honor one's father and mother (Prov. 6:20; 20:20; 23:22–25; 30:17), prohibition against adultery (6:32), stealing (6:30–31), bearing false witness (6:19; 14:25; 19:9, 28; 21:28; 25:18), coveting your neighbor's wife (6:25, 29), and coveting in general (21:26).

The scope of the law is wide in the book of Proverbs. Not limited to references to the Ten Commandments, it also includes numerous allusions to an array of Mosaic teaching.[21] One teaching that may be familiar to many readers has to do with reciprocity and is based on Leviticus 19:18, "You shall not take vengeance or bear a grudge against any of your people, but you shall love your neighbor as yourself." An adaptation of it appears in Proverbs 20:22 (my italics):

Do not say, "I will repay evil";
    wait for the LORD, and *he* will help you.

It also appears in Proverbs 24:29, but with slightly different wording:

Do not say, "I will do to others as they have done to me;
    I will pay them back for what they have done."

Deuteronomy 6:4–9 is a passage from the Torah of particular significance as it provides the basic creed of Judaism known as the Shema:

"Hear, O Israel: The LORD is our God, the LORD alone. You shall love the LORD your God with all your heart, and with all your soul, and with all your might. Keep these words that I am commanding you today in your heart. Recite them to your children and talk about them when you are at home and when you are away, when you lie down and when you rise. Bind them as a sign on your hand, fix them as an emblem on your forehead, and write them on the doorposts of your house and on your gates."

The book of Proverbs repeatedly alludes to the Shema.[22] Proverbs 6:20–24, for example, provides a free adaptation of this watchword of the Jewish faith:

My child, keep your father's commandment,
    and do not forsake your mother's teaching.
Bind them upon your heart always;
    tie them around your neck.
When you walk, they will lead you;
    when you lie down, they will watch over you;
    and when you awake, they will talk with you.
For the commandment is a lamp and the teaching a light,
    and the reproofs of discipline are the way of life,
to preserve you from the wife of another,
    from the smooth tongue of the adulteress.

Israel's sages clearly believed that those who are wise accept God's law, strive to live it out in their daily lives, and seek to pass it on to their children.

Torah and the Good Life

Israel's sages believed that a fully integrated approach to the law would lead to the good life. To integrate means to bring together into a whole. It's related to the word *integral*, which means "complete" or "whole," and to the mathematical term "integer," which refers to a whole number, not a fraction.

In psychology, "integration" refers to the bringing together of a person's fundamental traits, behavioral patterns, and motives so that they function as a whole person without conflict. Therefore, someone with an integrated view of God's law has integrated it into every part of their life so that they follow it "faithfully and wholeheartedly" (2 Chron. 19:9; cf. Ps. 2:11). Norman Whybray suggests, "Of all the books of the Old Testament it is probably the Psalter that opens the largest window on how the ancient Israelites viewed the good life and the extent to which they believed that they had attained it or that it was within their grasp."[23]

It was no accident that there is a wisdom psalm at the very beginning of the book of Psalms. Psalm 1 not only introduces the book, but it also teaches that the key to the good life is constant meditation on God's law:

> Happy are those
> who do not follow the advice of the wicked
> or take the path that sinners tread
> or sit in the seat of scoffers,
> but their delight is in the law of the LORD,
> and on his law they meditate day and night.
> They are like trees
> planted by streams of water,
> which yield their fruit in its season,
> and their leaves do not wither.
> In all that they do, they prosper. (1–3)

The author of Psalm 1 commends the Psalter itself to the reader as law and promises that its embrace will produce a truly good life.[24]

The premier example of this view is probably Psalm 119. The longest psalm, it's a highly artistic hymn of praise to God's law.[25] In it, the psalmist talks consistently about how much he values the law. He begins by saying, "Happy are those . . . who walk in the law of the LORD" (v. 1), "who keep his decrees" (v. 2), who "walk in his ways" (v. 3). He prays, "O that my ways may be steadfast in keeping your statutes!" (v. 5). The psalmist continues by repeating similar adulations of the law, substituting a seemingly endless array of synonyms for the law, until he finally bursts into praise:

> Oh, how I love your law!
> It is my meditation all day long. (v. 97)

Such lavish praise for the law may sound bizarre to modern ears. We tend to think of law as something negative and restrictive that hems us in. But the biblical view is just the opposite: It sees the law as a gracious provision God gives to his people for their benefit. This idea is profoundly expressed in verse 45, where it literally says, "I will walk in a wide place, for I have sought out your precepts." The NRSVue translates it, "I will walk in liberty," and the NIV reads, "I will walk in freedom." Again, modern Western readers probably tend to think of law as setting *limits* or creating a *narrow* place to walk in, but the psalmist says that seeking out the Lord's precepts enables us to walk in a "wide place," in "liberty," or even "freedom." How can that be?

An example from my days as an undergraduate student might help to make sense of this. When I was in college, our school had a pretty strong reputation for basketball. Every summer, young men came from all over the region to our basketball camps. Here, coaches would shout at them until they were blue in the face, make them run until they threw up, and make them do drills until they were about ready to pass out. Although one might think these players felt this kind of hard-driving discipline was a burden, this wasn't the case at all. Instead, they ate it up because they had hopes that this training might make them into the next great basketball star.

Think about two young people studying the violin. One of them doesn't pay attention to his teacher, doesn't practice at home, and even misses his lessons half of the time. The other student takes her lessons seriously. She never misses a lesson, and when she's with her teacher, she listens closely to his instructions. She practices at night and on the weekends. After a few years, the young man can barely play his violin and finally gives up in despair, whereas the other student developed the ability to create beautiful music. She attends Julliard and lands a job with a symphony after her graduation. She's then able to make wonderful contributions to the world of music, but only because she embraced discipline and instruction. It opened up a "wide place" for her to walk in, and now she excels in her field.

Or consider another two young people growing up in the church. One of them doesn't like the teachings of the church and rebels. He becomes a partier, hangs out with drug users, and begins to experiment with those drugs himself. He becomes sexually active in high school, and between his junior and senior year, gets a girl pregnant but convinces her to have an abortion. He covers up his guilt with drugs and alcohol, and his later relationships are cycles of misery. The other young man embraces the teachings of the church, abstains from drugs and alcohol, and never gets in trouble with the law. He saves himself for marriage and later builds a solid family. He's trusted by his employers and is successful in his career. Which one of these young men had a wide place to walk in? The one who flouted discipline and instruction or the one who embraced it?

The point is obvious, and the author of Psalm 119 also sees it. Because he follows God's teachings, he won't be put to shame (v. 6), has been made wiser than his enemies (v. 98), understands more than the aged (v. 100), and has been held back from evil paths (v. 101). These are but a few of the benefits he enumerates. And because of these benefits of the law, the psalmist says that its words taste sweet in his mouth and are sweeter than honey (v. 103). They're a lamp to his feet and a light to his path (v. 105). They are his heritage forever and the joy of his heart (v. 111). They're better than "thousands of gold and silver pieces" (v. 72).

The sentiments expressed in Psalm 119 are those of someone who has a fully integrated view of God's law. Ancient Israel's sages taught that if God's people would fully integrate the Torah into their lives, then they would be empowered to live stable lives in flourishing communities. Many of the sayings of the wise attest to this, including these examples from Proverbs:

> Keep straight the path of your feet,
>   and all your ways will be sure. (4:26)

> The integrity of the upright guides them,
>   but the crookedness of the treacherous destroys them. (11:3)

> Whoever walks in integrity walks securely,
>   but whoever follows perverse ways will be found out. (10:9)

> One who walks in integrity will be safe,
>   but whoever follows crooked ways will all into the Pit. (28:18)

Toward the New Testament

The importance of a sense of reverential awe for God, a commitment to God's law, and the importance of a fully integrated approach to it are all prominent themes in the New Testament. Although Christians will easily accept the importance of a reverential awe of God, they may be less comfortable with the idea of committing to God's law and fully integrating it into their lives. There are significant disagreements in contemporary churches about whether or not Old Testament law is binding for Christians today and, if so, to what extent. These questions are not new. There were strong disagreements among the earliest Christians about whether the Old Testament law was binding for them.

One of the key passages in the debate is Romans 10:4, in which the apostle Paul claimed that Christ is "the end of the law so that there may be righteousness for everyone who believes." Some commentators argue that Paul was not claiming that the law came to an end or ceased with Christ, but that Christ was the goal and culmination (*telos*) of the law because he provided righteousness for those who believed in him.[26] Others insist, however, that while the concepts of "purpose," "goal," and "fulfillment" may legitimately be seen in Paul's use of "end" (*telos*) in this passage, "the feature the apostle highlights is 'termination,' 'end,' or 'cessation' of the Mosaic law in any positive or custodial fashion in this new age of salvation history, which is characterized by the Lordship of Christ and the ministry of God's Holy Spirit."[27]

The idea that the Torah had a temporary function and that it would be replaced by a new Torah was not unique to Paul; it was original to the Old Testament and current to Jewish tradition in Paul's day. In a recent study, Charles Quarles demonstrated that the Pentateuch itself foretold the coming of a prophet like Moses who would deliver new divine commandments, and Jews of the Second Temple era and the rabbinic period expected that this figure would mediate a new covenant and teach a new Torah.[28] He explains that "some rabbis argued that in the messianic age, God's people would receive a new Torah,"[29] and that "this Torah could even be described specifically as the 'Torah of the Messiah'" (*Midr. Eccl.* 11.8).[30]

Paul believed that Jesus was the prophet like Moses and that he had both fulfilled the Mosaic Torah and delivered a new one. In his epistles, Paul repeatedly says that Christians are subject to the "law of Christ."[31] Long ago, C. H. Dodd proposed that Paul's "law of Christ" was probably a reference to the Sermon on the Mount, and many interpreters have held to this view.[32] Others have suggested that "it means that law (Torah) as interpreted by the love command in the light of the Jesus tradition and the Christ event."[33] Although there is disagreement about precisely what Paul meant by the "law of Christ," it's clear that he put great stock in the Mosaic Torah, for he said that "obeying the commandments of God is everything" (1 Cor. 7:19). It's also clear that he integrated numerous Mosaic laws into his own teaching.[34]

A complete discussion, however, of the relationship between law and gospel goes far beyond the scope of this brief section.[35] Suffice it to say that the Mosaic Torah is epitomized by the Ten Commandments, which are the heart of what God expected from his covenant people.[36] The Ten Commandments can be broken into two halves, with the first four dealing with our relationship with God and the remaining six with relationships in the community. They basically explain how to love God and how to love one's neighbor as oneself, both of which provide the foundation for personal and communal ethics.[37]

When Jesus was asked which of the commandments in the law was the greatest, he answered by summarizing these two foci:

> When the Pharisees heard that he had silenced the Sadducees, they gathered together, and one of them, a lawyer, asked him a question to test him. "Teacher, which commandment in the law is the greatest?" He said to him, "'You shall love the LORD your God with all your heart, and with all your soul, and with all your mind.' This is the greatest and first commandment. And a second is like it: 'You shall love your neighbor as yourself.' On these two commandments hang all the law and the prophets." (Matt. 22:34–40)

When these principles guide our every thought, decision, and action, we will truly realize the good life.

COMMUNITY

In 1994, Jan Karon published *At Home in Mitford*, a novel about Father Timothy Kavanaugh, rector of Lord's Chapel in the fictional town of Mitford, North Carolina. As the story begins, Father Tim is about to turn sixty and feels like he's at a crossroads in his life. Although his bishop has asked him to continue as rector of Lord's Chapel, Father Tim is unsure whether or not he should. He finally agrees, although somewhat reluctantly, and resumes the busy life of a pastor ministering to his parishioners. He finds, however, that the ordinary duties of ministry tire him out and that he's frequently exhausted. After repeated badgering by his secretary, he goes to the doctor who diagnosis him with diabetes, and Father Tim has to learn to take care of himself and find some balance in his life.

Something Father Tim never expected happens when he ends up becoming the ward of a scruffy boy named Dooley, his caretaker's grandson. He also comes to own a huge dog named Barnabas who instantly follows commands when given in the form of quotations from Scripture. Father Tim, Dooley, and Barnabas become a family, and the town of Mitford embraces Dooley as one of their own. The plot thickens when a lovely woman named Cynthia Coppersmith moves into the little house next door to the rectory. She illustrates children's books, and Father Tim is struck by her beauty, intelligence, and creativity. Having never been married, he is surprised by the feelings he begins to develop for her.

But Father Tim doesn't have to navigate any of this alone. These storylines and many more play out in the landscape of Mitford, which is really a village. It has a "greasy spoon" restaurant called the Grill run by Percy and Velma Mosely and a refined tea shop that appeals to the more genteel. There's The Local, Mitford's Main Street grocery store, run by Avis Packard. Hope

Winchester runs a cozy little bookshop called Happy Endings Bookstore. And then there's Oxford Antiques run by Andrew Gregory, who's always wearing a signature cashmere jacket and playing classical music in his shop.

If Father Tim pops into the Grill at lunchtime, he usually finds friends there like Mule Skinner, the town realtor, and J. C. Hogan, the editor of the *Mitford Muse*. If he walks by Oxford Antiques, Andrew will invite him in for a fresh cup of steaming hot Antigua tea, and he may chat with Hope as he passes by Happy Endings.

Mitford is a small village where everybody knows everyone else's name. This is probably why the series became a *New York Times* bestseller: people have nostalgia for that kind of community, even if they've never experienced it themselves. In this chapter, we'll look at the loss of community and its replacement with a loneliness that has reached pandemic proportions, and then we'll consider the makeup of ancient Israelite communities. We'll consider the ways that Israel's sages conceived of community, and then we'll zero in on some of the basic building blocks of the community, including family, friends, and neighbors. We'll conclude with a brief foray into how themes connected with community feature in the New Testament.

The Epidemic of Loneliness

About twenty years ago, Harvard sociologist Robert Putnam wrote *Bowling Alone: The Collapse and Revival of American Community*.[1] In this book, he shows how since about 1980, Americans have become increasingly disconnected from family, friends, neighbors, and community structures—whether it's the PTA, church, recreation clubs, service clubs, political parties, or bowling leagues.

There are many reasons for the decline in community in our society. The shift from an agricultural to an industrial society led to an entire generation moving from the country to the city. Today, with the continued commercialization of our society, people have to go where they can find employment. We tend to end up in the suburbs where no one knows anyone, and there are no sidewalks because everyone leaves there to go to work. Instead of front porches, we prefer patios or decks behind the house where they're not visible from the street. In order to ensure our privacy, we put up fences or walls around the yard. All too often, suburbs have become places of isolation.[2]

Changing demographics also contribute to increasing isolation. In their book *The Lonely American*, Jacqueline Olds and Richard Schwartz point out that 25 percent of households in the United States consist of only one person. More people live alone in America today than ever before. The result of all these changes is that loneliness has become a "social epidemic."[3]

In March 2020, the problem of loneliness increased exponentially with the quarantines implemented in an attempt to stop or slow the spread of COVID-19. For the next several months, all so-called nonessential workers were locked down in their homes. As the months passed, there was a tremendous amount of debate at all levels of society about whether it was essential to "reopen." Many argued that it wasn't necessary to reopen everything like before, that society would change, that we just really don't need that much in-person contact, and that we can do more things from our homes. People can work remotely. They can even shop for cars online and have their groceries delivered. There was even debate about whether it was essential for churches to meet in person. Some said that it ought to be sufficient to just watch a service on television or on a computer screen.

The fact that these debates even occurred is surprising, because scientists have known for years that human beings have an inherent need for closeness with one another and that loneliness can have devastating consequences. In a famous study published in 1945, Dr. Rene Spitz looked at what happened to infants placed in a European hospital for children who had been exposed or abandoned during World War II. There was only one nurse for every twelve infants and so, while they received adequate medical attention and food, they were seldom handled or held by the busy nurses. Thirty percent of the children died within the first year, and those who survived could not stand, walk, or talk by the age of four, and many had become developmentally delayed. Dr. Spitz argued that the deaths of the 30 percent and the failure to thrive among those who survived was because of the lack of human contact, which included being held, coddled, and talked to.[4]

In 1990, John Cacioppo and William Patrick wrote a book on loneliness in which they summarized what scientists have come to understand about its harmful effects.[5] They explained that being disconnected diminishes happiness, health, and longevity; instead, it increases aggression and is connected to increasing rates of violent crime. They said that communities with fewer social bonds[6] have lower educational performance and more teen pregnancy, child suicide, low birth weight, and even prenatal mortality.

In a more recent work, behavioral scientist Susan Mettes confirms the profound physical, emotional, and social effects of loneliness, which she argues has increased to pandemic proportions.[7] The former prime minister of England, Boris Johnson, was appointed "minister of loneliness," and in the United States, the surgeon general declared that loneliness was an epidemic. In the wake of these grim pronouncements, we'll go back in time to see what communities looked like in ancient Israel and what their sages had to say about community itself.

Ancient Israelite Communities

In his pioneering article "The Archaeology of the Family in Ancient Israel," Lawrence Stager showed how early Israelite society was grounded in kinship.[8] The foundation of the community was the "house of the father" (בֵּית אָב), which included the senior male, his wife and children, and any other dependents, including unmarried daughters, daughters-in-law, or grandchildren. The house of the father made up a unit that lived together in a single home or cluster of homes. A number of such families living together in a village made up a "clan" (מִשְׁפָּחָה). Several clans, grouped in a region, constituted the "tribe" (שֵׁבֶט), which was a patrimonial group whose descendants maintained kinship with one another through marriage and bloodlines traced back through the male relatives to one of the twelve sons of Israel, the tribal ancestors.[9]

When the early Israelites first arrived in the land of Canaan, they established small villages in the highlands that reflected this kinship model. These were simple, elliptical villages that consisted of a band of broad rooms arranged in an ellipse with a large open space in the center. These broad rooms faced the center and encircled the settlement, forming a courtyard where the villagers could corral their herds at night. This pattern can be seen in the early Israelite village founded around the end of the thirteenth or beginning of the twelfth century BC at 'Izbet Sartah (fig. 4.1.).

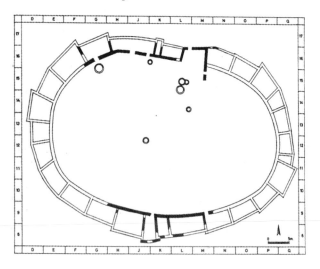

FIGURE 4.1. Schematic plan of Stratum III at 'Izbet Sartah. (Israel Finkelstein, *The Archaeology of the Israelite Settlement* [Jerusalem: Israel Exploration Society, 1988], 239. Used by permission.)

The population of 'Izbet Sartah comprised about a hundred people, with some twenty family units of four or five members each who practiced agriculture and animal husbandry.[10] The people who lived there were all part of the same clan and would have known each other well.

As the early Israelites made the transition to more permanent settlement, the villages they established began to look quite different. Instead of building a band of broad rooms arranged in an ellipse with a corral in the center, they covered the entire area of the settlement with dwellings. An example of this can be found at Ai, where the settlement extended over an area of almost two and a half acres without any peripheral belt of buildings (fig. 4.2.).

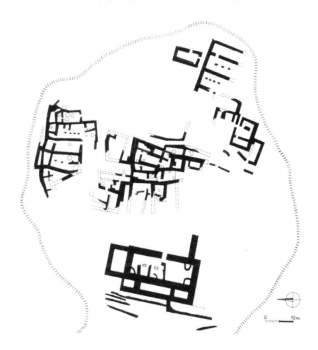

FIGURE 4.2. Ai in the Iron Age IA. (Ze'ev Herzog, *Archaeology of the City: Urban Planning in Ancient Israel and Its Social Implications* [Jerusalem: Emery and Claire Yass Archaeology Press, 1997], 196. Used by permission.)

The population is estimated to have been around fifteen hundred people, who had an economy based not only on agriculture but also various crafts such as metal working, pottery production, and wine making.[11] Although the population was denser, it would have still been established on this kinship model and therefore probably included many members of the same tribe.

As the population increased, Israel transitioned from a domestic-scale culture to a political-scale culture. From the middle of the tenth century BC, a radical change can be seen in urban planning.[12] Capital cities, which were central cities with a wide variety of functions, were established. Other cities were established for singular purposes, such as administrative centers, chariot cities, store cities, and cities with either a regional or national religious center.

Even after this urbanization, however, Israelite society was still a small-scale society. It may be hard for modern Americans to appreciate this since we are familiar with cities like New York with its population of 8.80 million people, or Chicago with 2.75 million people. The population of major urban centers in ancient Israel was nothing even remotely like this. By way of contrast, in the ninth century BC, the capital city of Samaria spread over only about four acres, and in the period between 1000 and 586 BC, the major administrative center at Megiddo encompassed only about thirteen acres. The population of the entirety of Iron Age Israel, including the coastal zones, was only about sixty to seventy thousand in 1200 BC, about one hundred fifty thousand in 1000 BC, and about four hundred thousand by the mid-eighth century BC.[13] Even in the towns and cities of ancient Israel, there were still domestic groupings that were probably organized along kinship lines.

The point is that early Israelite society was grounded in kinship and focused on community. Many or most of the people in small villages and towns would have known one another and most likely even been related. In the larger cities, kinship groups still lived together in domestic areas. The lives of ancient Israelites focused on family and kin to an extent that modern people no longer much experience. Although this would have been true of many ancient peoples, the Lord has provided them as an example for us in Scripture.

The Wisdom of Community

Ancient Israel's sages set a high value on community, and much of their teaching reinforces this or provides instruction about how to protect it.

A CLOSED COMMUNITY

Some parts of the book of Proverbs reflect the idea of a "closed community" that intentionally limited contact with outsiders and outside communities. This idea reflects Deuteronomic teaching that prohibited making covenants or intermarrying with those from the seven Canaanite nations, as well as worshiping or even inquiring about their gods.[14] The idea is also reflected in Proverbs 5:14, in which the sages refer to the "public assembly."

The NRSVue's "public assembly" is actually their translation of two Hebrew words: *qahal* [קָהָל], which refers to a legal assembly (Prov 26:26), and *'edah* [עֵדָה], which means "congregation." In Proverbs 5:14, the two words are linked together with a conjunction and literally read "assembly and congregation" [קָהָל וְעֵדָה]. This is the only time these two words are linked together in the entire Old Testament, and it may be a way of describing Israel as an exclusive religious community.[15]

The idea of Israel as a closed community is more clearly reflected in other ways. In Proverbs 5:1–23, for example, the pupil is repeatedly warned about "strangers": "strangers" (sg. נָכְרִי) who may want to acquire his wealth (v. 10), and "strangers" (זָרִים) who may want to enjoy being with his wife (v. 17). It may be that one or more foreigners had settled within the community. In any case, these warnings bring to mind the Deuteronomic instruction to maintain "a clear separation between Israel and foreigners."[16] The sages believed it was important to maintain some separation from foreigners since they could pose a threat to the religion of the Lord.

A RELIGIOUS COMMUNITY

In addition to the "assembly and congregation" (קָהָל וְעֵדָה) in Proverbs 5:14 as a distinct religious community, the sages also envisioned a community where people followed the Torah (תּוֹרָה). Furthermore, in Proverbs 7:14, there is a reference to the peace offering (שְׁלָמִים) in which a herd or flock animal was offered in sacrifice by the lay public in the outer area of the tabernacle/temple (Lev. 3; 7:11–35). The innards were burned in the fire on the altar, and then most of the animal was eaten after being divided between the priests and the family who brought the offering. The peace offering, therefore, was associated with feasting and was probably a festive occasion, much like an outdoor barbecue. It played an especially important role in ancient Israel as a social group, since it was associated with the extended family.

PASSING WISDOM TO THE NEXT GENERATION

The prologue to the book of Proverbs introduces its primary purposes:

For learning about wisdom and instruction,
    for understanding words of insight,
for gaining instruction in wise dealing,
    righteousness, justice, and equity;
to teach shrewdness to the simple,
    knowledge and prudence to the young—
let the wise also hear and gain in learning

> and the discerning acquire skill,
> to understand a proverb and a figure,
> the words of the wise and their riddles. (Prov. 1:2–6)

Ancient Israel's sages believed that training the "simple" and the "young" in wisdom would enable them to grow and mature and live into their responsibilities in the community. It would enable them to become valued members of the community.

WISDOM'S FOUNDATION

If the "simple" and the "young" are going to learn wisdom, then they must begin with the "fear of the LORD," which provides its only proper foundation:

> The fear of the LORD is the beginning of knowledge;
> fools despise wisdom and instruction. (Prov. 1:7)

Those who wanted to acquire true wisdom must be prepared at the outset to accept and embrace the fear of the Lord as its only true basis. A refusal to recognize this fear of the Lord is really symptomatic of a much broader failure to recognize the Lord himself. It's impossible for such a person to really learn wisdom, and in the end, they will remain a "fool" (1:7).

THE BASIS OF GOOD SOCIAL ORDER

"Righteousness" (צֶדֶק) and "justice" (מִשְׁפָּט), in addition to having positive effects in the lives of individuals, are the basic conditions of good social order. The scope of righteousness is wide, but its essence has to do with keeping God's will as conveyed in the Torah (e.g., Deut. 6:25).[17] The sages teach that "righteousness exalts a nation, but sin is a reproach to any people" (Prov. 14:34). It produces stability in government (Prov. 16:12), and "when the righteous are in authority, the people rejoice; but when the wicked rule, the people groan" (Prov. 29:2). When a nation conforms its life to God's moral standards, they will experience the benefits of power, peace, and prosperity.

Like righteousness, justice was also viewed as foundational for good social order. Justice has to do with treating people fairly and adjudicating impartially.[18] Ancient Israel's sages taught that the nation's leaders should implement justice in society. They envisioned the king as one who "winnows all evil with his eyes" (Prov. 20:8), which means he will separate out anything that is morally corrupt or socially disruptive to the well-being of the kingdom. Such a king removes wickedness from society (Prov. 20:26). When justice is done in society, it brings joy to the righteous and thwarts the plans of evildoers (Prov. 21:15), and it produces a society in which the rights of the poor are protected (Prov. 29:7).

WISDOM AND FOLLY

The sages urged their disciples to embrace their "teaching" (תּוֹרָה) and keep their "commandments" (מִצְוֹת) (Prov. 3:1). In an allusion to Deuteronomy 6:4–9, they admonish them, saying:

> Do not let loyalty and faithfulness forsake you;
>> bind them around your neck;
>> write them on the tablet of your heart. (Prov. 3:3)

If they did these things, they would "find favor and good repute in the sight of God and of people" (Prov. 3:4). This is an allusion to the blessings and curses of Deuteronomy 27:11–28:68, which are about how covenant loyalty plays out in the community.

Much of the sages' teaching on wisdom and folly has to do with the idea that behavior has social consequences in the community. When people live according to the precepts of wisdom, for example, this creates communities of trust. The wise themselves will live "securely" (Prov. 3:23), as well as the neighbor who lives beside them (3:29).

Their repeated teaching on "crooked speech" is not arbitrary, but because such speech can destroy a society from the inside out (e.g., Prov. 4:24; 6:12–19, esp. v. 12). Similarly, scoffing (e.g., Prov. 19:25) has a negative impact on the community. Many types of behavior, from speech to business practices, are cited as having an impact on the community (e.g., Prov. 11:9–15). Examples like these make it clear that wise instructions are given not only to individuals but also to the life of that individual in society. The book of Proverbs lays out the "preconditions for good social order," which include "righteousness, justice, and uprightness."[19] In other words, people who are wise live in ways that benefit their communities. Many sayings reflect this idea, including this example:

> When it goes well with the righteous, the city rejoices,
>> and when the wicked perish, there is jubilation.
> By the blessing of the upright the city is exalted,
>> but it is overthrown by the mouth of the wicked. (Prov. 11:10–11)

The Hebrew word translated here as "city" (עִיר) doesn't necessarily refer to an urban site; it can also mean a village, town, or even a tent encampment. The point is that the community that lives there is affected.

COMMUNITY FIRST

In ancient Israel, the concept of the "collectivist personality" took precedence over individual human rights.[20] This meant that communal concerns, group goals, dependence, and obedience and submission to authority all took precedence over individual human rights. From the moment the covenant was established at Sinai, God established Israel's corporate nature.[21] To live in the community of ancient Israel meant that everyone should subject their own interests to the interests of the community.[22]

Israel's sages certainly held to this view and taught that since the people of lived in community, they should put the community first.

> The one who lives alone is self-indulgent,
> showing contempt for all sound judgment.
> A fool takes no pleasure in understanding,
> but only in expressing personal opinion. (Prov. 18:1–2)

In these verses, the "one who lives alone" indulges the self and shows "contempt" for the wisdom that can be experienced only within community.[23] Those who don't comprehend this are fools who are interested only in their own "personal opinion."

Those who accept the "wholesome admonition" of the sages, on the other hand, will "lodge among the wise" (15:31). This is because they accepted the sages' teaching that true wisdom can only be found and lived out within the context of the covenant community. Accordingly, those who put community first don't act out of self-interest, but on behalf of their friends within that covenant community (12:26). They realize that their own personal work ethic affects their local community (18:9). There's even a recognition that how they treat their household animals is important because the animals' well-being is beneficial to society (12:10).

THE WISDOM OF STABLE COMMUNITIES

If the ancient Israelites valued community, then they also valued stability within those communities. A number of sayings reflect a society in which a "house and wealth are inherited from parents" (19:14). The ancient landmarks attested to the stability of these communities since the time of their ancestors (22:28; 23:10). Extended families lived together in these communities (e.g., 17:6), and kinfolk were nearby (17:17; 27:10).

LEADERSHIP IN THE COMMUNITY

When the sages made pronouncements on leadership, it was usually about how it could be exercised for the benefit of everyone. In Proverbs 11, for example, advice may have been directed toward a group of urban elites on what righteousness means in concrete terms and how it benefits the community.

Where there is no guidance, a nation falls,
> but in an abundance of counselors there is safety. (v. 14)

Since the guidance in this saying affects the destiny of the nation, the counselors who provide it may be civil or military leaders. This proverb makes the point that their leadership can have a major—even national—impact (see also Prov. 29:2, 4, 14, 16). There are several sayings that point out ways that the leadership of the king may impact society as well (e.g., Prov. 8:15–16, 14:28, 35; et al.).

Early Israelite society was grounded in kinship and focused on community, and its sages placed a high value on maintaining this community. They did this in part by maintaining some distance from outsiders, engaging in religious ceremonies together, and teaching their values to the next generation. They embraced the fear of the Lord as the foundation of wisdom and believed that righteousness and justice were the basic conditions of good social order. They understood that everything they did had consequences for the community, and they sought to take that into account when making decisions. They valued stability and sought to live where their ancestors had lived, with their extended family and kin nearby. Although modern people are removed from ancient Israel by thousands of years, the emphasis placed on community and its preservation can still be instructive for us today. God himself provided something of a blueprint for "the good life." In this respect, when we look at ancient Israel, we get a glimpse of how God means for us to live "the good life."

Families, Neighbors, and Friends

While ancient Israel's sages had a lot to say about the broader community, they also focused on the basic building blocks of communities: families, neighbors, and friends.

FAMILY

In wisdom literature, the family holds the pivotal place in society. While the kings of Israel indulged in polygamy, which was a doubtful luxury,[24] ancient Israel's sages clearly viewed the union of one man with one woman as the norm for marriage.[25]

Many people have the notion that women in ancient Israel were nothing but property that belonged to a man and that they weren't seen as good for anything other than bearing children. This is a misconception.[26] The book of Proverbs portrays marriage as a strong personal bond between husband and wife. The two share the children's training and appear to speak with one voice (Prov. 1:8–9; 6:20; et al.).

A man isn't supposed to be only loyal to his wife; he's also supposed to be enthusiastic about her and passionate toward her. Proverbs 5:19 says, "May you be intoxicated always by her love," and Proverbs 2:17 says that a broken marriage vow is a sin against an old friend. English translations usually translate this as "partner" or "companion," but the Hebrew word used here (אַלּוּף) is always a term for the closest of friends (cf. Prov. 16:28; 17:9; Ps. 55:13).

A woman in ancient Israel was in many ways the backbone of the family. The sage says that finding a good wife is a great benefit, an expression of the favor from the Lord (18:22). Elsewhere, he says that "a prudent wife is from the LORD" (19:14) and Proverbs 12:4 states that "a good wife is the crown of her husband."

This society is often referred to as "patriarchal," which means that men had more social power than women in society. While men certainly had more power in certain areas of society, women had more power in others, such as the market where they would barter, buy, and sell. Or such as the textile industry, which archaeology suggests was run primarily by women. Or in midwifery, which was a specialization of women.[27]

In many ways, Proverbs portrays women as having a great deal of authority in the home. While the man was out in the fields, it was the woman oversaw the success of her household. As Proverbs 14:1 says, "The wise woman builds her house."

If a woman has exceptional gifts, wisdom literature says she'll have plenty of opportunity to use them. The "valorous woman" of Psalm 31:10–31 is an administrator, a trader, craftswoman, philanthropist, and guide, and her influence reaches far beyond her home, though it's centered there and valued most of all for how it contributes to her family's well-being and especially to her husband's good reputation in the community.

The importance of the family features in three of the Ten Commandments, which come to life in wisdom literature with its pictures of parents joyfully united, working together for the good of the home, and faithfully bringing up children. It all illustrates the teaching of the fifth commandment: the result of strong families in society is that "you will live long in the land" (Exod. 20:12). Strong families produce a stable society and lay the foundation for healthy communities.

NEIGHBORS

A good "neighbor" (רֵעַ) should be a person of peace. This means they don't start trouble or conflict with their neighbors.

> Do not plan harm against your neighbor
>> who lives trustingly beside you.
> Do not quarrel with anyone without cause,
>> when no harm has been done to you. (Prov. 3:29–30)

If there is conflict between you and a neighbor, you shouldn't escalate it.

> What your eyes have seen
>> do not hastily bring into court;
> for what will you do in the end,
>> when your neighbor puts you to shame?
> Argue your case with your neighbor directly,
>> and do not disclose another's secret,
> or else someone who hears you will bring shame upon you,
>> and your ill repute will have no end. (Prov. 25:7–10)

Instead of being quarrelsome and escalating conflicts, good neighbors are disarmingly kind to others and generous in their judgments (e.g., Prov. 25:21–22) and don't criticize others (11:12). Instead of looking down on the poor in the community, they are kind to them (14:21). They want the best for everyone in their community and have mercy on those neighbors who need it (21:10).

This doesn't mean, however, that good neighbors put up with anyone and anything. They keep their distance from "those prone to anger," "hotheads" who enjoy conflict (22:24). They avoid becoming indebted to a neighbor (6:1–5) but will help a neighbor who needs it if they have the resources to do so (3:27–28).

Even though these passages don't use the word *love*, these examples of what it means to be a good neighbor all add up to Leviticus 19:18:

> "You shall not take vengeance or bear a grudge against any of your people, but you shall love your neighbor as yourself: I am the Lord."

THE GOOD FRIEND

The book of Proverbs identifies several characteristics of a good friend, of which we'll mention just a few. One of the most important features of a good friend is loyalty. Proverbs mentions many times what we call fair-weather friends. These are people who are your friends when times are good but at the first sign of trouble, they drop their relationship with you. A real friend, however, is someone who "sticks closer than a brother" (18:24) and "loves at all times" (17:17). My Nana used to always say that if you want to have a good friend, then you should *be* a good friend. The sages would agree: "Do not forsake your friend or the friend of your parent" (27:10).

Another thing a good friend does is provide counsel, which can take different forms. One proverb says that "the sweetness of a friend is better than self-counsel" (27:9 CSB). We can be our own worst enemies and harshest critics, and sometimes a friend can provide counsel that's truer than our own. Another proverb, though, says that "iron sharpens iron, and one person sharpens the wits of the other" (27:17). This could mean the kind of healthy discussion two friends might have that causes them to reconsider an issue, grow, and maybe think more clearly.

Another important feature of a good friend is honesty. Sometimes we don't want to hurt someone's feelings, so we flatter them to avoid any unpleasantness. But the sages say that "whoever flatters a neighbor is spreading a net for the neighbor's feet" (29:5). If we really care about someone, then we want them to know the honest truth: "Well meant are the wounds a friend inflicts" (27:6). It may be that the value of such truth-telling is not recognized until afterward: "Whoever rebukes a person will afterward find more favor than one who flatters with the tongue" (28:23).

A friend may provide wise and honest counsel, but they also need to be considerate. Good friends are sensitive to others, treating their friends with thoughtfulness and consideration. There are many proverbs that discuss being considerate of others in the simplest ways such as being too enthusiastic too early in the morning (27:14), overstaying one's welcome (25:17), not knowing when a joke has gone far enough (26:18–19), or being insensitive or even cruel (25:20). Good friends are mindful of the situation and attentive to the needs of their friends in any given situation.

Wisdom literature sees family, neighbors, and friends as vital ingredients of a healthy community. We move toward the "Good Society" by maintaining a loving relationship with our spouses, working together for the good of our homes, and faithfully bringing up our children. We move toward the Good Society by ceasing to view our neighbors as strangers to avoid by reaching across the fence and seeing them as friends. When we put our neighbor's interests before our own and be loyal to them, we can begin to move closer to what God desires for us.

Toward the New Testament

The emphasis on community in the Old Testament continues right into the New Testament. Although Jesus' healings may seem unrelated to community, they were actually one of the major ways in which he was restoring God's people. When Jesus healed the man with an unclean spirit (Mark 1:21–28), a leper (Mark 1:40–45), or a woman with a perpetual flow of blood (Luke 8:43–48), they were able to return to the synagogue and worship. Each of the Gospels portrays Jesus as a healer in its own unique way.[28]

When the early church was born, Luke makes the point that one of its immediate effects was the creation of true community:

> They devoted themselves to the apostles' teaching and fellowship, to the break-ing of bread and the prayers. Awe came upon everyone because many wonders and signs were being done through the apostles. All who believed were together and had all things in common; they would sell their possessions and goods and distribute the proceeds to all, as any had need. Day by day, as they spent much time together in the temple, they broke bread at home and ate their food with glad and generous hearts, praising God and having the goodwill of all the people. And day by day the Lord added to their number those who were being saved.
>
> (Acts 2:42–47)

The Greek word Luke uses for "fellowship" and having all things in "common" is *koinonia*. Although this word does mean fellowship, it also refers to a kind of relationship that goes much deeper than enjoying a pot-luck supper after church one Sunday. It has to do with living within a close-knit community that includes shared possessions as well as shared values, purposes, mission, and worship.

The apostle Paul places a heavy emphasis on community. He teaches that although people are estranged from God and from one another, God's purpose is to reconcile all humankind to himself and to one another (Eph. 2:14–19). The new congregations that Paul planted as he traveled around the Mediterranean world were communities, and he followed up with each of them by writing letters to provide guidance about, among other things, what it meant for them to live together in community and how they were to go about it.[29]

While the New Testament has a tremendous amount to say about commu-nity on a broader level, it also has a lot to say about the basic building blocks of the community, including family, friends, and neighbors. Paul would have shared the sages' view that the family was the basic building block of society, which meant it was one of the primary venues in which the principles of the gospel needed to be worked out. Paul does this in his "Household Codes," where he applies the gospel to every member of the family.[30] Through its trans-formative power, families themselves can experience true community, and they can also be agents of transformation in the broader communities around them.

Paul also spoke to the issue of how we're to relate to our neighbors. In his letter to the church at Rome, for example, he said, "We who are strong ought to put up with the failings of the weak, and not to please ourselves. Each of us must please our neighbor for the good purpose of building up the neighbor. For Christ did not please himself" (Rom. 15:1–3a). As we have seen, reaching out to a neighbor is part of what creates community.

Some Christians may think we should love everyone equally, but the New Testament affirms that we may have some friendships that go deeper than others. Even Jesus chose twelve disciples (Mark 3:13–14) whom he called "friends" (John 15:15). Among those Twelve, three comprised his "inner circle" whom he preferred for companionship (Luke 9:28). And among those three, there was one he particularly loved who came to be known as the "Beloved Disciple" (John 13:23). If our Lord needed friends, then certainly we do too.

CAUSE AND EFFECT

Y ou may have heard the one about the bricklayer's accident. Although there are many versions of this tale, here's one printed in the newsletter of the British version of the Workers' Compensation Board. It reads as follows:

Dear Sir:

I am writing in response to your request for additional information about how I filled out Block #3 of the accident reporting form. I put "Failure to Imple-ment the Principle of Cause and Effect" as the cause of my accident. In response to your request for a fuller explanation, I am providing the following details. I am a bricklayer by trade. On the day of the accident, I was working alone on the roof of a new six-story building. When I completed my work, I found I had some bricks left over which, when weighed later, were found to weigh 240 lbs. Instead of carrying the bricks down by hand, I decided to lower them in a barrel by using a pulley that was attached to the side of the building at the sixth floor. After securing the rope at ground level, I went up to the roof, swung the barrel out and loaded the bricks into it. Then I went down and untied the rope, holding it tightly to insure a slow descent of the 240 lbs. of bricks. You will note on the accident reporting form that my weight is 135 lbs. Due to my surprise at being jerked off the ground so suddenly, I lost my pres-ence of mind and forgot to let go of the rope. Needless to say, I proceeded at a rapid rate up the side of the building. Somewhere around the third floor, I met the barrel, which was now proceeding downward at an equally im-pressive speed. This explains the fractured skull, minor abrasions, and the broken collarbone, as listed in Section 3 of the accident reporting form. Slowed only slightly, I continued my rapid ascent, not stopping until the fingers of my right hand were two knuckles deep into the pulley, which I mentioned in Para-graph 2 of this correspondence. Fortunately, by this time, I had regained my pres-ence of mind and was able to hold tightly to the rope, in spite of the excruciating pain I was now beginning to experience. At approximately the same time, however, the barrel of bricks hit the ground, and the bottom fell out of the barrel. Now devoid of the weight of the bricks, the barrel weighed approximately 50 lbs. Note again that my weight is 135 lbs., as indicated in the Accident Reporting Form. As you might imagine, I began a rapid descent down the side of the building. In the vicinity of the third floor, I met the barrel coming up. This accounts for the two fractured ankles, broken tooth and severe lacerations of my legs and lower body. Here my luck began to change slightly. The encounter with the barrel seemed to slow me enough to lessen my injuries when I fell into the pile of bricks and, fortunately, only three vertebrae were cracked. I am sorry to report, however, that as I lay there on the pile of bricks, in pain, unable to move and staring at the empty barrel six stories above me, I again forgot the principle of cause and effect and let go of the rope.

The bricklayer who filed this accident report understood the principle of cause and effect—that every action has a specific and predictable effect, and that every effect has a specific and predictable cause. According to this principle, everything we experience in our lives is the result of a specific cause. On this basis, the bricklayer had to admit he was responsible for the injuries he had suffered—that he had caused his own effects!

Israel's sages believed in the principle of cause and effect. In this chapter, we will look at the background of this principle as it is found in the Pentateuch. We will study what these sages had to say about it and consider some examples, both positive and negative. Finally, we'll conclude with a brief look at how the concept finds expression in the New Testament.

Cause and Effect in the Ancient Near East and in the Pentateuch

In the ancient Near Eastern world, people believed in the principle of cause and effect, which we identified earlier as "retribution theology."[1] These people believed that the gods were responsible for the administration of justice in the human world and that they meted out a degree of suffering that corresponded to sins or offenses. In some instances, we might receive our just desserts in this life. In other cases, retribution may be carried out after death, when the gods would judge the deceased with either reward or punishment.

The ancient Egyptians believed that when they died, they would be judged on their behavior during their lifetime before being admitted into the afterlife. In this judgment ceremony, which was called the "Weighing of the Heart," the god Anubis weighed the heart of the deceased on a scale against the feather of the goddess Ma'at, who personified order, truth, and what is right. If the decedent's heart was lighter than the feather, then they would be admitted into the afterlife. If it outweighed the feather, however, then it would be immediately eaten by the goddess Ammit, the "devourer of the dead" (fig. 5.1.).[2]

FIGURE 5.1. Egyptian "Weighing of the Heart" ceremony. (Drawing by Sarah A. Hawkins.)

Whether it occurred in this life or the next, ancient Near Eastern peoples believed that everyone would get what they deserved.

In the Old Testament, this so-called principle of retribution theology is spelled out in the law of Moses, which taught that those who were faithful to the conditions of God's covenant would be blessed, while those who defied them and rebelled against God would be cursed (Deut. 27:11–28:68). It was a principle of cause and effect in which the righteous prospered and the wicked suffered, "both in proportion to their respective righteousness and wickedness."[3] This principle can be illustrated throughout Israel's history in the wilderness wanderings, period of the judges, throughout the monarchy, into the exile, and in Israelite society after their return from exile.[4]

Cause and Effect in Wisdom Literature

Israel's sages clearly believed that positive choices and behavior led to positive outcomes (rewards), while negative behavior produced negative consequences (punishments). They understood cause and effect as "an immutable law of God" on which the world operated.[5] They believed it functioned on the basis of how we choose. Good choices dictated positive results while unwise choices led to negative—even potentially disastrous—outcomes.

Since ancient Israel was an agricultural society, one of the most common metaphors in wisdom literature for the idea of cause and effect was sowing and reaping.[6] Everyone knew that whatever you sowed is you reaped. If you planted date seeds, then you'd get date palms, not corn. This allowed the principle of cause and effect to be applied to every area of life. Below, we will look at a few of the positive and negative examples of this in wisdom literature.

POSITIVE EXAMPLES

> The wicked earn no real gain,
>> but those who sow righteousness get a true reward. (Prov. 11:18)

Although this text doesn't specify what kind of righteousness is being sowed, the point is to encourage righteous deeds.[7] Proverbs 11:24–25 teaches that good consequences flow from generosity:

> Some give freely yet grow all the richer;
>> others withhold what is due, and only suffer want.
> A generous person will be enriched,
>> and one who gives water will get water.

Both of these verses contain a paradox. On the surface, it seems that the more you give, the more your resources are depleted. In God's economy, however, the more you give, the more you receive.[8] The text doesn't say what it is that's given—it could be money, help, or advice. The point is that when we pour into the lives of others, others will want to reciprocate. Other proverbs echo this idea.

> The perverse get what their ways deserve,
>> and the good, what their deeds deserve. (Prov. 14:14)

But the principle of cause and effect is not limited to the moral realm. It's also simply a principle of how life functions. In the realm of work, for example, we read that "in all labor there is profit, but idle chatter leads only to poverty" (14:23 NKJV). The NIV translates this verse, "All hard work brings a profit, but mere talk leads only to poverty." So much of wisdom literature subscribes to this view: Actions have consequences. Life is an exercise in volition, in which we cause our own effects.

This is not to say, however, that God is not at work in the world or that this principle represents a deistic view of reality in which God is only the "first cause."[9] For ancient Israel's sages, this principle represents divine retribution, and many of these sayings emphasize the Lord's active role.

> The good obtain favor from the LORD,
>> but those who devise evil he condemns. (Prov. 12:2)

> When the ways of people please the LORD,
>> he causes even their enemies to be at peace with them. (Prov. 16:7)

> Whoever is kind to the poor lends to the LORD,
>> and will be repaid in full. (Prov. 19:17)

Some of the proverbs among the further sayings of Solomon also reinforce this idea.

> If your enemies are hungry, give them bread to eat,
>> and if they are thirsty, give them water to drink,
> for you will heap coals of fire on their heads,
>> and the LORD will reward you. (Prov. 25:21–22)

> The greedy person stirs up strife,
>> but whoever trusts in the LORD will be enriched. (Prov. 28:25)

> The fear of others lays a snare,
>> but one who trusts in the LORD is secure.
> Many seek the favor of a ruler,
>> but it is from the LORD that one gets justice. (Prov. 29:25–26)

Bruce Waltke summarizes: "The sages believed in and taught a harmonious world order created and sustained by the LORD, but not an impersonal one."[10] They believed in the principle of cause and effect, but they also believed that God would ensure that justice would ultimately be meted out.

NEGATIVE EXAMPLES

At the beginning of the book of Proverbs, the sages talk about those who refuse to learn from wisdom:

> They shall eat the fruit of their way
>> and be sated with their own devices. (1:31)

The wicked will actually be entrapped by their own destructive choices:

> The iniquities of the wicked ensnare them,
>> and they are caught in the coils of their sin. (5:22)

When people constantly devise malicious schemes against others, they are eventually caught in such schemes.

> The crookedness of the treacherous destroys them. (11:3)
>
> The treacherous are taken captive by their schemes. (11:6)
>
> Whoever digs a pit will fall into it,
>   and a stone will come back on the one who starts it rolling. (26:27)

These and other sayings like them express the idea that those who plot against others "unknowingly set in motion an evil design that assumes a life of its own beyond his control that will destroy him."[11] This calls to mind the story of Haman, who hatched a plan to destroy the Jews but became the victim of his own plot (Esther 3:35; 7:10). In such cases, "this 'poetic justice' is in the hands of the Sovereign."[12] Those who engage in corrupt business practices will lose all respect in their communities:

> The people curse those who hold back grain,
>   but a blessing is on the head of those who sell it. (11:26)

No one wants to do business with anyone known for price gouging.

There are many sayings that apply the principle of cause and effect in cases of indifference toward the poor or others in distress in the community.

> If you close your ear to the cry of the poor,
>   you will cry out and not be heard. (Prov. 21:13)

In Proverbs 24:10–12, the sages explicitly state that the Lord will bring retribution against those who ignore those being "taken away to death":

> If you faint in the day of adversity,
>   your strength being small;
> if you hold back from rescuing those taken away to death,
>   those who go staggering to the slaughter;
> if you say, "Look, we did not know this"—
>   does not he who weighs the heart perceive it?
> Does not he who keeps watch over your soul know it?
>   And will he not repay all according to their deeds?

In cases where an innocent victim is in danger of death, we can't feign ignorance but must intervene. If we don't, then the Lord himself will bring retribution against us. Even rulers are not exempt from the principle of cause and effect, and there are plenty of warnings about the danger of abusing their authority.

> Whoever sows injustice will reap calamity,
>   and the rod of anger will fail. (22:8)

Those in authority who rule unjustly, impose unjust laws, or foster injustice in other ways will reap disaster in their jurisdiction. That king's oppressive "rod," a symbol of rulership, will eventually weaken and collapse.

As in the case of the positive examples, the negative cases are not limited to the moral or spiritual realm but appear in relation to every arena of life. Work, for example, is a frequent theme in wisdom literature, and poor work habits provide a negative example of cause and effect.

> I passed by the field of one who was lazy,
>> by the vineyard of a stupid person,
> and see, it was all overgrown with thorns;
>> the ground was covered with nettles,
>> and its stone wall was broken down.
> Then I saw and considered it;
>> I looked and received instruction.
> A little sleep, a little slumber,
>> a little folding of the hands to rest,
> and poverty will come upon you like a robber,
>> and want, like an armed warrior. (24:30–34)

We can easily see the principle of cause and effect at work here. Those who choose to relax and not tend their fields will have to cope with weeds. If they continue to neglect them, then they'll eventually find they have no livelihood; they will end up in poverty. They need to take the initiative to work to ensure a livelihood for themselves and their families.

Choice and Responsibility

For ancient Israel's sages, the principle of cause and effect was rooted in a "doctrine of the two ways," which included the way of the wise/righteous and the way of the fool/wicked.[13] In the proverbial sayings of wisdom literature, the sages invited people to follow the way of the righteous and to avoid the way of the wicked. This implies a degree of human freedom and responsibility. They believed that people were free to choose which of these ways they would follow and therefore shape their own destinies.

Studies in psychology have shown that responsible self-control is a key to mental health. Abraham Maslow (1908–1970) advocated that people have an inherent need for responsibility, which is the ability to make independent, pro-active decisions. Carl Rogers, William Glasser, David McClelland, Albert Bandura, Nathaniel Branden, and other prominent health scientists also adopted this view. Sometimes referred to as the theory of "responsibility psychology," the key idea is that irresponsibility leads to aberrant behavior, neurosis, and even mental deterioration. The treatment they proposed for people suffering from these symptoms didn't focus on extended psychoanalysis but on helping patients realize that they're responsible for their present actions as well as their future behavior. When people begin to assume personal responsibility, they're liberated to pursue positive goals.

In his book *Empires of the Mind*, behavioral scientist Dr. Denis Waitley further explores the impact that personal volition and responsibility have on a person's mental well-being.[14] He explains that those who believe they are the victims of chance, circumstance, or fate are more likely to give in to doubt and fear when faced with challenges. Conversely, people who believe that they have choices in life, that they are free to choose, and that they can exert at least some control over what happens to them, are happier than those who believe they're simply victims of fate. They tend to have a more positive outlook and are able to choose more appropriate responses to situations. They don't feel that they're victims of circumstances but that they have a choice in how they respond. They don't believe they're puppets dangling from the strings of circumstance or the conditions of their environment, but that they function on the basis of their own choices.

It's easy to fall into a negative mindset of thinking we "have to" do whatever we're doing. But when we feel we're only doing what we're doing because we "have to," we can become demotivated and even depressed. It's helpful to realize that everything in life *is* a choice. We don't have to work, pay taxes, exercise, eat right, go to church, or even get up in the morning. We don't *have* to do any of these things, but we decide to do them because they're profitable to us or good for us, and they're the best choices among the alternatives available to help us toward meeting our goals.

In this kind of thinking, those who don't make positive choices become the victims of negative fulfillment. Those who take the advice of the sages, on the other hand, choose positive causes that bring about positive effects. They sow positive seeds and reap beneficial harvests.

When It Doesn't Work

Retribution theology—or what we've been calling the principle of cause and effect—sounds awfully good. If we follow the path of the wise or the righteous, then we'll be blessed and find success and happiness in life. And while this principle may be generally true, it's not always true. There are times in life when you give to others and they take advantage of you. Or you pour your life into your spouse and they abandon you. Or you try to raise up your child in the faith only to watch them turn their back on it. Or you work hard but you don't advance. Or you save but one crisis after another means that instead of building that nest egg, you build up debt.

The sages of ancient Israel knew that the principle of cause and effect, or sowing and reaping, was not foolproof. They realized there were times when the wise lost while the fool won. There are two books in the wisdom literature that grapple with this reality—namely, Job and Ecclesiastes.

JOB

Job is probably the most famous story of a righteous sufferer. It's about a man who was deeply religious and lived a righteous life. In accordance with retribution theology, he had been richly rewarded. At the beginning of the book, we learn about his religious devotion and his wealth: "There were born to him seven sons and three daughters. He had seven thousand sheep, three thousand camels, five hundred yoke of oxen, five hundred donkeys, and very many servants, so that this man was the greatest of all the people of the East" (Job 1:2–3).

Then Job lost everything. In one day, his entire family died, his sheep burned up, and his camels were stolen. He lost all his children and property in one day, and only he and his wife were left alive (1:13–19). After that, he was afflicted with "loathsome sores" that covered him "from the sole of his foot to the crown of his head" (2:7). Job was, of course, devastated by all the tragedy that had afflicted him, but he maintained his piety.

> Then his wife said to him, "Do you still persist in your integrity? Curse God and die." But he said to her, "You speak as any foolish woman would speak. Shall we receive good from God and not receive evil?" In all this Job did not sin with his lips. (2:9–10)

Although Job did not sin, he was deeply distressed about what had happened to him. The principle of cause and effect taught that the righteous would be rewarded while the wicked would be punished, and yet his life had been destroyed.

The rest of the book is one long debate between Job, his three so-called friends, and a man named Eliphaz. Throughout the book, the four argue about why Job was suffering and how his suffering related to the principle of cause and effect. While Job's friends said he must have sinned, he insisted he was innocent. Job argued that if God is just, then it goes against his character to allow righteous people to suffer. God finally appeared to Job and told him that ultimately humans cannot understand God's ways. It's important to note that at the end of the book, God restored Job, thus reemphasizing his commitment to the principle of retribution: The righteous will be rewarded while the wicked will be punished.[15]

ECCLESIASTES

Qoheleth, the author of the book of Ecclesiastes, would certainly have been aware of the principle of retribution and how it was supposed to play out in a process of cause and effect. But he also realized that wise and righteous people have experiences that contradict it:

> There is a vanity that takes place on earth, that there are righteous people who are treated according to the conduct of the wicked, and there are wicked people who are treated according to the conduct of the righteous. (Eccles. 8:14)

In this verse, Qoheleth says that there are times when the principle of cause and effect seems to work in reverse: the righteous suffer while the wicked prosper. When this happens, he calls it "vanity" (v. 14). The Hebrew word translated as "vanity" is *hebel* (הֶבֶל), which appears thirty-eight times in Ecclesiastes, sometimes as a refrain, and it is translated in the KJV as the "vanity of vanities."

There has been much debate about how the word ought to be translated. In addition to the KJV translation, it has also been rendered as "useless" (GNB), "absurd" (Fox), "transience" (Fredericks), and "meaningless" (NIV). In his book *Ecclesiastes and the Search for Meaning in an Upside-Down World*, Russell Meek argues that the word *hebel* is connected with the name Abel (הבל), the second son of Adam and Eve.[16] He observes that Abel's life story defies retribution theology. Abel offers an acceptable sacrifice to God, while Cain does not. When God rejects Cain's offering, Cain becomes bitter and eventually kills his brother. Before this happens, God warns Cain that he needed to control his anger, but he didn't do so. Instead, he kills Abel and buries his body in a field. God curses Cain and says that, from that point on, he will have difficulty making a living and he'll be a fugitive and a wanderer on the earth (Gen. 4:11–12). When Cain complains that the punishment is too harsh, God puts a mark of protection on him (4:13–15). As Meek points out,

> The righteous Abel (Matt 23:35) suffers the consequences of disobedience: his life is cut short, leaving him with no children, no heritage, no material wealth. The one-to-one relationship between disobedience and curses, obedience and blessing, has been reversed.[17]

Meek suggests that the writer of Ecclesiastes picks up on the inconsistencies of Abel's life and uses Abel's name as a thematic word to describe the "Abel-ness" of all things—that is, vanity or a mere breath.[18]

To return to Ecclesiastes 8:14, when the author of Ecclesiastes observes that "there are righteous people who are treated according to the conduct of the wicked and wicked people who are treated according to the conduct of the righteous," he concludes that this is "vanity." Qoheleth seems to be saying that life is unfair, like the experience of Abel.

Despite these contradictions in the way things ought to be, Ecclesiastes advises that it still goes better for those who fear God:

> Though sinners do evil a hundred times and prolong their lives, yet I know that it will be well with those who fear God, because they stand in fear before him, but it will not be well with the wicked, neither will they prolong their days like a shadow, because they do not stand in fear before God. (Eccles. 8:12–13)

Even though there are exceptions, Qoheleth maintains that people should live as if the principle of cause and effect is true.[19]

Toward the New Testament

As a Jew, Jesus would have been familiar with the principle of retribution and how it was supposed to play out in a process of cause and effect. He certainly believed in sowing and reaping as seen in his famous parable below:

> Again he began to teach beside the sea. Such a very large crowd gathered around him that he got into a boat on the sea and sat there, while the whole crowd was beside the sea on the land. He began to teach them many things in parables, and in his teaching he said to them: "Listen! A sower went out to sow. And as he sowed, some seed fell on a path, and the birds came and ate it up. Other seed fell on rocky ground, where it did not have much soil, and it sprang up quickly, since it had no depth of soil. And when the sun rose, it was scorched, and since it had no root it withered away. Other seed fell among thorns, and the thorns grew up and choked it, and it yielded no grain. Other seed fell into good soil and brought forth grain, growing up and increasing and yielding thirty and sixty and a hundredfold." And he said, "If you have ears to hear, then hear!" (Mark 4:1–9)

This parable is one of only a few that Jesus explains when asked:

> He said to them, "Do you not understand this parable? Then how will you understand all the parables? The sower sows the word. These are the ones on the path where the word is sown: when they hear, Satan immediately comes and takes away the word that is sown in them. And these are the ones sown on rocky ground:

when they hear the word, they immediately receive it with joy. But they have no root and endure only for a while; then, when trouble or persecution arises on account of the word, immediately they fall away. And others are those sown among the thorns: these are the ones who hear the word, but the cares of the age and the lure of wealth and the desire for other things come in and choke the word, and it yields nothing. And these are the ones sown on the good soil: they hear the word and accept it and bear fruit, thirty and sixty and a hundredfold." (Mark 4:13–20)

In the same way that the effectiveness of seed is predicated on the kind of soil into which it is sown, the gospel produces fruit only when it is sown among those who are receptive. Jesus told his disciples this parable before he sent them out on their mission throughout Galilee, which is perhaps why it's included in Matthew, Mark, and Luke.[20]

Some might conclude that if success isn't guaranteed, then we shouldn't bother sowing at all. In the parable of the ten pounds, however, Jesus taught his disciples that this was the real risk. In this parable, a nobleman gave ten pounds (or talents) to ten of his servants before leaving on a journey, along with instructions to do business with those monies until his return. When he returned, he asked them to give an account of what they had gained by trading. The first had doubled the money, the second had increased the original ten pounds by five, but the third had only the original pound to return because he'd been afraid to invest it. He explained: "Lord, here is your pound: I wrapped it up in a piece of cloth, for I was afraid of you, because you are a harsh man; you take what you did not deposit, and reap what you did not sow" (Luke 19:20–21). The nobleman rebuked this servant because he didn't even try to put his money to work. This is an important parable, because it teaches that the Lord expects us to take risks and invest in the kingdom. If you sow nothing, then you'll reap nothing. The principle taught in this parable is so important that it's recorded in the Synoptic Gospels.[21]

Jesus' commitment to the principle of retribution is evident in his teaching that the righteous will be rewarded while the wicked will be punished. In the parable of the sheep and the goats, for example, he teaches that people will be judged according to their behavior during their lifetime (Matt. 25:31–46). What people sow in this life they will reap in the next.

Retribution theology, and its illustration in sowing and reaping, features elsewhere in the New Testament as well. In one passage, the apostle Paul draws on it in a discussion about divine justice:

Do not be deceived; God is not mocked, for you reap whatever you sow. If you sow to your own flesh, you will reap corruption from the flesh; but if you sow to the Spirit, you will reap eternal life from the Spirit. So let us not grow weary in doing what is right, for we will reap at harvest time, if we do not give up. So then, whenever we have an opportunity, let us work for the good of all and especially for those of the family of faith. (Gal. 6:7–10)

The principle of sowing and reaping should inspire us to sow good in the world so that there will be good to reap.

Just as in wisdom literature, however, there is also a recognition that what happens in this world cannot always be interpreted simply on the basis of cause and effect. On one occasion when Jesus was teaching, some people brought up a case in which Pilate had killed some Galileans, which they apparently interpreted as an example of retribution theology. Jesus responded, "Do you think that because these Galileans suffered in this way they were worse sinners than all other Galileans? No, I tell you, but unless you repent you will all perish as they did" (Luke 13:2–3). Jesus then explained that the eighteen people who had recently died when the tower of Siloam fell on them could likewise not be explained by retribution theology; it was just an unfortunate tragedy (Luke 13:4–5). Even though there are exceptions to this, however, the cumulative teaching of the New Testament is that we reap what we sow, whether for good or ill, and that justice and righteousness will prevail in the end.

COMMUNICATION

There's a story about a wagon train of pioneers headed across the Western plains. They knew they were in trouble when one of their lookouts spotted a cloud of dust in the distance moving toward them. Sure enough, after a short time, they could see a group of Native American braves thundering toward them. The leader of the settlers ordered the wagon train to form a circle behind a hill to establish at least a modicum of defense. They soon saw the imposing figure of the chief silhouetted against the sky as he surveyed them from on top of the hill. The leader of the settlers decided to try to communicate with the chief however he could. The pioneers nervously watched from a distance as the two men bent down and took turns drawing in the dust. After a little while, they saw the chief back away and return to his men.

When their leader returned to the wagon train, he explained what had happened. "Since we couldn't speak each other's language, we used sign language. I drew a circle in the dust to show him that we're all one in this land. He looked at the circle and drew a line through it. What he meant, of course, is that there are two nations—his and ours. But I pointed to the sky to say that we're all one under God. He reached into his pouch, took out an onion, and handed it to me. Naturally, I understood that he meant that there are multiple layers of understanding available to everyone. To show him I understood what he meant, I took the onion and ate it. Then I reached into my coat pocket, took out an egg, and offered it to him as a symbol of our good will. But he was too proud to accept it and simply walked away. We can relax now, since the chief and I clearly reached a peaceful agreement."

Meanwhile, the Native American warriors were getting ready to attack the wagon train and were just waiting for the order from their chief. When he returned, he told his warriors what had happened. "Since we didn't speak the same language, the white man drew a circle in the dust, and I knew he was telling me that they have us surrounded. I drew a line through his circle to show him that we would cut their forces in half. But then he raised his finger toward the sky to tell me that he would take us on all by himself. I held up an onion to show him how wrong he was and that he would soon taste the bitter tears of defeat and death. But he took the onion from my hand and ate it in defiance. Then he held out an egg to tell me just how fragile our position really is. They must have reinforcements nearby, so we should get out of here!"[1]

These two leaders didn't realize it, but they had serious miscommunication! Although it worked out well, it could have just as easily gone terribly wrong. In this chapter, we'll look at some of the ways that communication has gone wrong today, what ancient Israel's sages had to say about it, and how its importance continues to feature in the New Testament.

The Collapse of Communication

It's been estimated that about 51 percent of the American population are introverts, which means they are shy or reticent and may be happier alone with a book than with other people. We've all faced uncomfortable situations when we've entered a room full of strangers and didn't know what to say to anyone. In this kind of situation, many of us just grab a beverage and find an isolated wall to lean against, away from the crowd, hence the term "wallflower."

An introvert by nature, I struggled with this when I started out in the pastorate. I made convenient excuses not to call on visitors, avoided public involvement, and spent hours in my office studying and preparing Sunday school lessons and sermons. I was fortunate to have a mentor, Mike Beatty, a Georgia businessman and politician, who told me outright that I wasn't going to make it in ministry—or in any other form of leadership, for that matter—unless I learned to communicate with people. He gave me three books that forever changed my life: Frank Bettger's sales classic, *How I Raised Myself from Failure to Success in Selling*, Dale Carnegie's *How to Win Friends and Influence People*, and Les Giblin's *How to Have Confidence and Power in Dealing with People*.[2] I read and reread these books, and they helped me begin to develop the skills I needed to feel comfortable interacting with people.

As we're coming to see, technology has not helped in the area of human communication. It's become almost second nature to use instant messaging, email, and social media as handy escape hatches from having to interact with others in person. Social scientists have shown that the more time people spend with technology, the less adept they become at in-person communication. Daniel

Goleman has demonstrated how important human communication is for brain development in babies, and how it continues to play a vital role in our ongoing social and emotional development.[3] When children spend time with people, they learn how to be in a relationship with people. When they spend all their time with technology, they learn how to be in a relationship with technology.

Sherry Turkle, who has spent more than two decades studying the relationship people have with technology, recently wrote about the impact cell phones have on in-person conversation. She explains that when people spend time on devices in simulation, it prepares them for more time in simulation. The result of this immersion in simulation is a flight from conversation.[4] These effects seem especially pronounced on young people who have grown up with these devices. Educators note that students don't seem to make friends as easily as before, that it's difficult to get them to directly address one another in class, and that they sit and look at their phones during meals.[5] The rise in technology has meant a decline in the skills needed for human communication.

In order to grow, to learn to empathize with other people, to fully understand and engage with the world around us, and to develop the ability to love and be loved, we have to communicate with one another. This requires relearning the basic skills of communication.

Ancient Israel's Sages on Communication

The book of Proverbs has a lot to say about communication. In fact, it has more to say about the tongue and a person's words than probably any other topic. In the two major sections of Proverbs that are attributed to Solomon (10:1–22:17; 25:1–29:27), there are a total of 514 verses, and 174 of them have something to do with speech. The reason that such a large portion of these are devoted to speech is that it is the primary way people communicate directly with one another. If we are ever going to experience the good life, then we must recover the skills of in-person communication. In this section, we'll look at a selection of those sayings devoted to speech, beginning with negative speech and then move on to positive speech.

NEGATIVE SPEECH

A number of sayings recorded in the book of Proverbs warn us about the dangers of negative speech:

> Put away from you crooked speech,
>   and put devious talk far from you. (4:24)

> A fool's lips bring strife,
>> and a fool's mouth invites a flogging.
> The mouths of fools are their ruin,
>> and their lips a snare to themselves. (18:6–7)

The forms of negative speech that follow are some of the most prominent in this book.

LYING

There are many sayings about lying. One of the reasons it's mentioned so frequently is because of its harmful effects. The sages explain that it "breaks the spirit" (15:4). The language here is particularly forceful and means that it causes "despair in another's inmost being."[6] When we lie to someone, we betray their trust, and this can cause severe emotional harm.

In addition to the emotional damage that lies can cause, they can also wreak all kinds of calamity. The sages illustrate their potential for destruction by comparing a liar with a maniac who brandishes deadly weaponry:

> Like a maniac who shoots deadly firebrands and arrows,
> so is one who deceives a neighbor
>> and says, "I am only joking!" (Prov. 26:18–19)

While this may have been just a joke, it only adds insult to injury.

One context in which lying can be particularly damaging and destructive is in the court system, in which witnesses might be called either by the prosecution or the defense to testify (e.g., 1 Kings 21:10, 13; Prov. 14:25; Isa. 43:9–10, 12). If the truth is to be established, then it's essential that the witnesses be reliable. Giving false testimony in court was considered a serious crime in ancient Israel (and it still is in the modern world, of course), and the punishments for perjury ranged from fines to capital punishment. Since witnesses might provide the primary evidence for bringing a conviction, their honesty was vital for guaranteeing justice. This was so crucial that God enshrined it among the Ten Commandments: "You shall not bear false witness against your neighbor" (Exod. 20:16). This prohibition requires that witnesses tell the truth if called on to testify in court.

There are a number of proverbs that caution against getting involved in litigation in the first place; they stress that, if unavoidable, an honest testimony must be given. One example is found in Proverbs 24:28, where the sages advise,

> Do not be a witness against your neighbor without cause,
>> and do not deceive with your lips.

Other sayings stress the need for truthfulness in court and threaten those who lie on the witness stand with severe punishment.

> A false witness will not go unpunished,
>> and a liar will not escape. (Prov. 19:5)

Proverbs 25:18 emphasizes the devastating harm that can be brought about by a false testimony:

> Like a war club, a sword, or a sharp arrow
>> is the one who bears false witness against a neighbor.

Each of these sayings—as well as many others—reflects the background of the ninth commandment. The sages argue that the root cause of a liar's dishonesty is disdain for others:

> Lying lips conceal hatred,
>> and whoever utters slander is a fool. (Prov. 10:18)[7]

This idea that hatred motivates the liar is repeated in other sayings:

> A lying tongue hates its victims,
>> and a flattering mouth works ruin. (Prov. 26:28)

The sages taught that liars would eventually be destroyed by their own duplicitousness.

> The mouths of fools are their ruin,
>> and their lips a snare to themselves. (Prov. 18:7)

Chronic liars who are always trying to entrap others will eventually be entrapped by their own devices. This reflects a principle often repeated in the Psalms and wisdom literature.[8]

Those in leadership positions must maintain an impeccable reputation for honesty in themselves and their administrative staff, otherwise people's trust in them and their organization will erode.

> Excess speech is not becoming to a fool;
>> still less is false speech to a ruler. (Prov. 17:7)

If leaders are always fudging the truth, their administration will attract corrupt officials:

> If a ruler listens to falsehood,
>> all his officials will be wicked. (Prov. 29:12)

A leader must be intolerant of lies and maintain a reputation of total honesty.

GOSSIP

Gossip is one of the sins of the tongue widely condemned throughout all of Scripture, but no place more so than in the book of Proverbs. Gossip is something most people struggle with, but part of the problem may be defining the term itself. In the church, gossip is often simply defined as talking about someone or repeating something that you've heard about someone. As a pastor, I recall a couple of times when parishioners shared with me their concern that discussing the prayer list in church may be gossip. But gossip is not simply sharing information about someone, which could be positive or negative. Michael Zigarelli defines it as "discrediting talk about someone who is not present."[9] It's talking about someone with malicious intent. The Hebrew word translated in our English Bibles as "gossip" literally means "to murmur," "whisper," "backbite," or "slander."[10] It's that kind of malicious talk that can really cause damage to relationships.

> A gossip goes about telling secrets,
>> but one who is trustworthy in spirit keeps a confidence. (Prov. 11:13)

> A perverse person spreads strife,
>> and a whisperer separates close friends. (Prov. 16:28)

It's strange that even though we all know the damage gossip can cause, we're still strangely attracted to it. It reminds me of the story of the four preachers who decided they were going to support one another by having a time of confession together. The first one said, "Well, you know, I sometimes watch movies that I shouldn't be watching." The second one said, "Well, you know, I go to the casino and gamble occasionally." And then the third one said, "You know, when I'm by myself, I smoke cigarettes and cigars." And, lastly, the fourth one said, "Well, my sin is gossip, and I can't wait to get out of here!"[11] The sages observed this peculiar phenomenon when they said,

> The words of a gossip are like choice morsels;
>> they go down to the inmost parts. (Prov. 18:8 NIV)

In the same way that people are attracted to good food, they're also attracted to the words of gossip. But like food, once the words of gossip are taken in, they penetrate into our innermost parts. In other words, they have a deep impact on us, which is why we're urged to avoid gossip.

> For lack of wood the fire goes out,
>> and where there is no whisperer, quarreling ceases. (26:20)

A gossip reveals secrets;
>
> therefore do not associate with a babbler. (20:19)

FOOLISH TALK

In Proverbs 10:8, the sages provide a contrast between the ideal wise person and a particular kind of fool:

The wise of heart will heed commandments,
>
> but one with foolish lips will come to ruin.

This saying reflects a norm among the sages that true wisdom is found in the divine will as expressed in the Torah. In this view, those with a truly wise heart will obey "commandments" (מִצְוֹת); they are contrasted with those with "foolish lips." Instead of following commandments, "The fool is so full of himself that instead of having the capacity to accept wisdom he dangerously prattles on about his own 'clever opinions,' which are devoid of true wisdom (cf. 10:13) and scorch like fire (cf. 16:27)," and "by his undisciplined words he entangles himself and comes to ruin."[12]

SLANDER

Slander is saying something false about someone that's damaging to their reputation. In an example of climactic parallelism, the sages explain that "lying lips conceal hatred, and whoever utters slander is a fool" (10:18). Concealing our hatred by lying is bad enough, but slander is worse. Concealing your hatred of someone makes you a hypocrite, but spreading lies about them can destroy their reputation in the community.

ARGUING

Another type of negative speech is arguing, and the sages often address the strife and conflict stirred up by people who like to argue. There are several verses that use the Hebrew word (*rib*) that can be translated "argue" or "argumentative." It literally means "strife" or "dispute." Here are a few examples from Proverbs:

Those who are hot-tempered stir up strife,
>
> but those who are slow to anger calm contention. (15:18)

It is honorable to refrain from strife,
>
> but every fool is quick to quarrel. (20:3)

Like someone who takes a passing dog by the ears
>
> is one who meddles in the quarrel of another. (26:17)

For lack of wood the fire goes out,
    and where there is no whisperer, quarreling ceases.
As charcoal is to hot embers and wood to fire,
    so is a quarrelsome person for kindling strife. (26:20–21)

One given to anger stirs up strife,
    and the hothead causes much transgression. (29:22)

For as pressing milk produces curds
    and pressing the nose produces blood,
    so pressing anger produces strife. (30:33)

Arguing is a sin of the tongue that often has its roots in anger, a bad temper, or simply a contentious, argumentative spirit.

One of the virtues of wisdom is the ability to avert needless quarreling and live in harmony with others. A number of passages give advice about how to stay out of arguments. Proverbs 19:11–12 give two strategies, including exercising patience and overlooking and offense.

Those with good sense are slow to anger,
    and it is their glory to overlook an offense.
A king's anger is like the growling of a lion,
    but his favor is like dew on the grass.

Simply exercising patience and choosing to ignore something that might otherwise offend you are two strategies for staying out of arguments. This reminds me of the saying, "Pick your battles." Every little thing is not worth going to the mat over. Every disagreement is not worth fighting about. It's important to know what battles are worth fighting.

Another piece of advice the sages give here is to respond to hostility in a way that diffuses the conflict rather than escalates it.

A soft answer turns away wrath,
    but a harsh word stirs up anger. (Prov. 15:1)

Conflict is like a fire, and how we respond to it is key. We can either pour gasoline on it, which will cause it to grow out of control, or we can pour water on it and put it out.

SPEAKING RASHLY

Speaking rashly, without thinking through the effects our words may have, is another negative form of speech.

Do you see someone who is hasty in speech?
    There is more hope for a fool than for anyone like that. (Prov. 29:20)

One way people often get in trouble is by making rash financial commitments. In one example, the sages advise against hastily putting up your possessions as collateral for a loan.

> Do not be one of those who give pledges,
>   who become surety for debts.
> If you have nothing with which to pay,
>   why should your bed be taken from under you? (22:26–27)

If the loan comes due and you can't pay, then your creditors will take what you've put up as collateral, even if it's your very last possession (i.e., "your bed"). People who make such rash financial commitments end up going deeper into debt and run the risk of losing it all.[13]

One of the main forms of rash speech that concerned the sages was making religious vows. A vow was a pledge made to God in exchange for God's fulfillment of a prayer (see Lev. 7:16–17; 22:18–23). For example, when Hannah prayed for a child, she vowed that if the Lord answered her prayer, then she would dedicate the child to the Lord as a Nazirite for his entire life (1 Sam. 1:11). Since such vows were promises to God, the sages cautioned against making them rashly.

> It is a snare for one to say rashly, "It is holy,"
>   and begin to reflect only after making a vow. (20:25)

Fulfilling a religious vow was required in the Torah, and failure to keep it was the violation of an oath to God (cf. Num. 30:3; Deut. 23:22–24). Since these vows were serious, we should enter into them only after careful forethought.

The underlying principle in these sayings can, of course, be applied to the making of any kind of commitment without ample forethought. If we make a promise without thinking about whether we can realistically fulfill it, then we may end up realizing later that we don't have the means to do so. In cases like this, we may end up unable to make good on our word.

BOASTING

Boasting is exaggerated bragging about what you own, have accomplished, or some ability you may have. Although boasting may seem to stem from narcissism, it can also arise from insecurity. In either case, it hints at an inner emptiness. In one saying that deals with boasting, the sages underline the emptiness of the promises a boaster makes:

> Like clouds and wind without rain
>   is one who boasts of a gift never given. (Prov. 25:14)

Clouds and wind usually lead us to expect rain, and when they don't, they're a disappointment. In the same way, boasters brag about gifts they claim they will give but never actually deliver. They too are a disappointment and will come to be viewed as unreliable. While the saying clearly advises against making false promises, it may also be applied more generally as a caution against boasting.

MOCKERY

The last form of negative speech we'll mention is what is traditionally called "mockery," but this is a term we don't use much in the English language today. It means to "ridicule," "sneer at," "make fun of," "laugh at," or "scoff at." In Proverbs, the sages just about always associate the mocker with the fool. They see mockery as extremely unwise for a variety of reasons that will become clear as we consider some examples below.

Mockers are glad to scorn just about anything. They ridicule the poor (Prov. 6:6–11; 10:4–5; 17:5), they mock justice (19:28), they deride authority, and they disparage personal integrity. Proverbs 21:24 uncovers what is at the root of the mocker's problem:

> The proud, haughty person, named Scoffer,
>> acts with arrogant pride.

Why do mockers behave the way they do? Because they're arrogant. These kinds of people can have a tremendously negative effect on the quality of life in a community or an organization. The sages recognized this when they said,

> Scoffers set a city aflame,
>> but the wise turn away wrath. (29:8)

> Drive out a scoffer, and strife goes out;
>> quarreling and abuse will cease. (22:10)

Both of these sayings indicate the range of damage mockers can cause with their strife, quarrels, and insults. They can literally "set a city aflame."

It's not always the situation that's the problem; sometimes it's the people involved in a situation. In his classic commentary on the book of Proverbs, Derek Kidner explains:

> Disagreement and bad blood sometimes arise not from the facts of a situation but from a person with a wrong attitude, who makes mischief. That is to say, what an institution sometimes needs is not reforms, but the expulsion of a member.[14]

A mocker or scoffer can sometimes poison a community, an institution, or an organization, and the sages advise that in such a case, this person may need to be expelled for the sake of peace and concord.

In Proverbs 29:8, while the scoffer stirs up the city, the wise person is the voice of quiet reason who acts as a peacemaker to turn away anger from the city. The mocker is associated with impulsive, passionate, incendiary behavior, while the wise person with a calm bearing is the voice of reason.

POSITIVE SPEECH

Just as there are all kinds of negative speech, there are also all kinds of positive speech. The following examples include some of the most important ways that speech can contribute to the good life.

IMPARTING KNOWLEDGE AND WISDOM

The wise use their tongues to impart wisdom and knowledge.

> The tongue of the wise adorns knowledge,
>> but the mouths of fools pour out folly. (Prov. 15:2)

> The lips of the wise spread knowledge;
>> not so the minds of fools. (Prov. 15:7)

Their "pleasant words promote instruction" (16:23). These verses tell us that wise people disseminate knowledge and wisdom. They're teachers. The sages note, though, that there are few who can share knowledge.

> There is gold and abundance of costly stones,
>> but the lips informed by knowledge are a precious jewel. (Prov. 20:15)

This is why the sages spoke so frequently about the importance of acquiring wisdom. We can't share what we don't have, so we should invest time, energy, and resources in trying to acquire it.

> Incline your ear and hear my words
>> and apply your mind to my teaching,
> for it will be pleasant if you keep them within you,
>> if all of them are ready on your lips. (Prov. 22:17–18)

This reminds me of the apostle Peter's words, when he advised believers to "always be ready to make your defense to anyone who demands from you an accounting for the hope that is in you" (1 Pet. 3:15).

HEALING

The wise use of the tongue can bring healing to others. There are four verses that talk about how the tongue can bring healing.

> Rash words are like sword thrusts,
>> but the tongue of the wise brings healing. (12:18)

> A gentle tongue is a tree of life,
>> but perverseness in it breaks the spirit. (15:4)

> The light of the eyes rejoices the heart,
>> and good news refreshes the body. (15:30)

> Pleasant words are like a honeycomb,
>> sweetness to the soul and health to the body. (16:24)

These proverbs all say that the wise choose their words carefully because they realize they have the power to wound or to heal. Biting or hurtful speech is direct result of the fall. Proverbs 15:4, cited above, compares the tongue that brings healing to the "tree of life" in the Garden of Eden. In the same way that those who ate of the tree of life in the garden received life, there's a sense in which we can "restore Paradise in a broken world through healing speech" that gives life.[15] A Christian's speech should always be seasoned with grace and kindness instead of meanness or cruelty. Our intent should never be to wound or crush someone's spirit, but to bring healing to it.

Another of the sayings cited above, Proverbs 15:30, uses an interesting Hebrew expression. In English, it says that uplifting words give "health to the bones" (NIV). Robert Alter translates this as putting "sap in the bones"[16] and Michael Fox says it "fattens the bones."[17] While the word *fat* may have negative connotations for some today, in the ancient world, it was a sign of prosperity and good health. So, when the sage says that positive speech "fattens the bones," it suggests "abundance, full satisfaction, and health."[18] Words have the power to impact both physical and mental health, and positive words have positive psychological benefits that go all the way to the bones, to the depths of a person's being.

ENCOURAGEMENT

Another important positive use of the tongue is encouragement.

> Anxiety weighs down the human heart,
>> but a good word cheers it up. (Prov. 12:25)

People in the ancient world didn't have a scientific understanding of the terrible effects that stress has on the human body. They didn't know that stress exacerbates diseases like heart disease and diabetes. But they knew that it could "weigh a man down" in debilitating ways.

Anxiety can certainly be debilitating. It can lead to depression and a complete inability to function, but one kind word can have a miraculous impact on an anxious heart. A pleasant, timely, and thoughtful word can have a tremendously restorative effect. Proverbs 25:11 talks about the impact a timely word can have:

> A word fitly spoken
>> is like apples of gold in a setting of silver.

In this case, the *timeliness* of these words is as important as the content of the message itself.

Whether we're talking with our spouse, parent, child, manager, or employee, we find it's much easier to motivate someone with "a word aptly spoken" than with criticism or harsh words. In their excellent book *The Leadership Challenge*,[19] James Kouzes and Barry Posner discuss what they consider to be the "Five Practices of Exemplary Leadership." The fifth practice of exemplary leadership they identify is to "Encourage the Heart," and they devote two chapters to teaching leaders how to encourage others. They explain that "the climb to the top is arduous and steep. People become exhausted, frustrated, and disenchanted, and are often tempted to give up."[20]

Encouragement is a great way to use our words. Being an encourager is an idea that's repeated in the New Testament. For example, the author of the book of Hebrews tells us to "exhort one another every day, as long as it is called 'today,' so that none of you may be hardened by the deceitfulness of sin" (3:13).

TELLING THE TRUTH

The sages saw honesty as a great virtue to be exalted. Proverbs 12 includes a number of verses that speak to this.

> Whoever speaks the truth gives honest evidence,
>> but a false witness speaks deceitfully. (v. 17)

This verse seems to be talking about a law court, although the principle certainly applies outside the courtroom. The legal setting really makes it all the more dramatic, and it's so important that it's repeated often in the book of Proverbs (6:19; 14:5, 25; 19:5, 9; 21:28).

> Truthful lips endure forever,
>> but a lying tongue lasts only a moment. (12:19)

There's a contrast here in terms of the durability of lies and truths. A lie may last for a moment because people might temporarily think it's true. In other words, a lie will eventually be found out. Truth, on the other hand, endures.

> Lying lips are an abomination to the LORD,
>> but those who act faithfully are his delight. (12:22)

When the sages talk about "telling" the truth, they use a verb (*puah*) that basically means "to breathe."[21] Roland Murphy explains that "truth is to be something as natural as breathing."[22]

REBUKE

Sometimes telling the truth might mean we have to rebuke someone. While this may sound like a negative form of speech, the sages see it as positive. The following examples speak to the value of a rebuke:

> A rebuke strikes deeper into a discerning person
>> than a hundred blows into a fool. (17:10)

> Strike a scoffer, and the simple will learn prudence;
>> reprove the intelligent, and they will gain knowledge. (19:25)

> Like a gold ring or an ornament of gold
>> is a wise rebuke to a listening ear. (25:12)

> Whoever rebukes a person will afterward find more favor
>> than one who flatters with the tongue. (28:23)

All these sayings teach that although we may prefer flattery, there are times when a sincere rebuke may be warranted and much more valuable in the end. Even if a rebuke is necessary and helpful, fools won't learn anything from it because they're stiff-necked and unresponsive. A person with "discernment," on the other hand, will be impressed by it and will learn from it.

DISCRETION

Although a rebuke may be appropriate at times, this doesn't mean we should be fast and free with our speech and rebuke everybody all the time. Rebuking is serious business, and it's not always appropriate. This leads us to another form of positive communication, which I'm calling "discretion." Really, it's not so much a form of communication as much as knowing *when* and *how* to communicate. Sometimes it's better to remain silent than to speak (see Prov. 12:23; 17:27–28; 23:9). It takes wisdom to know when and how to communicate, and the following passages provide some examples of the sages' teaching on this subject:

> One who is clever conceals knowledge,
>> but the mind of a fool broadcasts folly. (12:23)

> To make an apt answer is a joy to anyone,
>> and a word in season, how good it is! (15:23)

> A word fitly spoken
>> is like apples of gold in a setting of silver. (25:11)

The wise use discretion and develop the skill of knowing what to say to whom in the right context, as well as when it's best to say nothing at all.

PROTECTION

Another positive use of the tongue is to protect others. Proverbs 12:6 says,

> The words of the wicked are a deadly ambush,
>> but the speech of the upright delivers them.

The sages don't specify the situation here; it could refer to an actual ambush, some kind of judicial situation, or a plot against someone. The emphasis is not on the fate of the one being ambushed; it's on how the upright use their speech to rescue them. If the righteous learn about a situation where someone is in danger or at risk because of a "plot of the wicked," they should warn them and protect them from the wicked. They should plead the cause of the oppressed and use their words in their defense.[23]

Sometimes we're reluctant to speak out—maybe because we don't want to be associated with a controversial position. The sages, however, advise:

> If you faint in the day of adversity,
>> your strength being small;
> if you hold back from rescuing those taken away to death,
>> those who go staggering to the slaughter;
> if you say, "Look, we did not know this"—
>> does not he who weighs the heart perceive it?
> Does not he who keeps watch over your soul know it?
>> And will he not repay all according to their deeds? (Prov. 24:10–12)

This passage could certainly apply to cases where someone's life is in danger and it's up to us to speak out on their behalf.

I'm reminded of the example of Martin Niemöller (1892–1984), a prominent pastor who emerged as an outspoken public foe of Adolf Hitler and spent the last seven years of Nazi rule in concentration camps. After the war, Niemöller lectured often about his experiences leading up to and during the war. Today, he is well known for his lament over the German church's silence in the face of the Nazi's persecution of the Jews:

> First they came for the Socialists, and I did not speak out—
> because I was not a Socialist.
>
> Then they came for the Trade Unionists, and I did not speak out—
> because I was not a Trade Unionist.
>
> Then they came for the Jews, and I did not speak out—
> because I was not a Jew.
>
> Then they came for me—and there was no one left to speak for me.[24]

Niemöller's point was that Germans—in particular, the leaders of the Protestant churches—shared the blame for the Nazis' imprisonment, persecution, and murder of millions of people because they remained silent while the Nazis committed those atrocities.[25] Proverbs 12:6 says that "cowardice in the face of injustice is reprehensible."[26]

Likewise, in his historic "Letter from a Birmingham Jail" addressed to "fellow clergymen," Martin Luther King Jr. reminds us that we are still called to seek justice and therefore follow Christ in loving our neighbor, wherever or whoever that neighbor might be:

> I cannot sit idly by in Atlanta and not be concerned about what happens in Birmingham. *Injustice anywhere is a threat to justice everywhere.* We are caught in an inescapable network of mutuality, tied in a single garment of destiny. Whatever affects one directly, affects all indirectly.[27]

Unfortunately, it took over fifty years before the church actually responded to his call for help and support.

Proverbs 12:6 may also be figurative. It could refer to someone being led away to destruction by getting involved in some kind of foolish behavior. For example, Proverbs 7:6–23 pictures a young man who goes off with a promiscuous woman, and the sages compare him to an ox going off to the slaughter. If the passage is imagining this kind of situation, then the sages are encouraging readers to stop people from their foolish behavior with its destructive consequences.

CONCILIATORY SPEECH

When we get into an argument, the way we answer can either escalate or deescalate it.

> A soft answer turns away wrath,
>> but a harsh word stirs up anger. (Prov. 15:1)

A "soft answer" isn't necessarily soft in the sense of quiet, but rather conciliatory. Conciliatory speech is the kind of answer that ends an argument and restores good temper and reasonableness.

> Those who are hot-tempered stir up strife,
>> but those who are slow to anger calm contention. (Prov. 15:18)

It can take a lot of patience and calmness to maintain peaceful relationships. There are some people who thrive on arguing and are always looking for ways to turn every dispute into a bitter disagreement. And then there's the opposite when someone does everything in their power to minimize disagreements and to get along. One saying that relates to this theme is often misunderstood.

> If your enemies are hungry, give them bread to eat,
>> and if they are thirsty, give them water to drink,
> for you will heap coals of fire on their heads,
>> and the LORD will reward you. (Prov. 25:21–22)

This has sometimes been misconstrued as teaching that if you want to get revenge on someone, you can do it through kindness. However, this turns kindness into sarcasm. The real meaning of the saying has to do with conciliatory speech and behavior. If we treat our enemies with kindness, then it may cause them to feel remorse. The imagery of "burning coals" represents pangs of conscience, which will happen more quickly as a result of kindness than by criticism. If we want someone to change their negative behavior, then they're much more likely to do it as a result of our kindness than our criticism. In his Sermon on the Mount, Jesus reaffirms this point:

> "You have heard that it was said, 'You shall love your neighbor and hate your enemy.' But I say to you: Love your enemies and pray for those who persecute you, so that you may be children of your Father in heaven, for he makes his sun rise on the evil and on the good and sends rain on the righteous and on the unrighteous." (Matt. 5:43–45)

MAKING AMENDS

When we hurt someone, we should make amends. The sages observe that "fools mock at making amends for sin, but goodwill is found among the upright" (Prov. 14:9 NIV). This teaches that those who are stupid value their own pride over their relationships, whereas those who are wise make amends with people. The unrighteous tend to lie, deny, or find an alibi when they've done something wrong. The righteous, however, have the humility and willingness and therefore the power to mend relationships.

PRAISE

Another form of speech that should be included in any discussion of positive communication is praise in the sense of applauding others.

> One is commended for good sense,
> but a perverse mind is despised. (Prov. 12:8)

Ancient Israel was what social scientists call an "honor-and-shame" culture, which means they praised those who upheld the community's standards of good and shamed those who violated those standards.[28] Praising and shaming can both be powerful ways of reinforcing behavior. The shame of a verbal reprimand or a form of punishment, such as a low grade or a demotion, can serve as a deterrent to undesirable behavior. A word of praise, a gold star, or a financial reward, on the other hand, are all forms of praise that foster and encourage the right kind of behavior.

A number of years ago, Kenneth Erickson wrote *The Power of Praise*, in which he studied a number of famous historical and contemporary people.[29] In every case, he showed how affirmation or praise from someone special changed the lives of certain people and set them on a trajectory for success. Erickson demonstrated that affirmation and praise can change a life or even a society. If we want to encourage a behavior, praise is where it's at.

In *Management by Proverbs*, Michael Zigarelli applies this principle to the workplace, suggesting that it's easier to motivate others with praise than with criticism. This is especially the case in a volunteer organization. People might come to work even if you criticize them because they'll lose their job otherwise. But in an organization that relies on a volunteer workforce, you can't heckle or criticize your people or they'll just leave! You have to motivate them in positive ways, and praise is one of the premier ways to do it. In this book, Zigarelli offers several practical suggestions for how to encourage or praise others: giving praise as a reward, praising people in public whenever possible, offering timely praise, and giving nonverbal praise in regular interactions.[30]

One of my favorite verses in all the wisdom literature is Proverbs 31:10–31, which is often referred to as "The Wife of Noble Character," but I think it's better translated as an "Ode to a Woman of Valor" or an "Ode to a Strong Woman." It's about a woman whose character is so outstanding that "her children rise up and call her happy; her husband, too, and he praises her"

(31:28). The last two verses of the book of Proverbs use the word *praise* twice with reference to this woman.

> Charm is deceitful and beauty is vain,
>> but a woman who fears the LORD is to be praised.
> Give her a share in the fruit of her hands,
>> and let her works praise her in the city gates. (31:30–31)

This woman is worthy of praise because she exemplifies the concepts of wisdom outlined in the book of Proverbs, and every godly person should strive to be like her. What I want to point out here, however, is that the writer praises her and doesn't hold back. Likewise, we too should be willing to give praise when it's due.

Toward the New Testament

The theme of the tongue's power is prominent throughout the New Testament. In keeping with the wisdom tradition, Jesus echoed the proverbial teaching that "death and life are in the power of the tongue" (Prov. 18:21) when he said,

> "I tell you, on the day of judgment you will have to give an account for every careless word you utter, for by your words you will be justified, and by your words you will be condemned." (Matt. 12:36–37)

He also explains how our words manifest what's in our hearts:

> "But what comes out of the mouth proceeds from the heart, and this is what defiles. For out of the heart come evil intentions, murder, adultery, fornication, theft, false witness, slander. These are what defile a person." (Matt. 15:18–20)

James's letter represents the wisdom tradition of the Torah and is very much concerned with right behavior, especially about how we control what we say.[31] "If anyone thinks they are religious, and do not bridle their tongues but deceive their hearts, their religion is worthless" (1:26). He explains that although the tongue is one of the smallest parts of the body, it has tremendous power for good and evil (3:1–12).

Instructions about the influence of our words feature throughout the New Testament epistles. In one example, Paul instructs the Ephesians: "Let no evil talk come out of your mouths, but only what is useful for building up, as there is need, so that your words may give grace to those who hear" (4:29). Lynn Cohick points out that the word the NRSVue translates here as "evil" is used elsewhere for putrid or rotten fruit or fish.[32] Instead of talking "trash," as it were, Paul wants believers to say "only what is useful for building up," using words that "give grace to those who hear." Similarly, the author of the epistle to the Hebrews writes,

> Let us consider how to provoke one another to love and good deeds, not neglecting to meet together, as is the habit of some, but encouraging one another, and all the more as you see the Day approaching. (Heb. 10:24–25)

When believers use positive communication that edifies those around them, they help create a good life for themselves and others.

SEX AND MARRIAGE

Is sex simply a way of escaping from one's own loneliness for a night? Is it just something that's fun to do for recreation? Is it animalistic behavior? A way of asserting one's independence or even power over others? Could it be that the sex act itself is the only true and authentic experience of spirituality available to humankind? In this chapter, we'll consider the contemporary situation in our society with regard to sex and marriage, how we got here, its impact on the family, and what ancient Israel's sages can teach us about these profoundly important subjects.

The Sexual Revolution

Before his death in 2012, Charles Colson claimed that the entire culture war is rooted in sex.[1] Indeed, studies of the American cultural revolution of the 1960s show that the desire for sexual "liberation" played a key part in it.[2] The notion of sexual utopianism can be traced back to at least the eighteenth century, with the writings of the likes of Jean-Jacques Rousseau (1712–1778) and Charles Fourier (1772–1837). At this early stage, calls for sexual liberation were infrequent and limited to nonconformists among the elite.

In the early twentieth century, however, interest in sexuality began to move into the limelight. Sigmund Freud (1856–1939) pioneered a new culture of psychoanalysis that encouraged people to sexualize everything. Alfred Kinsey (1894–1956), who presented himself as a scientist, sought to bring a moral revolution centered on sexual liberation. In 1948 and 1953, he published the Kinsey Reports, which advanced the notion of unbridled sexual experimentation. His message, which has been summarized as "fornicate early, fornicate often, fornicate in every possible way," became "the mantra of a sex ridden age."[3] In 1953, Hugh Hefner began publishing *Playboy*. An atmosphere of sexual liberation was becoming an ever more prominent part of American life.

While there were a number of writers in the 1950s who advanced the cause of sexual liberation during this period, one of the most influential may have been Herbert Marcuse (1898–1979), the author of *Eros and Civilization: A Philosophical Inquiry into Freud*. In it, he outlined a vision of emancipation based on the abolition of repression through, among other things, polymorphous, narcissistic sexuality. He protested against "the repressive order of procreative sexuality." Freeing sex from such restrictions "would lead to a disintegration of the institutions in which the private interpersonal relations have been organized, particularly the monogamic and patriarchal family."[4] This volume became a "bible" for the counterculture.

In the 1960s, rock music, drugs, and the demand for sexual liberation were the key instruments in a cultural revolution that rebelled against traditional culture. There may be a popular conception that "free love" was confined to "hippies," but this is not true at all. Instead, sexual liberation became an everyday fact of middle-class life. This was a result of several factors, including greater affluence, increased mobility, and the perfection of the birth-control pill. Pornography dissociated sex from marriage and promoted the possibility of arbitrary sexual relationships. The sexual revolution produced a society that spoke more graphically about sex than ever before, with cover stories about sexual techniques in mainstream "lifestyle" magazines such as *Marie Claire*, *Redbook*, *Cosmopolitan*, and *Maxim* featured at the checkout counter of every grocery or convenience store. These kinds of publications "represent the triumph of the Kinsey view of sex filtered through the ethic of *Playboy* and recast in the consumerist idiom of magazines like *Vanity Fair*."[5]

In her 1970 book *Sexual Politics*, American feminist writer Kate Millett articulated the vision of a "fully realized sexual revolution." Among other things, she explained that it would lead to "an end to traditional sexual inhibitions and taboos, particularly those that most threaten patriarchal monogamous marriage: homosexuality, 'illegitimacy,' adolescent, and pre- and extra-marital sexuality."[6] The goal, as she articulated it, was that every possible kind of sexual behavior would be welcomed with equal public approval. The National Organization for Women lobbied for abortion on demand, which became legally available in 1973 with the passage of *Roe v. Wade*. Hugh Hefner, the founder of Playboy Enterprises, was a major proponent of abortion and often filed amicus curiae briefs in abortion cases that went before the Supreme Court.

The goals of the sexual revolution were carried into the 1980s and promoted by activists such as Ellen Willis, who argued that feminists especially had an urgent duty to continue the revolution. She endorsed sexual freedom for women "to engage in sexual activity for our own pleasure, to have sex and bear children outside marriage, to control our fertility, to refuse sex with any particular man or all men, to be lesbians."[7] In the 1990s, the term "sex positivity" began to be used for a movement to change cultural attitudes and norms around sexuality. The sex-positive movement promoted sexual experimentation, the pursuit of sexual pleasure, and the idea that all consensual sexual activities are equal, acceptable, and fundamentally positive.[8]

By the 2000s, the acceptability of alternative forms of sexuality had become mainstream, and the familiar acronym LGBTQ+ continues to expand "to keep pace with the range of sexual minorities that it represents, so that it often now ends with a '+' sign to indicate its somewhat open-ended nature."[9] Numerous Supreme Court decisions illustrate the mainstreaming of alternative forms of sexuality, with the most famous example being the 2015 ruling in *Obergefell v. Hodges* in which the Supreme Court found a right to gay marriage in the constitution. This ruling represented the achievement of one of the major goals of the sexual revolution, which was to liberate sex from its restriction to the "repressive order of procreative sexuality." Since Obergefell, the idea that "love is love" has become conventional wisdom, and there has been a rise in efforts to overturn laws barring incest, polyamory, and polygamy.

Sex-positivity has become so culturally pervasive that it has redefined the sexual ethics of progressive churches. Lutheran pastor Nadia Bolz-Weber, for example, argues that traditional sexual ethics have oppressed people and hindered their sexual flourishing, and that churches need to undergo a "sexual reformation." She compares not having sex to Jesus' parable of burying one's talents,[10] and she insists that God wouldn't disapprove of any kind of sexual activity that people might think would help them thrive, as long as it's consensual and those involved believe it's mutually beneficial.[11] In this ethic, there's nothing wrong with using pornography and casual sex is beautiful.[12] Christians should work hard, she explains, to "help silence the voice of the Accuser," by which she means "the crippling messages on repeat in our heads that might suggest to us that some sexual behavior we're engaged in might be wrong."[13]

Many are familiar with the rise of the "Nones," which includes those who have no religious affiliation. Tara Isabella Burton chronicles the rise of an even broader category, the "Remixed," who aren't rejecting religion but rather remixing it on their own terms.[14] The Remixed don't just want to choose what and how they worship, but "they also want to apply that ethos in their most intimate spaces, envisioning nontraditional sexual, romantic, and familiar bonds outside the script of heterosexual marriage."[15] For the Remixed, sexual desire is inherently good and consent is the only standard. Whether it's "within a marriage, outside a marriage, in a one-night stand, within a polyamorous triad, or with multiple unfamiliar partners," consensual sex is "inherently empowering, an act of emotional and physical honesty, allowing your external actions to reflect your internal desires."[16]

The ongoing sexual revolution is also fostering new sexual-social identities, including polyamory and "kink." Polyamory is the practice of having multiple partners, all of whom consent to be in a sexual relationship together. Kink includes nontraditional sexual practices such as bondage, discipline, sadism, and masochism (BDSM). Polyamory and kink culture are both predicated on opposition to the strictures of heterosexual marriage, which is viewed as fundamentally unjust and immoral. Polyamorous and kink activists frequently refer to "toxic monogamy culture" as something that needs to be challenged and overcome. In recent years, reality shows like *Polyamory: Married and Dating*, movies like *Fifty Shades of Grey*, feature stories in magazines such as *Scientific American* and the *Atlantic*, and headline articles in newspapers like the *Guardian*, the *Observer*, and the *New York Times* have not only raised public awareness about polyamory and BDSM but also increased their social acceptance.

One of the major implications of the sexual revolution is that people in our society are marrying later and less often. Although there are certainly a number of factors that have contributed to this trend, two of the major causes are the personal ease of sexual access and the social perceptions of sexual activity. Mark Regnerus explores the impact of these factors in his 2017 book *Cheap Sex*, which he summarizes in *The Future of Christian Marriage*, as follows:

> Economically speaking, women *have* what men *want*. Thus, they possess something of considerable value to men, something that conceivably "costs" men to access. Historically, men have had to give something in exchange, most typically significant (economic and relational) commitments or promises, to gain access to her body. I affirm that men appreciate women for other reasons, but that fact doesn't make this claim less true. Sex is "cheap" if women expect little from men in return for sex, and if men do not have to supply much time, attention, resources, recognition, or fidelity in order to experience sex. Cheap sex is characterized not only by *personal* ease of sexual access but also *social* perceptions of the same.[17]

The resultant decline in marriage rates are so significant that some social scientists now refer to the "Fragile Family."[18] More than ever, America is made up of a multiplicity of family types that include two-parent families, blended families, one-parent families, cohabiting couples, gay and lesbian families, and extended family households. In a recent article, social scientists Jay Teachman, Lucky Tedrow, and Gina Kim survey these changing family demographics. Their study shows that there has been a decline in the rate of first marriage and ever-marriage since 1960.[19] Marriage is at its lowest point in years.

While marriage has declined, the rate of childbearing outside of marriage has increased dramatically. In 2005, about 32 percent of white births, 48 percent of Hispanic/Latino births, and 69 percent of African American births occurred outside of marriage. Married couples have declined as a fraction of all households, from over 70 percent in 1970 to just 51 percent in 2007. Since then, cohabitation has become acceptable and even normative, so that the numbers have increased exponentially.[20] Among those who do marry, there's an increase in marital dissolution, and children are experiencing higher numbers of transitions in living arrangements as parental unions form and dissolve more frequently.[21]

While the sexual revolution has made sex freer and more open than ever before, it has stymied the development of committed relationships and the formation of families. Many young people today are disillusioned with the prevailing sexual ethic. In one recent study of thousands of college students at religious, state, and secular private schools, for example, Donna Freitas found that many of them—both male and female—are deeply unhappy with hookup culture. In her 2013 book *The End of Sex*, she presents the results of the surveys and one-on-one interviews she conducted among these students: Many of them now associate sexuality with ambivalence, boredom, isolation, and loneliness.[22] In another example, Christine Emba, a columnist for *The Washington Post*, questions the prevailing sexual ethic and suggests that sexual liberation might actually be the source of our sexual discontent rather than its solution.[23]

Although we might think the sexual revolution would have peaked by now, political scientist Scott Yenor argues that "we are still only in [its] infancy," and that this is especially problematic because it moves forward "without a frame of reference."[24] For those who seek to find solid ground in the shifting sands of the continuing sexual revolution, the wisdom of the sages can provide it.

Sex and the Family

Just as sex is a frequent subject in culture, it's also a frequent topic in wisdom literature. Ancient Israel's sages had a lot to say about sex and its role in individual and communal life, its place and purpose in marriage, and its relationship to the family.

CHEAP SEX

As we saw in our overview of the sexual revolution, sex has become "cheap" in modern American society. But the cheapening of sex is not strictly a modern American phenomenon, and ancient Israel's sages were certainly familiar with it. They viewed this as crass and even dangerous:

> This is the way of an adulteress:
>> she eats, and wipes her mouth,
>> and says, "I have done no wrong." (Prov. 30:20)

This proverb portrays a married woman who doesn't see any harm in her sexual assignations with another man. For her, it was just a fling to satisfy a sexual urge and nothing more, without any personal implications, either for herself or the man. This sounds very modern and echoes current arguments that sex is nothing more than a biological function without any psychological or moral connotations.

It actually takes time to become so nonchalant about sex. Our natural inclination is to view it as something profoundly intimate that binds two people together in a mysteriously inextricable way. This penchant for taking sex so seriously is not a social construct; it actually reflects human biology and psychology. The very act of physical contact between two people, all by itself, releases the hormone oxytocin, which causes them to feel close to each other emotionally and psychologically. It also reduces the levels of cortisol, which is a stress hormone. Physical contact actually facilitates person-to-person bonding. This means that the act of sex literally creates intimacy and bonds people together emotionally and psychologically, even if they're not seeking this. Although the woman portrayed in this proverb insists she has done nothing wrong, she has disrupted the emotional, psychological, and relational bond she once shared with her husband alone. In doing so, she "shatters the network of family relationships, which are God's foundation stones for an ordered society."[25]

Other passages in the book of Proverbs warn against adulterous relationships. Proverbs 5:1–23, 6:20–35, and 7:6–27, for example, all provide extended teaching about the temptation of adulterous relationships and their dangerous results. Unlike the woman in Proverbs 30:20, these make it clear that men are also culpable in such liaisons. In any case, regardless of who initiates an adulterous liaison, the results are the same: destruction.

Incredibly, some researchers argue that the decline of the American family is to women's advantage,[26] though it seems to be men who derive the most satisfaction from arrangements such as cohabitation, where they get all the benefits of marriage without the commitment.[27] The reality is that these nonmarital arrangements are much less stable than marital unions.[28] Studies of marriage worldwide show that it has compelling advantages both for individuals and for society.[29] The decline of the American family holds negative consequences for every citizen.[30]

MARRIED SEX

In contrast to negative portrayals of illicit sex, wisdom literature as a whole celebrates the enjoyment of married sex as a wonderful blessing from God. The Song of Songs plays an especially important role in this positive portrayal of sex. In chapter 2, we discussed how as a result of the fall desire came to be viewed as something negative and dangerous that needed to be suppressed and controlled. In the Pentateuch, laws were set in place to regulate sexual relations, and the historical books tell stories of men whose desire got the best of them and ruined their careers or even their lives. The Song of Songs was written to turn this negative expression of desire into something positive. It "pictures the restoration of human love to its pre-Fall bliss."[31]

Although the Song of Songs is a celebration of sexual love, it's not advocating hookup culture or kink. It's not advocating sex positivity or proclaiming that sex is the one true path to authentic spirituality. Instead, the relationship celebrated in the Song is one of marriage.[32] It is full of the idea that marital sexuality is revered and even sacred.[33] Karl Möller insists that the Song invites us to consider human sexuality from a perspective of "good news, with God's good creation, with original blessing rather than original sin." He identifies three kinds of rhetoric that pervade the Song of Songs, including aesthetic appreciation, desire, and intoxicating pleasure.[34] The poems in the Song are deeply erotic (see chapter 2), and the book culminates with the woman saying to her lover:

> Set me as a seal upon your heart,
>   as a seal upon your arm,
> for love is strong as death,
>   passion fierce as the grave.
> Its flashes are flashes of fire,
>   a raging flame.
> Many waters cannot quench love,
>   neither can floods drown it.
> If one offered for love
>   all the wealth of one's house,
>   it would be utterly scorned. (Song 8:6–7)

The female in the Song wants to be set upon her lover's heart or bound upon his arm like a seal that established identity or authenticated ownership, much like the stamp seal of a notary public today. In other words, she wants to share his identity, not only physically but also legally. In other words, she wants to be his wife.

The reason for her longing is her recognition that "love is as strong as death, passion fierce as the grave" (8:6). These are powerful metaphors for the permanence of death. "No mere mortal can escape these, and thus they testify to the most powerful forces known. Their power cannot be overcome, and their hold is eternal."[35] The sparks of love are compared to "flashes of fire, a raging flame" (8:6). Fire is powerful, and its heat can overcome those who get too close. Similarly, love inflames the passions of those overcome by it.

The last line of verse 6 is especially significant and deserves special consideration. In it, love is also compared to "a raging flame," but I would argue that the Hebrew expression should be translated as "a flame of the LORD."[36] For various reasons, most commentators argue against this translation and prefer to understand the phrase as an expression of intensity, such as the NRSVue's rendering of it as "a raging flame." If the translation "a flame of the LORD" is correct, however, it would be the only occurrence of the divine name in the entire book and would make a significant contribution to the book's message. Its appearance in the Song's epilogue would serve as a concluding argument that "God is the ultimate author of this arousal of love and the heat of passion" that has been the subject of the book.[37]

Verse 7 seeks to express the endurance of this love. "Many waters" can't extinguish it, nor can floods drown it. These are powerful images. Floods can destroy businesses, wash away houses and even cars, and destroy lives. The fact that floodwaters can't wash away love testifies to love's unshakable durability. Finally, the value of love is inestimable. It can't be bought, and even if someone offered all their wealth, it wouldn't be enough. Love has an impact that's permanent; it can never be removed.

This is a profound view of erotic love. Many people think that restrictions on sex in the Old Testament—such as prohibitions against premarital sex and adultery[38]—are based on a negative view of sex. Nothing could be further from the truth, and the reality is that such prohibitions are based on a *high* view of sex. If sexual love binds two people together intractably, then having sex with multiple people over many years must have an adverse impact on one's emotional, psychological, and spiritual health. Marriage is not a social construct; it was designed by God as the best context in which to cultivate the love, security, and trust needed for sexual intimacy to flourish (Gen. 2:24).

The wisdom collected in the book of Proverbs shares this view that sex should be enjoyed in a marital relationship. While adultery is forbidden, sex

within marriage is celebrated. In Proverbs 5:15–19, for example, a father un-
ashamedly encourages his son to find sexual pleasure with his wife:

> Drink water from your own cistern,
>> flowing water from your own well.
> Should your springs be scattered abroad,
>> streams of water in the streets?
> Let them be for yourself alone,
>> and not for sharing with strangers.
> Let your fountain be blessed,
>> and rejoice in the wife of your youth,
>> a lovely deer, a graceful doe.
> May her breasts satisfy you at all times;
>> may you be intoxicated always by her love.

In these verses, the father uses vivid imagery to describe how the sexual pleasure his son can enjoy with his wife is far better than a "hookup" with a
"strange woman" (Prov. 5:1–23). While a man might find the idea of an as-
signation with an adulterous woman tempting, the sexuality of his own wife
is likened to a "cistern" or a "well," which provides a continuous supply of
water throughout the year. It's clear from ancient Near Eastern analogy and
from Song 4:10–15 that these highly erotic images are metaphorical references
to female pudendum.[39] While a liaison with an adulterous woman is fleeting
and ends in destruction, a husband can enjoy sexual fulfillment with his own
wife throughout the year.

The father uses similar imagery to refer to his son's own sexuality (v. 16).
It too is likened to "springs" that emit waters and may be a metaphor for male
ejaculation.[40] The father rhetorically asks whether his son's "springs" should be
scattered abroad or in the streets, and the implied answer is no, they should
not. Instead, the sexuality a husband and wife enjoy should be kept in the
home and not shared with anyone else (v. 17).

In verses 18–19, the father concludes with a benediction for his son's connubial relationship. He pronounces a blessing upon his son's "fountain," which
suggests the emission of waters and could either refer to male ejaculation or
to the female pudendum. In either case, the point is the same, which is that
he wants his son to enjoy a fulfilling sexual relationship at home with his wife.
The benediction also includes the wish that this sexual relationship will be a
cause for rejoicing (v. 18) and that her breasts might satisfy him "at all times"
or at "any time" (v. 19), which means "whenever the son is thirsty."[41] The blessing concludes with a desire that he always be "intoxicated" by his wife's love
(v. 19). Lovemaking can have the same effect as drinking an alcoholic drink,

which can make one lightheaded (e.g., Song 5:1). In sum, the benediction is a prayer for God's blessing on the son's sexual relationship with his wife, that it would a source of regular renewal and fulfillment in his marriage.

Marriage

In light of the sages' laudatory teaching about sex in marriage, we should probably also consider what they had to say about marriage itself. There are numerous aspects of marriage and family life mentioned in wisdom literature, and we'll discuss a selection of these.

A BLESSING AS PART OF THE CREATED ORDER

A high doctrine of creation pervades wisdom literature as a whole.[42] In the Song of Songs, the beauty of God's handiwork during the six days of creation is echoed in the description of the natural surroundings of the lovers. In the same way the creation narrative of Genesis 2 emphasizes the paradisiacal garden home of the first human couple, so the Song accentuates the lush natural setting of the lovers. In the Song, sexuality is assumed to be a creation ordinance (Gen. 2:24) created for human enjoyment in marriage (Song 8:6).[43] The Song revels in it.

Ancient Israel's sages shared the view that marriage is a blessing that's part of the created order and numerous proverbs attest to this:

> A good wife is the crown of her husband. (Prov. 12:4)

> He who finds a wife finds a good thing,
>   and obtains favor from the LORD. (Prov. 18:22)

Both of these proverbs use the word *tov* (טוֹב), which is the same word used to describe the goodness of God's creation in Genesis 1. A wife is a profound gift to a husband and may have a bearing on his success or failure in life.[44] While these proverbs are written from a male perspective, the affirmation that a spouse is a divine gift applies equally to women.

QUALITIES TO SEEK IN A SPOUSE

If a spouse is such a blessing, then what kind of person should one look for? While we might be tempted to place beauty or sex appeal at the top of the list, ancient Israel's sages did not rank it as highly. One of the sayings attributed to King Lemuel's mother says,

> Charm is deceitful, and beauty is vain,
>> but a woman who fears the LORD is to be praised. (Prov. 31:30)

Charm and beauty are deceitful because they promise more than they can deliver. The reason has to do with the very nature of physical beauty, which the NRSVue says is "vain." However, the Hebrew word is *hebel* (הֶבֶל), which would be better translated as "transient" or "temporary."[45] Physical beauty is deceitful because it's temporary and doesn't last. Likewise, sex appeal is temporary and probably won't last through the entire marriage.

Although physical beauty is most likely part of the reason we're attracted to a potential spouse, there are other factors we should regard as even more important: primarily, whether or not that person fears the Lord. As discussed earlier, the fear of the Lord refers to a reverential awe of God.[46] If someone's entire character is shaped by an underlying reverential awe of God, then this is probably a good indication they will also be characterized by love, joy, peace, patience, and other virtues identified with the way of the Lord. This is the kind of person who is truly worthy of praise and marriage.

A LIFELONG COMMITMENT

When people write their own wedding vows, they often focus on the feelings they have for each other and declare their intention to hold onto those feelings so that they will never fade. Traditional wedding vows, however, do not merely express the love we feel today but are a commitment for a lifetime. Israel's sages certainly viewed the marriage commitment as a permanent one. They urge husbands to rejoice in the woman they married when they were young (Prov. 5:18–19). They repeatedly praise wives as a gift from the Lord (e.g., Prov. 18:22; 19:14; 31:10). In a description of a "loose woman," she is someone "who forsakes the partner of her youth and forgets her sacred covenant" (Prov. 2:17). By way of contrast, the famous "Proverbs 31 wife" is lauded for her lifelong commitment to her husband:

> She does him good and not harm
>> all the days of her life. (v. 12)

Marriage is a covenant that calls for a lifelong commitment and, as such, provides a context of safety and trust in which two people can completely give themselves to each other.

DOMESTICITY

In ancient Israel, the family was understood as the foundation of society and the cultivation of the home as central to its development. The maintenance and development of the home were responsibilities largely managed by women. They were involved in numerous "maintenance activities," which is a term some gender archaeologists use for "practices and experiences concerning the sustenance, welfare, and long-term reproduction of the household."[47] While men undeniably held more numerous and more visible roles in community life, women also had power in the household and in the wider community. The "maintenance activities" they managed were "the basic tasks of daily life; many required specialized knowledge and were essential to regulate and stabilize both household and community life. They include economic, social, political, and religious activities."[48]

Although there are a number of passages in wisdom literature that laud women as wives, mothers, and teachers, none brings out the breadth of the contribution women made to ancient Israelite society more than Proverbs 31:10–31. The author begins by asking, "A capable wife who can find?" The Hebrew word the NRSVue translates as "capable" is *hayil* (חַיִל), which actually refers to physical strength, military action, strong moral character, or even material wealth. Fox translates it "strength."[49] Ellen Davis translates it "valor," which she suggests "better captures the tone of the extravagant" description that follows.[50]

That extravagant description is presented in the form of an acrostic. This means that as the writer reviews the characteristics of this woman, he's literally singing his A-B-Cs.[51] Proverbs 31:10–31, therefore, is a highly artistic song that works its way through the alphabet, and "the point is to sing the lady's praises 'from A to Z.' "[52] It's a song similar to a ballad sung in tribute to a heroic warrior and is essentially an "Ode to a Woman of Valor."

While the entirety of Proverbs 31:10–31 is worthy of study, I will point out just a few verses that mark some of this woman's involvement both in domestic production and in the commercial realm. In verses 21–22, for example, she is described as manufacturing fine clothing for herself and her family:

> She is not afraid for her household when it snows,
> for all her household are clothed in crimson.
> She makes herself coverings;
> her clothing is fine linen and purple.

At the same time, she is described in verse 24 as manufacturing and supplying local merchants:

> She makes linen garments and sells them;
> she supplies the merchant with sashes.

This wife and mother is deeply committed to her home life, and yet she also puts her gifts and talents to work in the marketplace. The Proverbs 31 wife breaks down the either-or categories of "stay-at-home mom" versus "working mom." She approaches her tasks with "strength and dignity" and "laughs at the time to come" (v. 25).

The Proverbs 31 wife is not an example of oppression but of how highly the sages regarded "the central significance of women's skilled work in a household-based economy."[53] Today, however, we live in a commercial-based economy, and it may be difficult or even impossible for a family to get by on one income, and so both spouses may have to work. While this used to mean they had to travel to a place of employment, people are now increasingly working remotely from home. This now allows for both partners to run the household. Mom can attend a video conference meeting while Dad gets dinner on the table. Regardless of how we live our modern lives, the family is still the foundation of society and central to its development, and we must do all we can to make it a haven for one another.

MUTUAL HONOR

Husbands and wives should honor each other. The poem in Proverbs 31:10–31 again provides a wonderful example. The text says that the valiant wife's "husband is known in the city gates, taking his seat among the elders of the land" (v. 23). In ancient Israel, the area just inside the city gates was the public meeting area and functioned like a city hall. The elders would meet there to discuss important matters, make decisions, and render judgments. That this woman's husband was known in the city gates means he was a leader in the community, and the fact that he takes his seat among the elders means he was an elder himself. The text clearly implies that he only attained this important level of status because of her support. Because she takes care of the "maintenance activities" of their household, he is able to rise to this position of leadership. Her own accomplishments and good reputation enable his promotion and success, while she herself is highly honored and respected.

> Her children arise and call her happy;
>> her husband also, and he praises her:
> "Many women have done excellently,
>> but you surpass them all." (Prov. 31:28–29)

They call her "blessed," which is a way of saying they hold her in the highest regard and believe she is living her best life, in the way God intended, and is reaping all of wisdom's benefits. In the end, her works are praised in the city gate itself (v. 31). The honor a husband and wife give each other has a ripple effect, producing multidimensional flourishing in their lives.

Children and Parenting

If the exclusivity and commitment of marriage is the best context for sex, then it's also the best context for bearing and raising children, the product of that physical act. Children are a frequent subject in wisdom literature, and we'll highlight some of the most frequent themes.

CHILDREN ARE A BLESSING FROM THE LORD

In ancient Israel's household-based economy, every child was an important addition to the family workforce. In today's commercial-based economy, however, both parents may have to work outside the home. When this is the case, the care and raising of children present a problem, not the least of which is the added expense of childcare. This is one of the great traps of modernity, which tends to lead people to eschew having children. They may not feel they can afford a family or be able to give children the life they desire to give them. Another issue is that people are having to wait too long to begin a family. They need to finish college and get a start on their careers before they can even consider it. Some people simply don't want to bring children into such a world. Since about the 1970s, whatever the reason, Americans have been having fewer babies so that population growth has been slowing and there's an impending population contraction. Concern over this demographic shift stems from more than just sentimentality; it also has potential social and economic implications.[54]

In her dystopian novel *Children of Men* set in 2021, P. D. James imagines a world where no babies have been born since 1995, when all males suddenly became infertile. As the years pass, a growing despair is reflected in the gradual crumbling of society. When a young woman is found to be pregnant, a group of revolutionaries spare no effort to ensure that she and her unborn child are protected. An Oxford historian is charged with her protection. The story concludes when she gives birth, and he makes the sign of the cross on the baby's forehead.[55] This haunting fictional story imagines a society that had lost its appreciation for the importance of children and regained it only when there were no more children. Today, in an age of continually declining fertility rates, it seems alarmingly prophetic.

In light of our situation in the twenty-first century, ancient Israel's sages' high view of children as a tremendous blessing from the Lord is timely. Two examples that immediately come to mind are Psalms 127 and 128.[56] Psalm 127 is about building a house, in the sense of establishing a family. A key part of establishing a family is having children, which the author of Psalm 127 exclaims are God's gift:

Sons are indeed a heritage from the LORD,
    the fruit of the womb a reward.
Like arrows in the hand of a warrior
    are the sons of one's youth.
Happy is the man who has
    his quiver full of them.
He shall not be put to shame
    when he speaks with his enemies in the gate. (vv. 3–5)

The psalmist's statement that children are a "heritage from the LORD" points to the idea that they provide access to life and a future.[57] The comparison of sons to arrows is particularly apt. If parents raise their children to love and fear the Lord, then they can "shoot" them into the world to make a positive impact. Similarly, Psalm 128 "articulates a theology of blessing as it celebrates the daily realms of work and family as gifts of God."[58]

Your wife will be like a fruitful vine
    within your house;
your children will be like olive shoots
    around your table. (Ps. 128:3)

In this worldview, children are not viewed as just a matter of personal preference but as a social investment.

INSTRUCTION

In this ancient view, the ultimate goal of parenting is to teach children to become wise and righteous. This is a frequent theme in wisdom literature, especially in Proverbs. In one case, the sage recalls how when he was young, his own father urged him to embrace wisdom:

When I was a son with my father,
    tender and my mother's favorite,
he taught me and said to me,
"Let your heart hold fast my words;
    keep my commandments and live." (Prov. 4:3–4)

The sages urge young people to listen to their parents and embrace the wisdom they want to transmit to them:

Listen to your father who begot you,
    and do not despise your mother when she is old.
Buy truth, and do not sell it;
    buy wisdom, instruction, and understanding.

The father of the righteous will greatly rejoice;
>he who fathers a wise son will be glad in him. (Prov. 23:22–24)

There are a number of sayings that talk about how glad parents will be if their children embrace wisdom and how disappointed they will be if they reject it.

A wise child makes a glad father,
>but the foolish despise their mothers. (Prov. 15:20)

There are those who curse their fathers
>and do not bless their mothers. (Prov. 30:11)

The eye that mocks a father
>and scorns to obey a mother
will be pecked out by the ravens of the valley
and eaten by the vultures. (Prov. 30:17)

DISCIPLINE

Today, many people assume that children are inherently good and that it is society that teaches them how to be bad. Ancient Israel's sages, however, believed that corruption was innate and could only be purged from a child through discipline:

Folly is bound up in the heart of a child,
>but the rod of discipline drives it far away. (Prov. 22:15)

It's true that children are naturally self-centered. Jean Piaget (1896–1980), the famous Swiss psychologist, demonstrated this in his work on child development. He argued that cognition develops throughout childhood and that children move through four stages in this developmental process. He called the stage that spans from ages two to seven the "pre-operational" stage and observed that children tend to be egocentric and have difficulty seeing things from someone else's perspective. It's only during the "concrete operational" period, which spans from ages seven to twelve, that the self-centeredness of the previous stage begins to disappear as kids become better at thinking about how others might view a situation and about how they might think and feel. They begin to understand that their thoughts are unique to them and that not everyone else necessarily shares their thoughts, feelings, and opinions. Children really are naturally self-centered, don't understand how other people feel, and can't grasp how their behavior will affect others. All of these things must be taught, and the lessons must be reinforced with discipline.

The failure to understand children's potential for folly can lead parents to ignore or dismiss their misbehavior with disastrous consequences. A number of proverbs warn about this, including the following examples:

> Those who spare the rod hate their children,
>> but those who love them are diligent to discipline them. (Prov. 13:24)

> Discipline your children while there is hope;
>> do not set your heart on their destruction. (Prov. 19:18)

> The rod and reproof give wisdom,
>> but a mother is disgraced by a neglected child. (Prov. 29:15)

While physical abuse is unacceptable, a child needs to be disciplined in a way that helps them learn what they need to learn (e.g., not being allowed to do something or go somewhere). Whatever the punishment, it must have real consequences in order to be effective.

THE BENEFITS OF TEACHING WISDOM TO CHILDREN

The sages promise benefits to young people who accept the teachings of wisdom:

> The righteous walk in integrity—
>> happy are the children who follow them! (Prov. 20:7)

The sages also promise that if children are properly trained in wisdom, they will adhere to it throughout their lives:

> Train children in the right way,
>> and when old, they will not stray. (Prov. 22:6)

While these are generalizations, they emphasize the positive impact parents can have on their children by raising them in the instruction of the Lord.

Toward the New Testament

The sages' views on sex, marriage, and parenting reflect traditional Jewish wisdom that's also found in the New Testament. Only a few sayings of Jesus that deal directly with sex and marriage have been preserved, but they are enough to make it clear that he held to traditional Jewish teaching on these subjects. In his words to the woman caught in adultery, for example, it's clear he viewed adultery as sinful (John 8:11). In another case, when some Pharisees sought to test him with questions about divorce, he cited the marriage mandate of Genesis 2:24 (Matt. 19:4–5; Mark 10:7).

In his correspondence with early Christian congregations, the apostle Paul wrote about sex and marriage. These subjects are especially frequent themes in his first letter to the Corinthians. Corinth was the "city of Aphrodite" and had a reputation for depravity. Some in the congregation at Corinth apparently believed that sexual sin had no effect on an individual believer's commitment to the Lord, while others apparently understood it as the individual believer's problem but of no concern to the community.[59] Paul definitely disagreed with both of these positions and warned the Corinthians about even associating with sexually immoral people (1 Cor. 5:9–11). He argued that sexual sin among those in the congregation was everyone's concern.

> Shun sexual immorality! Every sin that a person commits is outside the body, but the sexually immoral person sins against the body itself. Or do you not know that your body is a temple of the Holy Spirit within you, which you have from God, and that you are not your own? For you were bought with a price; therefore glorify God in your body. (1 Cor. 6:18–20)

Paul argued that sexual sin has a profound effect on those who engage in it and that it's harmful to the believing community as well.

The New Testament also teaches that sex is important to a marriage. Paul insists that in a marriage sex is not optional but essential (1 Cor. 7:2, 5). He assumes that marriage is a monogamous relationship between one man and one woman, each of whom share equal sexual authority and neither of whom should deprive the other except temporarily and by agreement for prayer (vv. 2–5). Paul also edifies marriage in the Household Codes, in the midst of which he cites the marriage mandate to reinforce his arguments about marriage (Eph. 5:31).[60] The author of the epistle to the Hebrews warns fornicators and adulterers about God's judgment and teaches that the entire believing community should hold marriage in honor and that the marriage bed should be kept undefiled, warning that God will judge fornicators and adulterers (Heb. 13:1–6).

Although there is not a lot of direct teaching in the New Testament about parenthood and parenting, there are indirect references that point to the value of children and the importance of parenting. For example, Jesus told the disciples to let the children come to him (Matt. 19:14; Mark 10:14; Luke 18:16). Jesus may have been referring to children as the "little ones" when he said, "It would be better for you if a millstone were hung around your neck and you were thrown into the sea than for you to cause one of these little ones to stumble" (Luke 17:2). He also taught that believers must have a childlike faith in order to enter the kingdom of God (Luke 18:17). Paul affirms the importance of godly parenting in the Household Codes.[61]

These and many other passages in the New Testament show that sex, marriage, and parenting were of vital interest to the early church. In today's culture, when the sexual revolution is ongoing, the New Testament's sexual ethics are themselves revolutionary.

· **8** ·

HEALTH

A few years ago, I had a parishioner in his mid-fifties named Tom who began to experience an array of seemingly unrelated physical symptoms. The first was difficulty sleeping, which his family doctor attributed to sleep apnea and treated by prescribing him a CPAP machine.

Sometime later, Tom's wife Nancy came to my office and confided that he had lost interest in sex. She was concerned that he may be having an affair. I encouraged her to talk with Tom about her concerns and, although it made her uncomfortable to do so, she spoke with him about it. When he assured her that he wasn't having an affair but that he just couldn't seem to get interested in sex these days, she convinced him to talk with a physician. Tom did so, and the doctor prescribed testosterone therapy.

Tom began to have trouble at work. He missed important deadlines and was reprimanded by his supervisor. He also stopped attending the meetings for the church's finance committee, of which he'd been a loyal member for several years. At the beginning of what would be the third meeting he'd missed, I called to see if everything was okay. When Nancy answered, I explained that the finance meeting was about to begin and asked if he was attending. She said no. When I asked if everything was okay and asked where he was, she said he was watching television. She explained that he just didn't seem to be interested in anything anymore.

A few weeks later, she noticed that Tom seemed to be having trouble thinking clearly, concentrating, making decisions, and remembering things. She took him to the family doctor, who referred him to a neurologist, who ran several kinds of tests including CT, MRI, and PET scans to identify possible causes for these symptoms. These tests failed to reveal dementia, but the neurologist pointed out that the symptoms Tom was experiencing could indicate depression and that he should see a psychiatrist. Nancy was outraged and, through gritted teeth, she said, "Tom does *not* have depression. He has a *real* problem!"

Nancy continued taking Tom to various specialists to try to "get to the bottom" of his myriad problems with sleep, intimacy, lack of interest in normal activities, and cognition, but she refused to consider the possibility that Tom could be suffering from a major depressive disorder. It wasn't until one of their adult children found him unconscious in bed with a half-empty bottle of pills on his nightstand and called 911 that he was admitted to the psychiatric ward at their local hospital where he was diagnosed with a major depressive disorder.

Tom and Nancy were victims of a modern mechanized approach to medicine in which the body is basically viewed as a machine that can be "fixed" by pills or "worked on" by a physician or a surgeon, kind of like the way a car might be put up on blocks and worked on by a mechanic. They believed that if they could just find doctors who could correctly identify the malfunctions in Tom's body-machine, then that doctor could prescribe the appropriate pill to fix it.

The reality, however, is that modern scientific remedies are only useful with about 25 percent of the illnesses that bring a typical patient to the doctor. The other 75 percent get better on their own, or they're related to interactions between the body and the mind. For a long time, Western medical practice was stubbornly resistant to the idea of mind-body interactions, like stress, as being related to the development and progression of disease. In the 1990s, Herbert Benson, the founder and former president of the Mind/Body Institute at Massachusetts General Hospital in Boston, called this "medicine's spiritual crisis."[1]

In recent years, the mechanized approach to medicine in Western culture has begun to reverse with the development of a "wellness culture," in which people are increasingly interested in learning about their health and taking care of their bodies. They are rejecting the chemical-filled lifestyle of previous generations. They are refusing to tolerate inhumane farms and slaughter houses. They are buying better food that is locally sourced. They are exercising more. And although they may not necessarily be "religious," they are increasingly spiritually minded.[2] In this chapter, we'll take a brief look at the medicalization of health in America and the rise of wellness culture, what ancient Israel's sages have to say about health and wellness, and then conclude with a brief look at how these themes are developed in the New Testament.

The Medicalization of Health Care and the Rise of Wellness Culture

Throughout human history, there was always a close relationship between religion and medicine.[3] In the United States, this can be traced back to the founding period. In early America, physicians were scarce and since ministers tended to be the best-educated members of their communities, it usually fell to them to provide some measure of medical care through the distribution of medicines, the use of botanical remedies, and homeopathy, as well as prayers for healing. When commercial society began to develop in the eighteenth-century colonies, however, this led to an increased segmentation of society into different spheres, including those of religion and medicine.

The influence of the Enlightenment, with its emphasis on rationalism and skepticism, drove a further wedge between religion and medicine. Physicians reacted by seeking to establish the authority of their theories, delegitimize alternative approaches, and professionalize under the banner of science. The transition to modern scientific medicine was marked by the founding of the American Medical Association (AMA) in 1847 and the passage of the Food and Drug Act of 1906. By the early twentieth century, the separation of medicine and religion was basically complete.

There was a revolt against the professionalization of health care that manifested itself in the increasing popularity of homeopathy, as well as the rise of several new religious movements that disagreed with the medical establishment's monopoly over it. For example, Joseph Smith (1805–1844) and his successor Brigham Young (1801–1877), founders of the Mormon movement, advocated for the use of botanical remedies.[4] In another case, the pioneers of Seventh-day Adventism promoted temperance, vegetarianism, and foods rich in whole grains and free of chemical additives. In yet another example, Mary Baker Eddy (1821–1910), the author of *Science and Health* (1875) and founder of the Christian Science movement, taught that disease and suffering are false notions rooted in misguided thinking and that we can reject this by changing how we think.

One of the most influential such groups was the New Thought movement, which stressed the unity, goodness, and spiritual nature of all beings and taught positive thinking, the law of attraction, and in some cases even the divinity of the self. Some of its practitioners believed they could tap into and manipulate the life force. The influence of this movement was profound, and it inspired the positive thinking movement of the 1950s, epitomized by the teachings of Norman Vincent Peale (1898–1993), whose bestseller *The Power of Positive*

Thinking (1952) inspired millions of readers to associate positive thinking with health and wealth.

After 1870, faith healing became more and more prominent in the Holiness and Pentecostal movements. Faith healers like Aimee Semple McPherson (1890–1944) taught that just as Jesus had paid for our sins on the cross, he also paid for our diseases. Therefore, if believers have faith in Christ, they will be healed. In a more radical example, John Alexander Dowie (1847–1907) taught that faith required the rejection of doctors and saw medicine as Satanic instruments designed to lure believers away from faith in God. In order to provide a setting where his disciples could live without such temptations, he founded a Christian "utopian" community in Zion City, Illinois.

Although these and other groups of medical dissenters drew many followers, they served only to drive the wedge deeper between religion and medicine. "As medicine became more grounded in science it prized itself on being disinterested, data-driven, and specialized, [which] had the effect of segmenting patient care into ever more tightly defined disciplines."[5] This biomedical approach—also known as conventional, mainstream, or Western medicine[6]—has certainly become the dominant medical model in modern times.

The mechanized approach to medicine and healing has continued to spawn dissenters in both the medical and religious spheres. In the medical sphere, critics argue that the ideology of the medical establishment has actually become detrimental to health. For example, in his 1976 book *Medical Nemesis*, Ivan Illich argued that the medical approach treated the body as a machine and that this was fostering sickness rather than health.[7] Modern life, he explained almost fifty years ago, actually deprecates human health. We atrophy our legs by immobilizing them in a car for hours each week. We drug our minds and nerves with narcotics and stimulants in appalling quantities. We poison our food. We breathe carcinogenic air. And then we think we have access to health because we can go to a modern hospital when we hurt or malfunction.

The gigantic medical facilities that are the new cathedrals of our society, however, are not signs of health but of sickness, as only an unprecedentedly sick society would provide a market for such complexes. With the medicalization of life itself, the incidence of disease and sickness rises exponentially, while the sizes of our hospitals increase and medical technology becomes more and more refined.[8] It is ironic that modern nations with the greatest access to medical technology are the sickest.[9]

Since the 1970s, these realizations have led to the swing of the pendulum away from the dominant biomedical model toward a wellness culture, in which there has been a huge growth in complementary and alternative medicine. Proponents of alternative approaches argue that biomedicine treats patients' bodies as machines that can be "worked on" by a surgeon or "fixed" by a pill. Practitioners of alternative approaches, on the other hand, seek to take a holistic approach to medicine, which seeks "to understand the body in the full context of personhood, in all its complex and mysterious dimensions, rather than simply as a physical organism driven by biochemistry subject to medical manipulation."[10]

Health in Wisdom Literature

The view of health in wisdom literature is far different from the medicalized model. Ancient Israel's sages often talk about "life" (חַיִּים or נֶפֶשׁ), and when they use that term, it's clear they mean everything that's good for people. They're talking about the ability to enjoy life to the fullest, with health and prosperity. When they talk about life, they're talking about the good life and the ability to appreciate it.

In Job 2:4, even the accuser (i.e., "the satan") recognizes that "all that a man has he will give for his life," and that's certainly true. We all want to live, and we want to live as long as we can with the best quality of life we can enjoy.[11] For ancient Israel's sages, that kind of "life"—well-lived and enjoyed—is reserved for the good and the wise. They say that whoever finds *wisdom* finds *life* (Prov. 8:35). For them, this life is the result of at least two things. First, health is the result of a certain lifestyle. Specifically, it's a lifestyle devoted to following God's instructions of the sages (e.g., Prov. 3:2; 10:11).

> The teaching of the wise is a fountain of life,
> so that one may avoid the snares of death. (Prov. 13:14)

The word the NRSVue translates as "teaching" in the verse above is "torah" (תּוֹרָה) for which the standard definition is "law," though it can also mean "instruction" or "teaching." Here, a metaphor is used to try to capture the life-giving nature of this teaching. It's like a "fountain" because "water" provides life, and a "fountain" of water—compared to stagnant water—exemplifies energy and life. This teaching is a fountain of *life* because it instructs people to avoid the "snares" that could lead to their death. These snares include all the negative things wisdom literature teaches us to avoid such as bad speech and deeds, wicked men and women, and other dangers.

A number of proverbs talk about health and disease in relationship to moral behavior. Proverbs 4:22, for example, talks about words of wisdom and that "they are life to those who find them, and healing to all their flesh." The parallel of "life" and "healing" suggests that someone who missed out on a full experience of life will be restored by rediscovering the words of wisdom. Bruce Waltke says, "Sound teaching preserves a person better than medicine, though the two should not be pitted against each other."[12]

Following the ways of wisdom leads to life, but rejecting them leads to death. "Those who are repeatedly warned about behavior that has potentially dangerous consequences but do not listen . . . will find all of a sudden that the consequences have caught up with them, and they will have moved beyond the point where an easy fix is possible."[13]

> One who is often reproved, yet remains stubborn,
> will suddenly be broken beyond healing. (Prov. 29:1)

For someone who is constantly malicious, "on such a one calamity will descend suddenly, in a moment, damage beyond repair" (6:15). In the book of Proverbs, bodily health is always attributed to a moral cause.[14]

Some proverbs particularly emphasize that those who obey God's commands will enjoy long life (3:2, 16). Wisdom says,

> For by me your days will be multiplied,
> and years will be added to your life. (9:11)

> Gray hair is a crown of glory;
> it is gained in a righteous life. (16:31)

Wisdom leads to long life because it provides "insight into life and the way the world works, so that people avoid the pitfalls that might lead to an early death or a damaged reputation."[15]

Health is also the reward of those who fear the Lord.

> It will be a healing for your flesh
> and a refreshment for your body. (3:8)

> The fear of the LORD is a fountain of life,
> so that one may avoid the snares of death. (14:27)

> The fear of the LORD prolongs life,
> but the years of the wicked will be short. (10:27)

If people have a reverential awe for the Lord and shun evil, then they will enjoy health and nourishment in their bodies.

Psychological Criticism and the Book of Proverbs

Within the broader field of biblical studies, there is an emerging discipline known as psychological biblical criticism, or psychological hermeneutics, that seeks to provide psychological insight into biblical texts.[16] Although ancient Israel's sages did not have modern scientific knowledge, there are many passages in wisdom literature that may be illuminated by psychological hermeneutics. In this section, we will look at some select examples from Proverbs.

THE PSYCHOSOMATIC EFFECT

There are a number of fascinating proverbs that show an early awareness of what we call today the "psychosomatic effect." The word *psychosomatic* refers to the relationship between the mind (*psyche*) and the body (*soma*). The psychosomatic effect happens when something we *think* in our mind is manifested in our body. This includes relaxation, tranquility, stress, anxiety, and even sickness. The mind has such a powerful effect on the body that it can produce improvements in symptoms or even healing of various conditions.

When medical researchers test new drugs, they have to compensate for this power of the mind. They do this by giving some patients the real drug and others a placebo (literally, "I will please"), a fake drug consisting of an inactive substance like sugar, distilled water, or a saline solution. While the placebo doesn't do anything, the patient may improve simply because they *believe* it will make them well. Researchers then compare the impact of the *real* medicine on the patient with the effects of the placebo to determine if the medicine works or if it's just the mind's power of suggestion that heals the patient.[17]

Although the ancient sages would certainly not have known about placebos, they were clearly aware of the amazing power of the mind. Proverbs 23:7 says: "For as [a man] thinks in his heart, so *is* he" (NKJV).[18] In other words, what we think about and dwell on becomes reality. This truth applies in both negative and positive ways.

THE POWER OF EMOTION

Ancient Israel's sages recognized the incredible impact that emotions have on our health, for good or ill:

A tranquil mind gives life to the flesh,
but jealousy makes the bones rot. (14:30)

This proverb is basically saying that serenity fosters good health, whereas ill feelings eat us up from the inside out. People who are shameful (12:4) or jealous (14:30) will experience rotten bones. Both of these proverbs affirm that negative dispositions have negative effects on our health.

HOPELESSNESS, GRIEF, AND RESIGNATION

> Hope deferred makes the heart sick,
>> but a desire fulfilled is a tree of life. (Prov. 13:12)

Dr. George Engel, professor of psychiatry at the University of Rochester Medical Center, found that extreme feelings of hopelessness and helplessness can produce sudden death. He referred to this as the "Giving-Up-Given-Up Complex."[19] In newspaper clippings from around the world, he found one hundred examples of sudden deaths in unusual circumstances in which someone's sense of powerlessness and inability to cope with life often led to their death.

In Proverbs 15:13, we read that the spirit can be broken by "sorrow of heart." We see frequent examples of this in widows and widowers who become sick right after the deaths of their spouses, and we say that these people "die from a broken heart."[20] My grandmother had always been a delicate woman who stayed indoors, whereas my grandfather was robust and loved to work outside. As they entered their later years, we always thought he would outlive her. She developed Parkinson's disease and began to deteriorate quickly. She lost her memory, her muscles atrophied, and she could no longer get out of bed. She had to be put in an assisted living facility. Sometimes when he visited her, she didn't know him, and he found the whole situation upsetting. One evening, to the whole family's shock, he just suddenly died. There hadn't been anything wrong with him. He died of a broken heart.

I had a parishioner whose wife had been in declining health for many years, and he had been her primary caregiver. They were both in their seventies, but while she was fragile and had been confined to her bed for some years, he remained healthy and vigorous. During my tenure at this congregation, she began to deteriorate. During her final days, her husband was conscientious about seeing that she was comfortable as she faced death. He arranged with me to serve them their last Communion together, and we planned her funeral together. He was healthy, able, and alert throughout this process. Then, within just a couple of weeks after her funeral, he took to his bed. In another week or two, he was moved to ICU, where he told me he was tired and ready to go. We prayed together, and within a few hours, he too was dead. Both of these cases are examples of Dr. Engel's "Giving-Up-Given-Up Complex."[21]

THE POWER OF FEAR

A strong negative emotion is fear, something that can have paralyzing, even lethal, effects.

> What the wicked dread will come upon them,
>> but the desire of the righteous will be granted. (Prov. 10:24)

This contains the idea of the "self-fulfilling prophecy," which is that we get what we expect, whether bad or good. For years, medical researchers have been fascinated by this phenomenon. A classic case of the fatal power of the self-fulfilling prophecy among the Māori aborigines of New Zealand is recounted by Dr. Walter Cannon, a famous Harvard Medical School physiologist around the turn of the twentieth century. In this case, a young aborigine stayed at an older friend's home while traveling. At breakfast the next morning, the elder served a meal that contained wild hen, which was a food that younger generations were strictly prohibited from eating. The young man asked his host several times if his breakfast had any wild hen in it, but the elder assured him it didn't.

A few years later, the friends were reunited, and the older man asked the younger if he would eat wild hen now. The young man said that of course he wouldn't, since it was forbidden by his tribal elders. The elder laughed at him and explained how he had tricked him into eating the hen years earlier. This discovery upset the younger man, who became afraid and began to experience physical distress. Within twenty-four hours, he was dead.[22]

This of course is an extreme example, but there are certainly plenty of instances closer to home. One often repeated case is that of Nick, a strong, healthy man who worked as a yardman for a railroad company. He was an honest worker who got along well with his coworkers and was reliable on the job. His one obvious fault was that he was a notorious worrier. He was pessimistic about everything. He always feared the worst and always explained everything in negative terms.

One summer day, the train crews were told they could quit an hour early in honor of the foreman's birthday. By accident, Nick got locked in an empty refrigerator boxcar that was in the yard for repairs. The rest of the workmen left the site, and Nick remained trapped in the isolated boxcar. He panicked, and fear welled up inside him. He banged and shouted until his fists were bloody and his voice was hoarse. But no one could hear him.

Nick thought to himself, "It must be 0 degrees in here. If I can't get out, I'll freeze to death." Shivering uncontrollably, he scrawled a message to his wife and family on a cardboard box: "So cold, body is getting numb. If I could just go to sleep. These may be my last words."

The next morning, the crew slid the heavy doors of the box car open and found Nick dead. An autopsy revealed that every physical sign in his body indicated that he had frozen to death. But the refrigeration unit was broken. There was plenty of fresh air in the boxcar, and the temperature inside had been steady through the night at about 61 degrees.[23]

Deep-rooted fears paralyze us and can have negative, even deadly, effects.

THE POWER OF TRANQUILITY AND JOY

On the positive side, Proverbs 14:30 tells us that "a tranquil mind gives life to the flesh." Tranquility is the quality or state of being calm, and so someone who is emotionally healthy enjoys greater physical health. Another positive example is that of joy.

A glad heart makes a cheerful countenance. (15:13)

A cheerful heart is a good medicine,
but a downcast spirit dries up the bones. (17:22)

A fascinating example of this is that of Norman Cousins (1915–1990), an adjunct professor of Medical Humanities at the School of Medicine at the University of California, Los Angeles, who did research on the biochemistry of human emotions, which he believed were the key to our success in fighting illness. All of a sudden, in midlife, he was hit with a mysterious, unidentified, crippling illness tentatively diagnosed as Ankylosing Spondylitis. He was told that he had little chance of surviving.

In the face of this mysterious disease, he forged an unusual collaboration with his doctor, and together they were able to beat the odds. His strategy involved the use of comedy, and he found that ten minutes of laughter—in his case, watching Marx Brothers movies or episodes of *Candid Camera*, gave him two hours of pain relief. Tests conducted by the hospital proved that laughter caused the Sed Rate (which monitors tissue inflammation) to drop, proving the strategy worked.[24] So, clearly in this case, a cheerful heart is literally good medicine!

The Healing Power of the Spiritual Life

There are literally hundreds of studies that show how maintaining a spiritual life has a measurable effect on our health. These studies represent a burgeoning field known as neurotheology, which studies the relationship between the brain and religious experience.[25] One of the pioneers in this field is Dr. Herbert Benson, a cardiologist and the founder of the Mind/Body Medical Institute at Massachusetts General Hospital in Boston, who has spent more than thirty years studying the relationship between the mind and the body. In his recent book *The Mind-Body Effect: The Power and Biology of Belief*, he unequivocally demonstrates that spirituality and religious life are good for people. He talks about the many reasons that religious activity and churchgoing are healthy. Religious groups tend to steer people away from unhealthy and destructive behaviors. Instead, they encourage health-affirming activities, including fellowship and socializing, prayer, volunteering, familiar rituals, and positive and healing music. Prayer in particular is therapeutic, both for those who pray and among those who have people praying on their behalf. What's more, specific religious beliefs also have specific health advantages. For example, church attendance is associated with decreased heart disease, blood pressure, emphysema, cirrhosis, and suicide.

Dr. Benson believes "that humans are wired for faith and that there is a special healing generated by people who rely on faith."[26] He says that when we're drawn to faith in an hour of need, we experience what the apostle Paul heard the Lord saying to him when he prayed for relief from a physical ailment: "My grace is sufficient for you, for power is made perfect in weakness" (2 Cor. 12:9).

Toward the New Testament

In the New Testament, there's a great deal of emphasis placed on health and healing. This emphasis is a continuation of an emphasis on healing in the Old Testament, in which the prophets appealed to God that he would heal his people, both individually and nationally. Isaiah prophesied that a Servant of the Lord would bring about this healing (e.g., Isa. 53:5). When Jesus gave his inaugural sermon at the synagogue in Nazareth (Luke 4:16–30), it described the nature of his ministry and the direction that it would take:[27]

> "The Spirit of the Lord is upon me,
>   because he has anointed me
>   to bring good news to the poor.
> He has sent me to proclaim release to the captives
>   and recovery of sight to the blind,
>   to set free those who are oppressed,
> to proclaim the year of the Lord's favor." (Luke 4:18–19)

With these words from Isaiah 61:1–2, Jesus interpreted his mission as the Lord's servant, a major part of which was the liberation of the poor and the oppressed. One of the primary ways Jesus enacted this ministry was by healing people of their diseases and infirmities and casting out demons.

After John the Baptist was arrested, he sent messengers to ask Jesus if he really was "the one who is to come" or whether he and his disciples were "to wait for another" (Luke 7:20). Luke records Jesus' reply:

> "Go and tell John what you have seen and heard: the blind receive their sight; the lame walk; those with a skin disease are cleansed; the deaf hear; the dead are raised; the poor have good news brought to them. And blessed is anyone who takes no offense at me." (Luke 7:22–23)

Jesus explained that his healings were evidence that he was "the one who is to come."[28] He believed that he was enacting God's saving purposes and that people sought him out for healing "to fulfill what had been spoken through the prophet Isaiah, 'He took our infirmities and bore our diseases' " (Matt. 8:17). Each of the Gospels portrays Jesus as a healer in its own unique way.[29] The aforementioned Gospel passages along with a number of other sayings from Jesus portray the kingdom of God as present in his ministry,[30] while in other passages, Jesus spoke of the coming of the kingdom as a future reality.[31] Many contemporary biblical interpreters reconcile this apparent tension by referring to the kingdom of God as being "now-and-not-yet." Although Jesus inaugurated the kingdom with his ministry, it won't be fully realized until the Parousia. During this "in-between-time," there will continue to be human conflict, war, sickness, and death. Even Christians of strong faith will get sick and not recover. It's all part of the reality of the fall.

The letters of the apostle Paul provide us with a case in point. Paul said that he was given "a thorn in the flesh" and that it was "a messenger of Satan" given to him to torment him (2 Cor. 12:7). There are good reasons to think this may have been a chronic health problem. In his letter to the Galatians, Paul says that an unspecified illness had kept him in Galatia (4:13), and just a couple of verses later, he adds, "Had it been possible, you would have torn out your eyes and given them to me" (4:15). Near the end of the letter, he added a personal greeting in his own handwriting: "See what large letters I make when I am writing in my own hand!" (6:11). If his "thorn" was some kind of eye disease, then it's possible it may have been bad enough to make him legally blind by today's standards.

Malaria is another chronic illness Paul may have had. This was first suggested in the 1800s by archaeologist William Ramsay. He speculated that Paul may have caught malaria on his first missionary journey while traveling through the coastal plains of Pamphylia, which would have bred disease-bearing mosquitos. Since malaria is a recurring disease, this would fit well with Paul's description of his thorn as one that continually tormented him.

Paul's theology also makes it clear that the kingdom of God has not fully arrived and that the entire created order still languishes under the effects of sin while it awaits its renewal. At the fall, creation itself was "subjected to futility" and is in the "bondage of decay" until the Last Day (Rom. 8:20–21). We're also in this bondage. Paul says, "We know that the whole creation has been groaning in labor pains until now; and not only the creation, but we ourselves, who have the first fruits of the Spirit, groan inwardly while we wait for adoption, the redemption of our bodies (Rom. 8:22–23).[32]

While we wait for the realization of the kingdom, healing is an integral part of the life of the Christian community. Paul lists "gifts of healing" among the varieties of spiritual gifts given in the church (1 Cor. 12:9).[33] Joel Green notes, however, that "Paul is generally reserved in speaking of such matters since weakness is an occasion for identifying with the suffering of Jesus and for communicating the power of the gospel (e.g., Gal. 4:13; 2 Cor. 12:7)."[34] James also instructs those who are sick to call for the elders of the church to pray over them and anoint them with oil in the name of the Lord (James 5:15–16). Healing may come but when it doesn't, we can find the same strength and comfort Paul found in the Lord, who assured him as he assures us: "My grace is sufficient for you, for power is made perfect in weakness" (2 Cor. 12:9).

WORK

I once had a colleague who, on Fridays when everyone was exhausted and eager to go home, would say, "Know what the best thing about Friday is? It's only two days 'till Monday!" He was, of course, playing on people's dislike of work. You hear it all the time: "Thank God it's Friday!" When Sunday night rolls around and we're thinking about having to go back to work in the morning, we often have the "Sunday night blues."

It seems that we've mostly always seen work as a curse. Many don't want to work, and many in our culture resent those who work hard to get ahead and scorn the investors or business owners who take the risks, while cheering for those who win the lottery or are awarded money in a lawsuit. In this chapter, we'll review God's original intention for work and its unraveling in the wake of the fall. We'll look at how ancient Israel's sages envisioned the transformation of work back into something positive and conclude with a glimpse at the New Testament's progressive view of work.

The Blessings and Curses of Work

Work is part of God's original created order. In fact, from the very beginning, the Lord is described as a God who works. The creation accounts in Genesis 1–2:3 and 2:4–24 emphasize different aspects of God's divine work. In Genesis 1–2:3, God's majesty and sovereignty are highlighted through God's creation by divine decree. On the other hand, Genesis 2:4–25 emphasize God's close proximity both to creation and humankind through the frequent use of anthropomorphic language. God "forms man" (Gen. 2:7), "plants a garden" (2:8), and "puts man in the garden" (2:15). The verb "to form" is often used for the craftsmanship of the potter (e.g., Jer. 18:1–11; Isa. 64:8), and "to plant" and "to put" are obvious anthropomorphisms that describe human work. Other verbs associated with various kinds of trades and crafts—such as building, threshing, and refining—are used throughout the Old Testament to describe God's work.

Work was part of God's original design for humankind. When God first created humankind, he gave us a mandate to be stewards of the earth (Gen. 1:28) and to till and keep the garden (Gen. 2:17). This mandate is based on the fact that God is a worker and people are created in his image, an idea enshrined in the theological term *imago Dei*.[1] The call to work is a call to live into the vocation of being image-bearers, and so part of what it means to be human is to work.

In Genesis 3, however, the blessing of work unraveled and from that point forward, the ground yielded food only through painful toil. It produced thorns and thistles, and humankind could only procure food by the sweat of their brows until they themselves returned to the dust from which they had come (Gen. 3:17–19). The original blessing of work had become a curse.

The author of Ecclesiastes, Qoheleth, illustrates this curse. In his search for personal satisfaction, he undertook making great works for himself (Eccles. 2:4). This included building impressive houses, planting vineyards, gardens, building parks and pools, and developing an international business (2:1–10). In the end, though, he considered everything he'd built for himself and concluded it was all "vanity" and "a chasing after the wind" (v. 11).

Qoheleth also found it troubling that in the end, he would have to leave the fruits of his labor to someone who hadn't worked for it, and there was no way he could know whether this heir would be worthy of that inheritance or not.

> I hated all my toil in which I had toiled under the sun, seeing that I must leave it to my successor, and who knows whether he will be wise or foolish? Yet he will be master of all for which I toiled and used my wisdom under the sun. This also is vanity. So I turned and gave my heart up to despair concerning all the toil of my labors under the sun, because sometimes one who has toiled with wisdom and knowledge and skill must leave all to be enjoyed by another who did not toil for it. This also is vanity and a great evil. What do mortals get from all the toil and strain with which they toil under the sun? For all their days are full of pain, and their work is a vexation; even at night their minds do not rest. This also is vanity. (Eccles. 2:18–23)

Qoheleth found these and other aspects of work troubling.

The Transformation of Work from Curse to Gift

Despite these troubling aspects, Qoheleth believed that the curse on work could be reversed, and he gives an account of its redemption in Ecclesiastes.

He teaches that there is a gain to the workers' labor (Eccles. 3:9): It is "to do good" (לַעֲשׂוֹת טוֹב). While English translations vary in how they render the Hebrew phrase, Tyler Atkinson suggests that it means "to do good" and that it provides "a clue into Qoheleth's thought about work's role in cultivating happiness."[2] Work is not about gaining wealth; it's about doing good in the world. It "consists in action that is inherently pleasing for the soul."[3]

The author of Ecclesiastes sees working for nothing more than an external reward as disappointing (4:4, 7–8). But when we work together as part of a community and for the good of others, then we feel a sense of personal reward (4:9–12). "There is nothing better for mortals than to eat and drink and find enjoyment in their toil. This also, I saw, is from the hand of God" (Eccles. 2:24). He's talking about working in the context of community, with people with whom we can eat and drink. This is rewarding. So, the book of Ecclesiastes shows a transformation of work from curse to gift, based in the continuing work of God in the world.[4]

Ancient Israel's Sages on Work

Wisdom literature reflects this positive view of work, and a host of sayings addresses many of its aspects. In what follows, we'll look at some of the most prominent themes.

THE VALUE OF HARD WORK AND DILIGENCE

Ancient Israel's sages placed tremendous value on hard work and diligence, which is taught in numerous proverbs, including the following:

Those who till their land will have plenty of food,
　　but those who follow worthless pursuits have no sense. (Prov. 12:11)[5]

In all toil there is profit,
　　but mere talk leads only to poverty. (14:23)

A slack hand causes poverty,
　　but the hand of the diligent makes rich. (10:4)

Do not love sleep, or else you will come to poverty;
　　open your eyes, and you will have plenty of bread. (20:13)

The craving of the lazy person is fatal,
　　for lazy hands refuse to labor. (21:25)

A little sleep, a little slumber,
　　a little folding of the hands to rest,

and poverty will come upon you like a robber,
and want, like an armed warrior. (6:10–11)[6]

PLANNING

If the sages believed it was good to work hard, then they also believed it was even better to work smart, which required planning. Proverbs 11:29 describes someone who failed to plan and the consequences they will suffer for that failure:

Those who trouble their households will inherit wind,
and the fool will be servant to the wise.

The second line of this proverb explains how they failed to plan their accounts in a way they could manage them and so they may have to become indebted to the wise (see Prov. 22:7). The point is that the trouble they brought on their family was the result of failing to plan their financial life with wisdom; consequently, their family has inherited nothing but "wind." In Proverbs 17:24, the sages contrast a person who makes plans with one who doesn't:

A discerning person looks to wisdom,
but the eyes of a fool to the ends of the earth.

The point is that the wise person keeps wisdom in view. In other words, they persist in following a course of wisdom and seek to implement the plans they've made in wisdom. The wise person comprehends the true issues of life and concentrates on wise plans based on that understanding. Fools, though, lack any kind of sustained concentration and can't keep their attention focused on anything, so they drift in the limitless sea of failure and lack of achievement. Wisdom literature teaches that the Lord is pleased with righteous plans, as seen in Proverbs 15:26:

Evil plans are an abomination to the Lord,
but gracious words are pure.

On the one hand, the "thoughts of the wicked" are intentions or plans that will harm others, and those kinds of thoughts are an abomination to the Lord. On the other hand, the Lord is pleased with plans that have righteous intentions.

Commit your work to the Lord,
and your plans will be established. (Prov. 16:3)

If this is true, then we ought to give careful thought to where we're headed with our lives and whether we have dedicated our plans to God.

> The wisdom of the prudent is to give thought to their ways,
> but the folly of fools is deception. (Prov. 14:8 NIV)

Not only is the Lord pleased with righteous plans but seeking advice and making plans is simply a wise thing to do.

> Without counsel, plans go wrong,
> but with many advisers they succeed. (Prov. 15:22)

You need good advice to make plans that will succeed. This applies especially to those who work on a national level.

> Where there is no guidance, a nation falls,
> but in an abundance of counselors there is safety. (Prov. 11:14)

Advice and plans are essential for the stability of a nation. The term used for "guidance" here (תַּחְבֻּלוֹת) is the same term used elsewhere for the guiding or steering of a ship; in this case, a "ship of state." Without proper control of the rudder—that is, by making plans based on good advice and counsel—the nation is in danger. Effective plans usually incorporate some sound advice.

> Plans are established by taking advice;
> wage war by following wise guidance. (Prov. 20:18)

It's wise to seek advice and make plans. And when it comes to war, wisdom is even more important than strength:

> Wise warriors are mightier than strong ones
> and those who have knowledge than those who have strength,
> for by wise guidance you can wage your war,
> and in abundance of counselors there is victory. (Prov. 24:5–6)

In other words, in order to attain victory, a wise strategy is much more important than strength. In fact, wisdom can even prevail over strength.

> One wise person went up against a city of warriors
> and brought down the stronghold in which they trusted. (Prov. 21:22)

This teaching about seeking advice and making plans is just as relevant today as it was in ancient Israel. Without plans, we can't accomplish anything in life. Without destinations, we'll just wander aimlessly. Imagine if you got in your car and turned on your GPS without entering a specific destination. In that case, the GPS wouldn't help you get anywhere, and you'd just wander around until you either ran out of gas or got too tired and had to stop at a hotel for the night. I'm reminded of when Alice became lost in Wonderland. She came across the Cheshire Cat perched on a branch in a tree and decided to ask it for directions.

> Alice asked the Cheshire Cat, who was sitting in a tree, "What road do I take?"
> The cat asked, "Where do you want to go?"
> "I don't know," Alice answered.
> "Then," said the cat, "it really doesn't matter, does it?"

Those who would live wisely will follow the wisdom in Proverbs by seeking advice and making plans for the future.

MOTIVATION

Motivation is another essential ingredient for successful work. Proverbs points out that one of the differences between the lazy person and the one who works hard is motivation.

> The appetite of the lazy craves and gets nothing,
>   while the appetite of the diligent is richly supplied. (13:4)

While this proverb's mention of "appetite" suggests a hunger for food, "the intention is to use this to state a principle that goes well beyond that of appetite."[7] It's really talking about motivation. The lazy and the diligent both have motives, but those of the lazy *don't* lead them to work, while those of the diligent *do*.

This proverb gets at the heart of understanding motivation. Some hold the mistaken notion that motivation is extrinsic and can be pumped in from the outside. The reality is that it comes from within.[8] Motivation is one's own personal motive in action.

Everyone is motivated, either a little or a lot. This reminds me of a story about a dispatcher in the Middle Ages who went out to determine how laborers felt about their work. Going to a construction site in France, he asked a worker what he was doing. The worker snapped at him and sarcastically asked, "What are you, blind? I'm cutting these impossible boulders with primitive tools and putting them together the way the foreman tells me. I'm sweating under this blazing sun. It's backbreaking work, and it's killing me. I don't even know why I'm doing this!"

The dispatcher found another worker and asked the same question. This second worker replied, "I'm shaping these boulders into useable forms, which are then assembled according to the architect's plans. It's hard work, and sometimes it gets repetitive, but I earn five francs a week, which is enough to support my family. It's a job, but it could be worse."

Somewhat encouraged, the dispatcher approached a third worker and asked the same question once again. "Why, can't you see?" this worker responded as he raised his arm toward the sky. "I'm building a cathedral."[9]

All three of these workers were building a cathedral, but only one had the real motivation to do so. Those who are diligent have a motive that compels them to work. Discovering our true motivation will help us to find joy in our work.

DIVERSIFIED WORK AND INVESTMENTS

In ancient Israel, many people were employed through a combination of agriculture and animal husbandry. Making a living based on rain-fed agriculture, however, can be difficult since the success or failure of a crop is dependent on the weather. In the face of such uncertainties, Qoheleth advises, "In the morning sow your seed, and at evening do not let your hands be idle, for you do not know which will prosper, this or that, or whether both alike will be good" (Eccles. 11:6). This advice was certainly not limited only to those who made their living by farming. As Michael Fox points out, "sowing" can represent "all gainful investments of work or wealth."[10]

Qoheleth also teaches that the lack of certainty about the outcome of our various pursuits suggests the need for diversification.

> Send out your bread upon the waters,
> for after many days you will get it back.
> Divide your means seven ways, or even eight,
> for you do not know what disaster may happen on earth. (Eccles. 11:1–2)

To "send out bread upon the waters" probably means to engage in commercial enterprises involving overseas trade.[11] Qoheleth advises that such investments will eventually bring a return. Dividing one's means "seven ways, or even eight" suggests a wide range of investments. It's important to be involved in multiple enterprises because we don't know when some kind of unforeseen calamity might cause one of them to fail.

USING THE RIGHT TOOLS

Ecclesiastes 10:10 talks about the importance of taking care of our tools in order to be effective in our work:

> If the iron is blunt and one does not whet the edge,
> then more strength must be exerted,
> but wisdom helps one to succeed.

If we're going to be successful, then we need to invest in the right tools for the work and then take care of them.

QUALITY WORK

Wisdom literature often talks about the value of doing quality work and notes that those who build a reputation for quality work will usually advance:

> Anyone who tends a fig tree will eat its fruit,
>   and anyone who takes care of a master will be honored. (Prov. 27:18)

> Again I saw that under the sun the race is not to the swift, nor the battle to the strong, nor bread to the wise, nor riches to the intelligent, nor favor to the skillful, but time and chance happen to them all. (Eccles. 9:11)

> Do you see those who are skillful in their work?
>   They will serve kings;
>   they will not serve common people. (Prov. 22:29)

> The hand of the diligent will rule,
>   while the lazy will be put to forced labor. (Prov. 12:24)

REST

While work is viewed highly, it must be balanced with rest, which is essential for individuals, communities, and the earth itself (e.g., Ps. 116:7; Jer. 6:16, Isa. 14:7). Rest is so vital that God blessed and hallowed the seventh day of the week as the Sabbath, a sacred day of rest (Exod. 20:9–11; Lev. 16:31). The Sabbath is not directly mentioned in the books traditionally associated with wisdom literature, which we've identified as Job, Proverbs, Ecclesiastes, and Song of Songs, and selected psalms. As we discussed in chapter 2, however, there's a growing awareness that genres are not pure forms with hard lines of separation and that texts can participate in multiple categories.[12] Recent research emphasizes that wisdom permeates all the different parts of the Old Testament.[13] There's a well-attested tradition, which goes all the way back into antiquity, that specifically links wisdom and creation.[14] In this view, the Lord created Wisdom at the beginning of creation and then created the cosmos with Wisdom (Prov. 8:22–36). When God created the heavens and the earth, he created "*all that exists concretely* and *the laws and norms* for all that exists."[15] This includes the principle of the Sabbath, which was established at creation. From this perspective, the Sabbath is a wisdom concept essential to wise living: Work must be balanced with rest.

In the past, Americans have worked more hours per week and taken fewer weeks of vacation than people in any other industrialized country. But many have become tired of this. No one wants to work their lives away; certainly not just for money. Even before the COVID-19 pandemic, work habits had started to change and some organizations had already begun to use—or investigate using—"Flexible Work Arrangements." During the pandemic, lockdown orders led to many people working from home. Since then, many have come to realize they enjoy working from home, which means they can forego a daily commute and enjoy greater flexibility and more frequent contact with family members. Another main driver of this trend is that a new generation of employees (Gen Z) expect organizations to offer these options to demonstrate that administrators are sensitive to work-life issues and the overall health and well-being of their employees.[16] These changes point to a recognition that work must be balanced by rest, and this is a change for the better.

The Consummate Example of Work

Many of the sayings about work that we have considered come from the book of Proverbs. Those who compiled this book chose to conclude it with the Proverbs 31 poem about a "capable" wife. The Hebrew word (חַיִל) that the NRSVue translates as "capable" actually refers to physical strength, military action, strong moral character, or even material wealth, and would be better translated here as "valor," which "better captures the tone of the extravagant" description that follows in verses 10–31.[17]

Important for our study in this chapter is the fact that after having presented a host of wisdom sayings collected from a variety of sources and contexts that spanned much of ancient Israel's history, the book of Proverbs concludes with this "Ode to a Woman of Valor." We might ask why it is a poem about a woman instead of a story about a king, a warrior, or even a farmer. The reason probably has to do with the wide range of skilled work for which women were responsible in a household-based economy. In this case, this poem provides a perfect case study for the flowering of wisdom in the home. With that in mind, the "Ode to a Woman of Valor" is a consummate example of wisdom at work in daily life.

The whole of Proverbs 31:10–31 certainly warrants a full study, but our concern here is to point out that almost every verse speaks directly about either her work or the benefits she brings to her family through her work.[18]

> A woman of strength who can find?
> She is far more precious than jewels.
> The heart of her husband trusts in her,
> and he will have no lack of gain.

She does him good and not harm
> all the days of her life.
She seeks wool and flax
> and works with willing hands.
She is like the ships of the merchant;
> she brings her food from far away.
She rises while it is still night
> and provides food for her household
> and tasks for her female servants.
She considers a field and buys it;
> with the fruit of her hands she plants a vineyard.
She girds herself with strength
> and makes her arms strong.
She perceives that her merchandise is profitable.
> Her lamp does not go out at night.
She puts her hands to the distaff,
> and her hands hold the spindle.
She opens her hand to the poor
> and reaches out her hands to the needy.
She is not afraid for her household when it snows,
> for all her household are clothed in crimson.
She makes herself coverings;
> her clothing is fine linen and purple.
Her husband is known in the city gates,
> taking his seat among the elders of the land.
She makes linen garments and sells them;
> she supplies the merchant with sashes.
Strength and dignity are her clothing,
> and she laughs at the time to come.
She opens her mouth with wisdom,
> and the teaching of kindness is on her tongue.
She looks well to the ways of her household
> and does not eat the bread of idleness.
Her children rise up and call her happy;
> her husband, too, and he praises her:
"Many women have done excellently,
> but you surpass them all."
Charm is deceitful and beauty is vain,
> but a woman who fears the Lord is to be praised.
Give her a share in the fruit of her hands,
> and let her works praise her in the city gates.

This woman's work is wide ranging indeed. She evaluates and purchases wool and flax in the marketplace and works them into products (v. 13). She's involved in purchasing food from other sources, as well as producing it in the household, and she is also able to create jobs for others (vv. 14–15).[19] She evaluates and purchases properties and is involved in viticulture (v. 16). She manufactures and sells products (v. 18), including textiles (v. 19). This woman is so industrious that she produces a surplus out of which she can give charity to the poor and needy (v. 20).[20] Those in her household don't have to be afraid of the elements because she's provided them with fine clothing (v. 21) and she herself is clothed with fine garments (v. 22). Her husband is well respected in the city gate, which implies that this is due, at least in part, to her good work (v. 23). The text again notes that she manufactures garments and sashes (this time of linen), which she provides to merchants (v. 24). This is a woman of strength and dignity who through her industriousness is prepared for the future (v. 25). She manages her household well and is never idle (v. 28). Her children praise her, and her husband lauds her as having surpassed all other women (vv. 28–29).

Why is this woman, who represents the flowering of wisdom in the home, to be praised so highly? It is because she fears the Lord (v. 30), and that is what has led her to live and work so effectively. In the end, this passage urges readers to "give her a share in the fruit of her hands, and let her works praise her in the city gates" (v. 31). The Proverbs 31 wife provides "a culmination and recapitulation, drawing together . . . the virtues [that the book of Proverbs] teaches throughout."[21] She is a model for all those who seek to walk in the way of wisdom.

Toward the New Testament

The positive view of work found in wisdom literature continues in the New Testament. In the same way that God is portrayed as a worker in the creation account and throughout the Old Testament, so Jesus is portrayed as a worker in the Gospels. Joseph was a "carpenter" (Matt. 13:54–55), and Jesus himself came to be known as the "carpenter" (Mark 6:3), which means that he probably inherited the family business from Joseph when Joseph died. The Greek word for their trade is *tektōn*, and although most translations follow the tradition of rendering it as "carpenter," it can also be translated as "builder." With the predominance of stone in the region, we might imagine that Joseph and Jesus were stonemasons rather than carpenters. During Jesus' youth, Herod Antipas launched a major building project at Sepphoris with a view to making it his capital. For decades, in order to staff the project, he recruited artisans from villages all around. Sepphoris became the "ornament of Galilee," and no doubt many artisans benefited from this massive government-sponsored project. Since Jesus would have spent much of his life working as a builder, we might imagine that he made regular trips to Sepphoris to work on its public buildings, such as the amphitheater that seated up to four thousand people. As a businessowner, he may have been more like a contractor who employed workers on such projects. In any case, he grew up working and spent most of his adult life working.[22] It is significant that the authors of the Gospels, who believed that Jesus was the Son of God, did not portray him as having come from royalty or the aristocracy, but from among those who owned small farms, businesses, or worked at a trade.[23]

The apostle Paul, who came from a socially privileged class and received training as a rabbi, was also a tentmaker (Acts 18:1–4). The term for "tentmaking" could apparently include a range of leatherworking activities. There are a number of passages suggesting that Paul's work was technical in nature and that he tended to work in metropolitan areas.[24] Paul frequently emphasized that when he worked with congregations, he also labored at his trade so that he wouldn't be a financial burden to them.[25] It was not uncommon for rabbis of the second and third centuries to work at a trade; and although we don't have data for the first century, we might presume it wasn't infrequent during that period as well.[26]

In his letters, Paul regularly emphasized the value of work. In 1 Corinthians 7:17, for example, he said that when people become Christians, they don't need to abandon their profession but should continue to do that "to which God called you." The word Paul uses here for their call (*kaleo*) to their ordinary work is the same one he uses for God's call to do ministry and build up the church (Rom. 12:3; 2 Cor. 10:13). Paul is saying that "secular" jobs are just as much a divine calling as "religious" jobs. This understanding should revolutionize the way Christians think of their work in this world.[27]

Paul also taught that work was a matter of equity in society. There were some in the Christian community at Thessalonica who were "living in idleness" and "not doing any work" (2 Thess. 3:11); they were dependent on food provided by other believers or served at the church's communal meals. The origin of this group of idlers in the church may have held the Greco-Roman aristocratic disdain for manual labor or, more likely, the influence of Cynic philosophy, in which work was viewed as a barrier to the truly good life. Aristotle, for example, said that the ability to live without having to work was one of the main requirements for a genuinely worthwhile life.[28] There may have been some converts in the church at Thessalonica who genuinely believed that since the kingdom of God had been inaugurated in Christ, work was no longer necessary.[29] Paul reminded them, however, that he and his coworkers had not been idle when they were with them. In fact, they worked to provide for themselves and never ate anything without paying for it, and he urged these idlers to imitate them (2 Thess. 3:7). He also said that "anyone unwilling to work should not eat" (3:10). It was unfair for these idlers to opt out of work when they should be working to provide for their families and contribute to the common good of the community.

Yet another reason Paul viewed work as paramount was that it enabled people to provide for their families, which Paul viewed as a vital component of Christian ethics. He taught that "whoever does not provide for their relatives, and especially for family members, has denied the faith and is worse than an unbeliever" (1 Tim. 5:8). In the first century, it was the responsibility of the senior male member of a household to provide for those under his care. James Dunn explains the seriousness with which Paul viewed this responsibility:

> Here we have a brief insight into the full sweep of responsibility of the paterfamilias. That responsibility included all his near relatives, whether living in his own immediate household or not, on whose behalf he had been appointed guardian. But he had a special responsibility for those of his immediate household, and here it is particularly his wife who is in view. The writer gives this responsibility the highest rank. To fail in it was tantamount to denying the faith. Such as one was "worse than an unbeliever." The importance of family and of family responsibilities as part of Christian faith and discipleship, and of the integration (not antithesis) of family and church responsibilities could hardly be more strongly stressed.[30]

As much as work is valued in the New Testament, its authors also shared the Old Testament belief that it must be balanced with rest. Jesus himself taught that the Sabbath was a gift of God to humankind (Mark 2:27). It was established to provide us with rest from labor and the opportunity for worship. In addition to observing the Sabbath, Jesus often went away to be by himself to rest and pray.[31] On one occasion, when the Twelve returned from a preaching and healing mission, Jesus instructed them, "Come away to a deserted place all by yourselves and rest a while" (Mark 6:31). Finding occasions for rest was a regular practice for Jesus, and so it should be for us as well.

Throughout the history of the church, all the great devotional writers have talked about the importance of solitude and rest for the Christian life. For example, in *The Imitation of Christ*, the unchallenged masterpiece of devotional literature for five hundred years, Thomas à Kempis has a section titled "On the Love of Solitude and Silence." Dietrich Bonhoeffer, the Lutheran pastor who led a resistance movement in World War II, wrote a devotional classic called *Life Together*. In it, he devotes a whole chapter to solitude and silence. Thomas Merton, the Roman Catholic monk, devoted a whole book to the subject, *Thoughts in Solitude*.

What these and other devotional writers understand is that solitude and silence before God is integral to the spiritual life and one of the keys to spiritual growth. Ruth Haley Barton, founder of the Transforming Center, explains:

> To enter into solitude is to take the spiritual life seriously. It is to take seriously our need to quiet the noise and constant stimulation of our lives, to cease the constant striving of human effort, to bring ourselves back from our absorption in human relationships *for a time* in order to give God full access to our souls. In solitude God begins to free us from our bondage to human expectations, for there we experience God as our ultimate reality—the one in whom we live and move and have our being (Acts 17:28). In solitude our thoughts and our mind, our will and our desires are reoriented Godward so we can become less and less attracted by external forces and can be more deeply responsive to God at work within us.[32]

When we learn to balance hard work with deep rest, we'll have fit together two of the most essential pieces into the puzzle of the good life.

WEALTH AND POVERTY

According to a recent *Atlantic* article by Alana Semuels, America is becoming a nation of hoarders.[1] In 2017, Americans spent 240 billion dollars on jewelry, watches, books, telephones, and other communication equipment. Even after adjusting the dollar value for inflation, this is twice as much as they spent in 2002. Spending on personal care products also doubled.

In order to contain all these purchases, Americans are supersizing their houses and building miles of storage units. In 2017, the average size of a single-family home was 2,426 square feet, which is an increase of nearly 25 percent of the square footage of an average American home twenty years ago. When I was growing up, I don't recall ever seeing a self-storage unit. By the end of 2019, there were 47,539 self-storage facilities in the United States with more than 1.9 billion square feet of self-storage space.

At the same time, charitable giving has declined. According to recent analyses, Christians today give only about 2.5 percent of their income, which amounts to about $17 per week. Nearly 40 percent of regular attendees, including evangelicals, don't give anything.

It would appear that Americans have bought into the idea that one of the primary ways to attain the good life is by shopping. In this chapter, we'll attempt to gain a more balanced perspective on how wealth and poverty relate to the good life. We'll begin with a broad overview of how the church has related to wealth and poverty throughout its history, and then we'll examine the general view of wealth and poverty in wisdom literature. We'll look at a number of ways of acquiring wealth viewed as honorable, and we'll conclude with a brief foray into wealth and poverty in the New Testament.

Wealth and Poverty in the History of the Church

Throughout the church's history, there has been disagreement about how Christians should properly relate to wealth and poverty. Below, we will discuss some of the issues.

CONTROVERSY OVER JESUS' ECONOMIC STATUS AND TEACHING ON WEALTH

These disagreements go all the way back to the Gospels, and they start with Jesus himself. Christians have disagreed about Jesus' own social and economic status. Throughout our history, it's been common to view Jesus as poor. In recent years, many scholars have argued that the young Jesus grew to adulthood in a society that was highly stratified and marked by extreme wealth on the one hand and extreme poverty on the other, and that there was really no one in between.[2] New Testament scholars who subscribe to this view have often portrayed Jesus as a peasant preacher whose main vocation was critiquing the wealthy and advantaged.[3] Recent archaeology, however, shows that economic conditions in Galilee were more diverse than that. While there were many who lived at a subsistence level, there were also homes with signs of wealth.[4] The region of Galilee showed more economic diversity than was once thought. Jesus' social and economic status, however, remains controversial. There has also been a great deal of disagreement about Jesus' teachings on wealth and how these should be interpreted. We'll say a bit more about all this below in "Toward the New Testament."

VENERATION OF POVERTY IN THE PATRISTIC PERIOD

In the patristic period, many early church fathers condemned private property and taught that the Christians in communities should all share the ownership of property. Many of them saw private property as a "necessary evil" that was a result of the fall. Saint Augustine, a major Christian theologian who lived from AD 354 to 430, urged Christians to turn away from the desire for material wealth and success. He taught that the accumulation of wealth was not a worthy goal for Christians. This scorn for wealth continued into the Middle Ages, and poverty came to be viewed as more spiritual than being wealthy.

THE RISE OF THE "PROSPERITY GOSPEL"

In nineteenth-century America, the New Thought movement began teaching a theology of healing and prosperity. A Prosperity Gospel developed out this and rose to prominence during the healing revivals of the 1950s. In the 1980s, prosperity teaching featured prominently in the Word of Faith movement and in televangelism. In the 1990s and 2000s, it was embraced by prominent leaders in the charismatic movement and taken all over the world by Christian missionaries, some of whom established megachurches that were bastions of prosperity theology.

Revivalists who preached prosperity argued that the atonement brought more than just spiritual healing; it also alleviated sickness and poverty. They emphasized that God's will is for people to be happy, healthy, and wealthy. One of the most popular leaders in this movement in recent years was Kenneth Hagin (1917–2003), who taught that the Bible contains numerous promises from God to believers, but that believers must "claim" them in order to activate them. Two of his most popular books were *"You Can Have What You Say!"* and *How to Write Your Own Ticket with God*.[5] This "Name-It-and-Claim-It" theology applies to healing from disease, driving out evil spirits, supernatural gifts, and financial prosperity.

These ideas have been modified and developed further by numerous preachers and teachers of prosperity. Charles Capps "systematized faith theology into an iron clad system of causality" and taught that "the spoken word, by activating faith, bound God to the individual's proclamation."[6] His most famous work, *The Tongue: A Creative Force*, sold more than three million copies.[7]

Prosperity preachers also taught that tithing was a key to wealth. Mid-twentieth-century revivalists generally taught that financial prosperity operated on a law of divine reciprocity. If believers gave to God, then he would in turn give back to them. Oral Roberts confidently proclaimed that "God will increase thirty-, sixty-, and a hundred-fold return on the tithe," and that "giving is not a debt you owe; it's a seed you *sow*."[8] Gordon Lindsay assured his disciples of a "hundredfold blessing," that God would reward givers a hundred times for their original donation.[9] Since then, many other prosperity preachers have taught the idea of the "hundredfold blessing," including Frederick Price, Joel Osteen, Kenneth Copeland, Frances Hunter, Marilyn Hickey, and others. What all these prosperity preachers have in common is the idea that obtaining wealth from God is an exact science, a sort of "calculus of God's 'money-back guarantee.'"[10] Prosperity can be obtained by speaking it into existence or by tithing or giving to prosperity ministries.

Some prosperity teachers even argue that Jesus himself was wealthy, which sets a precedent for believers to be wealthy.[11] Prosperity preachers have pointed to Mary and Joseph's donkey ride to Bethlehem, the gifts of the wise men to the baby Jesus, the fact that the guards divided Jesus' cloak among themselves at his crucifixion, and other clues in the Gospels as evidence of wealth. For some prosperity preachers, these and other so-called evidence of wealth provide justification for their own lavish living. Many prosperity preachers live opulent lifestyles purportedly to demonstrate the truth of their message to their audiences and inspire them to reach the same heights.[12] These teachings continue to be popular in charismatic churches.

BACKLASH: RENEWED RENUNCIATION OF WEALTH

The pendulum swung the other way again when many non-Pentecostal and non-charismatic traditions reacted by criticizing wealth in general. Some of these traditions look down on people with money and teach that Christians should shun wealth. They sometimes even teach that "money is the root of all evil," although what Paul says in 1 Timothy 6:10 is that it is "the *love* of money that is the root of all evil."

I grew up in a blue-collar town about twenty minutes outside of Birmingham, Alabama, and my family attended a congregation associated with a denomination with a long heritage of shunning wealth.[13] Early leaders of the tradition, such as David Lipscomb, taught that the church is for working people and that "the rich corrupt" the church.[14] He taught that preachers and other Christians should support themselves through manual labor. Lipscomb opposed education for ministers because he thought it would expose them to the surroundings of the rich. They should instead be trained to preach to the poor, and the church itself should be bound to material poverty. Those in the church should dress in styles and adopt manners that attract the poor rather than repel them, and church buildings should be simple. The Churches of Christ were opposed to organization because it smacked of denominationalism.[15] However, their resistance to organization was about more than simply opposing denominationalism; it was really about not being beholden to people with money.[16] In the congregation where I grew up, the preacher often criticized money and told the congregation how bad it is and that they shouldn't want it. I can't tell you how many times I heard sermons on how "money's the root of all evil."

There was even backlash from charismatic churches. Former Assemblies of God minister Jimmy Swaggart (born 1935), for example, called the hundredfold blessing an "outright fraud."[17] In his later years, Kenneth Hagin tempered his teaching and began to teach a more modest message of prosperity. In *The Midas Touch: A Balanced Approach to Biblical Prosperity*, he explained that he no longer told people to expect the hundredfold return on their offerings, but that he taught only what Scripture teaches in passages such as Luke 6:38, which is that for those who faithful in their tithes and offerings, blessings will always be "running over" in their lives.[18] Although other faith teachers protested such excesses as the hundredfold blessing, the message of prosperity remains popular.

Concluding Thoughts on the Prosperity Gospel

The Gospel of Wealth softened the rough edges of capitalism and industrialism with a theology that counters poverty, disease, and despair. It declared that the world was basically good and ripe with opportunity, despite all evidence to the contrary. The Prosperity Gospel held out hope to the poor.[19] It was the deification and ritualization of the "American Dream," which includes upward mobility and accumulation. The Prosperity Gospel appears to be the twin of American civil religion.

The emphasis on the individual's responsibility for their own fate resonated strongly with the American tradition of rugged self-reliance.[20] Americans have always loved the idea of individual freedom, which "was the sacred language of choice."[21] And the Prosperity Gospel guarantees believers the ability to change their circumstances by tapping into new spiritual powers. In its origins, it was a distinctly "American Gospel."[22]

Wealth and Poverty in Early Israelite Society and in Proverbs

The book of Proverbs talks about "the rich" and "the poor" as classes. But the way the proverbs talk about these groups suggests that their authors didn't see themselves as belonging to one or the other. It's as if they wrote the book from a neutral perspective. As a whole, Proverbs tends to disapprove of the wealthy as a class because their affluence enables them to abuse their power by mistreating the poor. On the other hand, wealth itself is not despised, and those who become rich through hard work and honest means are praised and encouraged. Many of the sayings recorded in the book of Proverbs appear to be addressed to people engaged in the cultivation of small, family-owned farms. This is suggested by the frequent references to agricultural pursuits.

In the society reflected in Proverbs, it seems that wealth was not a rarity. In one passage, for example, a father advises his son to honor the Lord by setting aside a portion of their produce so that their barns and wine vats would be full to overflowing (3:9–10). In another example, wealthy farmers are advised to sell to less fortunate neighbors in times of need instead of hoarding grain for themselves (11:26).

There are also examples of private luxury. In one example, scoundrels are on the lookout for "all kinds of costly things" in the houses of those they plan to rob (Prov. 1:13). In another example, a woman offers inducements of dinner and luxurious surroundings to her intended lover (7:6–27). Three passages refer to dinner parties where there seems to be a great deal of wealth (9:1–5; 17; 23:1–3). And the concluding chapter of the book describes the life of an obviously wealthy family, happy and well-adjusted (31:10–31), which shows that money, when properly obtained, doesn't necessarily corrupt. Since the book of Proverbs is written by various ancient writers, it contains a variety of perspectives as we will see below.

WEALTH AS A BLESSING FROM GOD

Proverbs teaches that wealth is a blessing from God (Prov. 10:22). This is an oft-repeated theme (cf. Prov. 3:9–10, 15–16; 10:15, 16; 14:24) and derives from the so-called principle of retribution theology spelled out in the law of Moses. As we've already seen, it teaches that those who are faithful to the conditions of God's covenant will be blessed, while those who defy them and rebel against God will be cursed (Deut. 27:11–28:68). According to retribution theology, it would be natural to expect that those who live wisely (8:21) and righteously (15:6) would acquire wealth.

ECONOMIC INEQUALITY IS TAKEN FOR GRANTED

Although ancient Israel's sages generally believed that wealth was a blessing from God, they also realized that not everyone would be wealthy and that some would be poor. There are several proverbs that echo Jesus' words: "The poor you will always have with you" (see Prov. 14:31; 22:16; 28:3, 6; 30:14). At the same time, many proverbs teach that those who are blessed with some measure of wealth should be generous to the poor (cf. Prov. 11:24, 25; 14:21; 19:17; 22:9; 28:27).

Being poor did not exempt someone from the prohibition against stealing (Exod. 20:15), and so those who are poor shouldn't try to steal from the rich. This was not viewed as an acceptable way for them to acquire wealth (Prov. 1:8–19). On the other hand, the sages taught that God's people should show some sympathy toward those who steal out of desperation and hunger (6:30; 30:9). They realized that anyone could fall into poverty. If this happened to our enemies, we should be kind even to them (25:21–22).

EQUALITY OF THE RICH AND THE POOR

Although economic inequality is taken for granted in Proverbs, it also teaches the equality of the rich and the poor. Some examples include:

> The rich and the poor have this in common:
> the LORD is the maker of them all. (22:2)

> The poor and the oppressor have this in common:
> the LORD gives light to the eyes of both. (29:13)

> Some pretend to be rich yet have nothing;
> others pretend to be poor yet have great wealth. (13:7)

PEOPLE WHO CAN NEVER ATTAIN WEALTH

Proverbs teaches that there are certain kinds of people who can never attain wealth or are destined to lose it if they get it. They're destined for poverty. These include the wicked (11:4), sinners (13:21), adulterers (5:10), those who are too eager to possess it (28:20, 22), those who are greedy for it (28:25), those with an inordinate desire for luxuries (21:17; 23:20–21), and those who are confident they'll never lose it (11:28).

SOME THINGS PREFERABLE TO WEALTH

Even though wealth is considered a blessing from God and righteousness generally leads to blessings, there are some things more important than wealth.

> Better is a little with the fear of the LORD
> than great treasure and trouble with it.
> Better is a dinner of vegetables where love is
> than a fatted ox and hatred with it. (15:16–17)

It is better to have just a "little" with righteousness than wealth with injustice (cf. Prov. 16:8; also 17:1; 28:6).

There's only one prayer in the entire book of Proverbs and, interestingly, it's about money:

> Two things I ask of you;
> do not deny them to me before I die:
> Remove far from me falsehood and lying;
> give me neither poverty nor riches;
> feed me with the food that I need,
> lest I be full and deny you
> and say, "Who is the LORD?"

or I be poor and steal
>and profane the name of my God. (30:7–9)

Apparently, both wealth and poverty can be conducive to sin, and our prayer should be to avoid extremes. Proverbs talks about a middle way between extreme wealth and extreme poverty. The best way is the way of righteousness, which is founded on the fear of the Lord and the love of neighbor.

Honorable Ways of Attaining Wealth

HARD WORK

Proverbs teaches that the number one way of attaining wealth is through hard work. Wisdom literature regularly points to the tilling of the land as work that produces "plenty of food" for one's family (Prov. 12:11; 27:23–27; 28:19).

The behavior of the lazy is often contrasted with that of the diligent in order to show the value of motivation, making plans, and hard work for success.

>The lazy do not roast their game,
>>but the diligent obtain precious wealth. (12:27)

>The appetite of the lazy craves and gets nothing,
>>while the appetite of the diligent is richly supplied. (13:4)

>In all toil there is profit,
>>but mere talk leads only to poverty. (14:23)

>The plans of the diligent lead surely to abundance,
>>but everyone who is hasty comes only to want. (21:5)

Proverbs 24:30–36 provides us with an extended moral tale that illustrates the folly of laziness:

>I passed by the field of one who was lazy,
>>by the vineyard of a stupid person;
>and see, it was all overgrown with thorns;
>>the ground was covered with nettles,
>>and its stone wall was broken down.
>Then I saw and considered it;
>>I looked and received instruction.
>A little sleep, a little slumber,
>>a little folding of the hands to rest,
>and poverty will come upon you like a robber,
>>and want, like an armed warrior.

This passage is a parody of laziness and epitomizes an intolerance of laziness (cf. also the parody in Prov. 26:13–16). Tremper Longman explains that laziness was seen as "the height of foolish behavior," because "it leads to difficult circumstances for both the individual and the community, and it is easily remedied."[23] That is, it could be remedied through hard work.

It's also taught that by developing skills and expertise, we can do more than break even but actually get ahead.

> Do you see those who are skillful in their work?
>> They will serve kings;
>>> they will not serve common people. (Prov. 22:29)

The word translated here as "skillful" means "skilled," "adept," or especially "trained."[24] It's not just working hard; developing special, unique, and valuable skills is what gives someone an advantage in the job market.[25]

In the "Ode to a Woman of Valor," which brings the book of Proverbs to its conclusion, the woman is praised because she wasn't lazy but industrious.

> She looks well to the ways of her household,
>> and does not eat the bread of idleness (Prov. 31:27)

AVOID BORROWING

> The rich rule over the poor,
>> and the borrower is the slave of the lender. (Prov. 22:7)

This proverb is probably picturing the rich person who charges interest from the poor borrower, who has no choice than to borrow from the rich person. The law of Moses, however, forbade charging interest from the poor (cf. Exod. 22:25 [24]; Lev. 25:36–37; Deut. 23:19 [20]), the prophets preached against it (cf. Ezek. 18:8, 13, 17; 22:12), and the sages condemned it (cf. Prov 28:18).[26] High interest is a form of entrapment. Those who take out high-interest loans do so because they're not able to make ends meet in the first place. Once they pay off that loan, they're even deeper in the hole and have to take out another one. It creates a vicious cycle.

This kind of high-interest, predatory lending is called "usury" and is forbidden in the Bible. Those who run businesses that make these high-interest loans are called "loan sharks," predatory animals. God's law forbids this practice because those who borrow money from these people become their "slaves" in the sense that they lose control over their money and are beholden to the lender.

BUILDING WEALTH SLOWLY

There's one proverb that's rather difficult to understand, but that's probably because it has multiple applications.

> Wealth hastily gotten will dwindle,
> but those who gather little by little will increase it. (13:11)

The Hebrew literally says, "Wealth gathered in a vapor will dwindle" (the Hebrew for "in a vapor" is *mēhebel*), and it's not totally clear what is meant by this. When we think of a "vapor" or a "puff of air," we think of something that lacks permanence. "The metaphor of getting money from a vapor suggests what English speakers call 'easy money' "[27] and might be intended to imply some kind of get-rich-quick scheme or even something illegal.

"Wealth gotten by a vapor" could also be translated "wealth gotten by a wind." It makes me think of the English word *windfall*. Maybe we could translate the verse, "Wealth gotten by a windfall won't last." A "windfall" is a piece of unexpected good fortune, typically one that involves receiving a large amount of money through inheritance or maybe the lottery.

Typically, those who receive a large sum of money by a windfall are not able to make it last. According to a 2015 Camelot Group Study, 44 percent of those who won a large lottery prize were broke within five years. The Certified Financial Planner Board of Standard says that nearly a third were so broke they had to declare bankruptcy, which means they were worse off than before they got the windfall. Other studies show that lottery winners often become estranged from family and friends and develop a greater incidence of depression, drug and alcohol abuse, divorce, and suicide than the average American.

The reason those who gain money through a sudden windfall are not able to make it last is that they don't understand the nature of wealth, how to relate to it, or how to build it. The second half of the proverb points to the *right* way to build wealth: "Those who gather little by little will increase it" (13:11). This describes a slow, small, steady accumulation of wealth by moonlighting, reinvesting in one's business, and saving.[28]

INVESTING

> Send out your bread upon the waters,
> for after many days you will get it back.
> Divide your means seven ways, or even eight,
> for you do not know what disaster may happen on earth. (Eccles. 11:1–2)

To cast "bread upon the waters" appears to be a metaphor for using capital to engage in trade, including trade across the seas.[29] But people are advised to be sensible and not to gamble everything on only one venture. The lack of certainty in financial investments points to the wisdom of diversification.

TITHING

Finally, ancient Israel's sages taught that people should give back to God some of their wealth as a sacrifice in recognition that it is God who gave it in the first place (cf. Exod. 23:19; Num. 28:26–27; Deut. 18:4; 26:1–2).

> Honor the LORD with your substance
> and with the first fruits of all your produce;
> then your barns will be filled with plenty,
> and your vats will be bursting with wine. (Prov. 3:9–10)

Although the text isn't explicit here, it's probably talking about giving a tithe to the temple.[30] The temple tithe was to be from the "firstfruits," which means that it was to be taken from the first revenue brought in from the produce.

What some commentators overlook in this passage is the promise that for those who honor God through faithfully giving their tithes to the temple, God will reward them by enhancing their own prosperity. Their "barns" will be full, and their "vats" will be "bursting with wine" (v. 10). Vats were receptacles that caught the wine that flowed out of the winepress after the grapes had been crushed. If we were to translate the Hebrew literally here, it says that the vats burst.[31] This, however, is not meant to be taken literally but is a metaphor for the way that God's blessings surpass the amount originally tithed. Barns are filled, and vats will burst.

Toward the New Testament

Wealth and poverty are significant themes in the New Testament that appear in all twenty-seven books.[32] Instead of trying to provide an overview of this teaching on the subject, I'd like to provide a brief look at two subjects that have had profound impacts on the way the church has thought about wealth and poverty throughout its history. The first is Jesus' own social and economic status as portrayed in the Gospels, and the second is the economic character of the early church as portrayed in Luke.

Earlier in the chapter, I mentioned that throughout much of church history, it has been common to view Jesus as having been poor. In recent years, many scholars have argued that he grew up in a society that was highly stratified and marked by extreme wealth on the one hand and extreme poverty on the other, with nothing like a middle class in between.[33] New Testament scholars who hold this view imagine that Jesus was a homeless, peasant preacher from the backwater of Galilee who would have been out of place in any kind of urban context and whose primary purpose was to critique the wealthy and advantaged.[34] Recent research has brought to light data that require us to radically revise this view of Jesus. First, as we discussed in chapter 9, the authors of the Gospels portray Jesus as a "carpenter" or "builder." He did not come from the masses of day laborers and landless tenets, but from the "middle class" of Galilee.

Second, Jesus' hometown of Nazareth may have been a small Jewish town, but it was no backwater. Trade routes connected the cities of Galilee with the Greek cities of the coastal plain, and Nazareth was also connected geographically to the Mediterranean Sea. All the towns in the region where Jesus was located were Greek-speaking and cosmopolitan, located on busy trade routes connected to Roman administrative centers.

Third, the idea that Jesus was homeless is incorrect. When Jesus launched his ministry, he concentrated on the towns and villages along the shoreline of the Sea of Galilee (Mark 1:16) with Capernaum as his base (Mark 1:21). When the Sabbath came, he went to the synagogue in Capernaum and taught (Mark 1:21). In the next episode, he leaves the synagogue and enters the house of Simon and Andrew (Mark 1:29), also in Capernaum. Then they went on a preaching tour in the Galilee (Mark 1:35), and after "some days," he "returned to Capernaum" and "it was reported that he was *at home*" (2:1). After Jesus recruited Levi, it appears he hosted a meal at "his house" (2:15).[35] Jesus conducted more ministry in Capernaum, engaged in debates and discussions, and then went back to the synagogue (3:1), presumably in Capernaum. He ministered along the seaside at Capernaum (Mark 3:7), and then he "went home" (3:20). The word spread about all Jesus had been doing in and around Capernaum, and people "came to him in great numbers from Judea, Jerusalem, Idumea, beyond the Jordan, and the region around Tyre and Sidon" (Mark 3:7). Apparently, Jesus had secured a home in Capernaum, and it was from there that he reached out to the villages in the Galilee region.

Much of Jesus' teaching is about rich people and their wealth. In the Sermon on the Mount, for example, he emphasized the importance of giving alms (Matt. 6:2–4), pronounced blessings on the poor (Luke 6:20),[36] and taught that people should focus on storing up treasures in heaven rather than on earth (Matt. 6:19–21). He stressed that people can't have two masters: they can't serve God and wealth at the same time (Matt. 6:24). Several of his parables are about the rich and their riches, including the parables of the rich fool (Luke 12:13–21), the dishonest manager (Luke 16:1–13), the rich man and Lazarus (Luke 16:19–31), and the ten pounds or talents (Luke 19:11–27).

While many students of the Bible assume that Jesus' teaching about money is entirely negative, this is not the case. The parables of the dishonest manager and of the ten pounds, for example, both present challenges to the rich to use their wealth to expand the kingdom of God. The parable of the dishonest manager is about how "in the critical moment, the manager does not hunker down, horde his wealth and hide from the world," but "rather bravely and shrewdly opens up, and in his nefarious manner gives himself to others, and others thus give themselves to him."[37] The parable of the ten pounds is about the "obligation to enter the world and to enlarge the master's power and dominion within it while he is away."[38] These parables do not condemn the rich but challenge them to use their wealth for the expansion of the kingdom.

The second subject we'll discuss here is Luke's description of the early Christian community as living communally and sharing their material possessions (Acts 2:42–45; 4:32–37). He specifically says that they "had all things in common" (2:44). Many interpreters throughout the history of the church have understood this to mean that the earliest Christians renounced private property. However, it's more likely that they retained ownership of their own property but would put it to use for the good of others.[39] The story of Ananias and Sapphira (Acts 5:1–11) confirms this interpretation. This couple sold a piece of property and pretended to give the proceeds to the community while holding back a portion of it. When Peter confronted them about the fraud, he said that both the property and the proceeds of its sale belonged to Ananias and Sapphira and that they were free to do whatever they wanted with it (Acts 5:4). Their story (as well as others) makes it clear that Luke's portrayal of the early Christian community as one that held "all things in common" entirely was exaggerated to make a theological point. He wanted to show that the Holy Spirit had brought about a community that realized the highest aspirations of human longing, including unity, peace, joy, and the praise of God.

Wealth and its use is a frequent theme throughout the rest of the New Testament, with many passages that laud its positive uses and others that warn of its potential dangers. In the end, money itself is neither good nor bad but is simply a medium of exchange. With regard to wealth, the good life is one of balance. Christians must guard themselves against "the *love* of money," which is indeed "a root of all kinds of evil" (1 Tim. 6:10), while using whatever financial resources they have for kingdom purposes.

TIME

In the late 1980s and early '90s, I was a college student trying to juggle two majors and two jobs. In between classes, I'd get in a few hours of work with the college's food services and then work a third shift as a night watchman a few nights a week. On the weekends, I often worked at a catering event. I had too many plates in the air and never enough time to focus on any one thing. One day, I was at a local bookstore and just happened to pick up a magazine with an article that predicted an upcoming "leisure revolution," driven by automation in industry and in the home. The author expressed some concern about the implications of "the end of work." What would people do with all their free time?

Fast-forward thirty years to a random weekday when I arrive in my office around 8:30 a.m. The light on my office phone is blinking, which means I have new voicemails, and as I boot up my computer, I find about fifty new emails in my inbox. There's no time to check them now, however, because I need to rush off to teach class. After class, I have to attend a committee meeting, and after that, I need to grade some papers during lunch since my afternoon class expects to receive them back today. Later, during my afternoon office hour, I listen to the voicemails and answer the first couple of emails, but then two students drop by, one after the other, to ask for some help with assignments. Once they've left, it's time for me to leave the office for the day. The next morning, the voicemail light is blinking and somewhere between twenty-five and fifty new emails appear after I boot up my computer.

So, what happened to this "leisure revolution"? When I was a college student working two and three jobs, I thought that as an adult I'd have more control over my time. Instead of a time surplus, however, it often feels like a time recession in which hours and minutes have become scarce resources. Instead of having time on my hands, it often feels like time is slipping through my fingers.

A Brief History of Time

People have not always related to time the same way we do in modern Western cultures. In fact, throughout human history, there have been many differences in the ways that time has been understood, experienced, and measured in various cultures. Tribal societies developed systems of measuring time based on regularities in the natural world, typically using astronomical phenomena such as the movement of the sun, phases of the moon, the changing positions of other heavenly bodies, tides, migrations of animals and birds, and so on. In his famous study of the African Nuer, for example, anthropologist E. E. Evans-Pritchard observed that their language doesn't even have a word for time. They seemed to perceive time differently, in a less hurried way.[1] In another example, studies of the Hopi language indicate that they experience time in terms of general cycles.[2] Among the Trobriand islanders, Branislow Malinowski observed that gardening activities rather than natural sequences seemed to be the ordinary means of reckoning time.[3] For those Australian Aborigines who live in the traditional way, it appears they view their daily activities as reenactments of the long-past activities of ancestors in the mythic "dream-time," which brings a sort of "timelessness" to their daily lives.[4]

The first clocks in Europe were not developed until the medieval period. They were invented by Benedictine monks in order to facilitate communal prayer. The monks engaged in spiritual activities together at set times during the day, and in order to make sure that everyone began each activity at the same time, a bell was rung to announce its commencement. The canonical hours, when the monks celebrate the Divine Offices, were especially important. Eventually, so that they wouldn't have to rely on bell ringers—who might oversleep!—they invented the mechanical clock. The whole meaning, purpose, and intention of these clocks were "to call the religious to spend time with God."[5] For the Benedictines, Swinton explains:

> Time had a purpose beyond the mundane and the instrumental. The chief end of time was to facilitate the glorification of God. Time's function and purpose was to ensure that humans remained faithful to their duty to worship God. The mechanical clock was a device brought into existence specifically in the service of God's people. In enabled people to spend their time faithfully.[6]

These early clocks were intended to facilitate spiritual practices in the monastery. By the middle of the fourteenth century, however, clocks were used outside of monasteries to synchronize and regulate the actions of workers.[7] Clocks were erected in town squares, where they replaced church bells as the center of community life.[8] Instead of calling people to worship, they called them to work.

Around the sixteenth century, the minute hand was created, and in early in the eighteenth century, the second hand followed. The clock made it possible to implement regular hours of production, standardize working hours, and produce a uniform product.[9] Since the clock now made it possible to be "as regular as clockwork," it literally made industrial life possible. Whereas time had once shaped, sustained, and guided the spiritual life, it soon became a tool for guiding the new economics.[10]

A completely new temporal consciousness began to develop. Originally, the clock had been invented to call people to the altar of God, but now it called people to the altar of competitiveness. The emphasis in traditional workplaces shifted so that using time more efficiently was the new norm. The goal was to be faster and more competitive than competing businesses, and by the end of the nineteenth century, people frequently referred to life as a "race" or even a "rat race."[11]

The invention of the railroad in the early nineteenth century had a huge impact on the way time was perceived, used, and eventually standardized.[12] Previous to train travel, it didn't make any difference if there were small differences in the time between cities. There was no direct or immediate way to communicate between towns, and no one could travel faster than a horse. Since people moved much more slowly, it was unnecessary for timekeeping to be entirely precise.[13] With the invention of the railroad, however, it became possible to travel hundreds of miles in an astonishingly short amount of time.

The increased speed of travel necessitated a correspondingly rapid means of communication, and inventors set to work to meet this need. Samuel Morse (1791–1872) and other inventors developed the telegraph in the 1830s and 1840s. It's difficult to overstate the importance of the telegraph, which could deliver a message at a fraction of the time it took to deliver a message by physical transport. Judy Wajcman explores the role of the telegraph in the massive social and technological changes that took place from the mid-nineteenth to the mid-twentieth century.[14] She notes that it altered the structure of social relations so significantly that it has been dubbed the "Victorian Internet."[15] In 1899, British prime minister Lord Salisbury pronounced that the telegraph "has, as it were, assembled all mankind upon one great plane, where they can see everything that is done and hear everything that is said, and judge of every policy that is pursued at the very moment those events take place."[16] The telegraph made it possible to establish standard "railway" time, and by 1883, America had synchronized its clocks and established five time zones.

A fundamental change had occurred in how time was viewed in society, culture, and business. With this new sense of temporal exactitude, time came to be equated with money—and "when time is money, then faster means better."[17] In this view, "speed becomes an unquestioned and unquestionable good."[18] Western societies have embraced this view and become what Hartmut Rosa calls "acceleration societies."[19] He notes that the most measurable forms of acceleration include transportation, communication, and production. Trains, cars, and airplanes have shortened travel time. The telegraph, telephone, radio, computer, and satellites have abbreviated communication time. These increases in the speed of transportation and communication contribute to an ever-increasing speed of innovation and production that only continues to accelerate. For example, while it took thirty-five years for radio usage to be adopted by fifty million listeners, it took only fifteen years for the television to achieve this, and barely four years for the internet.[20] This rate of acceleration is breathtaking.

Information and communication technology (ICT) continues to develop products that enable more efficient use of time and, thus, greater productivity. In corporate America, the computer, the internet, the web, and e-commerce have all dramatically altered the way we perform our work. By the mid-1990s, the private sector began to use email, which enabled nearly instantaneous communication between machines within an organization. In recent years, people have adopted the use of smartphones, tablets, and laptops, which allow us to be constantly connected to friends, family, and work. Theoretically, these ICTs have the potential to save time, speed up work, and allow knowledge workers to engage with their work "anytime, anywhere."

In the late-modern period, the good life seems to be tied to speed. There is an allure about being fast, and in capitalist modernity, there's an impulse to continually promote it.[21] A cultural shift has occurred in which busyness is viewed increasingly more positively. Wajcman explains, "Whereas a century ago those in the upper income bracket were defined by their leisure . . . nowadays prestige accords to those who work long hours and are busiest at work."[22] She notes, however, that busyness as a form of status is not limited to work; it also applies to leisure. "Those who work long hours in employment also have a greater leisure density"—that is, they're even busy when they're not at work.[23] Whether at work or at play, "there is prestige attached to a busy lifestyle."[24] A "good life is assumed to be an accelerating life."[25] We look to the latest technological gadgets to help us work more and play more and also to balance our busy lifestyles. Ultimately, technology takes on religious proportions and "replaces transcendence as the source of hope . . . and harmony."[26]

Time-Sickness

In 1982, American physician Larry Dossey coined the term "time-sickness" "to describe the obsessive belief that 'time is getting away, that there isn't enough of it, and that you must pedal faster and faster to keep up.' "[27] Carl Honoré observes, "These days, the whole world is time-sick," and "we all belong to the same cult of speed."[28] Andrew Root aptly captures this modern time-sickness:

> The more we speed up, the more we feel like we can't do it right, can't take advantage of all the convenience and opportunities, can't find the benefits of all these connections and avenues to curate and broadcast a truly unique identity. There is so much more available, yet not enough time for it all, though we are taking every step to speed up. We feel particularly guilty because others—those elite timekeepers with their flashy phones, witty Twitter accounts, and techno fashion—appear to be doing better, going faster, and flourishing inside the technology acceleration.[29]

Time-sickness is an existential angst fueled by the increasing acceleration of all aspects of our society.

The very technologies we rely on in order to accelerate are also afflicted with a form of time-sickness. French philosopher Paul Virilio (1932–2018) argued that technology has inherent countervailing tendencies.[30] His law of "dromology," which he defined as "science (or logic) of speed," states that increases in speed multiply the potential for gridlock.[31] Modern forms of transportation, for example, may compress time, but they have an inherent potential for gridlock. Although we can go fast in our car, we often end up sitting in traffic jams. Planes can go even faster than cars, but we end up standing in endless lines in crowded lobbies to check in, get through security, and wait for departures, and sometimes flights are delayed or even canceled. Similarly, the use of contemporary forms of instant communication "leads to an overload of information so extensive that taking advantage of only the tiniest fraction of it not only blows apart 'real-time' communication but also slows down operators to the point where they lose themselves in the eternity of electronically networked information, a 'black hole of globalized interconnectivity.' "[32] Humans cannot possibly absorb the overload of parallel information sources.

The way we interact with technology today makes us feel time-sick. In seeking solutions, we tend to look to ever-faster technology to save time, but this only compounds the problem. Time simply seems to accelerate. Ben Agger calls this kind of continually accelerating time "iTime," which is a frenzied, uncontrollable, extremely condensed time "weighing heavily on the person who always has too much to do, [and] not enough time to do it."[33]

Another byproduct of acceleration is severe social alienation, which is a major obstacle to the good life. In a study of the relationship between acceleration and alienation, Hartmut Rosa argues that the systematic distortion of the conditions of communication leads to social pathologies.[34] In the late-modern world, ICTs accelerate communication to a point where real arguments cannot be made and real meaning cannot be conveyed.[35] The concentration of people in cities, which are prime sites for intensified time use, creates a dense set of possible interactions in a small space that also contributes to alienation. Rosa explains that in previous ages, the cast of others someone encountered on a day-to-day basis was relatively stable. People rarely moved, and so they encountered the same people in the village each day, many of whom they knew by name. Today, however, we can encounter a staggering number of other people during the day. "In the morning," Rosa notes, "you encounter your family, people on the news, people on the commute to work. . . . You might encounter more people before noon than people in previous generations encounter in a month." As a result, "you shut off" because you're on overload.[36] In such contexts, it's no wonder we may feel alienated.

Rosa argues that in such settings, we become "increasingly detached, or disengaged, from the times and spaces of our life, from our actions and experiences, and from the [people] we live and work with."[37] He paints a grim picture of the future impact of continued social acceleration. He suggests that it's "about to pass certain thresholds beyond which human beings necessarily become alienated, not just from their actions, the objects they work and live with, nature, the social world and their self, but also from time and space themselves."[38] It sounds like time-sickness is reaching pandemic proportions.

Qoheleth on Time

If there was time-sickness in the ancient Near Eastern world, it didn't focus on acceleration but on the brevity of human life—which is an ever-present reality for everyone. As we saw in chapter 1, wisdom writers throughout the ancient world wrestled with this issue. Human life is fleeting, and this transience often leads people to question their value in the world. This is a major issue in the book of Ecclesiastes, and Qoheleth explores several aspects of this feeling of transience, including repetitiveness, timing, past and future, death, and the question of what lies beyond death.[39] Transience, however, is the aspect of time that pervades Ecclesiastes.[40] Since this book provides a dramatic contrast to the focus on constant acceleration that features so predominantly in contemporary

Western society, we'll highlight select passages in which Qoheleth grapples with the concept and its implications.

LIFE IS A FLEETING BREATH IN A BROKEN WORLD (ECCLES. 1:1–11)

As we noted in chapter 1, in order to understand the meaning of Ecclesiastes, the Hebrew word *hebel* must be rendered as "transience" rather than "vanity" and the refrain "under the sun" must be understood to refer to conditions in a world broken by sin. Throughout Ecclesiastes, Qoheleth uses wisdom to examine life "under the sun" and offer wise counsel on how to survive and flourish in a broken world. His central thesis is that "everything in life becomes nothing more than a fleeting breath with disappointing outcomes unless one has an orthodox fear of God."[41]

After introducing himself in verse 1, Qoheleth's rhetorical argument begins by the second verse of the book:

"Breath of breaths," said Qoheleth, "Breath of breaths. Everything is temporary!" What is the advantage to the one who labours laboriously under the sun?

A generation goes, a generation comes,
 yet the earth remains for ever.
So the sun rises,
 then the sun comes panting to its place,
 rising there again.
Going to the south and turning to the north,
 turning, turning, goes the wind,
 and upon its turns the wind returns.
All the rivers go to the sea,
 yet the sea is not full;
 to a place where rivers go,
 there they go again.
Everything is wearying beyond what one could say.
 Eyes are not satisfied by what they see,
 and ears are not full of hearing.
What has been, it will be,
 and what has been done is what will be done,
 so there is nothing new under the sun.
It is said, "See this? It's new!"
 Already it has existed for ages before us.
There is no memory of those who were earlier,
 nor of those to come will there be any memory by their successors.

(Eccles. 1:2–11 Fredericks)

The wording of verse 2—" 'Breath of breaths,' said Qoheleth, 'Breath of breaths. Everything is temporary!' "—is almost exactly the same as Ecclesiastes 12:8.

These two verses form bookends and encapsulate the entire meaning of the book. From an under-the-sun perspective, everything is like a breath from a temporal perspective. The opening poem summarizes everything that happens as an endlessly repetitive cycle of transient events. Qoheleth mentions work (1:3), the human cycle (1:4), and the natural rhythms of the cosmos (1:5–7). In light of these never-ending cycles, everything seems fleeting—and yet, our eyes are never satisfied by what we see, nor are our ears content with what we hear (1:8). We want to know more and hear new things, but our eyes and ears are unsatisfied because there's nothing new for us to experience (1:9–10). The poem concludes by pointing out the fact that once we die, everything we have done will be forgotten (1:11).

While some interpreters argue that this opening sets a cynical tone for the rest of the book, "it seems more likely that Qoheleth is attempting to compare the fleeting nature of human life to the longevity of the cosmos."[42] When the lives of finite people are compared to the cycles of nature, they seem fleeting indeed. This is why Qoheleth makes the case that we should put God in our lives (12:13–14). For those who decline to do so, "life in a broken world under the sun is all they have to look forward to" and "this, according to Qoheleth, is what defines true futility."[43]

THE FUTILITY OF QOHELETH'S EXPERIMENTS (ECCLES. 1:12–2:3)

In this section, Qoheleth draws a number of conclusions from his experiments "under the sun" or "under the skies." He writes:

> I, Qoheleth, have been king over Israel in Jerusalem and I have devoted myself to search and explore with wisdom everything done under the skies. It is a tragic affliction God has given to afflict the sons of men. I have observed all the activity done under the sun, and really, it is all temporary and like the whim of the wind. What has been twisted cannot be straightened, and what is lacking cannot be counted.
>
> I said to myself, "Really, I have amassed and increased wisdom beyond all my predecessors in Jerusalem because my heart has examined wisdom and knowledge thoroughly."
> Because I devoted myself to know wisdom and knowledge, madness and folly, I know this also is like the whim of the wind. Surely, in much wisdom there is much sorrow, and increasing knowledge increases grief.
> I said to myself, "Go ahead, and let me test you with pleasure, so enjoy what is good." But really it was also temporary. I said, "Laughter is madness, but joy—what does this accomplish?"
> I explored with my heart how to drag my flesh along with wine while my heart guided me along with wisdom in order to grasp folly until I might see

what is good for the sons of men to do under the skies the few days of their lives. (Eccles. 1:12–2:3 Fredericks)

Qoheleth here mentions his experimentation with pleasure (2:1), laughter (2:2), and wine (2:3), and then he recounts further experiments with massive building projects (2:4), the construction of gardens and parks (2:5), pools (2:6), the acquisition of male and female slaves (2:7), flocks and herds (2:7), the accumulation of silver, gold, and other treasures (2:8), and so on, all the way to 2:26. C. L. Seow explains that Qoheleth's presentation of himself and his pursuits presupposes the genre of royal propaganda, which lauded the wealth and power of kings in royal inscriptions.[44] After Qoheleth introduces himself as having been "king over Israel in Jerusalem" (1:12), "one expects, then, the text to tell of the king's extraordinary achievements and how the king is better off than other people."[45] Instead, he ironically "uses these very things as a foil to show the futility of using them as a goal in life."[46] Qoheleth makes the point that if wisdom, wine, women, song, building projects, or any other pursuits under the sun are the singular goal of one's existence, they won't bring fulfillment.

Qoheleth recounts at great length his experiments with pleasure and other pursuits, but he places all of them in the context of what people do "under the skies the few days of their lives" (2:3). He emphasizes how it seems that the time he spent engaged in these pursuits was only a "few days"—an expression that means "a limited number as opposed to an indefinite amount."[47] His point is that far from making an indelible impact on human history, these are transient pursuits undertaken in the course of a transient life. The few days of our lives cannot be crammed full of meaning by the frenetic pursuit of increased possessions or experiences.

TO EVERYTHING THERE IS A SEASON (ECCLES. 3:1–8)

These eight verses that comprise a poem about human activity and God's providence are probably the most well-known verses in the entire book. In 1965, they were made famous by The Byrds's remake of Pete Seeger's folksong *Turn, Turn, Turn*, which describes how there is a time for every purpose under heaven. In this poem, Qoheleth isn't exploring infinite time or eternity as concepts. Instead, knowing that life is finite, he uses Hebrew words that denote singular, temporary moments of time to reflect on the seasons of life.[48]

There is a definite time for everything,
    a suitable time for every choice under the skies.
A time for birthing, but a time for dying;
    a time for planting, but a time for plucking the planted;

A time for killing, but a time for healing;
    a time for demolishing, but a time for building;
A time for weeping, but a time for laughing;
    a time of mourning, but a time of dancing;
A time for discarding stones, but a time for collecting stones;
    A time for embracing, and a time for shunning embracing;
A time for seeking, but a time for destroying;
    A time for keeping, but a time for discarding;
A time for tearing, but a time for sewing;
    A time for being silent, but a time for speaking;
A time for loving, but a time for hating;
    A time for battling, but a time for peace. (Eccles. 3:1–8 Fredericks)

This poem is about the rhythm of the seasons in God's world. It evokes the same sense of order in time we find expressed in the creation account (Gen. 1:1–2:3). The first verse provides a heading and summarizes the poem's content. For all the different activities and events he describes, there appears to be a right time. He states this general principle is in 3:1 and then fleshes out in the rest of the poem.

The importance of time is a major concern in wisdom literature as a whole. Ancient Israel's sages were concerned with what is fitting or appropriate at a particular time.[49] This principle is based on their belief in creation and its orderliness. As Genesis 1 makes clear, part of God's shaping of creation as a wonderful home for humans are the seasons and rhythms he builds into it, to which humans are called to respond as they manifest God's image in the creation.

Some commentators argue that the poem portrays a deterministic world in which humans have no choice. There's a big debate in theology about the concepts of determinism and freedom. Some passages emphasize divine sovereignty, while others emphasize human freedom to make choices with real consequences. How these issues are understood leads to the different doctrinal positions of free will and predestination.[50] Roland Murphy argues that this poem reflects determinism: "Its purpose is to underscore that all events are determined by God and are beyond human control."[51] There are only two activities over which we have no control, and these are being born and dying. Aside from these, every other activity is one in which we can respond at the right time or choose not to. Qoheleth surveys the range of human life and activities in order to show that there's an order that extends across the entirety of God's world and the range of activities we experience in it. By listing fourteen pairs of opposites, he thereby evokes the completeness of human experience (Eccl. 3:2–8).

The first strophe (Eccl. 3:2–3) deals with beginnings and endings. There is a beginning and an end of human life, which includes a time to be born and a time to die. In the same way, there's a beginning and an end in agriculture, which includes a time to plant and a time to pull up what was planted.[52] The verse that says there's a time to kill and a time to heal might raise the question of when it's appropriate to kill. This could refer to legitimate capital punishment, "holy" war, or even the slaughter of an animal, while healing could refer to medical treatment or cultic restoration. The time for "demolishing" and "building" (3:3) could refer to knowing when to tear down a building and when to rebuild, or it could refer to the destruction and reconstruction of buildings in war.

Verses 4 and 5 deal in part with the expression and sharing of emotions. There's a time for grief and a time to celebrate, which have concrete expression in the second half of verse 4 where grief is manifested as mourning and celebration is manifested as dancing. It's not exactly clear to what the first part of verse 5 refers. It may mean clearing a field of stones to prepare it for sowing or some other kind of work. The gathering of stones may then refer to collecting them for building. The second half of verse 5 deals with embracing, which is an expression of affection or care, which is appropriate at certain times and inappropriate at others. Verse 6 probably has to do with possessions. There's a time to seek new ones and a time to let them go; a time to hold onto possessions and a time to get rid of them.

The context of verse 7 may have to do with mourning. It talks about "a time to tear," which could refer to the tearing of a garment during a time of grief. In this case, "a time to repair" would refer to the repairing of the garment at the end of the period of mourning. The theme of mourning continues into the second line of verse 7, which may be addressing the issue of appropriate responses during a time of mourning. If it's more general, then it may simply be addressing the fact that there are appropriate times to speak and appropriate times to remain silent. Verse 8 deals with personal emotions and their public correlates (war and peace). "Love" and "hate" can refer to emotions, but they can also have political implications.

Ultimately, the poem of Ecclesiastes 3:1–8 is about the "seasons" of life, which are finite periods of time established by God, and the discernment needed to make the right decisions during those seasons. It's important to make good decisions during these seasons because they're limited in duration. Like the seasons in nature, the seasons of life come and go.

ETERNITY IN THEIR HEARTS (ECCLES. 3:9–15)

In light of the poem of Ecclesiastes 3:1–8, Qoheleth recognizes that there's an order to creation, although it's difficult to grasp. When he looks at what he sees from an under-the-sun perspective, it all too often seems to lead to a dead end (3:9–10). There are, however, things he knows to be true from a beyond-the-sun perspective, which he presents in verses 14–15:

> What advantage has the worker in all his labour? I have seen the affliction God has given to afflict the sons of men.
>
> He has made everything beautiful in its time. He has also given them the sense of eternity in their hearts so that humanity will not understand the deeds God does from beginning to end. I know, then, there is nothing better for them than to be happy and to do good in their life. Surely, everyone should eat, drink and enjoy one's labour; it is God's gift.
>
> I know that everything God does will remain for eternity; nothing can be added on, and from it nothing can be taken, for God works so that they will revere him. Whatever is already has been, and whatever is to be already has been because God seeks what has been pursued before. (Eccles. 3:9–15 Fredericks)

The question with which Qoheleth begins (3:9) implies that humankind has no advantage apart from God (3:14). When viewed from a perspective under the sun, this is true. And yet Qoheleth knows that God has "made everything beautiful in its time" (3:11). This is a significant statement, and Peterson explains that "the rhythmic nature of life reveals a God of order, a similar picture painted in Genesis 1 with the rhythm of the creation days."[53] God has also placed "the sense of eternity in their hearts," even though they cannot fully comprehend the ways of God in this life (3:11). This "sense of eternity drives us to honour God and to submit to his will" in the "narrow window" available to us."[54]

JUDGMENT AND THE FUTURE BELONG TO GOD (ECCLES. 3:16–20)

In the following passage, Qoheleth addresses the problem of injustice "under the sun," in a world broken by sin:

> Furthermore, I have observed under the sun that in a place of justice there is wickedness instead, and in a place of fairness there is wickedness instead. I said to myself, "God will judge the righteous and the wicked, for there is a time for every choice and for every deed there."
>
> I said to myself concerning the sons of men, "God severely tests them to show them that they are themselves but an animal," since it happens to the sons of men and to the animal alike, the same for both—as one dies, so dies the other because there is one breath to both. So there is not an advantage to humanity over the beast, for both are temporary. Both go to one place. Both are from the dust, and both return to the dust. Who knows the breath of the sons of men, when it ascends above; and the breath of the beast, when it descends towards the earth?

> So I have observed that nothing is better than that one enjoys his activity, for it is his reward, since who will reveal to him what will succeed him?
>
> (3:16–20 Fredericks)

Despite the fact that too often the righteous suffer and the wicked prosper "under the sun," Qoheleth proclaims that judgment and the future belong to God. While some interpreters argue that there was no belief in resurrection or judgment beyond the grave at this point in ancient Israel's history, there are other passages in Ecclesiastes that suggest otherwise (cf. esp. Eccles. 11:9; 12:7). Likewise, by the time of the writing of Ecclesiastes, there were already other texts in circulation that contain the idea of judgment in the afterlife and even resurrection.[55]

IT IS FITTING TO FIND JOY DURING THE FEW DAYS OF OUR LIVES (ECCLES. 5:18–20)

Even in the midst of a life "under the sun," wisdom lies in finding joy in life as God blesses it. Qoheleth writes:

> Look at what I saw: it is good and beautiful to eat and to drink and to enjoy one's labour which one labours under the sun the few days of one's life that God gives, since it is one's reward. Really, everyone to whom God gives riches and wealth and has empowered him to eat from them and take his reward, happy is his labour—this is God's gift! So he will not dwell on the days of his life for long because God answers through the joy in his heart. (Eccles. 5:18–20 Fredericks)

While there are those who are unable to be satisfied with what they have in the present, this passage emphasizes that "to be able rightly and fully to enjoy the things of this world is a gift of God's grace."[56] It's appropriate to find enjoyment in life and in God's gifts during "the few days of one's life that God gives, since it is one's reward" (5:18).[57] In fact, "God has made it possible to forget about one's ephemeral life (see also 6:12; 9:9) through the enjoyment of life."[58]

THE FRUSTRATION OF DESIRES (ECCLES. 6:1–9)

In the following passage, Qoheleth returns to a theme he explored earlier in 5:18–20, which is the problem of enjoying the good gifts of life "under the sun." There may be several reasons, both internal and external, that we're unable to enjoy God's good gifts. Here, he provides several case studies:

> There is a tragedy I have seen under the sun, and it is overwhelming for humanity: a man to whom God gives riches, wealth and honour so that he lacks nothing he desires for himself, but God does not empower him to eat from them because a stranger eats from them. This is temporary and a sickening evil.

> If a man fathers a hundred children and lives many years—because there are so many days in his years—but his soul is not satisfied with goodness, or he has no gravesite, I say the miscarriage is better off. For he comes in brevity and leaves in darkness; in darkness even his name is covered. He does not even see or experience the sun. There is more rest for him than for the other. Even if the father lived two thousand years but did not enjoy any goodness, do not both go to the same place?
>
> All one's labour is for his mouth, but even the appetite is not satisfied. Really, what advantage does the wise have over the fool? What is there for the afflicted who know how to walk wisely before the living? The view of the eyes is better than the roving of the soul. This too is temporary and like the whim of the wind.
>
> (Eccles. 6:1–9 Fredericks)

In the first case, Qoheleth provides further examples of the transitory nature of the fruits of our labors (6:1–2). In the next case, he makes the point that our children—whether one or many—cannot assuage discontentedness (6:3). In another case, a stillborn child is better off than the person who lives a long life but is dissatisfied, since the child has more rest than the other (6:4–5). Rhetorically, Qoheleth asks whether, even if he lived two thousand years without contentedness, he would be any better off than the stillborn child (6:6). He may be able to feed his body, but he's unable to fill the hunger in his soul (6:7). Those of us who work to acquire riches or labor just to survive all share the same fate (6:8). In the end, it's better for us if we can find satisfaction with what we can already see with our eyes—that is, what we already have—rather than long for what we don't have (6:9a). Even if we find fulfillment in what we already have, we need to remember that this too is "temporary and like the whim of the wind" (6:9b).

A BALANCED VIEW OF LIFE (ECCLES. 6:10–7:14)

In this next passage, Qoheleth explores what can be known in light of the restrictions placed on humanity due to the fall and the limitations of living "under the sun."

> Whatever is, already has been identified and its nature known—a man indeed is unable to prevail against whatever is stronger than himself. Since there are many things that increase impermanence, what advantage is there for a man? Who knows what is good in life for a man the few days of his brief life, for he spends them as a shadow. For, who can tell him what will be after him under the sun? A good name is better than previous burial ointments, but the day of death is better than the day of his birth. Better to go to a funeral home than to a party house, since it is everybody's destination and the living take it to heart.

Sorrow is better than laughter,
>   for in a tragic face is a heart matured.
A wise heart is at a funeral home,
>   but a foolish heart is at a house of pleasure.
Better to hear rebuke from the wise
>   than for a man to hear a song of fools.
Really, as the crackling thorns under a pot,
>   is the fool's laughter.
>   Also this is temporary.
Surely extortion makes a fool of a wise person,
>   and a bribe destroys one's heart.
Better is the end of a matter than its beginning;
>   and the patient spirit is better than the proud spirit.
Do not rush your spirit to be angry,
>   for anger rests in the gut of fools.
Do not say, "what was it about the previous days that was better than these?"
>   since asking this does not come from wisdom.
Wisdom is good with an inheritance,
>   so there is an advantage for those who see the sun.
For wisdom is a shadow—money is a shadow;
>   yet the advantage to knowledge is that wisdom gives life to its masters.
Consider the work of God—for who can make straight what he has bent?
>   In the pleasant days, be pleased; but in a tragic day consider—surely God
>   has made the one as well as the other in order than man will not discover
>   anything after him. (Eccles. 6:10–7:14 Fredericks)

In this section, Qoheleth explains that in our lives "under the sun," we face an uphill battle against impermanence, since there are many things that increase it (6:11). He asks, "What is good in life" that is spent "as a shadow?" (6:12), and then he provides a series of instructions as sayings or proverbs (7:1–14). He cautions us not to think about how the "good old days" were better than today. Such questions don't arise from wisdom (7:10). Idealizations of the past are often inaccurate and unhelpful in the present. In the end, Qoheleth urges us to "take things as they come, accepting good when it is available and facing adversity when that is the reality" (7:14).[59] After all, neither is permanent.

Learning to Number Our Days

While the invention of the clock and the development of "clock time" has altered our view of time and led us to think we can master it and even find fulfillment through it, Qoheleth teaches us otherwise. Although there are many lessons he can teach us about time, I will highlight three of the most prescient.

First, we won't find our way back to the sacred by obliterating or escaping from time. In fact, quite the opposite is true: "The sacred will need to be found within time."[60] God has allotted all of us a "life span," and this is what defines us as human creatures. "In its particularity," writes Ephraim Radner, "this life span is the very means by which human beings relate to God."[61]

Second, while our culture of speed would lead us to believe that constant acceleration is the answer to managing our relationship to time, Qoheleth views time in terms of seasons (esp. Eccles. 3:1–8), something over which we have no control. Seasons come and seasons go. We can't force their arrival nor can we prevent their departure. Wajcman suggests, "Rather than being endemically pressed for time, perhaps we are confused about what time we are living in."[62] Qoheleth would agree. If we can learn to recognize the current season and then embrace it rather than wish it were another time of the year, we can learn to appreciate and enjoy those special things that belong to those times (Eccles. 3:11)—like watching ice crystals form on a window while sipping a hot beverage during the dead of winter or anticipating the first flowers in early spring. There is always something going on—if we're quiet and appreciative enough to notice it.

Third, Qoheleth's conclusions about coping with transience are liberating. In several of the passages we considered above, he identifies futile pursuits and advises their abandonment for those truly worthy of wise attention. Daniel Fredericks suggests that coping with transience in all its manifestations "involves resignation to some degree," and that "it should be a relief for the wise to know what potential success there is to any effort, and if it is nil, to be free to redirect one's time and energy."[63] If we, like Qoheleth, can learn to appreciate what is truly worthy of our attention during the brief time we have in this life, then we will have truly discovered "what is good for the sons of men to do under the skies the few days of their lives" (Eccles. 2:3 Fredericks).

Psalm 90 echoes all three of these concerns with time.[64] Its author asks the Lord to "teach us to count our days that we may gain a wise heart" (v. 12). The psalmist's concern is not that the Lord would simply help him "to count" his days in the sense of numbering them sequentially, but to help him "realize how short, how fleeting, life actually is."[65] He observes that "the days of our life are seventy years, or perhaps eighty, if we are strong," and that they "pass away . . . [and] come to an end like a sigh" (Ps. 90:9–10). In light of the transience of life, the psalmist prays that the Lord would teach us to count our days so "that we may gain a wise heart" (Ps. 90:12). Allen Ross explains that "a heart characterized by wisdom signifies a person who has the right affections and makes the proper choices." A person with such a heart would "live their lives with moral and ethical skill [and] produce things that are honoring to God and beneficial to the community. . . . In view of the brevity of life, people need to learn how to use what God has given them to live a righteous and productive life."[66] This is a wise prayer indeed.

Toward the New Testament

This belief in the transience of life reflects conventional Jewish wisdom that's also found in the New Testament. For example, Jesus urges his disciples not to worry about their lives (cf. Matt. 6:25–34; Luke 12:22–31) and rhetorically asks, "Which of you by worrying can add a single hour to your span of life?" (Matt. 6:27). He urges disciples to "seek first the kingdom of God and his righteousness, and all these things will be given to you as well" (Matt. 6:33). James, whose letter is often described as wisdom literature of the New Testament, closely mirrors Ecclesiastes when he talks about making plans for the future in light of life's transience. "Yet you do not even know what tomorrow will bring. What is your life? For you are a mist that appears for a little while and then vanishes" (James 4:14).

The apostle Paul likewise emphasizes the importance of wisdom for the Christian life. It is a frequent theme in Ephesians,[67] in which he urges the believers at Ephesus to be careful to live "not as unwise people but as wise, making the most of the time, because the days are evil" (Eph. 5:15–16). While Paul identifies the "days" or current age as "evil" rather than transient, his message is not dissimilar. In the immediate context, he writes in anticipation of the coming resurrection of the dead (5:13–14). When he writes that "the days are evil" (5:16), therefore, it's clear he's referring to the "last" days.[68] He believes that the return of Christ was immanent and therefore time was short. It's in light of this view that he urges the Ephesians to make the most of their time, by which he means that they should use it "with utmost effectiveness toward particular opportunities."[69] The need to use our time wisely in light of the coming resurrection is a theme Paul emphasized in his other epistles as well (see also Gal. 6:10; Col. 4:5).

Several decades ago, Oscar Cullman wrote a landmark study of time titled *Christ and Time*, in which he explained that all of human history relates back to the birth of Christ as its reference point.[70] Time is fulfilled in Christ, which means that everything that needs to be accomplished in human history has been accomplished in Christ.[71] He is the Alpha and the Omega, the beginning and the end (Rev. 22:13). John Swinton builds on this idea:

If everything that has to be done has been done for us in Jesus, human beings have no real need to race along trying to do everything on their own, in their own time, and by their own strength. . . .We are freed to slow down and learn what it looks like to accept that everything that is important for the redemption of the world has actually been achieved and, paradoxically, continues to be achieved by, in, and through Jesus.[72]

In light of this, he suggests that "the Christian calling will be to live out a different understanding of time and to learn how to dwell peaceably within God's time."[73]

Swinton points to the book *Three Mile an Hour God*, in which Japanese theologian Kosuke Koyama observes that the average speed at which a person walks is three miles an hour, and therefore when Jesus walked among the people of ancient Palestine, he walked three miles an hour.[74] This is so apropos to our culture of acceleration, in which we're always wanting to speed up. In *Becoming Friends of Time*, Swinton asks:

"Who are you following?" If Jesus is walking at three miles per hour and we are walking at six miles per hour, who are we following? God's love is slow; it takes time. Faithful discipleship is slow and attentive to the things that pass us by when we insist on traveling at high speed. There is a great power in slowness.[75]

Swinton concludes, "When we learn to slow down, we begin to see the world as God sees it."[76] He urges readers to become "friends of time" and explains that friends of time don't spend their days resisting and wrestling with time but learn instead to accept and cherish it.[77]

Time, slowness, gentleness, perseverance, and love: these are the qualities of people who have become friends of time. Time should not be our enemy; it should be our friend. The redemption of time has to do with turning time from an overbearing ruler into a gentle friend.[78]

I think Qoheleth would agree.

DEATH

When I was growing up in Alabama in the 1970s, Southern culture was quite formal. When there was a funeral at church, everyone was expected to go. It was customary for the body of the deceased to be presented in an open casket, which was placed at the front and center of the church's sanctuary. If the husband or wife of the deceased was living, they would stand beside the head of the casket. As people arrived, they walked down the center aisle to the casket, where they viewed the body and then expressed their sympathy to the spouse of the deceased before being seated. When there were funerals at church, my Nana had me walk with her down the aisle to view the body and greet the surviving spouse.

One of my earliest experiences of these funerals was that of Mrs. McAdams. I remember that when my Nana and I walked down the aisle and I saw Mrs. McAdams lying in the casket, I was baffled and uncomfortable. She was dressed in her Sunday best, with makeup on and a lovely hairdo, but she lay perfectly still inside the open casket. I wasn't sure what to think. As my Nana talked with some of Mrs. McAdams's family members who were standing at the head of the casket, I continued to watch Mrs. McAdams, wondering if I might detect movement.

While my Nana visited with the family, other ladies arrived at the casket, and they all stood around it together looking at Mrs. McAdams. I don't remember any of them crying, but I do remember them saying things like "Doesn't she look lovely?" or "Doesn't she look so natural?" or "Doesn't she just look so peaceful?" These remarks perplexed me because they seemed to suggest that Mrs. McAdams was only resting or something. Wasn't she dead? And, if she was dead, then what did that really mean? These early experiences left me confused about the meaning of death and its implications, and they did little to prepare me for encountering it as an adult.

The American Way of Death

The basic definition of death, according to Wikipedia, "is the cessation of all biological functions that sustain an organism."[1] Out of all human experiences, there is nothing more overwhelming in its implications than death. And yet, in contemporary American society, a culture of the denial of death has developed.[2] At least seven factors contribute to and perpetuate this.

First, death is a taboo subject. We just don't talk about it. In the 1918 Spanish flu pandemic, there were neighborhoods in the United States where corpses lined the streets and only a few people left alive to bury them. In order to keep up with the volume of bodies, the deceased often had to be buried in mass graves. This meant that the rituals and ceremonies that used to mark a loved one's death—such as displaying the body of the deceased in the parlor for a wake—were absent.[3] Geoffrey Gorer argues that when mourning rituals ceased to be practiced, people no longer had a way to process their grief. It became customary not to talk about death, and people eventually forgot how to do so.[4] Today, we find it nearly impossible to talk about our own personal grief, and the result is that the very topic of death has become off limits.

Second, indirect language is used to avoid talking or even thinking about death. Instead of saying that someone has died, we say they have "passed away." We don't say that someone is being embalmed, but that they are being "prepared." Instead of saying that the deceased is being buried, we say they are being "laid to rest." We don't describe the deceased as a corpse but refer to their "remains." We no longer use the term "undertaker" but have transformed this occupation into a "funeral director." These kinds of euphemisms are ways of trying to temper the bluntness of words that directly connote death.[5]

Third, death is treated as a medical crisis that can be avoided rather than a natural process. You never hear of people dying of mortality anymore. Instead, each death is viewed as a medical failure and explained as the product of a particular cause such as lung cancer, heart failure, a stroke, and so on. When someone's cause of death is "unexplained," friends and family members may be deeply troubled, as if their death may have been avoidable and contingent.[6]

Fourth, death is hidden. Beginning around 1945, the dying are hospitalized instead of remaining at home, which means we no longer see them in our day-to-day routines. Even more, as lifespans have increased over the past several generations, it's become more common for people to live with chronic disease and disability for months or even years before death. In such cases, full-time care may be required during the last days, weeks, months, or even years of life, and it's difficult to manage adequate care at home. The need for such care led to the rise of hospice and palliative care.[7] Although this eases the burden on the family, it further sequesters death and dying from our culture.

Fifth, the funerary industry puts a facade over the reality of death.[8] Tony Evans caricatures the ways the funerary industry does this.[9] He notes that funeral parlors have professional makeup artists who dress up the deceased and make them look as lifelike as possible: "I've seen some people look better dead than they ever looked alive." He observes that at the visitation, the head of the deceased is carefully positioned on a satin pillow, as if resting comfortably. He satirically notes how the casket is eased into the ground by a nickel-plated machine, so as not to wake the deceased. The entire funerary industry is designed to mute the reality of death.

Sixth, contemporary Christianity has even contributed to the denial of death through its insistence on personal immortality, or at least the inherent immortality of the soul.[10] This may be the most prevalent view of death in the Western world today, and many Christians take for granted that it's a Christian idea.[11] However, it actually has its origin in the teaching of the Greek philosophers Pythagoras (c. 570–495 BC), Plato (ca. 427–347 BC), and Plutarch (AD 46–after AD 119),[12] who taught that the body is physical and mortal but that the soul is nonphysical and immortal. In this view, the soul, which is housed in the physical body, is the true essence of a person, and when they die, it's released to live forever. While the Greeks were certainly saddened by the death of a loved one or a friend, their sorrow was mitigated by the belief that the deceased's essence would survive.[13]

Seventh, the trend toward the replacement of funerals with a "Celebration of Life" fosters the avoidance of the subject of death. Whereas a traditional funeral is structured around a liturgy, a "Celebration of Life" focuses on stories about the deceased.[14] The emphasis here is on remembering and celebrating the life of loved ones and honoring their achievements. Rev. Fleming Rutledge criticizes these because they are less biblical and "celebrate the person's life independently of the power of Death."[15]

In these and other ways, our culture helps us "deny, manipulate, distort, or camouflage death so that it is a less difficult threat with which to cope."[16] The denial of death in modern American society is fostered and reinforced by these seven factors. Death is removed from public spaces and kept at the margins of our personal lives. Even modern religion fails to deal effectively with death. The focus of our society—in both secular and religious realms—is on the individual, and the quintessentially modern individual is young and never dies.[17]

The denial of death and the refusal to face it are so deeply rooted in our culture that some seem to believe that death itself can actually be eliminated.

For example, Dr. David Sinclair, codirector of the Paul F. Glenn Labs for the Biology of Aging and Professor of Genetics at Harvard Medical School, argues that life can not only be extended and vitality prolonged, but that death itself can actually be conquered. In a recent book titled *Lifespan: Why We Age, and Why We Don't Have To*, to the question of what the upward limit might be for the human lifespan, he answers, "I don't think there is one . . . and many of my colleagues agree."[18] He asserts, "There is no biological law that says we must age. . . . Those who say there is don't know what they're talking about. We're probably a long way off from a world in which death is a rarity, but we're not far from pushing it ever further into the future."[19] Dr. Sinclair believes that it's possible for humankind to reach "a time of ending the inevitable."[20]

Beliefs about Death and the Afterlife in Ancient Israel

The ancient Israelite view of death and what happens to someone after they die is quite different from the contemporary views discussed above. In the ancient world, people generally believed that those who died went to the "abode of the dead." In the Old Testament, the most common term for this "abode" in the Old Testament is *Sheol* (שְׁאוֹל).[21]

SHEOL: ABODE OF THE DEAD

This term for the underworld occurs sixty-six times in the Old Testament. Although there is little description of it, there are some occasional glimpses. Some passages seem to describe it as a vast, subdivided burial chamber (see, e.g., Ezek. 32:21–28). It's also not entirely clear who was thought to go to Sheol. Some argue that only the wicked went there, but it appears these ancient people saw it as the place for everyone who died.[22]

Those who went to Sheol are sometimes called "shades" (רְפָאִים), which are "lifeless, nebulous, shadowy creatures in the underworld" who "never have any contact with the living."[23] It also seems they were thought to be completely alienated from God. In Psalm 88, for example, the psalmist complains that he is "like the slain who lie in the grave, whom you remember no more, who are cut off from your care" (v. 5 NIV). He goes on to ask the Lord about the state of those who die:

> Do you show your wonders to the dead?
> Do their spirits rise up and praise you?

Is your love declared in the grave,
  your faithfulness in Destruction?
Are your wonders known in the place of darkness,
  or your righteous deeds in the land of oblivion? (Ps. 88:10–12 NIV)

It seems that these shades were not able to praise the Lord (Ps. 88:10) and were thought to be so lethargic, they would have to be roused whenever somebody new arrived (Isa. 14:9–10). Sheol seems to have been conceived of as a lifeless place where its inhabitants were half asleep (e.g., Isa. 14:9–10).[24] These views about the afterlife and the state of the dead were not entirely unique to ancient Israel as many other Near Eastern cultures held similar views.[25]

THEODICY AND THE PRINCIPLE OF DIVINE RETRIBUTION

Contemporary Christian readers, who are accustomed to the idea of rewards and punishments in the afterlife, may find ancient Israel's views troubling. If the righteous and the wicked all have the same destiny in the hereafter, then how can God be just? The technical term for this conundrum is "theodicy," which combines the Greek words for "God" (*theos*) and "justice" (*dikē*), and literally means "God-justice."[26] The question of theodicy is concerned with the justice of God in a seemingly unjust world.

The ancient Israelites were certainly concerned with the justice of God, but they also believed in the principle of retribution (as we discussed in an earlier chapter). The book of Deuteronomy, which was essentially ancient Israel's constitutional document, articulated the principle of retribution in a passage often referred to as the "blessings and curses" (Deut. 28).[27] This passage teaches that those who are faithful to God's covenant will be rewarded with long and prosperous lives, while those who defy it and live wickedly will experience curses and may even have their lives cut short. In other words, God's retributive justice would be brought to bear in this life.[28]

Theodicy, Retribution, and Death
in Wisdom Literature

Ancient Israel's sages clearly believed in the principle of retribution, and it is reflected in many of the wisdom psalms as we will see below.

DIVINE RETRIBUTION IN WISDOM LITERATURE

Deuteronomy 28:1–14 states that the righteous will be given long life as a reward, and Psalm 91 assures the righteous of God's protection.

> Those who love me, I will deliver;
>> I will protect those who know my name.
> When they call to me, I will answer them;
>> I will be with them in trouble,
>> I will rescue them and honor them.
> With long life I will satisfy them,
>> and show them my salvation. (vv. 14–16)

Several psalms describe how faithfulness to the covenant and its command-ments leads to blessing. Psalm 111 explains that because God "is ever mindful of his covenant," he provided food for his people and established them in the land (vv. 5–6).[29] The rest of the psalm lauds the covenant and the blessings that come from being obedient:

> The works of his hands are faithful and just;
>> all his precepts are trustworthy.
> They are established forever and ever,
>> to be performed with faithfulness and uprightness.
> He sent redemption to his people;
>> he has commanded his covenant forever.
>> Holy and awesome is his name.
> The fear of the LORD is the beginning of wisdom;
>> all those who practice it have a good understanding.
> His praise endures forever. (vv. 7–10)

Although it doesn't specifically mention long life, Psalm 112 likewise praises God for his faithfulness to his covenant. For those who delight in his commandments (112:1), blessings will ensue (112:2–10). Psalm 119, a hymn to God's law, exclaims that "if your law had not been my delight, I would have perished in my misery" (119:92). However, the psalmist remembers the Lord's precepts and how through them, God gave him life (119:93). The psalmist repeatedly appeals to the Lord to preserve his life according to God's promise or on the basis of God's justice (e.g., Pss. 119:149, 154, 156, 159).

Just as the ancient Israelites believed that the righteous would be given long life as a reward for covenant obedience, they also believed that the lives of the wicked would be cut short (Deut. 28:15–68). Psalm 49, for example, warns those who put their trust in riches that they "cannot abide in their pomp," but that "they are like the animals that perish" (49:12).

> Such is the fate of the foolhardy,
>> the end of those who are pleased with their lot. *Selah*
> Like sheep they are appointed for Sheol;
>> Death shall be their shepherd;

straight to the grave they descend,
    and their form shall waste away;
    Sheol shall be their home. (vv. 13–14)

Likewise, Psalm 52 pronounces judgment on the deceitful. Although they plot destruction (52:1–4), God will not let them get away with it:

But God will break you down forever;
    he will snatch and tear you from your tent;
    he will uproot you from the land of the living. (v. 5)

The righteous will see and fear and continue to put their trust in God and find their refuge in him (52:5–7). As a result, while the wicked die, the righteous are established "like a green olive tree in the house of God" (52:8).

Psalm 53 emphasizes the permanence of death as a punishment for the wicked who deny God and commit abominable acts (53:1).

There they shall be in great terror,
    in terror such as has not been.
For God will scatter the bones of the ungodly
    they will be put to shame, for God has rejected them. (v. 5)

If someone's bones were scattered, it meant they couldn't receive a proper burial (e.g., Jer. 8:1–2; 2 Chron. 34:5). Allowing a body to decay above ground or be destroyed was a great dishonor (e.g., 1 Kings 14:10–14; 2 Kings 9: 34–37) and a sign of divine judgment.[30] The Israelites may also have believed that the scattering of someone's bones prevented them from being able to rest in the underworld.[31] For God to scatter the bones of the ungodly, therefore, is a way of saying that he would leave them permanently destroyed.

In Psalm 73, the psalmist explains that, at first, he was envious of the wicked since they seem to prosper despite their wickedness (vv. 1–2). They seem to cruise through life without difficulty, experiencing good health and great wealth, while they scoffed at both the poor and at God (vv. 4–9). Ultimately, however, they will not end well:

Truly you set them in slippery places;
    you make them fall to ruin.
How they are destroyed in a moment,
    swept away utterly by terrors!
They are like a dream when one awakes;
    on awaking you despise their phantoms. (vv. 18–20)

Psalm 92:7 pronounces that although the wicked sprout like grass and appear to flourish, they "are doomed to destruction forever."[32] Psalm 94 focuses on how God will avenge the righteous and exclaims that although the wicked seek to oppress the righteous, God will strike them down.[33]

> He will repay them for their iniquity
>> and wipe them out for their wickedness;
>> the LORD our God will wipe them out. (v. 23)

While the wicked will be destroyed, the life of the righteous will be preserved.

> Do not put your trust in princes,
>> in mortals, in whom there is no help.
> When their breath departs, they return to the earth;
>> on that very day their plans perish. (Ps. 146:3–4)

ALL HUMANKIND SHARES THE SAME FATE

The ancient Israelites were not under any illusion, however, that while the wicked prospered they would somehow live forever. They recognized that in the end, everyone dies.

> For the ransom of life is costly,
>> and can never suffice,
> that one should live on forever
>> and never see the pit.
>
> When we look at the wise, they die;
>> fool and dolt perish together
>> and leave their wealth to others.
> Their graves are their homes forever,
>> their dwelling places to all generations,
>> though they named lands their own. (Ps. 49:8–11)

The entirety of Psalm 90 is a lengthy meditation on the transitory nature of human life,[34] contrasting God's eternality with human frailty. After praising God as having existed from "everlasting to everlasting" (v. 2), the psalmist writes,

> You turn us back to dust,
>> and say, "Turn back, you mortals."
> For a thousand years in your sight
>> are like yesterday when it is past,
>> or like a watch in the night.
>
> You sweep them away; they are like a dream,
>> like grass that is renewed in the morning;

in the morning it flourishes and is renewed;
in the evening it fades and withers. . . .
For all our days pass away under your wrath;
our years come to an end like a sigh.
The days of our life are seventy years,
or perhaps eighty, if we are strong;
even then their span is only toil and trouble;
they are soon gone, and we fly away. (vv. 3–6, 9–10)

In spite of the theology of retribution, we understand that life naturally ends in death for everyone. Some scriptural traditions seem to hold to an idea of a "good" death, which was when someone died with plenty of children and at an old age (e.g., Gen. 25:8; 46:30). The report about the death of Abraham, for example, reads this way:

This is the length of Abraham's life, one hundred seventy-five years. Abraham breathed his last and died in a good old age, old and full of years, and was gathered to his people. (Gen. 25:7–8)

VIEWS ABOUT DEATH IN WISDOM LITERATURE

When we turn to wisdom literature, however, we find mixed views about death. In the book of Job, Job's suffering was so great that he cursed the day he was born and wished he was among the dead, as shown here in his heart-breaking lament:

"Why did I not die at birth,
come forth from the womb and expire?
Why were there knees to receive me,
or breasts for me to suck?
Now I would be lying down and quiet;
I would be asleep; then I would be at rest
with kings and counselors of the earth
who rebuild ruins for themselves,
or with princes who have gold,
who fill their houses with silver.
Or why was I not buried like a stillborn child,
like an infant that never sees the light?
There the wicked cease from troubling,
and there the weary are at rest.
There the prisoners are at ease together;
they do not hear the voice of the taskmaster.
The small and the great are there,
and the slaves are free from their masters." (3:11–19)

Apparently, Job believed that in the underworld, he would find peace and rest. The portrayal of Sheol as a place of peace and rest, however, is idiosyncratic and almost without parallel in the Old Testament.[35] David Clines calls Job's account of the underworld in these verses "eccentric."[36] Norman Habel describes it as a "desperate reversal of traditional understandings of that unhappy domain."[37] As we already noted, Sheol spelled gloom, darkness, and forgetfulness (Ps. 88:11–13). It was the bitter reality of his present condition, though, that led him to his preference for death:

> "Why is light given to one in misery,
>   and life to the bitter in soul,
> who long for death, but it does not come,
>   and dig for it more than for hidden treasures;
> who rejoice exceedingly,
>   and are glad when they find the grave?
> Why is light given to one who cannot see the way,
>   whom God has fenced in?
> For my sighing comes like my bread,
>   and my groanings are poured out like water.
> Truly the thing that I fear comes upon me,
>   and what I dread befalls me.
> I am not at ease, nor am I quiet;
>   I have no rest; but trouble comes." (3:20–26)

In these verses, Job compares the intensity of his longing for death to the urgency of treasure hunters who search for hidden riches (3:21). If he could only "find" his grave, he would be happier than those who discover a fortune (3:22). Later, however, he expresses a more traditional view of Sheol:

> "Remember that my life is a breath;
>   my eye will never again see good.
> The eye that beholds me will see me no more;
>   while your eyes are upon me, I shall be gone.
> As the cloud fades and vanishes,
>   so those who go down to Sheol do not come up;
> they return no more to their houses,
>   nor do their places know them any more." (7:7–10)

When he says that those who see him now will never see him again, Job believed he would be "gone" (7:8). The Hebrew literally reads, "I shall not be," which essentially means he will have ceased to exist.[38] Job then uses several analogies, including the dissolution of a cloud, a descent from which there is no ascent, and the cessation of the routine return home after a day's work

(7:10). In the face of such depressing and frightening prospects, Job bursts out in a passionate but despairing prayer to God:

> "Therefore I will not restrain my mouth;
>> I will speak in the anguish of my spirit;
>> I will complain in the bitterness of my soul.
> Am I the Sea or the Dragon,
>> that you set a guard over me?
> When I say, 'My bed will comfort me,
>> my couch will ease my complaint,'
> then you scare me with dreams
>> and terrify me with visions,
> so that I would choose strangling
>> and death rather than this body.
> I loathe my life; I would not live forever.
>> Let me alone, for my days are a breath.
> What are humans, that you make so much of them,
>> that you set your mind on them,
> visit them every morning,
>> test them every moment?
> Will you not look away from me for a while,
>> let me alone until I swallow my spittle?
> If I sin, what do I do to you, you watcher of humanity?
>> Why have you made me your target?
>> Why have I become a burden to you?
> Why do you not pardon my transgression
>> and take away my iniquity?
> For now I shall lie in the earth;
>> you will seek me, but I shall not be." (7:11–21)

Job's prayer ends dramatically with an echo of his earlier lament that his fate was unalterable. He concludes that even if the Lord were to seek him out, he wouldn't be able to find him because he "shall not be" (7:21).

A few chapters later, Job complains of life's brevity and expresses the common Israelite belief in the finality of death:

> "Why did you bring me forth from the womb?
>> Would that I had died before any eye had seen me,
> and were as though I had not been,
>> carried from the womb to the grave.
> Are not the days of my life few?
>> Let me alone, that I may find a little comfort
> before I go, never to return,
>> to the land of gloom and deep darkness,

the land of gloom and chaos,
        where light is like darkness." (10:18–22)

Job's bleak portrayal of the land of death (10:21–22) is in sharp contrast to his earlier description of an underworld where one could have peace, quiet, and rest, and be at ease with those from any station in life (3:13–19). Here, he describes a land of no return, characterized by "gloom and deep darkness" and "gloom and chaos" (10:21–22), which may be intended to recall the conditions that prevailed before creation.[39] In a setting where even "light is like darkness," chaos prevails.

THE FINALITY OF DEATH IN ECCLESIASTES

Death is a major theme in the book of Ecclesiastes, and Qoheleth was fixated on its finality.[40] Death is the great equalizer for all humankind. In the end, both the wise and the foolish die, a fact that troubles Qoheleth, for he asks, "How can the wise die just like fools?" (Eccles. 2:16; cf. also Ps. 49:10, 12). He views the recurring curse of death as God's way of proving to humanity that they are animals, finite mammals who are also merely God's creations:

> I said to myself with regard to humans that God is testing them to show that they are but animals. For the fate of humans and the fate of animals is the same; as one dies, so dies the other. They all have the same breath, and humans have no advantage over the animals, for all is vanity. All go to one place, all are from the dust, and all turn to dust again. Who knows whether the human spirit goes upward and the spirit of animals goes downward to the earth? (Eccles. 3:18–21)

Humans have the same breath as animals, are equally dust, and share the same fate.[41] Qoheleth seems uncertain about whether or not there is any difference in their fate. This is not to say that there is no difference between humans and animals, since humans are made in the image of God (Gen. 1:27).[42] What Qoheleth is certain about, however, is that the lives of both humans and animals are temporary.[43]

Qoheleth seems most troubled that the wise die just like the foolish—or even like animals—which seems to contradict the principle of retribution. This contradiction is a recurrent theme in this book.[44] Ecclesiastes 9 explores some of these tragic inversions of justices:

> Indeed, I devoted myself to all of this so to explain it, because the righteous and the wise and their actions are in God's hands. Furthermore, no one knows when either love or hatred will come—both are ahead. Both occur to everyone the same: for the righteous and the wicked, for the good and for the clean and for

the unclean, for those sacrificing and for those not sacrificing; as for the good as for the sinner, the one who swears an oath as the one who fears an oath. This is a tragedy in all that is done under the sun; indeed, there is the same event to both, since even the heart of the sons of man is full of evil, and madness is in their heart in their lives. Afterwards—to the dead! (9:1–3 Fredericks)

These same occurrences happen to everyone and are followed by death.

One of the most poignant passages is found at the end of Ecclesiastes with the description of aging and death:[45]

Remember your creator in the days of your youth, before the days of trouble come, and the years draw near when you will say, "I have no pleasure in them"; before the sun and the light and the moon and the stars are darkened and the clouds return with the rain; in the day when the guards of the house tremble, and the strong men are bent, and the women who grind cease working because they are few, and those who look through the windows see dimly; when the doors on the street are shut, and the sound of the grinding is low, and one rises up at the sound of a bird, and all the daughters of song are brought low; when one is afraid of heights, and terrors are in the road; the almond tree blossoms, the grasshopper drags itself along, and the caper bud falls; because all must go to their eternal home, and the mourners will go about the streets; before the silver cord is snapped, and the golden bowl is broken, and the pitcher is broken at the fountain, and the wheel broken at the cistern, and the dust returns to the earth as it was, and the breath returns to God who gave it. (12:1–7)

Qoheleth uses metaphor to describe the aging process. As Shannon Burkes summarizes: "The keepers could be the hands, the mighty men the back, the grinders the teeth, and the window-peerers the eyes. Thus, the hands tremble, the back is bent, the teeth are few, and the eyes dim."[46] More images of aging appear in these verses.[47] The climax of the passage comes in verses 6 and 7, where Qoheleth uses a number of metaphors for a person's death (v. 6), followed by the return of their body to dust and their breath to God (v. 7), concluding with the refrain, "Breath of breaths, everything is temporary!" (v. 8 Fredericks).[48]

Some scholars have argued that these views are unorthodox and inconsistent with conventional ancient Israelite thinking.[49] Some have understood it as so negative that they've even compared it to Greek pessimistic literature.[50] These kinds of negative evaluations, however, miss the point. As we noted in chapter 1, Brian Neil Peterson convincingly demonstrates that Qoheleth was evaluating life in light of the fall and its repercussions.[51] When he said that humans are no more than mere beasts who share the same fate as animals (Eccles. 3:18–21), he was admitting that this was how it appeared "under the sun" (3:16) but that only God really knows where humans and animals go after death (3:21–22).[52] When he considers how the same fate comes to both the righteous and the wicked (9:1–3), Qoheleth alerts us to the fact that he was observing the plight of humanity "under the sun" (9:3), where it often seems like there's no difference in outcomes for either lifestyle.[53] As we see in his meditation on aging and death (12:1–7), the realization that a person will experience decline and eventually death should lead us to appreciate the brevity of life and compel us turn to our Creator while we can, especially in the days of our youth (12:1).[54] Peterson argues:

> Qoheleth's instruction on death is not of necessity related to a pessimistic outlook on life, but rather a realist's perspective on the brevity of life. From this vantage point, Qoheleth teaches a very orthodox message on the importance of keeping one's mortality in the forefront of all that one does in life (cf. Ps 144:4). Further, Qoheleth seems to be reflecting on the effects of the fall and how that has shaped all aspects of human existence, none more so than the problem of death (Gen 3:19). This causes a person to think about, and value, the most important aspects of life—God's good gifts—as well as causing one to fear God, a common refrain throughout the book.[55]

Because of life's brevity and the apparent finality of death, Qoheleth wants us to make the most of our lives and, most importantly, to fear the God who gave us life (12:1) along with the ability to enjoy it (2:24; 5:18). This isn't pessimism but a "religious" message that "fits well within the wisdom tradition."[56] If we understand the finality of death through this lens, it can then lead us to both enjoy every moment of our lives and keep the Lord at the forefront of our minds.

Future Hope in Wisdom Literature

The fate of the righteous became an issue especially after the return of the Jews from exile in Babylon. Even though the exiles had returned to the promised land, the Davidic throne could not be reinstated because Israel was still subject to the Persian Empire. Ezra and Nehemiah both viewed the conditions of the returnees as "slavery" (Ezra 9:8; Neh. 9:17). The principle of theodicy seemed to have been subverted and justice had been perverted. Jews who observed the law were experiencing the curses that should have been reserved for the wicked, while the wicked were enjoying the blessings that had been promised to the righteous.[57] Jews reasoned that if God's people were not going to receive justice in this life, then it must be that the Lord would provide it in the afterlife.[58] Although the righteous may suffer and even die prematurely or at the hands of the unjust, and although the wicked may prevail in the here and now, God would set everything straight in the afterlife by giving the righteous their proper reward and the wicked their just punishment.

Job wished he had died at birth (3:11) and said he would rather be strangled than continue suffering (7:15). In the midst of his suffering, however, he exclaimed:

> "For there is hope for a tree,
>> if it is cut down, that it will sprout again,
>> and that its shoots will not cease.
> Though its root grows old in the earth,
>> and its stump dies in the ground,
> yet at the scent of water it will bud
>> and put forth branches like a young plant." (14:7–9)

In the ancient biblical world, trees were symbols of the blessings of shade, protection, and refreshment.[59] They played a special role in ancient Egypt's cult of the dead and since, as we noted in chapter 1, the book of Job reflects some Egyptian vocabulary and thought, Christopher Hays suggests that Job 14:7 may contain an allusion to such trees.[60] There were various tree goddesses in Egyptian lore who were thought to protect and sustain the deceased in the underworld, including Nut, Isis, and Hathor.[61] In the Book of the Dead, various decedents are described as sitting under these trees and enjoying their protection and sustenance.[62] In addition to these tree goddesses, there was also a tradition in which the decedent was explicitly linked to the afterlife tree by means of a connection to the deity Osiris.[63] Late in the New Kingdom period, funerary imagery often contained an "Osirian mound," in which Osiris lay in a crypt buried under a mound topped with a tree planted in the center (fig. 12.1.).[64]

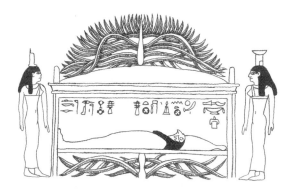

FIGURE 12.1. Sokaris-Osiris buried in an Osirian mound. (Drawing by Sarah A. Hawkins.)

The blossoming tree symbolized the rebirth or resurrection of the deceased. By the Persian period, the belief that one could share in Osiris's rebirth had become widespread in Egypt, and there would have been an awareness of the Osiris-tree myth in the wider Levant, including among Judean authors.[65] Hays suggests that Job may have intended to use this Egyptian belief as a springboard, reasoning that "if there is hope for a tree, how much more should there be hope for a human being?"[66]

Although Hays explores several other passages in Job that express a hope for something beyond death, I will mention only two of the most profound. The first is in Job 14, where Job prays that after he had descended to Sheol, the Lord would "remember" him (14:13). Hays translates the Hebrew verb instead as "summon," in which case it could mean that Job held out hope that God would summon him back from the dead.[67] Job then expresses uncertainty about whether mortals could possibly live again once they had died, but he says he would be willing to wait in the underworld in case release did come (14:14).

> "You would call, and I would answer you;
> you would long for the work of your hands." (14:15)

It seems clear that although Job had made some pessimistic statements about death, he had not given up hope.

The second passage is in Job 29, where he expresses hope for an afterlife using terms that would have been familiar in Egypt. Hays provides the following translation:

> Then I thought, "I shall perish among my clan,
> And I shall multiply my days like the sand;
> My roots spread out to the waters,
> With the dew all night on my branches;
> My soul shall be new within me,
> And my "bow" renewed in my hand. (29:18–20)[68]

Although he would die among his clan, Job hoped that God might "multiply" his days "like sand," even in the afterlife (29:18). Again, recalling the tree image from 14:7, he hopes he might be like a tree with its roots spread out to the waters (29:19).

Among the wisdom psalms, there are a few powerful hints at a hope for something beyond the grave. In Psalm 49, after elaborating on the folly of riches and warning that the wise and foolish alike will perish (49:1–14), the psalmist proclaims,

> But God will ransom my soul from the power of Sheol,
> for he will receive me. (49:15)

The use of the verb "ransom" here provides a contrast to its use in verses 8–9:

> For the ransom of life is costly
>> and can never suffice,
> that one should live on forever
>> and never see the Pit.

While death itself would be the shepherd of the ungodly (49:14), God will ransom the righteous from the power of death. But the psalmist's claim that God would receive him (49:15) is crucial to the meaning of this portion of the psalm. The expression "he will receive me" is used sometimes for being rescued from oppression or potential death (e.g., Ps. 18:16 [17]; Ezek. 36:24; 37:21; Hos. 13:14). However, it can also be translated literally as "he will take me"[69] and is used to describe the psalmist being "taken" so that he did not see death (see 2 Kings 2:3, 5, 9–10). While the psalmist may have meant to refer to his deliverance from worldly oppression in the present, the broader context of the psalm as a whole that deals with death suggests that he meant much more than that. Allen Ross writes, "How much the psalmist actually understood is unclear, but the words convey the idea of a hope that contrasts with the death and descent of the wicked to an unseen world."[70]

In Ecclesiastes, at the end of the Qoheleth's description of aging and death, he writes that "the dust returns to the earth as it was, and the breath returns to God who gave it" (12:7). This may be an allusion to the afterlife. In support of this view, Peterson points to other passages in Ecclesiastes that "seem to reflect some type of hope for the righting of wrongs, namely, retribution, beyond death (3:17; 11:9)." He also points out that this is how the later authors of the Targum on Ecclesiastes understood it: "The spirit will return to stand in judgment before God who gave it."[71]

Toward the New Testament

Over time, the hope for life and justice beyond the grave that began to develop in the Old Testament burgeoned into the idea that a general resurrection would eventually occur when all humankind would be raised from the dead and judged by God (e.g., Dan. 12:1–3). This wasn't the same as the Greek idea of the immortality of the soul, since Jews believed that all substantive life ceased at death. Instead, this was the idea that God would bring the dead back to life in order to mete out rewards and punishments.

Some scholars view the development of a belief in resurrection among the Jews as a process of natural development shaped by foreign religious influences, cultural forces, and political pressures.[72] Others, however, view it as the result of a process of progressive revelation, in which "earlier revelation became the foundation for later revelation."[73] Regardless of how one understands the development to have occurred, a belief in a bodily resurrection became mainstream in both surviving strands of Second Temple Judaism in rabbinic Judaism and Christianity.

In rabbinic Judaism, belief in the resurrection was viewed as having been established in the law, and that questioning it disqualified a person from any share in the world to come.[74] In the early church, Christian belief focused on the resurrection of Jesus Christ, which is the very foundation of Christianity itself (e.g., Rom. 6:1–8; 1 Cor. 15; 1 Pet. 1:3–4). Jesus' resurrection provides the guarantee of a future general resurrection (1 Cor. 15:20). If Christ is not raised, as Paul says, then the entire Christian faith is in vain (1 Cor. 15:14) since the dead will remain in their tombs.

If death is not real and people simply live forever via an immortal soul, then Christianity is irrelevant. But ancient Israel's sages understood that death was real and that it's the harsh conclusion to life in a broken world. The fact that it's disappeared from the proclamation of Christian preachers and teachers as part of the gospel they announce is indicative of contemporary forgetfulness. But no matter how we avoid the subject of death, use indirect language to avoid talking about it, sequester it from daily life or put a facade over it, we cannot eliminate it. It is real. "There is something important here to grasp," writes Ephraim Radner, and it is that "part of our Christian vocation is to proclaim the reality of death itself."[75] When we come to see the reality of death, we may also come to appreciate the promise of the good news of the gospel.

EPILOGUE: COUNT IT ALL JOY

In this book, we've been looking at what God said through ancient Israel's sages to teach us about the quest for the good life. We've looked at what they said about a whole host of topics related to society and family, love and sex, the meaning of life, the moral structure, and our relationship with God. And we've seen how, when we look at wisdom literature as a whole, it's evident that it all interlocks to cover the entire field of wisdom and every aspect of our lives. Its purpose is to help us develop a unified worldview with God at the center. For ancient Israel, it's this cultivation of such a unified worldview that represents the good life.

As we conclude our study, I thought it would be appropriate to reflect briefly on the experience of Qoheleth, the author of Ecclesiastes, since he too was on a quest for the good life. Seeking to find meaning, joy, and satisfaction in life, he looked everywhere for these things. He tried spending money, pursuing relationships, throwing himself into his work, undertaking great construction projects, and everything else we can imagine.

But he discovered that it was all "vanity" (Eccles. 1:2 KVJ). In chapter 2, we discussed the Hebrew word *hebel* (הֶבֶל), which lies behind this translation, and saw that it has more to do with transience than meaninglessness. We saw that it may be connected with the name of Adam and Eve's son "Abel" (הֶבֶל), whose life story is one of unfairness. Abel offered an acceptable sacrifice, while his brother Cain did not. God rejected the offering of Cain, who became bitter and eventually killed Abel. God warned Cain that he needed to get his anger under control, but he failed to do so and instead murdered his brother and then buried his body in a field. As a result, God cursed Cain and proclaimed that from that point on that he would have difficulty making a living and would be a fugitive and a wanderer on the earth (Gen. 4:11–12). When Cain complained that this punishment was too harsh and that anyone could kill him, God put a mark of protection on him (4:13–15).

Russell Meek concludes that it's "the righteous Abel (Matt. 23:35) [who] suffers the consequences of disobedience: his life is cut short, leaving him with no children, no heritage, no material wealth" and, in Abel's case, any association of disobedience with the curse of God seems to be totally reversed.[1] Abel's story is one of complete injustice. Meek suggests that the writer of Ecclesiastes picks up on the inconsistencies of Abel's life and uses Abel's name as a thematic word to describe the "Abel-ness" of all things.[2] Everything on this earth is like the experience of Abel: it's all unfair.

This is what the Teacher (Qoheleth) found when he set out on his quest for the good life. He saw injustice to the poor (4:1–3), crooked politics (5:8), incompetent leaders (10:6–7), guilty people allowed to commit more crimes (8:11), materialism (5:10), and the longing for "the good old days" (7:10). He then concluded that it was "all vanity and a vexation of the spirit" (1:14). Like Abel's life, it was all unfair.

Scholars have struggled to find a clear meaning in the book of Ecclesiastes, with some concluding that it's just a random collection of pessimistic reflections. Norman Whybray, however, innovatively argues that Qoheleth is trying to teach us to find joy in the midst of the unfairness of life.[3] T. A. Perry developed this view in a commentary titled *The Book of Ecclesiastes (Qohelet) and the Path to Joyous Living*.[4] He reinforces the idea that while the author of Ecclesiastes surveys all the negative and unfair aspects of life, he rejects it and insists that with all our woes we need to find enjoyment every single day (11:8).

This approach to Ecclesiastes has much to recommend it. After all, throughout the book after each discussion of unfairness in life, Qoheleth commends a joyous response. Here are seven of these passages:

> There is nothing better for mortals than to eat and drink and find enjoyment in their toil. This also, I saw, is from the hand of God. (2:24)

> I know that there is nothing better for them than to be happy and enjoy themselves as long as they live. (3:12)

> So I saw that there is nothing better than that all should enjoy their work, for that is their lot; who can bring them to see what will be after them? (3:22)

> This is what I have seen to be good: it is fitting to eat and drink and find enjoyment in all the toil with which one toils under the sun the few days of the life God gives us, for this is our lot. (5:18)

> So I commend enjoyment, for there is nothing better for people under the sun than to eat and drink and enjoy themselves. (8:15)

> Go, eat your bread with enjoyment and drink your wine with a merry heart. . . .
> Let your garments always be white; do not let oil be lacking on your head. Enjoy
> life with the wife whom you love. (9:7–9)

> Rejoice, young man, while you are young, and let your heart cheer you in the
> days of your youth. Follow the inclination of your heart and desire of your eyes.
> . . . Banish anxiety from your mind, and put away pain from your body. . . . Re-
> member your creator. (11:9–10; 12:1)

In each of these passages, Qoheleth wants us to realize that "the opportunity
to enjoy life is given by God himself."[5]

We might ask that if the writer of Ecclesiastes was so committed to
preaching about joy, then why did he spend so much time talking about
how he's discovered that everything is unfair? Perry suggests, "Perhaps it was
important to experience the emptiness of it all, not only to then be able to
turn from its pursuit but also to discover, beneath the rubble, the seeds of
rebirth into a better wisdom."[6] Qoheleth doesn't want us to have a superficial,
unrealistic joy. He doesn't want us to wear plastic smiles. He wants us to go
into life with our "eyes wide open" and with an awareness that we'll have
many experiences in life similar to Abel's. They're simply unfair. It's only when
we're aware of the transience and unfairness of life that we can truly discover
the joy of the Lord.

This idea may sound familiar to Christian readers since it reverberates
throughout the New Testament. The Gospels contain numerous passages
about Jesus and joy. Even though the disciples seemed to frustrate him to no
end, Jesus still found joy in them (John 15:11). He found joy in sinners who
returned to the fold (Luke 15:5–7). He wanted people in "the world" to have
"complete joy" (John 17:13). Jesus endured the cross because of "the joy set
before him" (Heb. 12:2). And he told his disciples that although they would
be grieved when he left them, their sadness would eventually turn to joy
when he returned (John 16:20–22). The apostle Paul, even as he languished
in prison, proclaimed,

> Rejoice in the Lord always; again I will say, Rejoice. . . . I have learned to be con-
> tent with whatever I have. I know what it is to have little, and I know what it is to
> have plenty. In any and all circumstances I have learned the secret of being well-
> fed and of going hungry, of having plenty and of being in need. (Phil. 4:4, 11–12)

In his letter, James, Jesus' brother, reminded the members of the Jerusalem
church that whenever they faced trials of any kind, they should "consider it
nothing but joy" (1:2).

None of these passages teach naive or fake joy. They acknowledge that life is full of pain and unfairness, but when we recognize this, we can then grasp the source of true joy—which is found in God himself. Therein lies the secret to the good life.

BIBLIOGRAPHY

Adam, Barbara. "Reflexive Modernization Temporalized." *Theory, Culture & Society* 20, no. 2 (2003): 59–78.

Agger, Ben. "iTime: Labor and Life in a Smartphone Era." *Time & Society* 20, no. 1 (2011): 119–36.

Alexander, Thomas C. "Mormon Primitivism and Modernization." Pp. 167–96 in *The Primitive Church in the Modern World*. Edited by Richard T. Hughes. Urbana: University of Illinois Press, 1995.

Allen, Frances. *Saving Normal: An Insider's Revolt against Out-of-Control Psychiatric Diagnosis, DSM-5, Big Pharma, and the Medicalization of Ordinary Life*. New York: William Morrow, 2014.

Alter, Robert. *The Wisdom Books*. New York: W. W. Norton, 2010.

Alvaré, Helen M. *Putting Children's Interests First in U.S. Family Law and Policy*. Cambridge: Cambridge University Press, 2018.

Anderson, Francis I. *Job*. TOTC. Downers Grove, IL: InterVarsity Press, 1976.

Anderson, William H. U. *Qoheleth and Its Pessimistic Theology: Hermeneutical Struggles in Wisdom Literature*. MBPS 54. Lewiston, NY: Mellen Biblical, 1997.

Andruska, Jennifer L. "The Song of Songs." Pp. 200–18 in *The Cambridge Companion to Biblical Wisdom Literature*. Edited by Katharine J. Dell, Suzanna R. Millar, and Arthur Jan Keefer. Cambridge: Cambridge University Press, 2022.

Astell, Ann W. "The Saving of Fear: An Introduction." Pp. 10–18 in *Saving Fear in Christian Spirituality*. Edited by Ann W. Astell. Notre Dame: University of Notre Dame Press, 2019.

Atkinson, Tyler. *Singing at the Winepress: Ecclesiastes and the Ethics of Work*. London: Bloomsbury T & T Clark, 2015.

Augustine. *Confessions*. Trans. Henry Chadwick. Oxford: Oxford University Press, 1991.

Averbeck, Richard E. *The Old Testament Law for the Life of the Church: Reading the Torah in the Light of Christ*. Downers Grove, IL: IVP Academic, 2022.

Baer, Jonathan R. "Health, Disease, and Medicine." Pp. 954–65 in vol. 2 of *Encyclopedia of Religion in America*. Edited by Charles H. Lippy and Peter R. Williams. Washington, DC: CQ Press, 2010.

Balentine, Samuel E. *Job*. SHBC. Macon, GA: Smyth & Helwys, 2006.

_____. *Wisdom Literature*. CBS. Nashville: Abingdon, 2018.

Barr, James. *Biblical Words for Time*. 2nd ed. London: SCM Press, 1969.

_____. *The Garden of Eden and the Hope of Immortality*. Minneapolis, MN: Fortress Press, 1992.

Bartlett, David L. "The First Letter of Peter." Pp. 227–319 in vol. 12 of *The New Interpreter's Bible*. Edited by Leander E. Keck. Nashville: Abingdon Press, 1998.

Barton, Ruth Haley. "Solitude." P. 762 in *Dictionary of Christian Spirituality*. Edited by G. G. Scorgie. Grand Rapids: Zondervan, 2011.

Becker, Ernest. *The Denial of Death*. Florence, MA: Free Press, 1985.

Beckwith, R. *The Old Testament Canon in the New Testament Church*. Grand Rapids: Eerdmans, 1985.

Belcher Jr., Richard P. *Finding Favour in the Sight of God: A Theology of Wisdom Literature*. NSBT 46. Downers Grove, IL: IVP Academic, 2018.

Beldman, David J. H. "Framed! Structure in Ecclesiastes." Pp. 137–61 in *The Words of the Wise Are Like Goads: Engaging Qohelet in the 21st Century*. Edited by Mark J. Boda, Tremper Longman III, and Christian Rata. Winona Lake, IN: Eisenbrauns, 2013.

Bell, Rob. *Love Wins: A Book about Heaven, Hell, and the Fate of Every Person Who Ever Lived*. New York: HarperCollins, 2011.

Bellah, Robert N., and Phillip E. Hammond. *Varieties of Civil Religion*. New York: Harper & Row, 1980.

Bennett, Harold V. "Justice, OT." *NIDB* 3:476–77.

Benson, Herbert. *Timeless Healing: The Power and Biology of Belief.* New York: Scribner, 1996.

Bergant, Dianne. *The Song of Songs.* Berit Olam. Collegeville, MN: The Liturgical Press, 2001.

Bettger, Frank. *How I Raised Myself from Failure to Success in Selling.* New York: Simon & Schuster, 1977.

Bivins, Jason C. *Religion of Fear: The Politics of Horror in Conservative Evangelicalism.* New York: Oxford University Press, 2008.

Bland, Dave. *Proverbs and the Formation of Character.* Eugene, OR: Cascade Books, 2015.

Blenkinsopp, Joseph. "The Family in First Temple Israel." Pp. 48–103 in *Families in Ancient Israel.* Edited by Leo G. Perdue, Joseph Blenkinsopp, John J. Collins, and Carol Meyers. Louisville, KY: Westminster John Knox Press, 1997.

_____. *Sage, Priest, Prophet: Religious and Intellectual Leadership in Ancient Israel.* LAI. Louisville, KY: Westminster John Knox, 1995.

_____. *Wisdom and Law in the Old Testament: The Ordering of Life in Israel and Early Judaism.* The Oxford Bible Series. Oxford: Oxford University Press, 1983.

Blocher, H. "The Fear of the Lord as the 'Principle' of Wisdom." *TynBul* 28 (1977): 3–28.

Boda, Mark J. "Speaking into the Silence: The Epilogue of Ecclesiastes." Pp. 257–79 in *The Words of the Wise Are Like Goads: Engaging Qohelet in the 21st Century.* Edited by Mark J. Boda, Tremper Longman III, and Christian Rata. Winona Lake, IN: Eisenbrauns, 2013.

Bolt, Peter G. "Life, Death, and the Afterlife in the Greco-Roman World." Pp. 51–79 in *Life in the Face of Death: The Resurrection Message of the New Testament.* Edited by Richard N. Longenecker. Grand Rapids: Eerdmans, 1998.

Bolz-Weber, Nadia. *Shameless: A Sexual Reformation.* New York: Convergent, 2019.

Bonhoeffer, Dietrich. *Life Together.* Translated by John W. Doberstein. San Francisco: Harper & Row, 1954.

Boring, M. Eugene. "The Gospel of Matthew." Pp. 87–505 in vol. 8 of *The New Interpreter's Bible*. Edited by Leander E. Keck. Nashville: Abingdon Press, 1995.

Bowler, Kate. *Blessed: A History of the American Prosperity Gospel*. Oxford: Oxford University Press, 2013.

Braver, Sanford L., and Michael E. Lamb. "Marital Dissolution." Pp. 487–516 in *Handbook of Marriage and the Family*. 3rd ed. Edited by Gary W. Peterson and Kevin R. Bush. New York: Springer, 2013.

Brecht, Martin. *Martin Luther: His Road to Reformation, 1483–1521*. Translated by James L. Schaaf. Minneapolis, MN: Fortress Press, 1985.

Brettler, Marc Zvi. "Acrostic." *NIDB* 1:32–33.

Brooks, David. *The Road to Character*. New York: Random House, 2015.

_____. *The Second Mountain: The Quest for a Moral Life*. New York: Random House, 2019.

Broshi, Magen. "The Population of Iron Age Palestine." Pp. 14–18 in *Biblical Archaeology Today, 1990, Proceedings of the Second International Congress on Biblical Archaeology; Supplement: Pre-Congress Symposium: Population, Production and Power*. Edited by A. Biran and J. Aviram. Jerusalem: Ketepress Enterprises, 1993.

Brough, Sonia. *Langenscheidt's New College German Dictionary*. New York: Langenscheidt, 1995.

Brown, Francis. *The New Brown-Driver-Briggs-Gesenius Hebrew and English Lexicon*. Peabody, MA: Hendrickson, 1979.

Brown, Raymond E. *The Epistles of John*. AB 30. New York: Doubleday, 1982.

_____. *An Introduction to the New Testament*. New York: Doubleday, 1997.

Brown, William P. "The Law and the Sages: A Reexamination of *Tôrâ* in Proverbs." Pp. 251–80 in *Constituting the Community: Studies on the Polity of Ancient Israel in Honor of S. Dean McBride*. Edited by John T. Strong and Steven S. Tuell. Winona Lake, IN: Eisenbrauns, 2005.

Brueggemann, Walter. *Reverberations of Faith: A Theological Handbook of Old Testament Themes*. Louisville, KY: Westminster John Knox Press, 2002.

Buber, M. *Israel and the World: Essays in a Time of Crisis*. New York: Shocken Books, 1948.

Burkes, Shannon. *Death in Qoheleth and Egyptian Biographies of the Late Period*. SBLDS 170. Atlanta: SBL, 1999.

Burnside, Jonathan P. "Law and Wisdom Literature." Pp. 423–39 in *The Oxford Handbook of Wisdom and the Bible*. Edited by Will Kynes. Oxford: Oxford University Press, 2021.

Burton, Tara Isabella. *Strange Rites: New Religions for a Godless World*. New York: Public Affairs, 2020.

Cacioppo, John T., and William Patrick. *Loneliness: Human Nature and the Need for Social Connection*. New York: W. W. Norton, 2009.

Cannon, W. B. " 'Voodoo' Death." *American Anthropologist* 44 (1942): 169–81.

Capps, Charles. *God's Creative Power: Gift Collection*. England, AR: Capps, 2004.

_____. *The Tongue: A Creative Force*. England, AR: Capps, 1976.

Carlson, M., S. McLanahan, and P. England. "Union Formation in Fragile Families." *Demography* 41 (2004): 237–61.

Carnegie, Dale. *How to Win Friends and Influence People*. New York: Pocket Books, 1990.

Carney, Timothy P. *Alienated America: Why Some Places Thrive While Others Collapse*. New York: Harper, 2019.

Carr, D. *The Erotic Word: Sexuality, Spirituality, and the Bible*. New York: Oxford University Press, 2005.

Ceresko, Anthony R. "The ABC's of Wisdom in Psalm xxxiv." *VT* 35 (1985): 99–104.

Charen, Mona. *Sex Matters: How Modern Feminism Lost Touch with Science, Love, and Common Sense*. New York: Crown Forum, 2018.

Cheung, Simon Chi-Chung. "Wisdom Psalms." Pp. 219–38 in *The Cambridge Companion to Biblical Wisdom Literature*. Edited by Katharine J. Dell, Suzanna R. Millar, and Arthur Jan Keefer. Cambridge: Cambridge University Press, 2022.

Childs, Brevard S. *Introduction to the Old Testament as Scripture*. London: SCM, 1979.

Clarke, Rosalind. "Seeking Wisdom in the Song of Songs." Pp. 100–12 in *Interpreting Old Testament Wisdom Literature*. Edited by David G. Firth and Lindsay Wilson. Downers Grove, IL: IVP Academic, 2017.

Clifford, Richard J. "Introduction to Wisdom Literature." Pp. 1–16 in vol. 5 of *The New Interpreter's Bible*. Edited by Leander E. Keck. Nashville: Abingdon Press, 1997.

Clines, David J. A. *Job 1–20*. WBC 17. Dallas: Word Books, 1989.

———. *Job 21–37*. WBC 18A. Grand Rapids: Zondervan, 2006.

———. *Job 38–42*. WBC 18B. Grand Rapids: Zondervan, 2011.

———. "Why Is There a Song of Songs and What Does It Do to You If You Read It?" *Jian Dao* 1 (1994): 1–27.

Cockerill, Gareth Lee. *The Epistle to the Hebrews*. Grand Rapids: Eerdmans, 2012.

Cohick, Lynn H. *The Letter to the Ephesians*. Grand Rapids: Eerdmans, 2020.

Collins, John J. *Introduction to the Hebrew Bible*. 3rd ed. Minneapolis: Fortress Press, 2018.

Collins, Raymond F. *Wealth, Wages, and the Wealthy: New Testament Insights for Preachers and Teachers*. Collegeville, MN: Liturgical Press, 2017.

Colson, Charles W., with Anne Morse. *My Final Word: Holding Tight to the Issues That Matter Most*. Grand Rapids: Zondervan, 2015.

Conrad, Peter. *The Medicalization of Society: On the Transformation of Human Conditions in to Treatable Disorders*. Baltimore: The Johns Hopkins University Press, 2007.

Coogan, Michael D., and Cynthia R. Chapman. *The Old Testament: A Historical and Literary Introduction to the Hebrew Scriptures*. 4th ed. Oxford: Oxford University Press, 2018.

Coombs, R. "Marital Status and Personal Well-Being: A Literature Review." *Family Relations* 40 (1991): 97–102.

Copeland, Gloria. *Live Long, Finish Strong: The Divine Secret to Living Healthy, Happy, and Healed*. Reprint, Nashville: FaithWords, 2011.

Copeland, Kenneth. *Walking in the Realm of the Miraculous*. Fort Worth, TX: Kenneth Copeland, 1979.

Cousins, Norman. *Anatomy of an Illness: As Perceived by the Patient*. New York: W. W. Norton, 2005.

Craigie, Peter C. *Psalms 1–50*. WBC 19. Waco: Word Books, 1983.

Crenshaw, James L. "The Contemplative Life in the Ancient Near East." Pp. 2445–57 in vol. 1 of CANE. Edited by Jack M. Sasson. New York: Charles Scribner's Sons, 1995.

_____. *Education in Ancient Israel: Across the Deadening Silence*. ABRL. New York: Doubleday, 1998.

_____. *Old Testament Wisdom: An Introduction*. Revised ed. Louisville, KY: 1998.

_____. *Old Testament Wisdom Literature*. Atlanta: John Knox Press, 1981.

_____, ed. *Theodicy in the Old Testament*. IRT 4. Philadelphia: Fortress Press, 1983.

Crossan, John Dominic. *The Historical Jesus: The Life of a Mediterranean Jewish Peasant*. New York: HarperCollins, 1992.

Cullman, Oscar. *Christ and Time: The Primitive Christian Conception of Time and History*. 3rd ed. Translated by Floyd V. Filson. London: SCM, 1962.

Dale Carnegie & Associates, with Brent Cole. *How to Win Friends and Influence People in the Digital Age*. New York: Simon & Schuster, 2011.

Danby, Herbert. *The Mishnah: Translated from the Hebrew with Introduction and Brief Explanatory Notes*. Oxford: Oxford University Press, 1933. Reprint, Peabody, MA: Hendrickson, 2011.

Davidson, Richard M. *Flame of Yahweh: Sexuality in the Old Testament*. Peabody, MA: Hendrickson, 2007.

_____. "The Literary Structure of the Song of Songs Redivivus." *JATS* 14/2 (2003): 44–65.

Davies, John. "Theodicy." Pp. 808–17 in *Dictionary of the Old Testament: Wisdom, Poetry and Writings*. Edited by Tremper Longman III and Peter Enns. Downers Grove, IL: IVP Academic, 2008.

Davies, John G. *Holy Week: A Short History*. ESW 11. Richmond: John Knox Press, 1963.

Davies, W. D. *Paul and Rabbinic Judaism*. London: SPCK, 1955.

_____. *Torah in the Messianic Age and/or the Age to Come*. SBLMS 7. Philadelphia: SBL, 1952.

Davis, Ellen F. *Proverbs, Ecclesiastes, and the Song of Songs*. WBC. Louisville, KY: Westminster John Knox Press, 2000.

de Villiers, Pieter G. R. " 'In awe of the Mighty Deeds of God': The Fear of God in Early Christianity from the Perspective of Biblical Spirituality." Pp. 20–37 in *Saving Fear in Christian Spirituality*. Edited by Ann W. Astell. Notre Dame: University of Notre Dame Press, 2019.

deClaissé-Walford, Nancy L. *Introduction to the Psalms: A Song from Ancient Israel*. St. Louis: Chalice Press, 2004.

_____. "Psalm 49." Pp. 440–46 in *The Book of Psalms*. By Nancy deClaissé-Walford, Rolf A. Jacobson, and Beth LaNeel Tanner. NICOT. Grand Rapids: Eerdmans, 2014.

_____. "Psalm 111." Pp. 839–42 in *The Book of Psalms*. By Nancy deClaissé-Walford, Rolf A. Jacobson, and Beth LaNeel Tanner. NICOT. Grand Rapids: Eerdmans, 2014.

_____. "Righteousness in the OT." *NIDB* 4:818–23.

deClaissé-Walford, Nancy L., Rold A. Jacobson, and Beth LaNeel Tanner. *The Book of Psalms*. NICOT. Grand Rapids: Eerdmans, 2014.

Dell, Katherine J. *The Solomonic Corpus of 'Wisdom' and Its Influence*. Oxford: Oxford University Press, 2020.

_____. "Does the Song of Songs Have Any Connections to Wisdom?" in Anselm C. Hagedorn, ed., *Perspectives on the Song of Songs*. BZAW. Berlin: de Gruyter, 2005.

Dempster, Stephen G. "Ecclesiastes and the Canon." Pp. 387–400 in *The Words of the Wise Are Like Goads: Engaging Qohelet in the 21st Century*. Edited by Mark J. Boda, Tremper Longman III, and Christian Rata. Winona Lake, IN: Eisenbrauns, 2013.

DeSpelder, Lynne Ann, and Albert Lee Strickland. *The Last Dance: Encountering Death and Dying*. 11th ed. New York: McGraw-Hill, 2020.

Devine, Minos. *Ecclesiastes or the Confessions of an Adventurous Soul*. London: Macmillan, 1916.

Dillard, Raymond B. and Tremper Longman, III. *An Introduction to the Old Testament*. Grand Rapids, MI: Zondervan, 1994.

Dodd, C. H. *The Gospel and the Law of Christ*. London: Longmans Green, 1947.

Douglas, Susan J., and Meredith W. Michaels. *The Mommy Myth: The Idealization of Motherhood and How It Has Undermined Women*. New York: Free Press, 2004.

Dumbrell, William J. "The Purpose of the Book of Job." Pp. 91–105 in *The Way of Wisdom: Essays in Honor of Bruce K. Waltke*. Edited by J. I. Packer and Sven K. Soderlund. Grand Rapids: Zondervan, 2000.

Dunn, J. D. G. *The Epistle to the Galatians.* BNTC. London: A & C Black, 1993.

———. "The First and Second Letters to Timothy and the Letter to Titus." Pp. 775–880 in vol. 11 of *The New Interpreter's Bible.* Edited by Leander E. Keck. Nashville: Abingdon Press, 2000.

———. *The Theology of the Apostle Paul.* Grand Rapids: Eerdmans, 1998.

Dunnavant, Anthony L. "David Lipscomb and the 'Preferential Option for the Poor' among Post-Bellum Churches of Christ." Pp. 27–50 in *Poverty and Ecclesiology: Nineteenth-Century Evangelicals in the Light of Liberation Theology.* Edited by Anthony L. Dunnavant. Collegeville, MN: The Liturgical Press, 1992.

Eaton, Michael A. *Ecclesiastes: An Introduction & Commentary.* TOTC. Leicester, UK: InterVarsity, 1983.

Eichrodt, Walter. *Theology of the Old Testament.* 2 vols. Translated by J. A. Baker. Philadelphia: Westminster Press, 1967.

Eissfeldt, Otto. *The Old Testament: An Introduction.* Translated by Peter R. Ackroyd. New York: Harper & Row, 1965.

Elledge, Cassey D. *Resurrection of the Dead in Early Judaism: 200 BCE – CE 200.* Oxford: Oxford University Press, 2017.

Ellens, J. Harold. *Psychological Hermeneutics for Biblical Themes and Texts: A Festschrift in Honor of Wayne G. Rollins.* London: T & T Clark Biblical Studies, 2014.

Emba, Christine. *Rethinking Sex: A Provocation.* New York: Sentinel, 2022.

Eng, Milton. *The Days of Our Years: A Lexical Semantic Study of the Life Cycle in Biblical Israel.* LHB/OTS 464. London: T & T Clark, 2011.

Engel, George. "A Life Setting Conducive to Illness: The Giving-Up-Given-Up Complex." *Bulletin of the Menninger Clinic* 32 (1968): 355–65.

———. "Sudden and Rapids Death During Psychological Stress: Folklore or Folk Wisdom?" *Annals of Internal Medicine* 74 (1971): 771–82.

Enns, Peter. "Ecclesiastes 1: Book of." Pp. 121–32 in *Dictionary of the Old Testament: Wisdom, Poetry & Writings.* Edited by Tremper Longman III and Peter Enns. Downers Grove, IL: IVP Academic, 2008.

Epstein, Joseph. "The Secret Life of Alfred Kinsey." *Commentary* (January 1998): 35–39.

Erickson, Kenneth. *The Power of Praise.* St. Louis, MO: Concordia, 1984.

Evans, Tony. *Tony Evans' Book of Illustrations.* Chicago: Moody, 2009.

Exum, J. Cheryl. "A Literary and Structural Analysis of the Song of Songs." *ZAW* 8 (1973): 47–79.

_____. *Song of Songs: A Commentary.* OTL. Louisville, KY: Westminster John Knox, 2005.

Falk, Maria. *Love Lyrics from the Bible.* Sheffield: Almond, 1982.

Faust, Katy, and Stacy Manning. *Them Before Us: Why We Need a Global Children's Rights Movement.* New York: Post Hill Press, 2021.

Fiensy, David A. *The Archaeology of Daily Life: Ordinary Persons in Late Second Temple Israel.* Eugene, OR: Cascade Books, 2020.

_____. *Christian Origins and the Ancient Economy.* Eugene, OR: Wipf & Stock, 2014.

Fiensy, David, and Ralph K. Hawkins, eds. *The Galilean Economy in the Time of Jesus.* Atlanta: Society of Biblical Literature, 2013.

Finkelstein, Israel. *'Izbet Sartah: An Early Iron Age Site near Rosh Ha'ayin, Israel.* Oxford: BAR, 1986.

Fishbane, Michael. *Song of Songs.* JPSBC. Philadelphia: JPS, 2015.

Fitzmyer, Joseph A. *The Acts of the Apostles: A New Translation with Introduction and Commentary.* AB 31. New York: Doubleday, 1998.

_____. *The Gospel According to Luke (I-IX).* AB 28. New York: Doubleday, 1970.

Foer, Franklin. *World without Mind: The Existential Threat of Big Tech.* New York: Penguin Press, 2017.

Fox, Matthew. *The Reinvention of Work: A New Vision of Livelihood for Our Time.* San Francisco: Harper San Francisco, 1994.

Fox, Michael V. *Ecclesiastes.* JPSBC. Philadelphia: The Jewish Publication Society, 2004.

_____. *Proverbs 10–31: A New Translation with Introduction and Commentary.* AYB 18B. New Haven: Yale University Press, 2009.

_____. *The Song of Songs and the Ancient Egyptian Love Songs.* Madison: University of Wisconsin Press, 1985.

Fredericks, Daniel C. *Coping with Transience: Ecclesiastes on Brevity in Life.* TBS 18. Sheffield: JSOT Press, 1993.

_____. "Ecclesiastes." Pp. 15–203 in *Ecclesiastes and Song of Songs*. By Daniel C. Fredericks and Daniel J. Estes. AOTC 16. Nottingham: Apollos, 2010.

_____. *Qoheleth's Language: Reevaluating Its Nature and Date*. Lewiston, NY: The Edwin Mellen Press, 1988.

Freedman, David Noel. *Psalm 119: The Exaltation of Torah*. BJS 6. Winona Lake, IN: Eisenbrauns, 1999.

Freitas, Donna. *The End of Sex: How Hookup Culture is Leaving a Generation Unhappy, Sexually Unfulfilled, and Confused about Intimacy*. New York: Basic Books, 2013.

Friedan, Betty. *The Feminine Mystique*. New York: W. W. Norton, 1963.

Fuhs, H. F. "ירא *yārē'*." Pp. 290–315 in vol. 6 of *Theological Dictionary of the Old Testament*. Edited by G. Johannes Botterweck and Helmer Ringgren. Translated by David E. Green. Grand Rapids: Eerdmans, 1990.

Gallagher, Maggie. *The Abolition of Marriage: How We Destroy Lasting Love*. Washington, DC: Regnery, 1996.

Gammie, John G., and Leo G. Perdue, eds. *The Sage in Israel and the Ancient Near East*. Winona Lake, IN: Eisenbrauns, 1990.

Gane, Roy E. *Old Testament Law for Christians: Original Context and Enduring Application*. Grand Rapids: Baker Academic, 2017.

Garber, Steven. *Visions of Vocation: Common Grace for the Common Good*. Downers Grove, IL: IVP Books, 2014.

Garrett, Duane A. *Proverbs, Ecclesiastes, Song of Songs*. NAC 14. Nashville: Broadman, 1993.

Gay, Craig M. *The Way of the (Modern) World Or, Why It's Tempting to Live As If God Doesn't Exist*. Grand Rapids: Eerdmans, 1998.

Gay, Hannah. "Clock Synchrony, Time Distribution and Electrical Timekeeping in Britain 1880–1925." *Past & Present* 181, no. 1 (2003): 107–40.

Gell, Alfred. *The Anthropology of Time: Cultural Constructions of Temporal Maps and Images*. Oxford: Berg, 1992.

Gerlach, Wolfgang. *And the Witnesses were Silent: The Confessing Church and the Jews*. Lincoln: University of Nebraska Press, 2000.

Gerstenberger, Erhard. "Psalms." Pp. 179–223 in *Old Testament Form Criticism*. Edited by John H. Hayes. San Antonio: Trinity University Press, 1974.

Ghosh, Palash. "Managers Say the Future of Work is Hybrid: New Structure Provides Management Firms with the Best of Both Worlds." *Pensions & Investments* 49/25 (2021): 3.

Giblin, Les. *How to Have Confidence and Power in Dealing with People.* New Jersey: Prentice-Hall, 1959.

Gillick, Muriel R. *Old and Sick in America: The Journey Through the Health Care System.* Chapel Hill: The University of North Carolina Press, 2017.

Gleick, James. *Faster: The Acceleration of Just about Everything.* New York: Pantheon Books, 1999.

Goldberg, Herb. *The Hazards of Being Male: Surviving the Myth of Masculine Privilege.* New York: Signet, 1987.

Goldingay, John. *The First Testament: A New Translation.* Downers Grove, IL: IVP Academic, 2018.

_____. *Psalms. Volume 1: Psalms 1–41.* BCOTWP. Grand Rapids: Baker Academic, 2006.

_____. *Psalms. Volume 2: Psalms 42–89.* BCOTWP. Grand Rapids: Baker Academic, 2007.

_____. Psalms. *Volume 3: Psalms 90–150.* BCOTWP. Grand Rapids: Baker Academic, 2008.

Goldsworthy, Graeme. *According to Plan: The Unfolding Revelation of God in the Bible.* Downers Grove, IL: InterVarsity Press, 1991.

Goleman, Daniel. *Social Intelligence: The New Science of Human Relationships.* New York: Bantam Books, 2006.

Golka, F. W. *The Leopard's Spots: Biblical and African Wisdom in Proverbs.* Edinburgh: T & T Clark, 1993.

González, Justo L. *Faith and Wealth.* San Francisco: Harper & Row, 1990.

Gorer, Geoffrey. *Death, Grief, and Mourning in Contemporary Britain.* London: The Cresset Press, 1965.

Green, Joel B. "Healing." *NIDB* 2:755–59.

Greenberg, Moshe. *Biblical Prose Prayer.* Berkeley: University of California Press, 1983.

Greenstein, Edward L. *Job: A New Translation.* New Haven: Yale University Press, 2019.

Greer, Peter, and Phil Smith. *Created to Flourish: How Employment-Based Solutions Help Eradicate Poverty*. Lancaster, PA: Hope International, 2016.

Grenz, Stanley J. *Created For Community: Connecting Christian Belief with Christian Living*. 2nd ed. Grand Rapids: BridgePoint, 1998.

Gunkel, Hermann. *Introduction to Psalms: The Genres of the Religious Lyric of Israel*. Macon, GA: Mercer University Press, 1998. Reprint, Eugene, OR: Wipf & Stock, 2020.

_____. *The Psalms: A Form-Critical Introduction*. Philadelphia: Fortress Press, 1967.

Habel, Norman C. *The Book of Job: A Commentary*. Philadelphia: The Westminster Press, 1985.

Hagin, Kenneth E. *How to Write Your Own Ticket with God*. Broken Arrow, OK: Faith Library, 2000.

_____. *The Midas Touch: A Balanced Approach to Biblical Prosperity*. Tulsa, OK: Kenneth Hagin Ministries, 2000.

_____. *"You Can Have What You Say!"* Broken Arrow, OK: Faith Library, 1988.

Harrell Jr., David Edwin. *Oral Roberts: An American Life*. Bloomington: Indiana University Press, 1985.

Harrington, Anne, ed. *The Placebo Effect: An Interdisciplinary Exploration*. Cambridge, MA: Harvard University Press, 1997.

Hart, Archibald D. *The Sexual Man: Masculinity without Guilt*. Dallas: Word, 1994.

Hart, Archibald D., and Sylvia Hart Frejd. *The Digital Invasion: How Technology Is Shaping You and Your Relationships*. Grand Rapids: Baker Books, 2013.

Hawkins, Ralph K. *Discovering Exodus: Content, Interpretation, Reception*. Grand Rapids: Eerdmans, 2021.

_____. *A Heritage in Crisis: Where We've Been, Where We Are, and Where We're Going in the Churches of Christ*. Lanham, MD: University Press of America, 2001.

_____. *How Israel Became a People*. Nashville: Abingdon Press, 2013.

Hays, Christopher B. " 'There Is Hope for a Tree': Job's Hope for the Afterlife in the Light of Egyptian Tree Imagery." *CBQ* 77 (2015): 42–68.

Hayslip Jr., Bert. "Death Denial: Hiding and Camouflaging Death. Pp. 31–42 in *Handbook of Death and Dying*. Edited by Clifton D. Bryant. Thousand Oaks, CA: Sage, 2003.

Heider, G. C. "Marriage and Sex." Pp. 451–57 in *Dictionary of the Old Testament: Wisdom, Poetry & Writings*. Edited by T. Longman III and P. Enns. Downers Grove, IL: InterVarsity Press, 2008.

Heim, Knut Martin. *Ecclesiastes*. TOTC. Downers Grove, IL: Inter Varsity, 2019.

Heinze, R. W. "Luther, Martin." Pp. 717–19 in *Evangelical Dictionary of Theology*. 2nd ed. Edited by Walter A. Elwell. Grand Rapids: Baker Academic, 2001.

Hendrix, Scott H. *Martin Luther: Visionary Reformer*. New Haven: Yale University Press, 2017.

Herzog, Zeev. "Settlement and Fortification Planning in the Iron Age." Pp. 231–74 in *The Architecture of Ancient Israel: From the Prehistoric to the Persian Empire*. Edited by Aharon Kempinski and Ronny Reich. Jerusalem: Israel Exploration Society, 1992.

Hess, Richard S. *The Old Testament: A Historical, Theological, and Critical Introduction*. Grand Rapids: Baker Academic, 2016.

———. *Song of Songs*. BCOTWP. Grand Rapids: Baker Academic, 2005.

———. "Song of Songs: Not Just a Dirty Book." *Bible Review* 21/5 (2005): 30–40.

Hodge, Charles. *Systematic Theology*, Vol 1: *Theology*. Grand Rapids: Eerdmans, 1872–1873. Reprint, Peabody, MA: Hendrickson, 1999.

Holladay, William L. *A Concise Hebrew and Aramaic Lexicon of the Old Testament*. Grand Rapids: Eerdmans, 1988.

Honey, Michael K. *To the Promised Land: Martin Luther King and the Fight for Economic Justice*. New York: W. W. Norton, 2018.

Honoré, Carl. *In Praise of Slowness: Challenging the Cult of Speed*. San Francisco: HarperOne, 2004.

Hooker, Morna D. "The Letter to the Philippians." Pp. 467–549 in vol. 11 of *The New Interpreter's Bible*. Edited by Leander E. Keck. Nashville: Abingdon Press, 2000.

Horne, Milton P. *Proverbs-Ecclesiastes*. SHBC. Macon, GA: Smyth & Helwys, 2003.

Huntington, Enders, and John A. Hostetler. *The Hutterites in North America.* Australia: Cengage Learning, 2002.

Illich, Ivan. *Medical Nemesis: The Expropriation of Health.* New York: Random House, 1976.

Jacobson, Diane. "Wisdom Language in the Psalms." Pp. 147–57 in *The Oxford Handbook of the Psalms.* Edited by William P. Brown. Oxford: Oxford University Press, 2014.

Jacobson, Rolf A. "Form Criticism and Historical Approaches to Interpretation." In deClaissé-Walford et al., *The Book of Psalms,* pp. 13–21.

_____. "Psalm 1: The Way of Life." In deClaissé-Walford et al., *The Book of Psalms,* pp. 58–64.

_____. "Psalm 14." In deClaissé-Walford et al., *The Book of Psalms,* pp. 164–69.

_____. "Psalm 34." In deClaissé-Walford et al., *The Book of Psalms,* pp. 321–30.

Jaeger, W. *The Theology of the Early Greek Philosophers.* Oxford: Oxford University Press, 1947.

James, P. D. *The Children of Men.* New York: Alfred A. Knopf, 1993.

James, William. *Varieties of Religious Experience: A Study in Human Nature.* Centennial Edition. London: Routledge, 2002.

Jewett, Robert. *Romans: A Commentary.* Hermeneia. Minneapolis, MN: Fortress Press, 2006.

Johnson, Luke Timothy. *The Acts of the Apostles.* SP Series 5. Collegeville, MN: The Liturgical Press, 1992.

_____. "The Letter of James." Pp. 175–225 in vol. 12 of *The New Interpreter's Bible.* Edited by Leander E. Keck. Nashville: Abingdon Press, 1998.

Jones, Jordan. *She Opens Her Hand to the Poor: Gestures and Social Values in Proverbs.* PHSC 30. Piscataway, NJ: Gorgias Press, 2019.

Jones, Martyn Wendell. "Kingdom Come in California?" *Christianity Today* 60/4 (2016): 30–37.

Jones, Scott C. *Rumors of Wisdom: Job 28 as Poetry.* BZFAW. Berlin: De Gruyter, 2009.

Kaiser Jr., Walter C. "True Marital Love in Proverbs 5:15–23 and the Interpretation of the Song of Songs." Pp. 106–16 in *The Way of Wisdom: Essays in Honor of Bruce K. Waltke.* Edited by J. I. Packer and Sven K. Soderlund. Grand Rapids: Zondervan, 2000.

Keel, Othmar. *The Song of Songs: A Continental Commentary*. Translated by Frederick J. Gaiser. Minneapolis: Fortress Press, 1994.

Keen, Ralph. "The Reformation Recovery of the Wrath of God." Pp. 96–102 in *Saving Fear in Christian Spirituality*. Edited by Ann W. Astell. Notre Dame: University of Notre Dame Press, 2019.

Keener, Craig S. "Family and Household." Pp. 353–68 in *Dictionary of New Testament Background*. Edited by Craig A. Evans and Stanley E. Porter. Downers Grove, IL: InterVarsity Press, 2000.

Keller, Timothy, with Katherine Leary Alsdorf. *Every Good Endeavor: Connecting Your Work to God's Work*. New York: Viking, 2012.

Keller, Timothy, with Kathy Keller. *The Meaning of Marriage: Facing the Complexities of Commitment with the Wisdom of God*. New York: Dutton, 2011.

Kidner, Derek. *The Proverbs: An Introduction and Commentary*. TOTC. Downers Grove: InterVarsity, 1964.

Kille, D. Andrew. *Psychological Biblical Criticism*. GBSOT. Minneapolis, MN: Fortress Press, 2000.

Kimball, Roger. *The Long March: How the Cultural Revolution of the 1960s Changed America*. San Francisco: Encounter Books, 2000.

King, Philip J., and Lawrence E. Stager. *Life in Biblical Israel*. Louisville, KY: Westminster John Knox, 2001.

Knibb, Michael A. "Life and Death in the Old Testament." Pp. 395–415 in *The World of Ancient Israel*. Edited by R. E. Clements. Cambridge: Cambridge University Press, 1989.

Knight, George R. "Seventh-day Adventists." Pp. 2065–68 in vol. 4 of *Encyclopedia of Religion in America*. Edited by Charles H. Lippy and Peter R. Williams. Washington, DC: CQ Press, 2010.

Kouzes, James M., and Barry Z. Posner. *The Leadership Challenge*. 4th ed. San Francisco: John Wiley & Sons, 2007.

Koyama, Koyama. *Three Mile an Hour God: Biblical Reflections*. New York: Orbis, 1979.

Krüger, Thomas. *Qoheleth*. Hermeneia. Minneapolis, MN: Fortress Press, 2004.

Kynes, Will. *An Obituary for "Wisdom Literature": The Birth, Death, and Intertextual Reintegration of a Biblical Corpus*. Oxford: Oxford University Press, 2019.

Lambert, W. G. *Babylonian Wisdom Literature*. Oxford: Oxford University Press, 1960.

Lamm, Julia A. "Casting Out Fear: The Logic of 'God is Love' in Julian of Norwich and Friedrich Schleiermacher." Pp. 231–57 in *Saving Fear in Christian Spirituality*. Edited by Ann W. Astell. Notre Dame: University of Notre Dame Press, 2019.

Last, Jonathan V. *What to Expect When No One's Expecting: America's Coming Demographic Disaster*. New York: Encounter Books, 2013.

Le Godff, Jacques. *Time, Work, and Culture in the Middle Ages*. Translated by Arthur Goldhammer. Chicago: Chicago University Press, 1977.

Leaf, Clifton. "The Shrinking Middle Class." *Fortune* 179.1 (2019): 52–79.

Lehmann, Paul L. *Ethics in a Christian Context*. New York: Harper & Row, 1963.

Leithart, Peter J. "Solomon's Sexual Wisdom: Qohelet and the Song of Songs." Pp. 443–60 in *The Words of the Wise Are Like Goads: Engaging Qohelet in the 21st Century*. Edited by Mark J. Boda, Tremper Longman III, and Cristian G. Rata. Winona Lake: Eisenbrauns, 2013.

Lemos, T. M. "Were Israelite Women Chattel?" Pp. 227–41 in *Worship, Women, and War: Essays in Honor of Susan Niditch*. Edited by John J. Collins, T. M. Lemos, and S. M. Olyan. Providence, RI: Brown Judaic Studies, 2015.

Levenson, Jon D. *Resurrection and the Restoration of Israel: The Ultimate Victory of the God of Life*. New Haven: Yale University Press, 2006.

Lindsay, Gordon. *God's Master Key to Prosperity*. Dallas: Christ for the Nations, 1998.

Liu, H., and D. Umberson. "The Times They are a Changin': Marital Status and Health Differentials from 1972 to 2003." *Journal of Health and Social Behavior* 49 (2008): 239–53.

Long, Thomas G. *Accompany Them with Singing: The Christian Funeral*. Louisville, KY: Westminster John Knox, 2009.

Longenecker, Richard N. *The Epistle to the Romans*. NIGTC. Grand Rapids: Eerdmans, 2016.

Longman III, Tremper. "Determining the Historical Context of Ecclesiastes." Pp. 89–102 in *The Words of the Wise Are Like Goads: Engaging Qohelet in the 21st Century*. Edited by Mark J. Boda, Tremper Longman III, and Cristian G. Rata. Winona Lake: Eisenbrauns, 2013.

_____. "The 'Fear of God' in the Book of Ecclesiastes." *BBR* 25.1 (2015): 13–21.

_____. *The Fear of the Lord Is the Wisdom: A Theological Introduction to Wisdom in Israel*. Grand Rapids: Baker Academic, 2017.

_____. "Israelite Genres in Their Ancient Near Eastern Context." Pp. 177–95 in *The Changing Face of Form Criticism in the Twenty-First Century*. Edited by M. A. Sweeney and Ehud Ben Zvi. Grand Rapids: Eerdmans, 2003.

_____. *Proverbs*. BCOTWP. Grand Rapids: Baker Academic, 2006.

_____. "The Scope of Wisdom Literature." Pp. 13–33 in *The Cambridge Companion to Biblical Wisdom Literature*. Edited by Katharine J. Dell, Suzanna R. Millar and Arthur Jan Keefer. Cambridge: Cambridge University Press, 2022.

_____. *Song of Songs*. NICOT. Grand Rapids: Eerdmans, 2001.

Longman III, Tremper, and Raymond B. Dillard. *An Introduction to the Old Testament*. 2nd ed. Grand Rapids: Zondervan, 2006.

Luckman, Thomas. *The Invisible Religion: The Problem of Religion in Modern Society*. New York: Macmillan, 1967.

Malina, B. J. "Collectivist Personality." *NIDB* 1: 699–700.

Marcuse, Herbert. *Eros and Civilization: A Philosophical Inquiry into Freud*. 8th ed. Boston: Beacon Press, 1974.

Martin, Ralph P. *2 Corinthians*. WBC 40. Waco: Word Books, 1986.

Maxwell, John C. *Everyone Communicates, Few Connect: What the Most Effective People Do Differently*. Nashville: Thomas Nelson, 2010.

McBride Jr., S. Dean. "Polity of the Covenant People: The Book of Deuteronomy." *Int* 41 (1987): 229–44.

McCann Jr., J. Clinton. "The Book of Psalms." Pp. 639–1280 in vol. 4 of the *New Interpreter's Bible*. Edited by Leander E. Keck. Nashville: Abingdon Press, 1998.

McCarthy, Margaret Harper. *Torn Asunder: Children, the Myth of the Good Divorce, and the Recovery of Origins*. Grand Rapids: Eerdmans, 2017.

McConville, J. Gordon. *Being Human in God's World: An Old Testament Theology of Humanity*. Grand Rapids: Baker Academic, 2016.

McDonald, Lee Martin, and James A. Sanders, eds. *The Canon Debate*. Peabody, MA: Hendrickson, 2002.

McLaughlin, John L. *An Introduction to Israel's Wisdom Traditions*. Grand Rapids: Eerdmans, 2018.

Meek, Russell L. *Ecclesiastes and the Search for Meaning in an Upside-Down World*. Peabody, MA: Hendrickson, 2022.

_____. "The Meaning of הבל in Qohelet: An Intertextual Suggestion." Pp. 241–56 in *The Words of the Wise Are Like Goads: Engaging Qohelet in the 21st Century*. Edited by Mark J. Boda, Tremper Longman III, and Christian Rata. Winona Lake, IN: Eisenbrauns, 2013.

_____. "Twentieth- and Twenty-First Century Readings of Hebel (הֶבֶל) in Ecclesiastes." *CurBR* 14/3 (2016): 279–97.

Meier, John P. *A Marginal Jew: Rethinking the Historical Jesus*, Vol. 2: *Mentor, Message, and Miracles*. New York: Doubleday, 1994.

Melanchthon, Philip. *Commonplaces: Loci Communes 1521*. Translated by Christian Preus. St. Louis: Concordia, 2014.

Mellor, Philip A., and Chris Shilling. "Modernity, Self-Identity and the Sequestration of Death." *Sociology* 27/3 (1993): 411–31.

Menninger, Karl. *Whatever Became of Sin?* New York: Hawthorn Books, 1974.

Mettes, Susan. *The Loneliness Epidemic: Why So Many of Us Feel Alone—and How Leaders Can Respond*. Grand Rapids: Brazos Press, 2021.

Meyers, Carol. "The Family in Early Israel." Pp. 1–47 in *Families in Ancient Israel*. Edited by Leo G. Perdue, Joseph Blenkinsopp, John J. Collins, and Carol Meyers. Louisville, KY: Westminster John Knox Press, 1997.

_____. *Rediscovering Eve: Ancient Israelite Women in Context*. New York: Oxford University Press, 2013.

_____. "Was Ancient Israel a Patriarchal Society?" *JBL* 133.1 (2014): 8–27.

Michaels, J. Ramsey. *1 Peter*. WBC 49. Waco: Word Books, 1988.

Miller, Corey. *In Search of the Good Life: Through the Eyes of Aristotle, Maimonides, and Aquinas*. Eugene, OR: Pickwick, 2019.

Miller, Dave. *Piloting the Strait: A Guidebook for Assessing Change in Churches of Christ*. Pulaski, TN: Sain, 1996.

Millett, Kate. *Sexual Politics*. Garden City, NY: Doubleday, 1970.

Mitford, Jessica. *The American Way of Death*. Camp Hill, PA: Simon and Schuster, 1963.

_____. *The American Way of Death Revisited*. Reprint, New York: Vintage, 2000.

Möller, Karl. *The Song of Songs: Beautiful Bodies, Erotic Desire and Intoxicating Pleasure*. Cambridge: Grove Books, 2018.

Moyer, James C. "Shades." Pp. 207–208 in vol. 5 of the *New Interpreter's Dictionary of the Bible*. Edited by K. D. Sakenfeld. Nashville: Abingdon Press, 2009.

Munn, N. D. "The Cultural Anthropology of Time: A Critical Essay." *ARA* 21 (1992): 93–123.

Murphy, Roland E. *Ecclesiastes*. WBC 23A. Dallas: Word, 1992.

_____. *Proverbs*. WBC 22. Nashville: Thomas Nelson, 1998.

_____. *The Tree of Life: An Exploration of Biblical Wisdom Literature*. 3rd ed. Grand Rapids: Eerdmans, 2002.

Newberg, Andrew B. *How God Changes Your Brain: Breakthrough Findings from a Leading Neuroscientist*. New York: Ballantine Books, 2010.

_____. *Principles of Neurotheology*. Abingdon, UK: Routledge, 2010.

Nickelsburg, George W. E. *Resurrection, Immortality, and Eternal Life in Intertestamental Judaism and Early Christianity*. Expanded ed. Harvard Theological Studies. Cambridge, MA: Harvard University Press, 2007.

Nicole, Roger R. "The Wisdom of Marriage." Pp. 280–96 in *The Way of Wisdom: Essays in Honor of Bruce K. Waltke*. Edited by J. I. Packer and Sven K. Soderlund. Grand Rapids: Zondervan, 2000.

Olds, Jacqueline, and Richard S. Schwartz. *The Lonely American: Drifting Apart in the Twenty- First Century*. Boston: Beacon Press, 2010.

O'Regan, Cyril. "Fear of God in John Henry Newman and Søren Kierkegaard." Pp. 258–84 in *Saving Fear in Christian Spirituality*. Edited by Ann W. Astell. Notre Dame: University of Notre Dame Press, 2019.

Osborne, William R. "The Tree of Life in Proverbs and Psalms." Pp. 100–21 in *The Tree of Life*. Edited by Douglas Estes. TBN 27. Leiden: Brill, 2020.

Otto, Rudolf. *The Idea of the Holy: An Inquiry into the Non-Rational Factor in the Idea of the Divine and Its Relation to the Rational*. Translated by John W. Harvey. New York: Oxford University Press, 1958.

Outka, Elizabeth. "'Wood for the Coffins Ran Out': Modernism and the Shadowed Afterlife of the Influenza Pandemic." *Modernism/Modernity* 21/4 (2015): 937–60.

Packer, James I. "Understanding the Bible: Evangelical Hermeneutics." Pp. 147–60 in *Honouring the Written Word of God: The Collected Shorter Writings of J. I. Packer*, vol. 3. Rep. ed. Carlisle, UK: Paternoster, 1999.

Pardes, Ilana. *The Song of Songs: A Biography*. LGRB. Princeton, NJ: Princeton University Press, 2019.

Pataki-Bittó, Fruzsina, and Kata Kapusy. "Work Environment Transformation in the Post Covid-19 based on Work Values of the Future Workforce." *Journal of Corporate Real Estate* 23/3 (2021): 151–69.

Pate, C. M., J. S. Duvall, J. D. Hays, E. R. Richards, W. D. Tucker Jr., and P. Vang. *The Story of Israel: A Biblical Theology*. Downers Grove, IL: InterVarsity Press, 2004.

Paul, Shalom. "A Lover's Garden of Verse: Literal and Metaphorical Imagery in Ancient Near Eastern Love Poetry." Pp. 99–110 in *Tehilla le-Moshe: Biblical and Judaic Studies in Honor of Moshe Greenberg*. Edited by Mordechai Cogan, Barry L. Eichler, and Jeffrey H. Tigay. Winona Lake, IN: Eisenbrauns, 1997.

Pemberton, Glenn. *A Life That Is Good: The Message of Proverbs in a World Wanting Wisdom*. Grand Rapids: Eerdmans, 2018.

Penchansky, David. *Understanding Wisdom Literature: Conflict and Dissonance in the Hebrew Text*. Grand Rapids: Eerdmans, 2012.

Perdue, Leo G. "The Household, Old Testament Theology, and Contemporary Hermeneutics." Pp. 223–57 in *Families in Ancient Israel*. Edited by Leo G. Perdue, Joseph Blenkinsopp, John J. Collins, and Carol Meyers. Louisville, KY: Westminster John Knox Press, 1997.

_____. *Proverbs*. Louisville: John Knox Press, 2000.

Perry, T. A. *The Book of Ecclesiastes (Qohelet) and the Path to Joyous Living*. New York: Cambridge University Press, 2015.

Peters, William. *A Class Divided: Then and Now*. New Haven: Yale University Press, 1987.

Peterson, Brian Neil. *Qoheleth's Hope: The Message of Ecclesiastes in a Broken World*. Lanham: Lexington Books, 2020.

Pfeiffer, R. H. "The Fear of God." *IEJ* 5/11 (1955): 41–48.

Phipps, William E. "The Plight of the Song of Songs." *JAAR* 42/1 (1974): 82–100.

Pickstone, Charles. *The Divinity of Sex: The Search for Ecstasy in a Secular Age*. New York: St. Martin's Press, 1996.

Pilch, John J., and Bruce J. Malina. *Biblical Social Values and Their Meaning*. Peabody, MA: Hendrickson, 1993.

Plaut, Gunther W. *The Book of Proverbs*. New York: Jewish Commentary for Bible Readers, 1961.

Pope, Marvin H. *The Song of Songs*. AB 7C. Garden City, NY: Doubleday, 1977.

Popenoe, David. "American Family Decline, 1960–1990: A Review and Appraisal." *Journal of Marriage and Family* 55 (1993): 527–42.

_____. *Disturbing the Nest: Family Change and Decline in Modern Society*. New York: Aldine de Gruyter, 1988.

_____. *Life without Father: Compelling New Evidence That Fatherhood and Marriage Are Indispensable for the Good of Children and Society*. Cambridge, MA: Harvard University Press, 1996.

_____. *War over the Family*. New Brunswick, NJ: Transaction, 2008.

Postman, Neil. *Technopoly: The Surrender of Culture to Technology*. New York: Vintage Books, 1993.

Provan, Iain. *Ecclesiastes/Song of Songs*. NIVAC. Grand Rapids: 2001.

_____. *Seeking What Is Right: The Old Testament and the Good Life*. Waco: Baylor University Press, 2020.

_____. "The Terrors of the Night: Love, Sex, and Power in Song of Songs 3." Pp. 150–67 in *The Way of Wisdom: Essays in Honor of Bruce K. Waltke*. Edited by J. I. Packer and Sven K. Soderlund. Grand Rapids: Zondervan, 2000.

Putnam, Robert D. *Bowling Alone: The Collapse and Revival of American Community*. New York: Simon & Schuster, 2000.

_____. *Our Kids: The American Dream in Crisis.* New York: Simon & Schuster, 2015.

Putnam, Robert D., and David E. Campbell. *American Grace: How Religion Divides and Unites Us.* New York: Simon & Schuster, 2010.

Putnam, Robert D., and Lewis M. Feldstein. *Better Together: Restoring the American Community.* New York: Simon & Schuster, 2003.

Quarles, Charles L. "Jesus as a Teacher of New Covenant Torah: An Examination of the Sermon on the Mount." In *Matthew as Teacher in the Gospel of Matthew.* Edited by Charles L. Quarles and Charles N. Ridlehoover. LNTS. Edinburgh: T & T Clark, 2023.

Quart, Alissa. *Squeezed: Why Our Families Can't Afford America.* New York: Ecco, 2018.

Rad, Gerhard von. *God at Work in Israel.* Translated by John H. Marks. Nashville: Abingdon Press, 1980.

_____. *Wisdom in Israel.* Translated by James D. Martin. Nashville: Abingdon Press, 1977.

Radner, Ephraim. *A Time to Keep: Theology, Mortality, and the Shape of a Human Life.* Waco: Baylor University Press, 2016.

Ray, J. D. "Egyptian Wisdom Literature." Pp. 17–29 in *Wisdom in Ancient Israel.* Edited by J. Day, R. P. Gordan, and H. G. M. Williamson. Cambridge: Cambridge University Press, 1995.

Regnerus, Mark. *Cheap Sex: The Transformation of Men, Marriage, and Monogamy.* Oxford: Oxford University Press, 2017.

_____. *The Future of Christian Marriage.* Oxford: Oxford University Press, 2020.

Richardson, M. E. J. Richardson, M. E. J. "חָכְמָה." *HALOT* 1:314.

Rifkin, Jeremy. *Time Wars: The Primary Conflict in Human History.* New York: Touchstone, 1989.

Robertson, Brian C. *There's No Place Like Work: How Business, Government, and Our Obsession with Work Have Driven Parents from Home.* Dallas: Spence, 2000.

Rollins, Wayne G., and D. Andrew Kille. *Psychological Insight into the Bible: Texts and Readings.* Grand Rapids: Eerdmans, 2007.

Root, Andrew. *The Congregation in a Secular Age: Keeping Sacred Time against the Speed of Modern Life.* Grand Rapids: Baker Academic, 2021.

Rosa, Hartmut. *Alienation and Acceleration: Towards a Critical Theory of Late-Modern Temporality*. NSU Summertalk, vol. 3. Malmö, Denmark: NSU Press, 2010.

_____. *Social Acceleration: A New Theory of Modernity*. New York: Columbia University Press, 2013.

Rose-Greenland, Fiona, and Pamela J. Smock. "Living Together Unmarried: What Do We Know about Cohabiting Families?" Pp. 255–73 in *Handbook of Marriage and the Family*. 3rd ed. Edited by Gary W. Peterson and Kevin R. Bush. New York: Springer, 2013.

Ross, Allen P. *A Commentary on the Psalms: Volume 1 (1–41)*. KEL. Grand Rapids: Kregel, 2011.

_____. *A Commentary on the Psalms: Volume 2 (42–89)*. KEL. Grand Rapids: Kregel, 2013.

_____. *A Commentary on the Psalms: Volume 3 (90–150)*. KEL. Grand Rapids: Kregel, 2016.

_____. "Proverbs." Pp. 881–1134 in vol. 5 of Expositor's Bible Commentary. Edited by F. E. Gaebelein. Grand Rapids: Zondervan, 1991.

Rowntree, Les, Martin Lewis, Marie Price, and William Wyckoff. *Diversity Amid Globalization: World Regions, Environment, Development*. 2nd ed. Upper Saddle River, NJ: Pearson Education, 2003.

Russell, Bertrand. *A History of Western Philosophy*. New York: Simon & Schuster, 1972.

_____. *Why I Am Not a Christian and Other Essays on Religion and Related Subjects*. Edited by Paul Edwards. New York: Touchstone, 1967.

Rutledge, Fleming. *The Undoing of Death: Sermons for Holy Week and Easter*. Grand Rapids: Eerdmans, 2002.

Sadgrove, Michael. "The Song of Songs as Wisdom Literature. Pp. 245–48 in *Studia Biblica 1978: I*. Edited by E. A. Livingstone. JSOTSup. Sheffield: JSOT, 1979.

Sampley, J. Paul. "The First Letter to the Corinthians." Pp. 771–1003 in vol. 10 of the *New Interpreter's Bible*. Edited by Leander E. Keck. Nashville: Abingdon Press, 2002.

Schipper, Bernd U. *Proverbs 1–15*. Translated by Thomas Krüger. Minneapolis, MN: Fortress Press, 2019.

Schloen, J. D. *The House of the Father as Fact and Symbol: Patrimonialism in Ugarit and the Ancient Near East.* Winona Lake, IN: Eisenbrauns, 2001.

Schneider, *Godly Materialism: Rethinking Money & Possessions.* Downers Grove, IL: InterVarsity Press, 1994.

Schultz, Richard. "'Fear God and Keep His Commandments' (Ecc 12:13): An Examination of Some Intertextual Relationships between Deuteronomy and Ecclesiastes." Pp. 327–43 in *For Our God Always: Studies on the Message and Influence of Deuteronomy in Honor of Daniel I. Block.* Edited by Jason S. DeRouchie, Jason Gile, and Kenneth J. Turner. Winona Lake, IN: Eisenbrauns, 2013.

Schwab, Zoltán. "Creation in the Wisdom Literature." Pp. 391–413 in *The Cambridge Companion to Biblical Wisdom Literature.* Edited by Katharine J. Dell, Suzanna R. Millar, and Arthur Jan Keefer. Cambridge: Cambridge University Press, 2022.

Semuels, Alana. "We are All Accumulating Mountains of Things: How Online Shopping and Cheap Prices are Turning Americans into Hoarders." *The Atlantic*, August 21, 2018. http://theatlantic.com/technology/archive/2018/08/online-shopping-and-accululation-of-junk/567985.

Seow, Choon-Leong. *Ecclesiastes: A New Translation with Introduction and Commentary.* AYB 18C. New Haven: Yale, 1997.

Sherman, Amy L. *Kingdom Calling: Vocational Stewardship for the Common Good.* Downers Grove, IL: IVP Books, 2011.

_____. *Restorers of Hope: Reaching the Poor in Your Community with Church-Based Ministries That Work.* Eugene, OR: Wipf & Stock, 2004.

Shields, M. A. *The End of Wisdom: A Reappraisal of the Historical and Canonical Function of Ecclesiastes.* Winona Lake, IN: Eisenbrauns, 2006.

Shrier, Abigail. *Irreversible Damage: The Transgender Craze Seducing Our Daughters.* Washington, DC: Regnery, 2020.

Shveka, Avi, and Avraham Faust. "Premarital Sex in Biblical Law: A Cross-Cultural Perspective." *VT* (2020): 1–24.

Sinclair, David A. *Lifespan: Why We Age, and Why We Don't Have to.* New York: Atria Books, 2019.

Smith, David W. *The Friendless American Male.* Ventura, CA: Regal Books, 1984.

Smith, James E. *The Wisdom Literature and Psalms*. Joplin, MO: College Press, 1996.

———. *The Social World of the Sages: An Introduction to Israelite and Jewish Wisdom Literature*. Minneapolis, MN: Fortress Press, 2015.

Smith, Nicholas D. "Wisdom." *REP* 9:752–55.

Sneed, Mark R. *The Politics of Pessimism in Ecclesiastes: A Social-Science Perspective*. SBLAILit 12. Atlanta: SBL, 2012.

Spencer, F. Scott. *Song of Songs*. WBC 25. Collegeville, MN: Liturgical Press, 2017.

Spitz, Rene. *Hospitalism: An Inquiry into the Genesis of Psychiatric Conditions in Early Childhood*. Vol. 1 of *The Psychoanalytic Study of the Child*. New York: International Universities Press, 1945.

Stacey, J. *Brave New Families: Stories of Domestic Upheaval in Late 20th Century America*. New York: Basic Books, 1990.

———. "Good Riddance to 'the Family': A Response to David Popenoe." *Journal of Marriage and Family* 55 (1993): 545–47.

Stafford, Tim. *The Sexual Christian*. Wheaton, IL: Victor Books, 1989.

Stager, L. A. "The Archaeology of the Family in Ancient Israel." *BASOR* 260 (1985): 1–36.

Standage, Tom. *The Victorian Internet: The Remarkable Story of the Telegraph and the Nineteenth Century's On-Line Pioneers*. London: Weidenfeld and Nicolson, 1998.

Stanton, Glenn T. *Why Marriage Matters: Reasons to Believe in Marriage in Postmodern Society*. Colorado Springs: Piñon Press, 1997.

Strawn, Brent A. "bě-rē' šît, with 'Wisdom,' in Genesis 1.1 (MT)." *JSOT* 46/3 (2022): 358–87.

Sullivan, Lawrence E., and Susan Sered. "Healing and Medicine: An Overview." *EncJud* 6:3808–16.

Surane, Jenny. "Bank Bucks U.S. Peers, Saying No One Should Return 5 Days a Week." Bloomberg.com, June 28, 2021. https://search.ebscohost.com/login.aspx?direct=true&db=bth&AN=151119821&site=ehost-live.

Swaggart, Jimmy. "Clean Up Our Act." *Charisma* (November 1982): 25–29.

Swinton, John. *Becoming Friends of Time: Disability, Timefulness, and Gentle Discipleship*. Waco: Baylor University Press, 2016.

Teachman, Jay, Lucky Tedrow, and Gina Kim. "The Demography of Families." Pp. 39–63 in *Handbook of Marriage and the Family*. 3rd ed. Edited by Gary W. Peterson and Kevin R. Bush. New York: Springer, 2013.

Tomlinson, John. *The Culture of Speed: The Coming of Immediacy*. London: Sage, 2007.

Towner, P. H. "Households and Household Codes." Pp. 417–19 in *Dictionary of Paul and His Letters*. Edited by Gerald F. Hawthorne and Ralph P. Martin. Downers Grove, IL: InterVarsity Press, 1993.

Trible, Phyllis. *God and the Rhetoric of Sexuality*. Minneapolis, MN: Fortress Press, 1978.

Trueman, Carl R. *The Rise and Triumph of the Modern Self: Cultural Amnesia, Expressive Individualism, and the Road to Sexual Revolution*. Wheaton, IL: Crossway, 2020.

Tucker Jr., W. Dennis. "Psalms 1: Book of." Pp. 578–93 in *Dictionary of the Old Testament: Wisdom, Poetry & Writings*. Edited by Tremper Longman III and Peter Enns. Downers Grove, IL: IVP Academic, 2008.

Turkle, Sherry. *Alone Together: Why We Expect More from Technology and Less from Each Other*. New York: Basic Books, 2011.

_____. *Reclaiming Conversation: The Power of Talk in a Digital Age*. New York: Penguin Press, 2015.

Van Leeuwen, Raymond C. "The Book of Proverbs." Pp. 17–264 in vol. 5 of *The New Interpreter's Bible*. Edited by Leander E. Keck. Nashville: Abingdon Press, 1997.

_____. "Theology, Creation, Wisdom, and Covenant." Pp. 6–83 in *The Oxford Handbook of Wisdom and the Bible*. Edited by Will Kynes. Oxford: Oxford University Press, 2021.

_____. "Wisdom Literature." Pp. 847–50 in *Dictionary for Theological Interpretation of the Bible*. Edited by K. J. Vanhoozer, C. G. Bartholomew, D. J. Treier, and N. T. Wright. Grand Rapids: Baker Academic, 2005.

Van Pelt, M. V., and W. C. Kaiser Jr. "ירא." *NIDOTTE* 2: 527–303.

Vermes, Geza. *The Complete Dead Sea Scrolls in English*. New York: Allen Lane, 1997.

Virilio, Paul. "Speed-Space: Interview with Chris Dercon." In *Virilio Live: Selected Interviews*. Edited by John Armitage. London: Sage, 2001.

Vos, Gerhardus. *Biblical Theology: Old and New Testaments*. Grand Rapids: Eerdmans, 1948.

Waite, L., and E. Lehrer. "The Benefits from Marriage and Religion in the United States: A Comparative Analysis." *Population and Development Review* 9 (2003): 255–75.

Waitley, Denis. *Empires of the Mind: Lessons to Lead and Succeed in a Knowledge-Based World*. New York: William Morrow, 1995.

_____. *The Psychology of Motivation*. Niles, IL: Nightingale Conant, 1997.

Waitley, Denis, and Reni L. Witt. *The Joy of Working*. New York: Dodd, Mead, 1985.

Wajcman, Judy. *Pressed for Time: The Acceleration of Life in Digital Capitalism*. Chicago: The University of Chicago Press, 2015.

Walsh, C. E. *Exquisite Desire: Religion, the Erotic, and the Song of Songs*. Minneapolis, MN: Fortress Press, 2000.

Walter, Tony. "Modern Death: Taboo or Not Taboo?" *Sociology* 25/2 (1991): 293–310.

Waltke, Bruce K. "The Fear of the Lord: The Foundation for a Relationship with God." Pp. 282–300 in *The Dance between God and Humanity: Reading the Bible Today as the People of God*. Grand Rapids: Eerdmans, 2013.

_____. *The Book of Proverbs: Chapters 1–15*. NICOT. Grand Rapids: Eerdmans, 2004.

_____. *The Book of Proverbs: Chapters 15–31*. NICOT. Grand Rapids: Eerdmans, 2005.

_____. "The Book of Proverbs and Ancient Wisdom Literature." *Bibliotheca Sacra* 136 (1979): 221–38.

Walton, John H. "The Psalms: A Cantata about the Davidic Covenant." *JETS* 34 (1991): 21–31.

_____. "Retribution." Pp. 647–55 in *Dictionary of Old Testament: Wisdom, Poetry, and Writings*. Edited by Tremper Longman III and Peter Enns. Downers Grove, IL: IVP Academic, 2008.

Weeks, Stuart. *An Introduction to the Study of Wisdom Literature*. TTCABS. London: T & T Clark, 2010.

Weems, Renita J. "The Song of Songs: Introduction, Commentary, and Reflections." Pp. 361–434 in vol. 5 of *The New Interpreter's Bible*. Edited by Leander E. Keck. Nashville: Abingdon Press, 1997.

Weiser, Artur. *The Psalms: A Commentary*. OTL. Philadelphia: The Westminster Press, 1962.

Westermann, Claus. *Roots of Wisdom: The Oldest Proverbs of Israel and Other Peoples*. Translated by J. Daryl Charles. Louisville, KY: Westminster John Knox, 1995.

Wharton, James A. *Job*. WBC. Louisville, KY: Westminster John Knox, 1999.

White, John B. *A Study of the Language of Love in the Song of Songs and Ancient Egyptian Poetry*. SBLDS. Missoula: Scholars Press, 1978.

Whybray, R. Norman. *Ecclesiastes*. Grand Rapids: Eerdmans, 1989.

_____. *The Good Life in the Old Testament*. London: T & T Clark, 2002.

_____. "Qohelet, Preacher of Joy." *JSOT* 23 (1982): 87–98.

Wilkinson, Richard H. *The Complete Gods and Goddesses of Ancient Egypt*. London: Thames & Hudson, 2003.

Williamson, Paul R. *Death and the Afterlife: Biblical Perspectives on Ultimate Questions*. London: Apollos, 2018.

Willis, Ellen. "Toward a Feminist Sexual Revolution." *Social Text* 6 (1982): 3–21.

Wilson, J. A. *The Burden of Egypt*. Chicago: University of Chicago Press, 1951.

Wilson, Lindsay. "The Book of Job and the Fear of God." *TynBul* 46.1 (1995): 59–79.

_____. "Job as a Problematic Book." Pp. 60–80 in *Interpreting Old Testament Wisdom Literature*. Edited by David G. Firth and Lindsay Wilson. Downers Grove, IL: IVP Academic, 2017.

_____. *Proverbs*. TOTC. Downers Grove, IL: InterVarsity, 2018.

Wilson-Hartgrove, Jonathan. *The Wisdom of Stability: Rooting Faith in a Mobile Culture*. Brewster: Paraclete Press, 2010.

Wright, C. J. H. "Family." *ABD* 2: 761–69.

Wright, Robert. "Infidelity—It May Be in Our Genes: Our Cheating Hearts." *Time*. http://canadiancrc.com/newspaper_articles/Time_Magazine_infidelity _in_genes_15AUG94.aspx. Accessed February 2, 2016.

Yamauchi, Edwin. "Life, Death, and the Afterlife in the Ancient Near East." Pp. 21–50 in *Life in the Face of Death: The Resurrection Message of the New Testament*. Edited by Richard N. Longenecker. Grand Rapids: Eerdmans, 1998.

Yenor, Scott. *The Recovery of Family Life: Exposing the Limits of Modern Ideologies*. Waco: Baylor University Press, 2020.

Yost, Robert A. *Leadership Secrets from the Proverbs: An Examination of Leadership Principles from the Book of Proverbs*. Eugene, OR: Wipf & Stock, 2013.

Youngblood, Ronald F., and Glen G. Scorgie. "Fear of the Lord." Pp. 444–46 in *Dictionary of Christian Spirituality*. Edited by Glen G. Scorgie. Grand Rapids: Zondervan, 2011.

Zerafa, P. *The Wisdom of God in the Book of Job*. Rome: Herder, 1978.

Zigarelli, Michael. *Management by Proverbs*. Otsgo, MI: PageFree, 2004.

NOTES

Introduction

1. Cf. "Pablo Escobar," *Wikipedia.com*, https://en.wikipedia.org/wiki/Pablo
_Escobar; "Pablo Escobar Biography," *Biography.com*, https://www.biography.com
/crime-figure/Pablo-escobar.

2. See Plato, "The Apology," in *Plato* I, trans. Harold North Fowler, LCL 36
(Cambridge, MA: Harvard University Press, 2001), 22C-D.

3. Nicholas D. Smith, "Wisdom," *REP* 9:753.

4. Smith, "Wisdom," *REP* 9:753.

5. Aristotle, *Nichomachean Ethics*, quoted in Paul L. Lehmann, *Ethics in a Christian Context* (New York: Harper & Row, 1963), 169. For a more detailed discussion of Aristotle's view of wisdom and the good life, see Corey Miller, *In Search of the Good Life: Through the Eyes of Aristotle, Maimonides, and Aquinas* (Eugene, OR: Pickwick, 2019).

6. James L. Crenshaw, "The Contemplative Life in the Ancient Near East," in *CANE* 42445–57.

7. R. Norman Whybray, *The Good Life in the Old Testament* (London: T & T Clark, 2002), 3–4.

8. For wisdom as a "path of life" and a "fountain of life," see Prov. 2:19; 5:6; 13:14; 14:27.

9. Contra William Osborne, who argues that the "tree of life" is used in Proverbs simply as a "stock image" for life and vitality. The expression "tree of life" also appears in the Psalms, where Osborne suggests that it takes on new meaning and is used to forge together various concepts associated with the implications of a right relationship with the Lord. Cf. William R. Osborne, "The Tree of Life in Proverbs and Psalms," in *The Tree of Life*, ed. Douglas Estes, TBN 27 (Leiden: Brill, 2020), 100–21.

Chapter 1

1. Tremper Longman III, "Israelite Genres in Their Ancient Near Eastern Context," in *The Changing Face of Form Criticism in the Twenty-First Century*, ed. M. A. Sweeney and Ehud Ben Zvi (Grand Rapids: Eerdmans, 2003), 183.

2. Katharine Dell, Will Kynes, and Mark Sneed are among those whose work has especially advocated for this idea. For an excellent and up-to-date discussion of recent developments in genre studies and wisdom, see Tremper Longman III, "The Scope of

Wisdom Literature," in *The Cambridge Companion to Biblical Wisdom Literature*, ed. Katharine J. Dell, Suzanna R. Millar, and Arthur Jan Keefer (Cambridge: Cambridge University Press, 2022), 13–33.

3. Longman, "The Scope of Wisdom Literature," 32.

4. M. E. J. Richardson, ed., "חָכְמָה," *HALOT* 1:314.

5. Raymond van Leeuwen, "Wisdom Literature," in *Dictionary for Theological Interpretation of the Bible*, ed. K. J. Vanhoozer, C. G. Bartholomew, D. J. Treier, and N. T. Wright (Grand Rapids: Baker Academic, 2005), 847–50.

6. Walther Eichrodt, *Theology of the Old Testament*, trans. J. A. Baker (Philadelphia: Westminster Press, 1967), 2:268.

7. Eichrodt, *Theology of the Old Testament* 2:268–69.

8. Bruce K. Waltke, "The Fear of the Lord: The Foundation for a Relationship with God," in *The Dance between God and Humanity: Reading the Bible Today as the People of God* (Grand Rapids: Eerdmans, 2013), 292.

9. Waltke, "The Fear of the Lord," 292.

10. The original German term is *Scheu*, which can be translated as "shyness," "timidity," "reserve," "awe," or "fright."

11. Eichrodt, 2:268–69. Cf. Gen. 20:11; 22:12; 42:18; Exod. 18:21; Deut. 4:10; 25:18; 2 Kings 4:1; Isa. 11:2; 29:13; 50:10; Ps. 90:11; Prov. 2:5; Job 1:1, 8; 2 Chron. 6:33; Eccles. 7:18; et al.

12. Gerhard von Rad, *Wisdom in Israel*, trans. J. D. Martin (London: SCM, 1970), 67–68.

13. J. A. Wilson, *The Burden of Egypt* (Chicago: University of Chicago Press, 1951), 48.

14. J. D. Ray, "Egyptian Wisdom Literature," in *Wisdom in Ancient Israel*, ed. J. Day, R. P. Gordan, and H. G. M. Williamson (Cambridge: Cambridge University Press, 1995), 18.

15. This chart draws on selected material from "The Instruction of Amen-Em-Opet," trans. John A. Wilson, *ANET*, 421–50.

16. See David J. A. Clines, *Job 1–20*, WBC 17 (Dallas: Word, 1989), 10–11.

17. It might have been relocated within the book at some point following its composition.

18. Francis I. Andersen, *Job*, TOTC (Downers Grove, IL: InterVarsity, 1976), 23–32.

19. W. G. Lambert, *Babylonian Wisdom Literature* (Oxford: Oxford University Press, 1960), 21–91.

20. P. Zerafa, *The Wisdom of God in the Book of Job* (Rome: Herder, 1978).

21. Anderson, *Job*, 73.

22. Cf. J. G. Davies, *Holy Week: A Short History*, ESW 11 (Richmond: John Knox Press, 1963), 23ff.

23. John H. Walton, "The Psalms: A Cantata about the Davidic Covenant," *JETS* 34 (1991): 21–31.

24. Hermann Gunkel, *The Psalms: A Form-Critical Introduction* (Philadelphia: Fortress Press, 1967). "Form criticism" is the investigation of the literary "form" or "genre" of a text.

25. Gunkel, *The Psalms*, 10–25.

26. E.g., Erhard Gerstenberger, "Psalms," in *Old Testament Form Criticism*, ed. John H. Hayes (San Antonio: Trinity University Press, 1974), 179–223.

27. E.g., Moshe Greenberg, *Biblical Prose Prayer* (Berkeley: University of California Press, 1983), 52.

28. Cf. Rolf A. Jacobson, "Form Criticism and Historical Approaches to Interpretation," in Nancy deClaissé-Walford, Rolf A. Jacobson, and Beth Laneel Tanner, *The Book of Psalms* (Grand Rapids: Eerdmans, 2014), 13–21.

29. For a summary of the discussion, see Diane Jacobson, "Wisdom Language in the Psalms," in *The Oxford Handbook of the Psalms*, ed. W. P. Brown (Oxford: Oxford University Press, 2014), 147–57. More recently, see Simon Chi-Chung Cheung, "Wisdom Psalms," in *The Cambridge Companion to Biblical Wisdom Literature*, ed. Katharine J. Dell, Suzanna R. Millar, and Arthur Jan Keefer (Cambridge: Cambridge University Press, 2022), 219–38.

30. In an alphabetic acrostic, the first word of each verse begins with a successive letter of the Hebrew alphabet so that it covers the whole alphabet.

31. This provides a contrast with other ancient Near Eastern views, in which the gods were elements of nature. In the Babylonian creation epic *Enuma Elish*, for example, the gods Apsu and Tiamat were freshwater and saltwater.

32. Examples of messianic psalms include Pss. 2, 16, 22, 45, 110.

33. In Acts 13:33, Paul quotes from Ps. 2:7, and in Acts 13:35, he quotes Ps. 16:10.

34. W. Dennis Tucker, Jr., "Psalms 1: Book of," in *Dictionary of the Old Testament: Wisdom, Poetry and Writings*, ed. Tremper Longman III and Peter Enns (Downers Grove, IL: IVP Academic, 2008), 592.

35. Otto Eissfeldt, *The Old Testament: An Introduction*, trans. P. R. Ackroyd (New York: Harper & Row, 1965), 476.

36. Ellen F. Davis, *Proverbs, Ecclesiastes, and the Song of Songs* (Louisville, KY: Westminster John Knox, 2000), 16.

37. Bruce Waltke, "The Book of Proverbs and Ancient Wisdom Literature," *Bibliotheca Sacra* 136 (1979): 221–38.

38. On sages in ancient Israel and the debate about their role in the production and dissemination of wisdom literature, see Joseph Blenkinsopp, *Sage, Priest, Prophet: Religious and Intellectual Leadership in Ancient Israel*, LAI (Louisville, KY: Westminster John Knox, 1995), 9–65; James L. Crenshaw, *Old Testament Wisdom Literature* (Atlanta: John Knox Press, 1981), 28–39; John G. Gammie and Leo G. Perdue, eds., *The Sage in Israel and the Ancient Near East* (Winona Lake, IN: Eisenbrauns, 1990); and Mark R. Sneed, *The Social World of the Sages: An Introduction to Israelite and Jewish Wisdom Literature* (Minneapolis: Fortress Press, 2015).

39. Davis, *Proverbs, Ecclesiastes, and the Song of Songs*, 15.

40. E.g., Claus Westermann, *Roots of Wisdom: The Oldest Proverbs of Israel and Other Peoples*, trans. J. Daryl Charles (Louisville, KY: Westminster John Knox, 1995).

41. See also F. W. Golka, *The Leopard's Spots: Biblical and African Wisdom in Proverbs* (Edinburgh: T & T Clark, 1993), which uses African parallels to make the case that early biblical wisdom originated as oral folk tradition.

42. Katharine J. Dell, *The Solomonic Corpus of "Wisdom" and Its Influence* (Oxford: Oxford University Press, 2020), 111.

43. This will be discussed in greater length in chapter 3.

44. Gunther W. Plaut, *Book of Proverbs* (New York: Jewish Commentary for Bible Readers, 1961), 7.

45. See R. Beckwith, *The Old Testament Canon in the New Testament Church* (Grand Rapids: Eerdmans, 1985), 297–304.

46. Traditionally (e.g., KJV), the term was rendered "preacher." More recent translations (e.g., NIV, NLT) prefer "teacher."

47. "The Dispute Between a Man and His Soul," *ANET* 405–7.

48. *ANET* 72–99.

49. *ANET* 437–38.

50. For a summary of the issues, see Peter Enns, "Ecclesiastes 1: Book of," in *Dictionary of the Old Testament: Wisdom, Poetry and Writings*, ed. Tremper Longman III and Peter Enns (Downers Grove, IL: IVP Academic, 2008), 123–24.

51. Daniel C. Fredericks, *Qoheleth's Language: Reevaluating Its Nature and Date* (Lewiston, NY: The Edwin Mellen Press, 1988).

52. E.g., M. A. Shields, *The End of Wisdom: A Reappraisal of the Historical and Canonical Function of Ecclesiastes* (Winona Lake, IN: Eisenbrauns, 2006), 96.

53. Mark J. Boda, "Speaking into the Silence: The Epilogue of Ecclesiastes," in *The Words of the Wise Are Like Goads: Engaging Qohelet in the 21st Century*, ed. Mark J. Boda, Tremper Longman III, and Christian Rata (Winona Lake, IN: Eisenbrauns, 2013), 257–79.

54. See Ecclesiastes 1:2–11; 2:12–26; 3:9–15; 5:13–20; 6:1–12; 8:1–15; 9:1–12; 11:7–12:7.

55. William H. Anderson, *Qoheleth and Its Pessimistic Theology: Hermeneutical Struggles in Wisdom Literature*, MBPS 54 (Lewiston, NY: Mellen Biblical, 1997), 61–65, 176.

56. Cf. Michael A. Eaton, *Ecclesiastes: An Introduction and Commentary* (Leicester, UK: InterVarsity Press, 1983), 46–47.

57. For a brief history of the interpretation of *hebel*, see Russell L. Meek, "The Meaning of הבל in Qohelet: An Intertextual Suggestion," in *The Words of the Wise Are Like Goads: Engaging Qohelet in the 21st Century*, ed. Mark J. Boda, Tremper Longman III, and Christian Rata (Winona Lake, IN: Eisenbrauns, 2013), 241–45.

58. Russel L. Meek, "Twentieth- and Twenty-First Century Readings of Hebel (הֶבֶל) in Ecclesiastes," *CurBR* 14/3 (2016), 284.

59. Daniel C. Fredericks, *Coping with Transience: Ecclesiastes on Brevity in Life*, TBS 18 (Sheffield: JSOT Press, 1993), 15–16.

60. Fredericks, *Coping with Transience*, 11–32.

61. Fredericks, *Coping with Transience*, 92.

62. Peterson, *Qoheleth's Hope*, 38–39.

63. Daniel C. Fredericks, "Ecclesiastes," in *Ecclesiastes & the Song of Songs*, AOTC 16 (Nottingham, UK: Apollos, 2010), 15–263.

64. Meek, "The Meaning of הבל in Qohelet," 245–55.

65. Meek, "The Meaning of הבל in Qohelet," 253–54.

66. David J. H. Beldman, "Framed! Structure in Ecclesiastes," in *The Words of the Wise Are Like Goads: Engaging Qohelet in the 21st Century*, ed. Mark J. Boda, Tremper Longman III, and Christian Rata (Winona Lake, IN: Eisenbrauns, 2013), 150–54.

67. Eaton, *Ecclesiastes*, 44.

68. Eaton, *Ecclesiastes*, 45.

69. Eaton, *Ecclesiastes*, 45.

70. Eaton, *Ecclesiastes*, 45.

71. Eaton, *Ecclesiastes*, 45.

72. Brian Neil Peterson, *Qoheleth's Hope: The Message of Ecclesiastes in a Broken World* (Lanham, MD: Lexington Books; Fortress Academic, 2020), 47.

73. Wright, "Ecclesiastes," 1146.

74. See *m. Yadayim* 3.5, in Herbert Danby, *The Mishnah: Translated from the Hebrew with Introduction and Brief Explanatory Notes* (Oxford: Oxford University Press, 1933; repr., Peabody, MA: Hendrickson, 2011), 782.

75. Solomon's name is mentioned in Song 1:5; 3:7, 9, 11; 8:11–12, and there are references to a "king" in 1:4, 12, and 7:5.

76. Maria Falk, *Love Lyrics from the Bible* (Sheffield: Almond, 1982), 4, 12–51.

77. Tremper Longman III, *Song of Songs*, NICOT (Grand Rapids: Eerdmans, 2001), viii.

78. John J. Collins, *Introduction to the Hebrew Bible*, 3rd ed. (Minneapolis: Fortress Press, 2018), 515.

79. See Lee Martin McDonald and James A. Sanders, eds., *The Canon Debate* (Peabody, MA: Hendrickson, 2002), 585–90.

80. Brevard S. Childs, *Introduction to the Old Testament as Scripture* (London: SCM, 1979), 574.

81. Rosalind Clarke, "Seeking Wisdom in the Song of Songs," in *Interpreting Old Testament Wisdom Literature*, ed. David G. Firth and Lindsay Wilson (Downers Grove, IL: IVP Academic, 2017), 103. See Song 1:4b, 5–6; 2:7; 3:5, 11; 5:1b, 8–16; 6:1–3; 8:4.

82. Michael Fishbane, *Song of Songs*, JPSBC (Philadelphia: JPS, 2015), xxiv–xlvii.

83. Michael Sadgrove, "The Song of Songs as Wisdom Literature," in *Studia Biblica 1978:* JSOTSup (Sheffield: JSOT, 1979), 247. Clarke suggests that he has overstated his case for the Song as a "wisdom puzzle." Clarke, "Seeking Wisdom in the Song of Songs," 102n11.

84. Gerhard von Rad, *Wisdom in Israel*, trans. J. D. Martin (Nashville: Abingdon, 1972), 166.

85. Katherine Dell, "Does the Song of Songs Have Any Connections to Wisdom?," in Anselm C. Hagedorn, ed., *Perspectives on the Song of Songs*, BZAW (Berlin: De Gruyter, 2005), 20.

86. Clarke, "Seeking Wisdom in the Song of Songs," 103. For a recent overview of the book's reception history, as well as an argument that the book should be identified as wisdom literature, see Jennifer L. Andruska, "The Song of Songs," in Katharine J. Dell, Suzanna R. Millar, and Arthur Jan Keefer, eds., *The Cambridge Companion to Biblical Wisdom Literature* (Cambridge: Cambridge University Press, 2022), 200–18.

87. This view goes back to at least the beginning of the fifth century BC, when the Codex Sinaiticus included rubrics in the margins to indicate the identity of the speakers.

88. Cf. Tremper Longman III and Raymond B. Dillard, *An Introduction to the Old Testament*, 2nd ed. (Grand Rapids: Zondervan, 2006), 290–92.

89. Michael V. Fox, *The Song of Songs and Ancient Egyptian Love Songs* (Madison: University of Wisconsin Press, 1985); and John B. White, *A Study of the Language of Love in the Song of Songs and Ancient Egyptian Poetry*, SBLDS (Missoula: Scholars Press, 1978).

90. E.g., Othmar Keel, *The Song of Songs: A Continental Commentary*, trans. Frederick J. Gaiser (Minneapolis: Fortress Press, 1994), 17.

91. E.g., J. Cheryl Exum, "A Literary and Structural Analysis of the Song of Songs, *ZAW* 8 (1973): 47–79; Fox, *The Song of Songs*, 194–5.

92. Richard S. Hess, *Song of Songs*, BCOTWP (Grand Rapids: Baker Academic, 2005), 34–35.

93. Clarke, "Seeking Wisdom in the Song of Songs," 103.

94. Clarke, "Seeking Wisdom in the Song of Songs," 103–4.

95. For a detailed study, see Richard M. Davidson, "The Literary Structure of the Song of Songs Redivivus," *JATS* 14/2 (2003): 44–65.

96. David J. A. Clines, "Why Is There a Song of Songs and What Does It Do to You If You Read It?," *Jian Dao* 1 (1994): 1–27.

97. Richard S. Hess, *Song of Songs*, BCOTWP (Grand Rapids: Baker Academic, 2005), 34–35. See also Hess, "Song of Songs: Not Just a Dirty Book," *Bible Review* 21/5 (2005), 30–40.

98. A detailed summary of the history of the interpretation of the Song can be found in Marvin H. Pope, *The Song of Songs*, AB 7C (Garden City, NY: Doubleday, 1977), 89–229. The most thorough history of Jewish interpretation of the Song is now found in Fishbane, *Song of Songs*, 245–304.

99. Coogan and Chapman, *The Old Testament*, 479.

100. Cf. Song of Songs 4:8–5:1 where the term "bride" occurs six times.

101. For a history of the book's interpretation and reception, see Ilana Pardes, *The Song of Songs: A Biography*, LGRB (Princeton: Princeton University Press, 2019).

102. See the discussion in William E. Phipps, "The Plight of the Song of Songs," *JAAR* 42/1 (1974): 82–100, esp. 95–98.

103. Katherine Dell, "Does the Song of Songs Have Any Connections to Wisdom?," in Anselm C. Hagedorn, ed., *Perspectives on the Song of Songs*, BZAW (Berlin: De Gruyter, 2005), 9.

104. Roland E. Murphy, *The Tree of Life: An Exploration of Biblical Wisdom Literature*, ABRL (New York: Doubleday, 1990), 106.

105. Richard S. Hess, *The Old Testament: A Historical, Theological, and Critical Introduction* (Grand Rapids: Baker Academic, 2016), 509.

106. Clarke, "Seeking Wisdom in the Song of Songs," 104.

107. Karl Möller, *The Song of Songs: Beautiful Bodies, Erotic Desire and Intoxicating Pleasure* (Cambridge: Grove Books, 2018), 4.

108. Möller, *The Song of Songs*, 15.

109. Möller, *The Song of Songs*, 15.

110. Möller, *The Song of Songs*, 19–20.

111. Shalom Paul, "A Lover's Garden of Verse: Literal and Metaphorical Imagery in Ancient Near Eastern Love Poetry," in *Tehilla le-Moshe: Biblical and Judaic Studies in Honor of Moshe Greenberg*, ed. M. Cogan et al. (Winona Lake, IN: Eisenbrauns, 1997), 99–110.

112. See the discussion in Othmar Keel, *The Song of Songs*, trans. Frederick J. Gaiser (Minneapolis, MN: Fortress Press, 1994), 174–76.

113. William L. Holladay, *A Concise Hebrew and Aramaic Lexicon of the Old Testament* (Grand Rapids: Eerdmans; Leiden: Brill, 1988), 34.

114. In 5:1, "I have come" is in the perfect form, which suggests that the action took place in the past. It should be noted, however, that in poetry this is not necessarily the case. See standard commentaries for alternatives.

115. Möller, *The Song of Songs*, 17.

116. Holladay, *A Concise Hebrew and Aramaic Lexicon of the Old Testament*, 396.

117. J. Cheryl Exum, *Song of Songs: A Commentary*, OTL (Louisville, KY: Westminster John Knox, 2005), 13–14.

118. Hess, "Song of Songs: Not Just a Dirty Book," 40.

119. Song of Songs 2:3–13; 4:12–5:1; 5:2–6:3; 6:11; 7:10–13; 8:13–14.

120. See the discussion and references in Richard M. Davidson, *Flame of Yahweh: Sexuality in the Old Testament* (Peabody, MA: Hendrickson, 2007), 552–53.

121. Raymond B. Dillard and Tremper Longman, III, *An Introduction to the Old Testament* (Grand Rapids: Zondervan, 1994), 265.

122. Renita J. Weems, "The Song of Songs: Introduction, Commentary, and Reflections," in vol. 5 of *The New Interpreter's Bible*, ed. Leander E. Keck (Nashville: Abingdon Press, 1997), 369.

123. Phylis Trible, *God and the Rhetoric of Sexuality* (Minneapolis: Fortress, 1978), 144.

124. Dillard and Longman, *An Introduction to the Old Testament*, 265.

125. Diane Bergant, *The Song of Songs*, Berit Olam (Collegeville, MN: Liturgical Press, 2001), 105.

126. In 1 Corinthians 7, Paul appears to be promoting an unmarried state, but he is probably addressing a particular situation. This single passage should not be used to counter the clear thrust of the rest of Scripture.

Chapter 2

1. E.g., Dave Miller, *Piloting the Strait: A Guidebook for Assessing Change in Churches of Christ* (Pulaski, TN: Sain, 1996), 454.

2. See W. Jaeger, *The Theology of the Early Greek Philosophers* (Oxford: Oxford University Press, 1947), 182–83, 250. Cited in R. H. Pfeiffer, "The Fear of God," *IEJ* 5/1 (1955): 41n1.

3. *Thebais* III, 661. Cited in Pfeiffer, "The Fear of God," 41.

4. Pfeiffer, "The Fear of God," 41.

5. H. F. Fuhs, "יָרֵא *yārē*'," in *Theological Dictionary of the Old Testament*, ed. G. Johannes Botterweck and Helmer Ringgren, trans. David E. Green (Grand Rapids: Eerdmans, 1990), 6:298–300.

6. Pieter G. R. de Villiers, " 'In Awe of the Mighty Deeds of God': The Fear of God in Early Christianity from the Perspective of Biblical Spirituality," in *Saving Fear in Christian Spirituality*, ed. Ann W. Astell (Notre Dame: University of Notre Dame Press, 2019), 23.

7. de Villiers, "In Awe of the Mighty Deeds of God," 23.

8. de Villiers, "In Awe of the Mighty Deeds of God," 23.

9. Cf. Bertrand Russell, *A History of Western Philosophy* (New York: Simon & Schuster, 1972), 246–51.

10. Ralph Keen, "The Reformation Recovery of the Wrath of God," in *Saving Fear in Christian Spirituality*, ed. Ann W. Astell (Notre Dame: University of Notre Dame Press, 2019), 170.

11. On the importance of this incident in Luther's life, see Martin Brecht, *Martin Luther: His Road to Reformation, 1483–1521*, trans. James L. Schaaf (Minneapolis, MN: Fortress Press, 1985), 44–50.

12. It is unlikely that the storm alone convinced Luther to suddenly become a monk. Cf. the thorough discussion of the numerous factors involved in Luther's decision in Scott H. Hendrix, *Martin Luther: Visionary Reformer* (New Haven: Yale University Press, 2017), 27–40.

13. R. W. Heinze, "Luther, Martin," in *Evangelical Dictionary of Theology*, 2nd ed., ed. Walter A. Elwell (Grand Rapids: Baker Academic, 2001), 717–19.

14. Keen, "The Reformation Recovery of the Wrath of God," 171.

15. Philip Melanchthon, *Commonplaces: Loci Communes 1521*, trans. Christian Preus (St. Louis: Concordia, 2014), 110. Cited in Keen, "The Reformation Recovery of the Wrath of God," 171.

16. Julia A. Lamm, "Casting out Fear: The Logic of 'God Is Love' in Julian of Norwich and Friedrich Schleiermacher," in *Saving Fear in Christian Spirituality*, ed. Ann W. Astell (Notre Dame: University of Notre Dame Press, 2019), 234n13.

17. Lamm, "Casting out Fear," 235.

18. Cyril O'Regan, "Fear of God in John Henry Newman and Søren Kierkegaard," in *Saving Fear in Christian Spirituality*, ed. Ann W. Astell (Notre Dame: University of Notre Dame Press, 2019), 261.

19. O'Regan, "Fear of God in John Henry Newman and Søren Kierkegaard," 276–77.

20. William James, *Varieties of Religious Experience: A Study in Human Nature* (London: Routledge, 2002).

21. James, *Varieties of Religious Experience*, 81, 77. Cited in Ann W. Astell, "The Saving of Fear: An Introduction," in *Saving Fear in Christian Spirituality*, ed. Ann W. Astell (Notre Dame: University of Notre Dame Press, 2019), 15.

22. James, *Varieties of Religious Experience*, 75–76. Cited in Astell, "The Saving of Fear," 75–76.

23. Bertrand Russell, *Why I Am Not a Christian and Other Essays on Religion and Related Subjects*, ed. Paul Edwards (New York: Touchstone, 1967), 20.

24. Quoted in Ronald F. Youngblood and Glen G. Scorgie, "Fear of the Lord," in *Dictionary of Christian Spirituality*, ed. Glen G. Scorgie (Grand Rapids: Zondervan, 2011), 446.

25. "The Religious Typology: A New Way to Categorize Americans by Religion," Pew Research Center, August 29, 2018, https://www.pewforum.org/2018/098/29/29 /religious-and-spiritual-practices-and-beliefs-2.

26. Rob Bell, *Love Wins: A Book about Heaven, Hell, and the Fate of Every Person Who Ever Lived* (New York: HarperCollins, 2011), viii.

27. Bell, *Love Wins*, 95.

28. Bell, *Love Wins*, 184.

29. Bell, *Love Wins*, 187.

30. Raymond van Leeuwen, "Wisdom Literature," in *Dictionary for Theological Interpretation of the Bible*, ed. K. J. Vanhoozer, C. G. Bartholomew, D. J. Treier, and N. T. Wright (Grand Rapids: Baker Academic, 2005), 848–49.

31. Rudolf Otto, *The Idea of the Holy: An Inquiry into the Non-Rational Factor in the Idea of the Divine and Its Relation to the Rational*, trans. John W. Harvey (New York: Oxford University Press, 1958), 12–24.

32. Otto, *The Idea of the Holy*, 13.

33. Otto, *The Idea of the Holy*, 13–14.

34. Sonia Brough, *Langenscheidt's New College German Dictionary* (New York: Langenscheidt, 1995), 523.

35. Otto, *The Idea of the Holy*, 31.

36. Walter Eichrodt, *Theology of the Old Testament*, trans. J. A. Baker (Philadelphia: Westminster Press, 1967), 2:268.

37. Eichrodt, *Theology of the Old Testament*, 2:268–77.

38. Eichrodt, *Theology of the Old Testament*, 2:268.

39. Bruce K. Waltke, "The Fear of the Lord: The Foundation for a Relationship with God," in *The Dance between God and Humanity: Reading the Bible Today as the People of God* (Grand Rapids: Eerdmans, 2013), 292.

40. Waltke, "The Fear of the Lord," 292.

41. Nancy deClaissé-Walford, "Psalm 111," in *The Book of Psalms*, ed. Nancy deClaissé-Walford, Rolf A. Jacobson, and Beth Laneel Tanner (Grand Rapids: Eerdmans, 2014), 841.

42. Daniel C. Fredericks, "Ecclesiastes," in Daniel C. Fredericks and Daniel J. Estes, *Ecclesiastes & Song of Songs*, AOT 16 (Nottingham, UK: Apollos; Downers Grove, IL: InterVarsity Press, 2010), 107ff.; John Goldingay, *The First Testament: A New Translation* (Downers Grove, IL: IVP Academic, 2018), 605ff.

43. Tremper Longman III, *The Fear of the Lord Is Wisdom: A Theological Introduction to Wisdom in Israel* (Grand Rapids: Baker Academic, 2017), 12–13.

44. For a discussion of the various aspects of the Hebrew word, see *NIDOTTE* 2:527–33.

45. Cf. H. Blocher, "The Fear of the Lord as the 'Principle' of Wisdom," *TynBul* 28 (1977): 3–28.

46. Gerhard von Rad, *Wisdom in Israel*, trans. J. D. Martin (London: SCM, 1970), 67–68.

47. Lindsay Wilson, "The Book of Job and the Fear of God," *TynBul* 46.1 (1995): 59–79. The precise expression "fear of the Lord" actually never occurs in the book of Job, but the idea of fearing God appears throughout it (Job 1:1, 8, 9; 2:3; 4:6; 6:14; 15:4; 22:4; 28:28; 37:24).

48. The fear of the Lord and turning away from evil are often coupled in Proverbs. E.g., Prov 3:7; 14:16; 16:6.

49. Lindsay Wilson, "The Book of Job and the Fear of God," *TynBul* 46.1 (1995): 67.

50. Cf. Job 5:8–9; 8:20; 11:7–20.

51. Wilson, "The Book of Job and the Fear of God," 69.

52. For a thorough study of Job 28 and its place and function in the book of Job, see Scott C. Jones, *Rumors of Wisdom: Job 28 as Poetry*, BZAW (Berlin: De Gruyter, 2009).

53. Wilson, "The Book of Job and the Fear of God," 69.

54. Wilson, "The Book of Job and the Fear of God," 72.

55. Wilson, "The Book of Job and the Fear of God," 75–78.

56. Cf. Marc Zvi Brettler, "Acrostic," *NIDB* 1:32–33.

57. E.g., Anthony R. Ceresko, "The ABC's of Wisdom in Psalm xxxiv," *VT* 35 (1985): 99–104.

58. In v. 9, fearing the Lord clearly means adopting God's way of life. This is evident by the fact that the three imperatives are in parallelism.

59. Rolf A. Jacobson, "Psalm 34," in *The Book of Psalms*, Nancy deClaissé-Walford, Rolf A. Jacobson, and Beth Laneel Tanner (Grand Rapids: Eerdmans, 2014), 327.

60. Peter C. Craigie, *Psalms 1–50*, WBC 19 (Waco: Word, 1983), 282.

61. Craigie, *Psalms 1–50*, 282.

62. E.g., Artur Weiser, *The Psalms: A Commentary*, OTL (Philadelphia: The Westminster Press, 1962), 697–702.

63. In Exodus 34:6, the text reads "merciful and gracious." While the psalmist wanted to evoke the Divine Attribute Formula, the acrostic structure of the psalm necessitated that he reverse the word order.

64. For a discussion of the Divine Attribute Formula in Exodus, its use in Old Testament and Apocryphal prayers, and its appropriation in later Jewish and Christian liturgy, see Ralph K. Hawkins, *Discovering Exodus: Content, Interpretation, Reception* (Grand Rapids: Eerdmans, 2021), 157–66.

65. Hawkins, *Discovering Exodus*, 158.

66. On the power of God in the exodus and the promise of the conquest of Canaan, cf. Hawkins, *Discovering Exodus*, 79–108, 127–28.

67. Allen P. Ross, *A Commentary on the Psalms: Volume 3 (90–150)* (Grand Rapids: Kregel, 2016), 369–70.

68. DeClaissé-Walford, "Psalm 111," 841.

69. Fuhs, "אֵרָי *yārē*'," *TDOT* 6:311.

70. In addition to Proverbs 1:7, see also 1:29; 2:5; 3: 7; 8:13; 10:27; 14:2, 26, 27; 15:16, 33; 16:6; 19:23; 22:4; 23:17; 24:21; 28:14; 29:25; 31:30.

71. See the discussions of retribution theology in chapter 2 above.

72. Bruce K. Waltke, *The Book of Proverbs: Chapters 15–31*, NICOT (Grand Rapids: Eerdmans, 2005), 8.

73. Once the heart has been corrupted, that corruption will be manifested in corrupt speech (see Matt. 15:10–20).

74. Goldingay, *The First Testament*, 623.

75. Tremper Longman III, *Proverbs*, BCOTWP (Grand Rapids: Baker Academic, 2006), 403–4.

76. See, however, the qualifications in Roland E. Murphy, *Proverbs*, WBC 22 (Nashville: Thomas Nelson, 1998), 166–67.

77. Fox, *Ecclesiastes*, xxxi.

78. Tremper Longman III, "The 'Fear of God' in the Book of Ecclesiastes," *BBR* 25.1 (2015): 13–21.

79. Brian Neil Peterson, *Qoheleth's Hope: The Message of Ecclesiastes in a Broken World* (Lanham, MD: Lexington Books; Fortress Academic, 2020), 47.

80. See further, Richard Schultz, " 'Fear God and Keep His commandments' (Ecc 12:13): An Examination of Some Intertextual Relationships between Deuteronomy and Ecclesiastes," in *For Our Good Always: Studies on the Message and Influence of Deuteronomy in Honor of Daniel I. Block*, ed. Jason S. DeRouchie, Jason Gile, and Kenneth J. Turner (Winona Lake, IN: Eisenbrauns, 2013), 327–43.

81. Longman, "The 'Fear of God' in the Book of Ecclesiastes," 16.

82. Peterson, *Qoheleth's Hope*, 75.

83. Michael V. Fox, *Ecclesiastes*, JPSBC (Philadelphia: JPS, 2004), 49.

84. See the discussion and notes in C. L. Seow, *Ecclesiastes*, AYB 18C (New Haven: Anchor Yale Bible, 1997), 252–53.

85. William H. U. Anderson, *Qoheleth and Its Pessimistic Theology: Hermeneutical Struggles in Wisdom Literature*, MBPS 54 (Lewiston, NY: Mellen Biblical, 1997), 109.

86. Knut Martin Heim, *Ecclesiastes: An Introduction and Commentary*, TOTC 18 (Downers Grove, IL: InterVarsity Press, 2019), 157.

87. At the end of v. 10, Qoheleth describes this example of injustice as *hebel* (הֶבֶל), which Fredericks translates here as "temporary." Cf. Fredericks, "Ecclesiastes," 188.

88. Heim, *Ecclesiastes*, 157.

89. For a brief discussion about whether the author of the epilogue was Qoheleth or a later editor, see chapter 2 above.

90. Fox, *Ecclesiastes*, 83.

91. Peterson, *Qoheleth's Hope*, 141.

92. Joseph A. Fitzmyer, S. J., *The Gospel According to Luke (I-IX)*, AB 28 (New York: Doubleday, 1970), 368.

93. M. Eugene Boring, "The Gospel of Matthew," in vol. 8 of *The New Interpreter's Bible*, ed. Leander E. Keck (Nashville: Abingdon Press, 1995), 261.

94. Luke Timothy Johnson, *The Acts of the Apostles*, Sacra Pagina Series 5 (Collegeville, MN: The Liturgical Press, 1992), 177.

95. Joseph A. Fitzmyer, S.J., *The Acts of the Apostles: A New Translation and Commentary*, AB 31 (New York: Doubleday, 1998), 440.

96. Ralph P. Martin, *2 Corinthians*, WBC 40 (Waco: Word Books, 1986), 211.

97. On the Household Codes, see P. H. Towner, "Households and Household Codes," in *Dictionary of Paul and His Letters*, ed. Gerald F. Hawthorne and Ralph P. Martin (Downers Grove, IL: InterVarsity Press, 1993), 417–19; and Craig S. Keener, "Family and Household," in *Dictionary of New Testament Background*, ed. Craig A. Evans and Stanley E. Porter (Downers Grove, IL: InterVarsity Press, 2000), 353–68.

98. Cf. Lynn H. Cohick, *The Letter to the Ephesians* (Grand Rapids: Eerdmans, 2020), 340.

99. Morna D. Hooker, "The Letter to the Philippians," in vol. 11 of *The New Interpreter's Bible*, ed. Leander E. Keck (Nashville: Abingdon Press, 2000), 512.

100. Cf. the discussion in Gareth Lee Cockerill, *The Epistle to the Hebrews* (Grand Rapids: Eerdmans, 2012), 642–60.

101. Cockerill, *The Epistle to the Hebrews*, 673.

102. David L. Bartlett, "The First Letter of Peter," in vol. 12 of *The New Interpreter's Bible*, ed. Leander E. Keck (Nashville: Abingdon Press, 1998), 258.

103. See the discussion in J. Ramsey Michaels, *1 Peter*, WBC 49 (Waco: Word Books, 1988), 132.

104. Lamm, "Casting Out Fear," 234n13.

105. de Villiers, "In Awe of the Mighty Deeds of God," 39.

106. Ann W. Astell, "The Saving of Fear: An Introduction," in *Saving Fear in Christian Spirituality*, ed. Ann W. Astell (Notre Dame: University of Notre Dame Press, 2020), 14.

Chapter 3

1. Denis Waitley, *Empires of the Mind: Lessons to Lead and Succeed in a Knowledge-Based World* (New York: William Morrow, 1995), 74–75.

2. "Cops: Man buys car after taking $150,000 left by ATM workers," *AP News*, July 31, 2015, https://apnews.com/article/e8e4d5cc9fd9401baa3e567525d261d6.

3. Karl Menninger, *Whatever Became of Sin?* (New York: Hawthorn Books, 1973).

4. Cf. Frances Allen, *Saving Normal: An Insider's Revolt against Out-of-Control Psychiatric Diagnosis, DSM-5, Big Pharma, and the Medicalization of Ordinary Life* (New York: William Morrow, 2014).

5. Robert Wright, "Infidelity—It May Be in Our Genes: Our Cheating Hearts," *Time: Online Edition*, http://canadiancrc.com/newspaper_articles/Time_Magazine _infidelity_in_genes_15AUG94.aspx.

6. Menninger, *Whatever Became of Sin?*, 13.

7. David Brooks, *The Road to Character* (New York: Random House, 2015), 24.

8. Walter Brueggemann, *Reverberations of Faith: A Theological Handbook of Old Testament Themes* (Louisville, KY: Westminster John Knox Press, 2002), 79–80.

9. See Rolf A. Jacobson, "Psalm 14," in Nancy deClaissé-Walford, Rolf A. Jacobson, and Beth Laneel Tanner, *The Book of Psalms*, NICOT (Grand Rapids: Eerdmans, 2014), 164.

10. Cf. the discussion of this passage in Bernd U. Schipper, *Proverbs 1–15*, trans. Thomas Krüger (Minneapolis, MN: Fortress Press, 2019), 338–39.

11. It is a problem of perception. See Tremper Longman III, *Proverbs*, BCOTWP (Grand Rapids: Baker Academic, 2006), 300.

12. This idea is also reflected in Ps. 143:2, Job 4:17–19, and Eccl. 7:20.

13. Although "torah" has traditionally been translated as "law," it comes from the verb *yarah*, which means "to point," and clearly has a more expansive meaning that includes "guidance," "instruction," or "teaching." In this discussion, we will simply use the transliterated form of the Hebrew word itself, Torah.

14. Cf. Exod. 20:20; cf. Neh. 5:9, 15; Job 6:14; Ps. 36:1; Prov. 8:13; 23:17.

15. Job 1:1, 8; 2:3; 28:28; Prov. 14:16; 16:6; cf. Isa. 59:15.

16. E.g., Joseph Blenkinsopp, *Wisdom and Law in the Old Testament: The Ordering of Life in Israel and Early Judaism*, The Oxford Bible Series (Oxford: Oxford University Press, 1983), 140–45; James L. Crenshaw, *Old Testament Wisdom: An Introduction*, rev. ed. (Louisville, KY: Westminster John Knox, 1998), 21.

17. See Katharine J. Dell, *The Solomonic Corpus of "Wisdom" and Its Influence* (Oxford: Oxford University Press, 2020), 19–31; Will Kynes, *An Obituary for "Wisdom Literature": The Birth, Death, and Intertextual Reintegration of a Biblical Corpus* (Oxford: Oxford University Press, 2019).

18. For an up-to-date overview of the discussion, along with current bibliography, see: Jonathan P. Burnside, "Law and Wisdom Literature," in *The Oxford Handbook of Wisdom and the Bible*, ed. Will Kynes (Oxford: Oxford University Press, 2021), 423–39.

19. William P. Brown, "The Law and the Sages: A reexamination of *Tôrâ* in Proverbs," in *Constituting the Community: Studies on the Polity of Ancient Israel in Honor of S. Dean McBride*, ed. John T. Strong and Steven S. Tuell (Winona Lake, IN: Eisenbrauns, 2005), 251–80.

20. Schipper, *Proverbs 1–15*, 450.

21. Brown, "A Reexamination of *Tôrâ* in Proverbs," 268–78.

22. Compare Prov. 1:9; 3:3, 22; 6:20–24; and 7:1–3.

23. R. Norman Whybray, *The Good Life in the Old Testament* (Edinburgh: T & T Clark, 2002), 142.

24. See the discussion in Rolf A. Jacobson, "Psalm 1: The Way of Life," in Nancy deClaissé-Walford, Rolf A. Jacobson, Beth Laneel Tanner, *The Book of Psalms* (Grand Rapids: Eerdmans, 2014), 58–64.

25. David Noel Freedman, *Psalm 119: The Exaltation of Torah*, BJS 6 (Winona Lake, IN: Eisenbrauns, 1999), 87–94.

26. Robert Jewett, *Romans: A Commentary*, Hermeneia (Minneapolis, MN: Fortress Press, 2006), 619.

27. Richard N. Longenecker, *The Epistle to the Romans*, NIGTC (Grand Rapids: Eerdmans, 2016), 850.

28. Charles L. Quarles, "Jesus as a Teacher of New Covenant Torah: An Examination of the Sermon on the Mount," in *Matthew as Teacher in the Gospel of Matthew*, ed. Charles L. Quarles and Charles N. Ridlehoover, LNTS (Edinburgh: T & T Clark, 2023.

29. *Lev. Rab.* 13.3; *Tg. Isa.* 12.3. *Tg. Ket.* on Songs 5.10; *Midr. Eccl.* 2.1; *Yal.* on Isa. 26.2.

30. Quarles, "Jesus as a Teacher of New Covenant Torah," For the idea that the Messiah would bring a "new" or "messianic" Torah, see W. D. Davies, *Paul and Rabbinic Judaism* (London: SPCK, 1955), 69–74, 142–45, 174–76; W. D. Davies, *Torah in the Messianic Age and/or the Age to Come*, SBLMS 7 (Philadelphia: SBL, 1952), 91ff.

31. Paul's expression "the Law of Christ" is equivalent to the "Torah of the Messiah."

32. C. H. Dodd, *The Gospel and the Law of Christ* (London: Longmans Green, 1947).

33. J. D. G. Dunn, *The Epistle to the Galatians*, BNTC (London: A & C Black, 1993), 323.

34. E.g., 1 Cor. 9:20–21; Gal. 6:2; Col. 3:20; etc.

35. For thorough discussions of this topic, see Richard E. Averbeck, *The Old Testament Law for the Life of the Church: Reading the Torah in the Light of Christ* (Downers Grove, IL: IVP Academic, 2022); and Roy E. Gane, *Old Testament Law for Christians: Original Context and Enduring Application* (Grand Rapids: Baker Academic, 2017).

36. For a brief introduction to and overview of the Ten Commandments, see Ralph K. Hawkins, *Discovering Exodus: Content, Interpretation, Reception* (Grand Rapids: Eerdmans, 2021), 118–26.

37. Cf. also Deut. 6:4–5; 10:12–13; Lev. 19:18.

Chapter 4

1. Robert D. Putnam, *Bowling Alone: The Collapse and Revival of American Community* (New York: Simon & Schuster, 2000).

2. Les Rowntree, Martin Lewis, Marie Price, and William Wyckoff, *Diversity Amid Globalization: World Regions, Environment, Development*, 2nd ed. (Upper Saddle River, NJ: Pearson Education, 2003), 92–94.

3. Jacqueline Olds and Richard S. Schwartz, *The Lonely American: Drifting Apart in the Twenty-First Century* (Boston: Beacon Press, 2010).

4. Rene Spitz, *Hospitalism: An Inquiry into the Genesis of Psychiatric Conditions in Early Childhood*, vol. 1 of *The Psychoanalytic Study of the Child* (New York: International Universities Press, 1945), 53–73.

5. John T. Cacioppo and William Patrick, *Loneliness: Human Nature and the Need for Social Connection* (New York: W. W. Norton, 2009).

6. Putnam uses the term "social capital."

7. Susan Mettes, *The Loneliness Epidemic: Why So Many of Us Feel Alone—and How Leaders Can Respond* (Grand Rapids: Brazos Press, 2021).

8. L. A. Stager, "The Archaeology of the Family in Ancient Israel," *BASOR* 260 (1985): 1–36.

9. J. D. Schloen, *The House of the Father as Fact and Symbol: Patrimonialism in Ugarity and the Ancient Near East* (Winona Lake, IN: Eisenbrauns, 2001), 113–15, 135–83; Stager, "The Archaeology of the Family," 18–23; C. J. H. Wright, "Family," ABD 2: 761.

10. Israel Finkelstein, *'Izbet Sartah: An Early Iron Age Site near rosh Ha'ayin, Israel* (Oxford: BAR, 1986), 174. For an overview of the site of 'Izbet Sartah and its archaeology, see Ralph K Hawkins, *How Israel Became a People* (Nashville: Abingdon Press, 2013), 159–73.

11. Zeev Herzog, "Settlement and Fortifications Planning in the Iron Age," in *The Architecture of Ancient Israel: From the Prehistoric to the Persian Empire*, ed. Aharon Kempinski and Ronny Reich (Jerusalem: Israel Exploration Society, 1992), 237.

12. Herzog, "Settlement and Fortifications Planning in the Iron Age," 247–65.

13. As estimated by Magen Broshi, "The Population of Iron Age Palestine," in *Biblical Archaeology Today, 1990, Proceedings of the Second International Congress on*

Biblical Archaeology; Supplement: Pre-Congress Symposium: Population, Production and Power, ed. A Biran and J. Aviram (Jerusalem: Ketepress, 1993), 14–18.

14. E.g., Deut. 6:10–15; 7:1–6; 11:16; 12:29–32.

15. Bernd U. Schipper, *Proverbs 1–15*, Hermeneia (Minneapolis, MN: Fortress Press, 2019), 198.

16. Schipper, *Proverbs 1–15*, 198.

17. For a broader discussion of the term, see Nancy deClaissé-Walford, "Righteousness in the OT," *NIDB* 4:818–23.

18. For a fuller discussion of the meaning of this term, see Harold V. Bennett, "Justice, OT," in *NIDB* 3:476–77.

19. Schipper, *Proverbs 1–15*, 26.

20. B. J. Malina, "Collectivist Personality," in *NIDB* 1:699.

21. M. Buber, *Israel and the World: Essays in a Time of Crisis* (New York: Shocken Books, 1948), 138.

22. This is similar to the Hutterite ideal of *Gelassenheit*, which means "voluntarily renouncing individual will and accepting the will of God as made manifest in the sacred writings and as interpreted and required by the [Hutterite] colony." See Gertrude Enders Huntington and John A. Hostetler, *The Hutterites in North America* (Australia: Cengage Learning, 2002), 18.

23. Roland E. Murphy, *Proverbs*, WBC 22 (Nashville: Thomas Nelson, 1998), 135.

24. The polygamous marriages of the patriarchs often led to conflict in the family. The "Regulations of the Kingship" (Deut. 17:14–20) did not specifically prohibit polygamy, but it did prohibit the king from accumulating "many wives."

25. Cf. G. C. Heider, "Marriage and Sex," in *Dictionary of the Old Testament: Wisdom, Poetry & Writings*, ed. T. Longman III and P. Enns (Downers Grove, IL: InterVarsity Press, 2008), 451–57.

26. Cf. T. M. Lemos, "Were Israelite Women Chattel?," in *Worship, Women, and War: Essays in Honor of Susan Niditch*, ed. J. J. Collins, T. M. Lemos, and S. M. Olyan (Providence, RI: Brown Judaic Studies, 2015), 227–41

27. Carol Meyers recently argued that the term "patriarchy," which implies that men held all the power in society, should be replaced with "heterarchy," which means that men and women alike had authority but in different arenas of society. Cf. Carol L. Meyers, "Presidential Address," *JBL* 133.1 (2014): 3–27.

28. See Joel B. Green, "Healing," *NIDB* 2:755–59, esp. 759.

29. See, for example, Robert J. Banks, *Paul's Idea of Community: Spirit and Culture in Early House Churches*, 3rd ed. (Grand Rapids: Baker Academic, 2020).

30. The two main texts that contain Household Codes are Eph. 5:22–6:9 and Col. 3:18–4:1. There also seems to be an underlying Household Code reflected in 1 Tim. 2:1–15; 3:1–13; 5:17–22; 6:1–2; Titus 2:1–10; and 1 Pet. 2:13–3:7.

Chapter 5

1. Cf. J. H. Walton, "Retribution," in *Dictionary of Old Testament: Wisdom, Poetry & Writings*, ed. T. Longman III and P. Enns (Downers Grove, IL: IVP Academic, 2008), 647–55.

2. The Weighing of the Heart ceremony is recorded in chapter 125 of the Book of the Dead.

3. Walton, "Retribution," 647.

4. Cf. C. M. Pate, J. S. Duvall, J. D. Hays, E. R. Richards, W. D. Tucker Jr., and P. Vang, *The Story of Israel: A Biblical Theology* (Downers Grove, IL: InterVarsity Press, 2004), 11–118.

5. James Montgomery Boice, "Galatians," EBC 10, ed. F. E. Gaebelein (Grand Rapids: Zondervan, 1976), 504.

6. The metaphor of sowing and harvesting is common in all ancient literature.

7. Tremper Longman III, *Proverbs* (Grand Rapids: Baker Academic, 2006), 259.

8. Raymond C. Van Leeuwen, "Proverbs," in vol. 5 of the *New Interpreter's Bible*, ed. Leander E. Keck (Nashville: Abingdon Press, 1997), 119.

9. See the discussion in Bruce K. Waltke, *The Book of Proverbs: Chapters 1–15*, NICOT (Grand Rapids: Eerdmans, 2004), 73–76.

10. Waltke, *The Book of Proverbs: Chapters 1–15*, 75.

11. Bruce K. Waltke, *The Book of Proverbs: Chapters 15–31* (Grand Rapids: Eerdmans, 2005), 366.

12. Waltke, *The Book of Proverbs: Chapters 15–31*, 366.

13. Richard J. Clifford, "Introduction to Wisdom Literature," in vol. 5 of the *New Interpreter's Bible*, ed. Leander E. Keck (Nashville: Abingdon Press, 1997), 12.

14. Denis Waitely, *Empires of the Mind: Lessons to Lead and Succeed in a Knowledge-Based World* (New York: William Morrow, 1995), 17–35.

15. For a more thorough discussion of Job, see chapter 2 of this book.

16. Russell L. Meek, *Ecclesiastes and the Search for Meaning in an Upside-Down World* (Peabody, MA: Hendrickson, 2022). See also Russell L. Meek, "The Meaning of הבל in Qohelet: An Intertextual Suggestion," in *The Words of the Wise are Like Goads: Engaging Qohelet in the 21st Century*, ed. M. J. Boda, T. Longman III, and C. G. Rata (Winona Lake, IN: Eisenbrauns, 2013), 241–56.

17. Meek, "The Meaning of הבל in Qohelet," 252–53.

18. Meek, "The Meaning of הבל in Qohelet," 254.

19. For a more thorough discussion of Ecclesiastes, see chapter 2 in this book.

20. In addition to the Mark's account, it appears in Matt. 13:1–9, 18–23; Luke 8:4–8, 11–15.

21. The parable appears in full in Matt. 25:14–30 and Luke 19:12–27 and is alluded to in Mark 13:34.

Chapter 6

1. Adapted from John C. Maxwell, *Everyone Communicates, Few Connect: What the Most Effective People Do Differently* (Nashville: Thomas Nelson, 2010), 99–100.

2. Frank Bettger, *How I Raised Myself from Failure to Success in Selling* (New York: Simon & Schuster, 1977); Dale Carnegie, *How to Win Friends and Influence People* (New York: Pocket Books, 1990); Les Giblen, *How to Have Confidence and Power in Dealing with People* (New Jersey: Prentice-Hall, 1959). In recent years, Dale Carnegie's

classic has been updated as Dale Carnegie & Associates, *How to Win Friends and Influence People in the Digital Age* (New York: Simon & Schuster, 2011).

3. Daniel Goleman, *Social Intelligence: The New Science of Human Relationships* (New York: Bantam Books, 2006), 27–37.

4. Sherry Turkle, *Reclaiming Conversation: The Power of Talk in a Digital Age* (New York: Penguin Press, 2015), 19–56.

5. Turkle, *Reclaiming Conversation*, 3–7.

6. Raymond C. Van Leeuwen, "The Book of Proverbs," in vol. 5 of *The New Interpreter's Bible*, ed. Leander E. Keck (Nashville: Abingdon Press, 1997), 148.

7. The idea that those who are constantly trying to entrap others will eventually be entrapped by their own devices is often repeated in the Psalms and wisdom literature. Cf. e.g., Pss. 7:15–16; 9:15–16; 35:7–8.

8. For some additional examples, see Pss. 7:15–16; 9:15–16; 35:7–8.

9. Michael Zigarelli, *Management by Proverbs* (Otsego, MI: PageFree, 2004), 185.

10. The Hebrew verb is *ragan* (רגן). Cf. Francis Brown, *The New Brown-Driver-Briggs-Gesenius Hebrew and English Lexicon* (Peabody, MA: Hendrickson, 1979), 920.

11. Tony Evans, *Tony Evans' Book of Illustrations: Stories, Quotes, and Anecdotes from More Than 30 Years of Preaching and Public Speaking* (Chicago: Moody, 2009), 139.

12. Bruce K. Waltke, *The Book of Proverbs: Chapters 1–15*, NICOT 11 (Grand Rapids: Eerdmans, 2005), 459.

13. This is a recurring theme that appears in a number of other proverbs. Cf. also Prov. 6:1–5; 11:15; 17:18; 20:16.

14. Derek Kidner, *Proverbs* (Downers Grove, IL: InterVarsity, 1964), 148.

15. Bruce K. Waltke, *The Book of Proverbs: Chapters 1–15*, NICOT 11 (Grand Rapids: Eerdmans, 2005), 615.

16. Robert Alter, *The Wisdom Books* (New York: W. W. Norton, 2010), 261.

17. Michael V. Fox, *Proverbs 10–31*, AYB 18B (New Haven: Yale University Press, 2009), 603.

18. Waltke, *The Book of Proverbs: Chapters 15–31*, 7.

19. James M. Kouzes and Barry Z. Posner, *The Leadership Challenge*, 4th ed. (San Francisco: John Wiley & Sons, 2007).

20. Kouzes & Posner, *The Leadership Challenge*, 23.

21. *HALOT* 2:916.

22. Roland E. Murphy, *Proverbs* (Nashville: Thomas Nelson, 1998), 91.

23. James E. Smith, *The Wisdom Literature and Psalms* (Joplin, MO: College Press, 1996), 549.

24. Martin Niemöller, "First they came for the Socialists. . . ," *Holocaust Encyclopedia*, United States Holocaust Memorial Museum, https://encyclopedia.ushmm.org/content/en/article/martin-niemoeller-first-they-came-for-the-socialists.

25. Cf. Wolfgang Gerlach, *And the Witnesses were Silent: The Confessing Church and the Jews* (Lincoln: University of Nebraska Press, 2000).

26. Murphy, *Proverbs*, 181.

27. Martin Luther King Jr., "Letter from a Birmingham Jail," April 16, 1963, https://www.africa.upenn.edu/Articles_Gen/Letter_Birmingham.html (italics added).

28. Cf. John J. Pilch and Bruce J. Malina, eds., *Biblical Social Values and Their Meaning* (Peabody, MA: Hendrickson, 1993), 95–104.

29. Kenneth Erickson, *The Power of Praise* (St. Louis, MO: Concordia, 1984).

30. Michael Zigarelli, *Management by Proverbs* (Otsego, MI: PageFree, 2004), 169–72.

31. On the book of James as wisdom writing, see Luke Timothy Johnson, "The Letter of James," in vol. 12 of *The New Interpreter's Bible*, ed. Leander E. Keck (Nashville: Abingdon Press, 1998), 179–80.

32. Lynn H. Cohick, *The Letter to the Ephesians*, NICNT (Grand Rapids: Eerdmans, 2020), 299.

Chapter 7

1. Charles W. Colson with Anne Morse, *My Final Word: Holding Tight to the Issues That Matter Most* (Grand Rapids: Zondervan, 2015), 137.

2. My review of the sexual revolution, from its inception up to the 1980s, draws from and builds on Roger Kimball, *The Long March: How the Cultural Revolution of the 1960s Changed America* (San Francisco: Encounter Books, 2000), 6–9.

3. Joseph Epstein, "The Secret Life of Alfred Kinsey," *Commentary* (1998), 39.

4. Herbert Marcuse, *Eros and Civilization: A Philosophical Inquiry into Freud*, 8th ed. (Boston: Beacon Press, 1974), 164, 171, 201.

5. Kimball, *The Long March*, 150.

6. Kate Millett, *Sexual Politics* (Garden City, NY: Doubleday, 1970), 62.

7. Ellen Willis, "Toward a Feminist Sexual Revolution," *Social Text* 6 (1982), 7.

8. See Millett, *Sexual Politics*, 62.

9. Carl R. Trueman, *The Rise and Triumph of the Modern Self: Cultural Amnesia, Expressive Individualism, and the Road to Sexual Revolution* (Wheaton, IL: Crossway, 2020), 340. For a history of the LGBTQ+ movement, see chapter 10 in Trueman's book.

10. Nadia Bolz-Weber, *Shameless: A Sexual Reformation* (New York: Convergent, 2019), 55–56.

11. Bolz-Weber, *Shameless*, 129–30.

12. Bolz-Weber, *Shameless*, 135–48, 163–75.

13. Bolz-Weber, *Shameless*, 180.

14. Tara Isabella Burton, *Strange Rites: New Religions for a Godless World* (New York: Public Affairs, 2020).

15. Burton, *Strange Rites*, 145.

16. Burton, *Strange Rites*, 145–46.

17. Mark Regnerus, *The Future of Christian Marriage* (Oxford: Oxford University Press, 2020), 91; Mark Regnerus, *Cheap Sex: The Transformation of Men, Marriage, and Monogamy* (Oxford: Oxford University Press, 2017).

18. M. Carlson, S. McLanahan, and P. England, "Union Formation in Fragile Families," *Demography* 41 (2004): 237–61.

19. Jay Teachman, Lucky Tedrow, and Gina Kim, "The Demography of Families," in *Handbook of Marriage and the Family*, 3rd ed., ed. Gary W. Peterson and Kevin R. Bush (New York: Springer, 2013), 39–63.

20. Fiona Rose-Greenland and Pamela J. Smock, "Living Together Unmarried: What Do We Know about Cohabiting Families?," in *Handbook of Marriage and the Family*, 3rd ed., ed. Gary W. Peterson and Kevin R. Bush (New York: Springer, 2013), 255–73.

21. Cf. Sanford L. Braver and Michael E. Lamb, "Marital Dissolution," in *Handbook of Marriage and the Family*, 3rd ed., ed. Gary W. Peterson and Kevin R. Bush (New York: Springer, 2013), 487–16.

22. Donna Freitas, *The End of Sex: How Hookup Culture is Leaving a Generation Unhappy, Sexually Unfulfilled, and Confused about Intimacy* (New York: Basic Books, 2013).

23. Christine Emba, *Rethinking Sex: A Provocation* (New York: Sentinel, 2022).

24. Scott Yenor, *The Recovery of Family Life: Exposing the Limits of Modern Ideologies* (Waco: Baylor University Press, 2020), ix.

25. Bruce K. Waltke, *The Book of Proverbs: Chapters 15–31*, NICOT (Grand Rapids: Eerdmans, 2005), 492.

26. J. Stacey, *Brave New Families: Stories of Domestic Upheaval in Late 20th Century America* (New York: Basic Books, 1990); and J. Stacey, "Good Riddance to 'the Family': A Response to David Popenoe," *Journal of Marriage and Family* 55 (1993): 545–47.

27. See, for example, the research of Liu and Umberson, who argue that men derive few benefits from marriage. H. Liu and D. Umberson, "The Times They are a Changin': Marital Status and Health Differentials from 1972 to 2003," *Journal of Health and Social Behavior* 49 (2008): 239–53.

28. Teachman, Tedrow, and Kim, "The Demography of Families," 46.

29. R. Coombs, "Marital Status and Personal Well-Being: A Literature Review," *Family Relations* 40 (1991): 97–102; L. Waite and E. Lehrer, "The Benefits from Marriage and Religion in the United States: A Comparative Analysis," *Population and Development Review* 9 (2003): 255–75.

30. D. Popenoe, *Disturbing the Nest: Family Change and Decline in Modern Society* (New York: Aldine de Gruyter, 1988); D. Popenoe, "American Family Decline, 1960–1990: A Review and Appraisal," *Journal of Marriage and Family* 55 (1993): 527–42; A. Skolnick, *Embattled Paradise: The American Family in an Age of Uncertainty* (New York: Basic Books, 1991).

31. Dillard and Longman, *An Introduction to the Old Testament*, 265.

32. Cf. Song of Songs 4:8–5:1, where the term "bride" occurs six times. Hess points out that "the use of 'bride' (*kallâ*) never occurs other than in contexts of legal marriages (unlike terms of kinship, such as 'sister,' that can be used to describe a close friendship rather than a blood relationship) or as reference to a daughter-in-law." See Richard S. Hess, *Song of Songs*, BCTWP (Grand Rapids: Baker Academic, 2005), 28. See also the detailed discussion in Richard M. Davidson, *Flame of Yahweh: Sexuality in the Old Testament* (Grand Rapids: Baker Academic, 2012), 561–69.

33. William E. Phipps, "The Plight of the song of Songs," *JAAR* 42/1 (1974): 95–98.

34. Karl Möller, *The Song of Songs: Beautiful Bodies, Erotic Desire and Intoxicating Pleasure* (Cambridge: Grove Books, 2018), 4.

35. Hess, *Song of Songs*, 239.

36. For a detailed discussion of the issues involved in the translation of this line, see Richard M. Davidson, *Flame of Yahweh: Sexuality in the Old Testament* (Grand Rapids: Baker Academic, 2012), 624–32.

37. Hess, *Song of Songs*, 240.

38. While there is no explicit prohibition of premarital sex in the Old Testament, it is clear from the law of the slandered bride (Deut. 22:13–22) that it was viewed negatively in ancient Israelite society. This view was in accordance with the values of practically all Mediterranean and ancient Near Eastern societies. For a detailed study, see Avi Shveka and Avraham Faust, "Premarital Sex in Biblical Law: A Cross-Cultural Perspective," *VT* (2020): 1–24. Adultery is prohibited in the seventh of the Ten Commandments (Exod. 20:14).

39. See Shalom Paul, "A Lover's Garden of Verse: Literal and metaphorical Imagery in Ancient Near Eastern Love Poetry," in *Tehilla le-Moshe: Biblical and Judaic Studies in Honor of Moshe Greenberg*, ed. M. Cogan et al. (Winona Lake, IN: Eisenbrauns, 1997), 99–110; and M. Fox, *The Song of Songs and the Ancient Egyptian Love Songs* (Madison: University of Wisconsin Press, 1985), 283–87.

40. Tremper Longman III, *Proverbs*, BCOTWP (Grand Rapids: Baker Academic, 2006), 162.

41. Bruce K. Waltke, *The Book of Proverbs: Chapters 1–15*, NICOT (Grand Rapids: Eerdmans, 2004), 322.

42. Cf. Raymond C. Van Leeuwen, "Theology: Creation, Wisdom, and Covenant," in *The Oxford Handbook of Wisdom and the Bible*, ed. Will Kynes (Oxford: Oxford University Press, 2021), 65–83; Zoltán Schwáb, "Creation in the Wisdom Literature," in *The Cambridge Companion to Biblical Wisdom Literature*, ed. Katharine J. Dell, Suzanna R. Millar, and Arthur Jan Keefer (Cambridge: Cambridge University Press, 2022), 391–413.

43. See the discussion of the Song and of Song 8:6 in chapter 2.

44. See also Prov. 19:13 and 21:9, which portray the adverse impact a negative wife may have.

45. See the discussion of *hebel* (הֶבֶל) in the section on Ecclesiastes in chapter 2.

46. See chapters 2 and 3.

47. See Carol L. Meyers, *Rediscovering Eve: Ancient Israelite Women in Context* (New York: Oxford University Press, 2013), 126–27.

48. Carol L. Meyers, "Was Ancient Israel a Patriarchal Society?" *JBL* 133/1 (2014): 8–27, esp. 20.

49. Michael V. Fox, *Proverbs 10–31*, AYBC (New Haven, CT: Yale University Press, 2009), 916.

50. Ellen F. Davis, *Proverbs, Ecclesiastes, and the Song of Songs*, WBC (Louisville, KY: Westminster John Knox, 2000), 152.

51. Allen Ross points out that Proverbs 31:10–31 looks like a hymn and proposes that it is modeled on Psalm 111. Cf. Allen P. Ross, "Proverbs," in vol. 5 of *Expositor's Bible Commentary*, ed. F. E. Gaebelein (Grand Rapids: Zondervan, 1991), 1129.

52. Davis, *Proverbs, Ecclesiastes, and the Song of Songs*, 151.

53. Davis, *Proverbs, Ecclesiastes, and the Song of Songs*, 154.

54. See, for example, the discussion in Jonathan V. Last, *What to Expect When No One's Expecting: America's Coming Demographic Disaster* (New York: Encounter Books, 2013).

55. P. D. James, *The Children of Men* (New York: Alfred A. Knopf, 1993).

56. Psalms 127 and 128 are both identified as wisdom psalms.

57. J. Clinton McCann Jr., "The Book of Psalms," in vol. 4 of the *New Interpreter's Bible*, ed. Leander E. Keck (Nashville: Abingdon Press), 1198.

58. McCann, "The Book of Psalms," 1201.

59. See the discussion in J. Paul Sampley, "The First Letter to the Corinthians," in vol. 10 of the *New Interpreter's Bible*, ed. Leander E. Keck (Nashville: Abingdon Press, 2002), 863–64.

60. The two main texts that contain Household Codes are Ephesians 5:22–6:9 and Colossians 3:18–4:1. There also seems to be an underlying Household Code reflected in 1 Timothy 2:1–15; 3:1–13; 5:17–22; 6:1–2; Titus 2:1–10; and 1 Peter 2:13–3:7.

61. See Sampley, "The First Letter to the Corinthians," 863–64.

Chapter 8

1. Herbert Benson, *Timeless Healing: The Power and Biology of Belief* (New York: Scribner, 1996), 97–121.

2. For many, wellness itself may be a religion, although we will not explore this aspect of wellness culture in this chapter. For those interested in wellness as religion, see Tara Isabella Burton, *Strange Rites: New Religions for a Godless World* (New York: PublicAffairs, 2020), 91–113.

3. Cf. Lawrence E. Sullivan and Susan Sered, "Healing and Medicine: An Overview," *EncJud* 6:3808–16.

4. Cf. Thomas C. Alexander, "Mormon Primitivism and Modernization," in *The Primitive Church in the Modern World*, ed. Richard T. Hughes (Urbana, IL: University of Illinois Press, 1995), 167–96; George R. Knight, "Seventh-day Adventists," in *Encyclopedia of Religion in America*, vol. 4, ed. Charles H. Lippy and Peter R. Williams (Washington, DC; CQ Press, 2010), 2065–68.

5. Jonathan R. Baer, "Health, Disease, and Medicine," in *Encyclopedia of Religion in America*, vol. 2, ed. Charles H. Lippy and Peter R. Williams (Washington, DC: CQ Press, 2010), 962.

6. "Biomedicine" definition, National Cancer Institute, https://www.cancer.gov/publications/dictionaries/cancer-terms/def/biomedicine.

7. Ivan Illich, *Medical Nemesis: The Expropriation of Health* (New York: Random House, 1976), 79.

8. Cf. Peter Conrad, *The Medicalization of Society: On the Transformation of Human Conditions into Treatable Disorders* (Baltimore: The Johns Hopkins University Press, 2007).

9. See the recent study by Muriel R. Gillick, *Old and Sick in America: The Journey through the Health Care System* (Chapel Hill: The University of North Carolina Press, 2017).

10. Baer, "Health, Disease, and Medicine," 963.

11. Although it is not entirely clear whether humankind was originally intended to be mortal, it is clear that after the fall, mortality is clearly our lot. The ancient Hebrews

believed that when someone was buried, their spirit descended into Sheol, the "world of the dead," which is described as a dark and dreary land of silence and forgetfulness (e.g., Pss. 6:5; 88:3–12; 115:17; Isa. 38:18). Everyone, whether good or evil, goes down to Sheol (Job 3:11–19), where they exist as mere shadows of their former selves. The ancient Hebrews believed that once they descended to Sheol, they ceased to exist in any substantive way and survived only as "shades" (Ps. 88:10). Cf. Michael A. Knibb, "Life and Death in the Old Testament," in *The World of Ancient Israel*, ed. R. E. Clements (Cambridge: Cambridge University Press, 1989), 395–415, esp. 402–7. While there may be inklings of life after death in the Old Testament, death is generally viewed as the end of one's substantive life. By the time of the NT, a belief in the resurrection of the dead had developed and was held by some Jews, such as the Pharisees, and was developed further by Jesus. For further discussion of beliefs about death and the afterlife in ancient Israel, see chapter 12 in this volume.

12. Bruce K. Waltke, *The Book of Proverbs: Chapters 1–15* (Grand Rapids: Eerdmans, 2004), 297.

13. Tremper Longman III, *Proverbs* (Grand Rapids: Baker Academic, 2006), 501.

14. There is only one exception to this: when good news is said to refresh the heart of the person who receives it (15:30).

15. Longman, *Proverbs*, 137.

16. See esp. D. Andrew Kille, *Psychological Biblical Criticism*, GBSOT (Minneapolis, MN: Fortress Press, 2000); Wayne G. Rollins and D. Andrew Kille, *Psychological Insight into the Bible: Texts and Readings* (Grand Rapids: Eerdmans, 2007); J. Harold Ellens, *Psychological Hermeneutics for Biblical Themes and Texts: A Festschrift in Honor of Wayne G. Rollins* (London: T & T Clark Biblical Studies, 2014).

17. There is ongoing debate in the medical community about the value and ethics of the use of placebos. Cf. the essays in Anne Harrington, ed., *The Placebo Effect: An Interdisciplinary Exploration* (Cambridge, MA: Harvard University Press, 1997).

18. The translation of this verse is disputed. See the standard commentaries for discussion. Waltke's translation is similar to that of the KJV: "as he calculates within himself, so is he." Cf. Bruce K. Waltke, *The Book of Proverbs: Chapters 15–31* (Grand Rapids: Eerdmans, 2005), 227.

19. Cf. George Engel, "A Life Setting Conducive to Illness: The Giving-Up-Given-Up Complex," *Bulletin of the Menninger Clinic* 32 (1968): 355–65; Engel, "Sudden and Rapid Death During Psychological Stress: Folklore or Folk Wisdom?," *Annals of Internal Medicine* 74 (1971): 771–82.

20. Cf. Engel, "A Life Setting Conducive to Illness," 355–65

21. Cf. Engel, "A Life Setting Conducive to Illness," 355–65.

22. W. B. Cannon, "'Voodoo' Death," *American Anthropologist* 44 (1942): 169–81.

23. Denis Waitley, *Empires of the Mind: Lessons to Lead and Succeed in a Knowledge-Based World* (New York: William Morrow, 1995). 126.

24. Norman Cousins, *Anatomy of an Illness: As Perceived by the Patient* (New York: W. W. Norton, 2005).

25. For an introduction to this burgeoning field, see Andrew B. Newberg, *Principles of Neurotheology* (Abingdon, UK: Routledge, 2010).

26. Benson, *Timeless Healing*, 171–91.

27. Raymond E. Brown, *An Introduction to the New Testament* (New York: Doubleday, 1997), 237.

28. Jesus' response to John the Baptist parallels Dead Sea Scrolls text 4Q521, which says that the Messiah "will heal the wounded, and revive the dead and bring good news to the poor." See Geza Vermes, *The Complete Dead Sea Scrolls in English* (New York: Allen Lane, 1997), 391–92.

29. See Joel B. Green, "Healing," *NIDB* 2:755–59, esp. 759.

30. Cf. Matt. 11:2–19 and parallels; Matt. 12:28 // Luke 11:20; Mark 3:24–27 and parallels; Luke 17:20–21; Mark 1:15. For a discussion of the kingdom as a present reality inaugurated with the ministry of Jesus, see John P. Meier, *A Marginal Jew: Rethinking the Historical Jesus*, vol. 2: *Mentor, Message, and Miracles* (New York: Doubleday, 1994), 398–506, esp. 450–54.

31. E.g., Matt. 6:10 // Luke 11:2; Mark 14:25; Matt. 8:11–12 // Luke 13:28–29. See the discussion in Meier, *A Marginal Jew* 2:289–97, esp. 348–51.

32. This passage mitigates against the "dominion" or "kingdom now" theology common in many charismatic churches, which teaches that while the kingdom of God has a future reality in the New Jerusalem, it is already an invisible, spiritual reality, fully functioning now, as promised by Jesus (John 14:12–14). This is an *over*-realized eschatology.

33. For a discussion of the nature and function of the spiritual gifts in the early church, see James D. G. Dunn, *The Theology of the Apostle Paul* (Grand Rapids: Eerdmans, 1998), 552–61.

34. Green, "Healing," *NIDB* 2:259.

Chapter 9

1. Walter Brueggemann, *Reverberations of Faith: A Theological Handbook of Old Testament Themes* (Louisville, KY: Westminster John Knox Press, 2002), 105–8.

2. Tyler Atkinson, *Singing at the Winepress: Ecclesiastes and the Ethics of Work* (London: Bloomsbury T & T Clark, 2015), 202.

3. Atkinson, *Singing at the Winepress*, 202.

4. Atkinson, *Singing at the Winepress*, 222.

5. The idea is repeated in a variant form in 28:19.

6. See the extended version of this proverb in 24:30–34.

7. Tremper Longman III, *Proverbs* (Grand Rapids: Baker Academic, 2006), 285.

8. See the discussion of intrinsic versus extrinsic motivation in Denis Waitley, *The Psychology of Motivation* (Niles, IL: Nightingale Conant, 1997), 23–24.

9. As told in Denis Waitley and Reni L. Witt, *The Joy of Working* (New York: Dodd, Mead, 1985), 23–24.

10. Michael V. Fox, *Ecclesiastes*, JPSBC (Philadelphia: The Jewish Publication Society, 2004), 74.

11. Some interpreters understand this passage to be referring to charitable giving. Cf., e.g., Thomas Krüger, *Qoheleth*, Hermeneia (Minneapolis: Fortress Press, 2004), 191–93. Duane Garrett points out, however, that charitable giving is never brought

up in Ecclesiastes and that 11:6 "confirms that this context concerns personal financial strategy." See Duane A. Garrett, *Proverbs, Ecclesiastes, Song of Songs* (Nashville: Broadman Press, 1993), 338n221.

12. Tremper Longman III, "Israelite Genres in Their Ancient Near Eastern Context," in *The Changing Face of Form Criticism in the Twenty-First Century*, ed. M. A. Sweeney and Ehud Ben Zvi (Grand Rapids: Eerdmans, 2003), 183.

13. Katharine Dell, Will Kynes, and Mark Sneed are among those whose work has especially advocated for this idea. For an excellent and up-to-date overview of recent developments in genre studies and wisdom, see Tremper Longman III, "The Scope of Wisdom Literature," in *The Cambridge Companion to Biblical Wisdom Literature*, ed. Katharine J. Dell, Suzanna R. Millar, and Arthur Jan Keefer (Cambridge: Cambridge University Press, 2022), 13–33.

14. See the discussion and bibliography in Brent A. Strawn, "bĕ-rēʾšît, 'With 'Wisdom,' in Genesis 1.1 (MT)," in *JSOT* 46/3 (2022): 358–87, esp. 375–77.

15. Raymond C. Van Leeuwen, "Theology: Creation, Wisdom, and Covenant," in *The Oxford Handbook of Wisdom and the Bible*, ed. Will Kynes (New York: Oxford University Press, 2021), 65–82, esp. 65–68.

16. For more on changing trends in American work patterns, cf. e.g., Fruzsina Pataki-Bittó and Kata Kapusy, "Work Environment Transformation in the Post-COVID-19 Based on Work Values of the Future Workforce," *Journal of Corporate Real Estate* 23/3 (2021): 151–69; Palash Ghosh, "Managers Say the Future of Work Is Hybrid: New Structure Provides Management Firms with the Best of Both Worlds," *Pensions & Investments* 49/25 (2021): 3; Jenny Surane, "Bank Bucks U.S. Peers, Saying No One Should Return 5 Days a Week," Bloomberg.com, June 28, 2021, https://search.ebscohost.com/login.aspx?direct=true&db=bth&AN=151119821&site=ehost-live.

17. Ellen F. Davis, *Proverbs, Ecclesiastes, and the Song of Songs*, WBC (Louisville, KY: Westminster John Knox, 2000), 152.

18. For thorough studies of Proverbs 31:10–31, see Michael V. Fox, *Proverbs 10–31*, AYB 18B (New Haven: Yale University Press, 2009), 888–917; Bruce K. Waltke, *The Book of Proverbs: Chapters 15–31*, NICOT (Grand Rapids: Eerdmans, 2005), 510–36.

19. The "servant-girls" of v. 15 could be slaves or hirelings.

20. The expressions "opens her hand to the poor" and "reaches out her hands to the needy" are metaphors for charity. See Jordan W. Jones, *She Opens Her Hand to the Poor: Gestures and Social Values in Proverbs*, PHSC 30 (Piscataway, NJ: Gorgias Press, 2019), 146–53.

21. Fox, *Proverbs 10–31*, 916.

22. The average life expectancy for males in first century Palestine was somewhere in the mid-thirties to early forties. Cf. David A. Fiensy, *The Archaeology of Daily Life: Ordinary Persons in Late Second Temple Israel* (Eugene, OR: Cascade Books, 2020), 229–41. If Jesus began apprenticing with his father at the age of ten, launched his ministry when he was "about thirty" (Luke 3:23), and died when he was about thirty-three, then it is evident that he had spent most of his life working as a carpenter/builder.

23. Roman society was highly stratified. The *honestiores* was the highest class of aristocrats, consisting of senators, equestrians, and decurions; the *humiliores* were the

free people who owned small farms or businesses, or worked in a trade; and the lowest class was comprised of slaves and *libertani*, or freedmen. It was a highly stratified society with no middle-class as we know it.

24. See Acts 20:34; 1 Cor. 4:12; 1 Thess. 2:9.

25. See: 1 Thess. 2:9; 2 Thess. 3:6–8; 1 Cor. 4:12; 9:6.

26. Cf. David A. Fiensy, *Christian Origins and the Ancient Economy* (Eugene, OR: Wipf & Stock, 2014), 18–19. Cf. also Luke Timothy Johnson, *The Acts of the Apostles*, Sacra Pagina 5 (Collegeville, MN: The Liturgical Press, 1992), 322.

27. For an excellent discussion of this idea, see Timothy Keller with Katherine Leary Alsdorf, *Every Good Endeavor: Connecting Your Work to God's Work* (New York: Viking, 2012), 64–80.

28. Aristotle, *Politics*, I.VIII 9, and *Nichomachean Ethics*, X.7.

29. For other interpretations of the idlers at Thessalonica, see the standard commentaries.

30. James D. G. Dunn, "The First and Second Letters to Timothy and the Letter to Titus," in *The New Interpreter's Bible*, vol. 11, ed. Leander E. Keck (Nashville: Abingdon Press, 2000), 775–880, quote from pp. 819–20.

31. E.g., Matt 14:13, 23; 17:1–9; 26:36–46; Mark 1:35; Luke 5:15; 6:12; et al.

32. Ruth Haley Barton, "Solitude," in *Dictionary of Christian Spirituality*, ed. G. G. Scorgie (Grand Rapids: Zondervan, 2011), 762.

Chapter 10

1. Alana Semuels, "We Are All Accumulating Mountains of Things: How Online Shopping and Cheap Prices are Turning Americans into Hoarders," *The Atlantic*, August 21, 2018, http://theatlantic.com/technology/archive/2018/08/online-shopping-and-accumulation-of-junk/567985.

2. E.g., Justo González, *Faith and Wealth* (San Francisco: Harper & Row, 1990), 72–75.

3. E.g., John Dominic Crossan, *The Historical Jesus: The Life of a Mediterranean Jewish Peasant* (New York: HarperCollins, 1992).

4. Cf. the papers collected in David A. Fiensy and Ralph K. Hawkins, eds., *The Galilean Economy in the Time of Jesus* (Atlanta: Society of Biblical Literature, 2013).

5. Kenneth E. Hagin, *"You Can Have What You Say!"* (Broken Arrow, OK: Faith Library, 1988); Hagin, *How to Write Your Own Ticket with God* (Broken Arrow, OK: Faith Library, 2000).

6. Kate Bowler, *Blessed: A History of the American Prosperity Gospel* (Oxford: Oxford University Press, 2013), 97.

7. Charles Capps, *The Tongue: A Creative Force* (England, AR: Capps, 1976).

8. Cf. David Edwin Harrell, Jr., *Oral Roberts: An American Life* (Bloomington: Indiana University Press, 1985), 284, 357, 411, 421, 460–62.

9. Gordon Lindsay, *God's Master Key to Prosperity* (Dallas: Christ for the Nations, 1998).

10. Bowler, *Blessed*, 99.

11. Bowler, *Blessed*, 96.

12. Bowler, *Blessed*, 77–138.

13. The idea of embracing poverty, of course, goes back to the earliest centuries of church history, but a review of this history goes beyond the scope of my interest in this chapter.

14. Cf. Anthony L. Dunnavant, "David Lipscomb and the 'Preferential Option for the Poor' among Post-Bellum Churches of Christ," in *Poverty and Ecclesiology: Nineteenth-Century Evangelicals in the Light of Liberation Theology*, ed. Anthony L. Dunnavant (Collegeville, MN: The Liturgical Press, 1992), 27–50.

15. Ralph K. Hawkins, *A Heritage in Crisis: Where We've Been, Where We Are, and Where We're Going in the Churches of Christ* (Lanham, MD: University Press of America, 2001), 111–22.

16. Dunnavant, "David Lipscomb and the 'Preferential Option for the Poor' among Post-Bellum Churches of Christ," 41.

17. Jimmy Swaggart, "Clean Up Our Act," *Charisma* (November 1982), 25–29.

18. Kenneth E. Hagin, *The Midas Touch: A Balanced Approach to Biblical Prosperity* (Tulsa, OK: Kenneth Hagin Ministries, 2000), 153.

19. The Prosperity Gospel has often been portrayed as a poor people's movement, but Bowker shows that there are reasons to question this. Cf. Bowker, *Blessed*, 233–37.

20. Bowker, *Blessed*, 227.

21. Bowker, *Blessed*, 227.

22. While it originated as a distinctly "American Gospel," it now flourishes globally. Cf. Bowker, *Blessed*, 230–32.

23. Tremper Longman III, *Proverbs* (Grand Rapids: Baker Academic, 2006), 443.

24. Cf. the discussion in Michael V. Fox, *Proverbs 10–31* (New Haven: Yale University Press, 2009), 718.

25. Cf. the discussion in Longman, *Proverbs*, 419.

26. Waltke notes that "exacting usury from the poor was allowed everywhere in the ancient Near East except in Israel." Cf. Waltke, *The Book of Proverbs: 15–31* (Grand Rapids: Eerdmans, 2005), 207n75.

27. Bruce K. Waltke, *The Book of Proverbs: Chapters 1–15* (Grand Rapids: Eerdmans, 2004), 561.

28. Note the value of saving. When we survey the early Israelite highland villages, it's clear that they produced a surplus. Cf. the chapter on Izbet Sartah in *How Israel Became a People*. There are also many proverbs that teach that it is self-defeating to get rich in a hurry (10:22; 13:11; 20:21; 28:20, 22).

29. Some interpret this as an exhortation to charity, such as C.-L. Seow, *Ecclesiastes* (New Haven: Anchor Yale Bible, 1997), 341–46. Long ago, however, Delitzsch observed that the idea of investment in charity does not belong to the Teacher's thought elsewhere.

30. Cf. the discussion in Michael V. Fox, *Proverbs 1–9* (New York: Doubleday, 2000), 151–52.

31. The Hebrew verb *prts* (פרץ) is used for breaking through a wall in Proverbs 25:28.

32. See Raymond F. Collins, *Wealth, Wages, and the Wealthy: New Testament Insights for Preachers and Teachers* (Collegeville, MN: Liturgical Press, 2017).

33. Cf. the discussion in Fox, *Proverbs 10–31*, 718.

34. Cf. the discussion in Longman, *Proverbs*, 419.

35. While English translations typically read that Jesus hosted the meal "in Levi's house," the Greek reads, "in his house."

36. Although Matthew adds "in spirit" to clarify that the poverty Jesus was speaking about was not necessarily economic.

37. John Schneider, *Godly Materialism: Rethinking Money and Possessions* (Downers Grove, IL: InterVarsity Press, 1994), 159.

38. Schneider, *Godly Materialism*, 162.

39. For thorough discussions of Acts 2:42–47, see Joseph A. Fitzmyer, *The Acts of the Apostles: A New Translation with Introduction and Commentary*, AB 31 (New York: Doubleday, 1997), 268–75; Luke Timothy Johnson, *The Acts of the Apostles*, SP 5 (Collegeville, MN: The Liturgical Press, 1992), 56–63.

Chapter 11

1. N. D. Munn, "The Cultural Anthropology of Time: A Critical Essay," *ARA* 21 (1992): 96.

2. A. Gell, *The Anthropology of Time: Cultural Constructions of Temporal Maps and Images* (Oxford: Berg, 1992), 126–28.

3. Munn, "The Cultural Anthropology of Time," 96.

4. Gell, *The Anthropology of Time*, 26–27.

5. John Swinton, *Becoming Friends of Time: Disability, Timefulness, and Gentle Discipleship* (Waco: Baylor University Press, 2016), 26.

6. Swinton, *Becoming Friends of Time*, 26.

7. Cf. Neil Postman, *Technopoly: The Surrender of Culture to Technology* (New York: Vintage Books, 1993), 14.

8. Cf. Jeremy Rifkin, *Time Wars: The Primary Conflict in Human History* (New York: Touchstone, 1989), 97.

9. Postman, *Technopoly*, 15.

10. Jacques Le Godff, *Time, Work, and Culture in the Middle Ages*, trans. Arthur Goldhammer (Chicago: Chicago University Press, 1977), 29–52.

11. Rifkin, *Time Wars*, 103.

12. James Gleick, *Faster: The Acceleration of Just about Everything* (New York: Pantheon Books, 1999), 44.

13. Carl Honoré, *In Praise of Slowness: Challenging the Cult of Speed* (San Francisco: HarperOne, 2004), 26.

14. Judy Wajcman, *Pressed for Time: The Acceleration of Life in Digital Capitalism* (Chicago: The University of Chicago Press, 2015),

15. Tom Standage, *The Victorian Internet: The Remarkable Story of the Telegraph and the Nineteenth Century's On-Line Pioneers* (London: Weidenfeld and Nicolson, 1998), cited in Wajcman, *Pressed for Time*, 44.

16. Lord Salisbury, quoted in Hannah Gay, "Clock Synchrony, Time Distribution and Electrical Timekeeping in Britain 1880–1925," *Past & Present* 181, no. 1 (2003): 127, quoted in Wajcman, *Pressed for Time*, 45.

17. Barbara Adam, "Reflexive Modernization Temporalized," *Theory, Culture & Society* 20, no. 2 (2003), 67. Quoted in Wajcman, *Pressed for Time*, 17.

18. Wajcman, *Pressed for Time*, 17.

19. Hartmut Rosa, *Social Acceleration: A New Theory of Modernity* (New York: Columbia University Press, 2013).

20. Rosa, *Social Acceleration*, 75.

21. John Tomlinson, *The Culture of Speed: The Coming of Immediacy* (London: Sage, 2007), 65.

22. Wajcman, *Pressed for Time*, 71.

23. Wajcman, *Pressed for Time*, 73.

24. Wajcman, *Pressed for Time*, 7.

25. Andrew Root, *The Congregation in a Secular Age* (Grand Rapids: Baker Academic, 2021), 32.

26. Root, *The Congregation in a Secular Age*, 68.

27. Carl Honoré, *In Praise of Slowness: Challenging the Cult of Speed* (New York: HarperCollins, 2004), 3.

28. Honoré, *In Praise of Slowness*, 3.

29. Root, *The Congregation in a Secular Age*, 69.

30. Paul Virilio, "Speed-Space: Interview with Chris Dercon," in *Virilio Live: Selected Interviews*, ed. John Armitage (London: Sage, 2001), 69–81.

31. *Dromos* is an Ancient Greek noun for race or racetrack. In "dromology," Virilio noted that the speed at which something happens may change its essential nature, and that which moves with speed quickly comes to dominate that which is slower. "Whoever controls the territory possesses it. Possession of territory is not primarily about laws and contracts, but first and foremost a matter of movement and circulation." John Armitage, "The Kosovo War Took Place in Orbital Space: Paul Virilio in Conversation," *Ctheory*, October 18, 2000.

32. Wajcman, *Pressed for Time*, 24.

33. Ben Agger, "iTime: Labor and Life in a Smartphone Era," *Time & Society* 20, no. 1 (2011): 124. Quoted in Wajcman, *Pressed for Time*, 173.

34. Hartmut Rosa, *Alienation and Acceleration: Towards a Critical Theory of Late Modern Temporality*, NSU Summertalk, vol. 3 (Mamlö, Denmark: NSU Press, 2010), 55.

35. Rosa, *Alienation and Acceleration*, 57.

36. Rosa, *Alienation and Acceleration*, 96.

37. Rosa, *Alienation and Acceleration*, 96.

38. Rosa, *Alienation and Acceleration*, 83.

39. Daniel C. Fredericks, "Ecclesiastes," in *Ecclesiastes & the Song of Songs* (Nottingham, UK: Apollos, 2010), 28–30.

40. Fredericks, "Ecclesiastes," 23–28.

41. Brian Neil Peterson, *Qoheleth's Hope: The Message of Ecclesiastes in a Broken World* (Lanham, MD: Lexington Books; Minneapolis: Fortress Academic, 2020), 55.

42. Peterson, *Qoheleth's Hope*, 46–47.

43. Peterson, *Qoheleth's Hope*, 47.

44. C. L. Seow, *Ecclesiastes: A New Translation with Introduction and Commentary*, AYB 18C (New Haven: Yale University Press, 1997), 144–45.

45. Seow, *Ecclesiastes*, 145.

46. Peterson, *Qoheleth's Hope*, 57.

47. Fredericks, "Ecclesiastes," 78.

48. In this passage, the NRSVue translates זְמָן as "season" and עֵת as "time." They are essentially synonyms that refer to a "set time," "season," or "hour." See further, James Barr, *Biblical Words for Time*, 2nd ed. (London: SCM Press, 1969), 86–109.

49. Cf. Gerhard von Rad, *Wisdom in Israel* (Nashville: Abingdon Press, 1977), 138–43.

50. Cf. Nancy Weatherwax, "Determinism," *NIDB* 2:106.

51. Roland Murphy, *Ecclesiastes*, WBC 23A (Dallas: Word, 1992), 33.

52. Planting could also have a metaphorical meaning. In Jeremiah's call story, God says, "See, today I appoint you over nations and over kingdoms, to pluck up and to pull down, to destroy and to overthrow, to build and to plant" (Jer. 1:10).

53. Peterson, *Qoheleth's Hope*, 73.

54. Fredericks, "Ecclesiastes," 118.

55. E.g., Job 14:7–15; 19:25–27; Dan. 12:1–3. Cf. the next chapter in this volume on death.

56. Duane A. Garrett, *Proverbs, Ecclesiastes, Song of Songs*, NAC 14 (Nashville: Broadman Press, 1993), 315.

57. Ecclesiastes 5:18–20 is related by vocabulary and content to 3:10–15, which also talks about what is appropriate, about the enjoyment of life, and the gift of God.

58. Seow, *Ecclesiastes*, 224.

59. Seow, *Ecclesiastes*, 251.

60. Root, *The Congregation in a Secular Age*, 254.

61. Radner, *A Time to Keep*, 11.

62. Wajcman, *Pressed for Time*, 183.

63. Daniel C. Fredericks, *Coping with Transience: Ecclesiastes on Brevity in Life*, TBS 18 (Sheffield: JSOT Press, 1993), 96.

64. Psalm 90 is typically categorized as a prayer psalm, but its lengthy meditation on the transitory nature of human life led Gerhard von Rad to view it as having derived from the same intellectual and theological situation as Ecclesiastes. Cf. Gerhard Von Rad, *God at Work in Israel*, trans. John H. Marks (Nashville: Abingdon Press, 1980), 214.

65. Allen P. Ross, *A Commentary on the Psalms, Vol. 3 (90–150)* (Grand Rapids: Kregel, 2016), 36.

66. Ross, *A Commentary on the Psalms*, 36.

67. Cf. Lynn H. Cohick, *The Letter to the Ephesians* (Grand Rapids: Eerdmans, 2020), 334.

68. Cohick, *The Letter to the Ephesians*, 335n422.

69. Cohick, *The Letter to the Ephesians*, 335.

70. Oscar Cullman, *Christ and Time: The Primitive Christian Conception of Time and History*, 3rd ed., trans. Floyd V. Filson (London: SCM, 1962).

71. Cullman, *Christ and Time*, 54.

72. John Swinton, *Becoming Friends of Time: Disability, Timefullness, and Gentle Discipleship* (Waco: Baylor University Press, 2016), 67.

73. Swinton, *Becoming Friends of Time*, 67.

74. Kosuke Koyama, *Three Mile an Hour God: Biblical Reflections* (New York: Orbis, 1979), 6–7. Cited in Swinton, *Becoming Friends of Time*, 68.

75. Swinton, *Becoming Friends of Time*, 69.

76. Swinton, *Becoming Friends of Time*, 73.

77. In sharing these thoughts, Swinton recalls some of the teachings of Jean Vanier of the L'Arche community in France (https://www.larche.org). Cf. Swinton, *Becoming Friends of Time*, 75.

78. Swinton, *Becoming Friends of Time*, 76.

Chapter 12

1. Cf. "Death," *Wikipedia.com*, https://en.wikipedia.org/wiki/Death.

2. Cf. Ernest Becker, *The Denial of Death* (Florence, MA: Free Press, 1985).

3. Cf. Elizabeth Outka, "'Wood for the Coffins Ran Out': Modernism and the Shadowed Afterlife of the Influenza Pandemic," *Modernism/Modernity* 21/4 (2015): 937–60, esp. 938.

4. Cf. Geoffrey Gorer, *Death, Grief and Mourning in Contemporary Britain* (London: Cresset, 1965).

5. Lynne Ann DeSpelder and Albert Lee Strickland note that "euphemisms, metaphors, and slang make up a large part of death talk," and they include a table listing several dozen metaphors, euphemisms, and slang for death. Cf. Lynne Ann DeSpelder and Albert Lee Strickland, *The Last Dance: Encountering Death and Dying* (New York: McGraw-Hill, 2020), 8.

6. Philip A Mellor and Chris Shilling, "Modernity, Self-Identity and the Sequestration of Death," *Sociology* 27/3 (1993), 425.

7. DeSpelder and Strickland, *The Last Dance*, 189–92.

8. Cf. Jessica Mitford, *The American Way of Death* (Camp Hill, PA: Simon and Schuster, 1963); Jessica Mitford, *The American Way of Death Revisited* (repr., New York: Vintage, 2000).

9. Evans, *Tony Evans' Book of Illustrations*, 72.

10. Mellor and Shilling, "Modernity, Self-Identity and the Sequestration of Death," 425.

11. Cf. Paul R. Williamson, *Death and the Afterlife: Biblical Perspectives on Ultimate Questions* (London: Apollos, 2018), 5–7.

12. See the brief overview in Peter G. Bolt, "Life, Death, and the Afterlife in the Greco-Roman World," in *Life in the Face of Death: The Resurrection Message of the New Testament*, ed. Richard N. Longenecker (Grand Rapids: Eerdmans, 1998), 51–79, esp. 69–70.

13. This view probably began to creep into Christian thought at least as early as the time of Augustine (AD 354–430), who was a Platonist. Cf. Saint Augustine, *Confessions*, trans. Henry Chadwick (Oxford: Oxford University Press, 1991).

14. Cf. Thomas G. Long, *Accompany Them with Singing: The Christian Funeral* (Louisville, KY: Westminster John Knox, 2009), 6–7.

15. Fleming Rutledge, *The Undoing of Death: Sermons for Holy Week and Easter* (Grand Rapids: Eerdmans, 2002), 276.

16. Bert Hayslip Jr., "Death Denial: Hiding and Camouflaging Death," in *Handbook of Death and Dying*, ed. Clifton D. Bryant (Thousand Oaks, CA: Sage, 2003), 35.

17. Thomas Luckman, *The Invisible Religion: The Problem of Religion in Modern Society* (New York: Macmillan, 1967), 114.

18. David A. Sinclair, *Lifespan: Why We Age, and Why We Don't Have To* (New York: Atria Books, 2019), xxii–xxiii.

19. Sinclair, *Lifespan*, xxiii.

20. Sinclair, *Lifespan*, xxiii.

21. Nancy deClaissé-Walford, "Psalm 49," in Nancy deClaissé-Walford, Rolf A. Jacobson, and Beth Laneel Tanner, *The Book of Psalms* (Grand Rapids: Eerdmans, 2014), 440.

22. E.g., James Barr, *The Garden of Eden and the Hope of Immortality* (Minneapolis: Fortress Press, 1992), 29–30.

23. Cf. James C. Moyer, "Shades," in vol. 5 of *New Interpreter's Dictionary of the Bible*, ed. K. D. Sakenfeld (Nashville: Abingdon Press, 2009), 207–8.

24. See, for example, Isaiah 14:9–10. Sleep is a common metaphor for death in the Old Testament (e.g., Ps. 90).

25. While there were similarities, there were also important differences. Cf. Edwin Yamauchi, "Life, Death, and the Afterlife in the Ancient Near East," in *Life in the Face of Death: The Resurrection Message of the New Testament*, ed. Richard N. Longenecker (Grand Rapids: Eerdmans, 1998), 21–50.

26. Cf. the classic essays compiled in James L. Crenshaw, ed., *Theodicy in the Old Testament*, IRT 4 (Philadelphia: Fortress Press, 1983). More recently, see Walter Brueggemann, *Reverberations of Faith: A Theological Handbook of Old Testament Themes* (Louisville, KY: Westminster John Knox Press, 2002), 212–14; and John Davies, "Theodicy," in *Dictionary of the Old Testament: Wisdom, Poetry & Writings*, ed. Tremper Longman III and Peter Enns (Downers Grove, IL: IVP Academic, 2008), 808–17.

27. For the idea of the book of Deuteronomy as ancient Israel's constitutional document, see S. Dean McBride Jr., "Polity of the Covenant People: The Book of Deuteronomy," *Int* 41 (1987): 229–44.

28. See further, Brueggemann, *Reverberations of Faith*, 174–77.

29. Psalm 111 is usually categorized as an individual hymn of thanksgiving, but it shares many of the same characteristics of Psalms 112 and 119, which are widely accepted as wisdom psalms. See deClaissé-Walford, "Psalm 111," in deClaissé-Walford, Jacobson, Tanner, *The Book of Psalms*, 839.

30. Philip J. King and Lawrence E. Stager, *Life in Biblical Israel* (Louisville, KY: Westminster John Knox, 2001), 363.

31. King and Stager, *Life in Biblical Israel*, 375.

32. While this psalm is usually classified as a thanksgiving psalm, its beginning (vv. 1–3) declares that it is good to praise the Lord, and it offers a hint that the testimony has a didactic tone. Verses 6–7 also have clear wisdom motifs. Cf. Goldingay, *Psalms*, vol. 3: *Psalms 90–150*, 52–53.

33. Psalm 94 is often categorized as a psalm of protest or trust, but it has didactic aspects that align it with the wisdom psalms. Cf. Goldingay, *Psalms*, vol. 3: *Psalms 90–150*, 75.

34. Psalm 90 is typically categorized as a prayer psalm. With its lengthy meditation on the transitory nature of human life, however, Gerhard von Rad viewed it as derived from the same intellectual and theological situation as Ecclesiastes. Cf. Gerhard von Rad, *God at Work in Israel*, trans. John H. Marks (Nashville: Abingdon Press, 1980), 214.

35. Cf. David J. A. Clines, *Job 1–20*, WBC 17 (Dallas: Word Books, 1989), 91–92.

36. Clines, *Job 1–20*, 92.

37. Norman C. Habel, *The Book of Job: Commentary* (Philadelphia: The Westminster Press, 1985), 110.

38. Clines, *Job 1–20*, 187.

39. The description of the earth prior to creation is described as "formless and void" (Gen. 1:2). This is a translation of the Hebrew expression *tohu wavohu*, which some interpret as having to do with the forces of chaos. Cf. the entry on "chaos" in Brueggemann, *Reverberations of Faith*, 28–29.

40. Ecclesiastes 1:2–11; 2:12–26; 3:9–15; 5:13–20; 6:1–12; 8:1–15; 9:1–12; 11:7–12:7.

41. Humans and animals both share the same breath of life (Gen. 2:7; 7:22) and return to dust (cf. Gen. 3:19; Job 10:9; 34:14–15; Pss. 104:29; 146:4).

42. On the image of God, see J. Gordon McConville, *Being Human in God's World: An Old Testament Theology of Humanity* (Grand Rapids: Baker Academic, 2016), 11–29.

43. R. Norman Whybray, *Ecclesiastes* (Grand Rapids: Eerdmans, 1989), 79.

44. E.g., many of the riddles of life that Qoheleth explores in Ecclesiastes 7:15–29 and 8:10–17 seem to contradict retribution theology.

45. There are other interpretive options, all of which are summarized in Minos Devine, *Ecclesiastes or the Confessions of an Adventurous Soul* (London: Macmillan, 1916), 224–27.

46. Shannon Burkes, *Death in Qoheleth and Egyptian Biographies of the Late Period*, SBLDS 170 (Atlanta: SBL, 1999), 216.

47. See Burkes, *Death in Qoheleth and Egyptian Biographies of the Late Period*, 53–59.

48. Fredericks, "Ecclesiastes," 229.

49. E.g., Michael D. Coogan and Cynthia R. Chapman, *The Old Testament: A Historical and Literary Introduction to the Hebrew Scriptures*, 4th ed. (Oxford: Oxford University Press, 2018), 472.

50. E.g., William H. U. Anderson, *Qoheleth and Its Pessimistic Theology: Hermeneutical Struggles in Wisdom Literature*, MBPS 54 (Lewiston, NY: Mellen Biblical, 1997). For an analysis of this approach, see Mark R. Sneed, *The Politics of Pessimism in Ecclesiastes: A Social-Science Perspective*, SBLAILit 12 (Atlanta: SBL, 2012). Seow makes a convincing case that there is no evidence of Greek influence on Ecclesiastes. Cf. Choon-Leong Seow, *Ecclesiastes*, AYB 18C (New Haven: Yale University Press, 1997), 16.

51. Brian Neil Peterson, *Qoheleth's Hope: The Message of Ecclesiastes in a Broken World* (Lanham: Lexington Books; Minneapolis: Fortress Academic, 2020), 15.

52. Peterson, *Qoheleth's Hope*, 77–78.

53. Peterson, *Qoheleth's Hope*, 119–20.

54. Peterson, *Qoheleth's Hope*, 135–37.

55. Peterson, *Qoheleth's Hope*, 157

56. Peterson, *Qoheleth's Hope*, 157.

57. See, however, the discussion of the return of the Judean exiles in Ralph K. Hawkins, *Discovering Exodus: Content, Interpretation, Reception* (Grand Rapids: Eerdmans, 2021), 206–7.

58. George W. E. Nickelsburg, *Resurrection, Immortality, and Eternal Life in Intertestamental Judaism and Early Christianity: Expanded Edition*, Harvard Theological Studies (Cambridge: Harvard University Press, 2007).

59. E.g., Ps. 104:16–17; Song 7:8–9; Ezek. 31:1–9; Dan. 4:10–12; et al.

60. Christopher B. Hays, "'There Is Hope for a Tree': Job's Hope for the Afterlife in the Light of Egyptian Tree Imagery," *CBQ* 77 (2015), 42–68.

61. Cf. Richard H. Wilkinson, *The Complete Gods and Goddesses of Ancient Egypt* (London: Thames & Hudson, 2003), 139–45, 146–49, 160–63.

62. Hays points to several examples in Hays, "'There Is Hope for a Tree,'" 45.

63. For Osiris, see Wilkinson, *The Complete Gods and Goddesses of Ancient Egypt*, 118–23.

64. Cf. Hays, "'There Is Hope for a Tree,'" 50–54.

65. Hays presents substantial evidence that the Osiris myth would have been known in the Levant and in Judah. Cf. Hays, "'There Is Hope for a Tree,'" 54–58.

66. Hays, "'There Is Hope for a Tree,'" 58.

67. Hays, "'There Is Hope for a Tree,'" 60. While the basic definition of the Hebrew verb *zakar* is "to mention" or "to remember," it also carries the meaning "to summon." Cf. William L. Holladay, *A Concise Hebrew and Aramaic Lexicon of the Old Testament* (Grand Rapids: Eerdmans; Leiden: Brill, 1988), 88.

68. Hays, "'There Is Hope for a Tree,'" 64–65.

69. The expression "he will receive me" is based on the Hebrew verb *laqah*, which means "to take."

70. Allen P. Ross, *A Commentary on the Psalms: Volume 2 (42–89)*, KEL (Grand Rapids: Kregel, 2013), 151.

71. Peterson, *Qoheleth's Hope*, 137. The Targums were Aramaic paraphrases of the Hebrew Bible created around the first century AD when Hebrew was declining as a spoken language.

72. E.g., Cassey D. Elledge, *Resurrection of the Dead in Early Judaism: 200 BCE –CE 200* (Oxford: Oxford University Press, 2017), 56–57; and Jon D. Levenson, *Resurrection and the Restoration of Israel: The Ultimate Victory of the God of Life* (New Haven: Yale University Press, 2006), xiii, 180.

73. James I. Packer, "Understanding the Bible: Evangelical Hermeneutics," in *Honouring the Written Word of God: The Collected Shorter Writings of J. I. Packer*, vol. 3 (repr., Carlisle, UK: Paternoster, 1999), 147–60. For classic articulations of progressive revelation, see Charles Hodge, *Systematic Theology*, vol. 1: *Theology* (Grand Rapids: Eerdmans, 1872–73; repr., Peabody, MA: Hendrickson, 1999), 446–47; Geerhardus Vos, *Biblical Theology: Old and New Testaments* (Grand Rapids: Eerdmans, 1948). For

a more recent discussion, see Graeme Goldsworthy, *According to Plan: The Unfolding Revelation of God in the Bible* (Downers Grove, IL: IVP Academic, 2002).

74. The rabbis taught that "all Israelites have a share in the world to come. . . . These are the ones who have no portion in the world to come: (1) He who says, the resurrection of the dead is a teaching which does not derive from the Torah, (2) and the Torah does not come from Heaven; and (3) an Epicurean" (*m. Sanh.* 10:1).

75. Ephraim Radner, *A Time to Keep: Theology, Mortality, and the Shape of a Human Life* (Waco: Baylor University Press, 2016), 152.

Chapter 13

1. Russell L. Meek, "The Meaning of הבל in Qohelet: An Intertextual Suggestion," in *The Words of the Wise are Like Goads: Engaging Qohelet in the 21st Century,* ed. M. J. Boda, T. Longman III, and C. G. Rata (Winona Lake, IN: Eisenbrauns, 2013), 252–53.

2. Meek, "The Meaning of הבל in Qohelet," 254.

3. One of the first to take this approach is R. Norman Whybray, "Qohelet, Preacher of Joy," *JSOT* 23 (1982): 87–98.

4. T. A. Perry, *The Book of Ecclesiastes (*Qohelet*) and the Path to Joyous Living* (New York: Cambridge University Press, 2015).

5. Whybray, "Qoheleth, Preacher of Joy," 88.

6. Perry, *The Book of Ecclesiastes (*Qohelet*) and the Path to Joyous Living*, xv.